A Nation on Fire

Hinduism Under Siege

A Nation on Fire

Hinduism Under Siege

Brig. BN Sharma (Retd.)

Manas Publications
New Delhi - 110 002 (India)

MANAS PUBLICATIONS
(Publishers, Distributors, Importers & Exporters)
4858, Prahlad Street,
24, Ansari Road, Darya Ganj,
New Delhi - 110 002 (INDIA)
Ph.: 23260783, 23265523 (O); 23842660(R)
Fax: 011- 23272766
E-mail: manaspublications@vsnl.com

First Published 2006

ISBN 81-7049-182-7
Rs. 795/-

Typeset at
Manas Publications

Printed in India at
Nice Printing Press, Delhi
and Published by Mrs Suman Lata for
Manas Publications, 4858, Prahlad Street,
24, Ansari Road, Darya Ganj,
New Delhi - 110 002 (INDIA)

Apologia

This book starts with an apology. Apology for writing a book that defends Hinduism, not in a language that speaks most with the essence of its identity and substance. Hindi, a proud language of 85 crore people and the national language of India that is Bharat and enshrined as such in our Constitution, has been long denied its rightful place by consistent continuation of English use by a few select elites who take pride in traducing their own culture in pathetic imitation of the West. I could have written in Hindi but due to reasons that soon follow, preferred to use English to defend a religion and people who have suffered the most through this weapon of communication. Right from the days of Macaulay, Marx and the Missionaries, the process of denigrating their ethnic and primal culture, religion and historic past had started, with a view to enslave not only the bodies of Indian subjects but also their minds. This language imposed by our erstwhile rulers, was avidly adopted by the Khadi-wearing flag-bearers of the freedom struggle, led by the great Nehru, the first 'Indian Viceroy' of Independent India. Of Nehru, Gandhiji once said, "He wants the *Angrez* to go but *Angreziat* to remain, but I want *Angreziat* to go and the *Angrez* can stay as friends". Despite strong opposition from scholars like P.D. Tandon and Dr. Rajendra Prasad, the anglicization of India continued, spawning a class of English loving elite. Most of today's English newspapers and their editorial chatterati, self-appointed social analysts, anchors of chat shows on foreign owned T.V. channels and hired pen-pushers, have caused the greatest damage to Hindi, the Hindu and Hindustan. Perhaps, it is poetic justice that I use the same weapon to defend what these self-styled oracles and prophets of doom have used to attack and destroy.

Now, the reasons. For good or for bad, today English has a wider reach. With a few honourable exceptions the vernacular press voices the news and views of their states and regions. Despite recent efforts, they have a limited circulation, lack a national canvas, and do not address issues concerning the totality of our country; nor do they have any significant access to international readership. But the damage control to Hinduism is urgently required, not only within the national boundaries but also overseas. Finally, the counter-assault on the loud mouths that carry out the political, cultural and religious discourses and lay down the paradigm of national debate within and outside the country can only be mounted effectively through their own weapon.

Publisher's Note

Alas! Brig. Sharma was snatched away by death just before this book was completing publication. This work will be a standing tribute to his orginality of thinking, his deep commitment to the glory of Indian culture and civilization which he so dearly loved and was forthright in putting its living elements across—without fear or favour. Our respectful salute to a distinguished soldier, an ultimate patriot, erudite scholar and an intense Indian. May his soul rest in peace!

Introduction

There is no doubt that in today's political lexicon in India, *Hindutva* is a dirty word. But many wise heads forget that *Hindutva* is nothing but the essence of Hinduism. Being a Hindu or being proud of one's Hindu identity is dubbed as a retrogressive impulse. It is not the done thing. Unless you underplay your Hindu identity, publicly abjure the use of the majority idiom or syntax, and loudly defend the minority cacophony of perceived grievances, regardless of the truth, you are sequestered from the 'know all' tribe as a social and political outcast. The subject of this book is not political. It is social and cultural. The thought processes that inform the Indian elite today make Hindu bashing the most favoured sport and a distinctive and desirable sign of modernity. To the 'secular' chatterati, *Hindutva* is an obscurantist cant, a fundamentalistic impulse amounting to terrorism. Despite living in the post 9/11 era of the human bombing of the World Trade Centre, which shows the true face of Islamic fundamentalism and its weapon of terror, our secularists prefer to live in a cloud cuckoo land of their own make-believe and turn a blind eye to the real threat to the world order. They focus their attention on the justified unease within the most tolerant religion in the world and label this as positively fascist. Let there be no mistake, *Hindutva* is the essence of being a Hindu, and so says the Supreme Court of India, which explains it as a way of life, the same as Hinduism. The trouble with the critics of Hinduism is that they have no knowledge of the roots of Hindu religion which dig deep into a ten millennia past and draw their cultural nutrition from the age-old Vedas, Upanishads, Samhitas and Brahmanas and the other subaltern literature emanating from this primal source. The corpus of the Vedas is the fundamental architecture of Hindu thought and embodies not only the tenets and praxis of religion, but also all forms of human knowledge most of which have not been surpassed even today. The achievements and striving during the age of the Vedas and the literature that followed later, became the foundation of Indian spirituality, and from it, according to Aurobindo, "gush still the life-saving waters of perennial never failing inspirations". In them you shall find eternal truths. "*Tamso Ma Jyotirgamaya*" (Lead me from darkness unto light) and "*Asato Ma Sadgamaya*" (From untruth lead me unto truth). To those who have not even read or written a word of Sanskrit, to claim knowledge of Hinduism is the biggest blasphemy. The worthy critics of Hinduism and its present form not only suffer from a total ignorance of the Vedic literature, but base their half-baked thoughts on translated, edited and distorted versions of our scriptures by foreign authors commissioned by our erstwhile rulers, to denigrate Hinduism. Foremost amongst these was Max Müller (1823-1901). With our illiterate literati it is a routine habit to quote foreign authors who they feel lend credence to their writings and are the repositories of all sense and sensibility. This slavery of the mind is all-pervasive. With few honourable exceptions of our home grown scientists, technical experts, information technologists and research scholars abroad, one strives in vain to find original talent or thought in our country, particularly in the field of Economics, Politics, Philosophy, Literature and Journalism. The purveyors of the last mentioned business, an Indian-born foreign breed, with one exception, who claim to be the opinion makers of our masses are the ones who have done the biggest disservice to our nation and stunted the mental growth of generations to come. Some of our English media, print or visual, does not inform. It peddles half-truths, sub-serving the interests of select lobbies and political formations. Under the rubric of 'freedom of press and speech', this class can stoop to any depth to serve the interests of their masters. How else does one explain the fact that the action or inaction of the Chief Minister of a riot-torn state qualify him for a place next to Slobdan Milosovich, the ruler of erstwhile Serbia, who was being tried for war crimes at The Hague. Another worthy compares the zeal of a few hot heads of a Hindu organization agitating for the restoration of national pride by constructing a temple at the birthsite of its most revered and cherished God – Rama—as a German Nazi tyranny. Cocooned in their airconditioned offices in the metro towns these species have never ventured out to the vast countryside that is real India. Their chosen correspondents who go out and report from the scenes of action are so naïve as to mistake the trees for the wood. Losing all perspective they get carried away by the local sights and sounds and send inflammatory reports to their Headquarters. The responsibility of constructing the overall picture is that of the editorial staff who are as good as, if not worse, than their observers and correspondents on the spot. Objectivity is not their strong point. Sensationalism gets the better of reporting facts. In war or a violence-affected area this could be dangerous. In the War Operations Room the Supreme Commander sifts battle reports that converge from all fronts giving in various details. Each Field Commander gives his own picture and tends to over-emphasize his own zone. But the Supreme Commander has to have a balanced and a total view of the war situation. He does not get carried away by local news or views. Our editors do precisely the opposite. I have read a large number of books on the four Arab-Israeli conflicts since Israel's declaration of Independence in 1948. The spot reports from war correspondents of different news agencies on the same local action differed so violently, that to arrive at a reasoned conclusion seemed almost impossible. Now looking back in retrospect after a cool analysis, the facts can be separated from fiction; the spot reportage becomes dimmer and a clearer picture emerges. The problem gets worse when a reporter goes out with pre-conceived ideas and a definite inherited bias. This is what happened in Gujarat on which our T.V. channels had not given up painting events larger than life. By repeating the same visuals under different dates they succeeded in their mission of inflaming communal passions. Gujarat is not the end of the world. India is much more than Gujarat alone. Admittedly violence must be condemned, wherever it occurs. But here again the treatment must not be discriminative and the leaders of political formations should not suffer from selective amnesia.

India's agriculture based settlements that formed the core of its civilizational architecture were constantly under attack by foreign invaders. The process was well known and documented as far as the north-west was concerned. But a similar silent and peaceful ingress of trans-Burman and Shan tribes into Assam and North-east went relatively unnoticed. Till the middle of the eighth century, all was quiet on the north-western front. Invaders came, attacked, settled down and were themselves assimilated into Indian ethnicity and culture. But with the advent of Islam things were different. The proselytizing zeal and iconoclastic fervour of the invaders whetted by the enormous riches of our temples and other places of worship caused a major civilizational upheaval, besides loss of territory and the establishment of Muslim kingdoms. State sponsored massacre of non-believers, read *kafirs*, removal and weighing of sacred threads after beheading Brahmins, looting and destruction continued unabated till the late seventeenth century. For details of Hindu shrines and temples destroyed by the Muslims, readers are referred to the book *Hindu Temples – What Happened To Them* by Sitaram Goel. As against this, the destruction of Babri Masjid, a non-mosque is described a national shame by the secularists brigade and is celebrated every year on 6th December as a day of national mourning!

Islam refused to reconcile to an ethnic co-existence with Hinduism till as late as the time of Aurangzeb, the cruelest of the Mughal rulers. Without getting into the record of his atrocities and inventory of temples destroyed by this single great faithful of Islamic purity, read fundamentalism, we can clearly see the dividing fault-line between Hinduism and Islam that refused to fade away with the march of time. To honour this great author of Hindu genocide, defacement of ethnic culture, record destruction of temples and imposition of survival tax, called *Jaziya* on Hindus, our secularists named a road after him in the heart of free India's capital city!

During the earlier part of the British rule, the civilizational fault-lines remained somewhat buried, but re-surfaced again in the early twentieth century under the British policy of divide and rule. The miniscule community of foreign invaders enlarged the Dar-ul-Islam beyond recognition. The forcible conversions, coercive policies and naked violence against Hindus carried through generations, created a religious fraternity, which today comprises 15% of India's population. And they wish to be treated as a special minority; a minority that has to its credit the onerous task of taking an active part in Jinnah's Movement for the creation of Pakistan. Consequent to the Partition, those who could migrate to Pakistan, their Islamic Fatherland, did so. But those who wanted but could not undertake this odyssey stayed behind and multiplied many times over since 1947. It is this segment of our Muslim population misguided by their leaders and mullahs, which has lost its moorings and are pining for a mini Pakistan within India. In the process they have become easy victims to the self-seeking, vote hungry politicians who never tire of instilling the fear of Hindus in their minds and force them into self-created ghettos.

In their persistent efforts to prey on the perceived insecurity of the Muslims these pseudo-secularists have perfected the art of slandering Hindus and Hinduism. The biggest danger to Hinduism in India today comes not from the militant Islam outside but from these 'secular fundamentalists' within. External threat can be perceived and defeated but the internal threat from these neo-secularists and secular fundamentalists is difficult to locate and counter. It is this fifth column within the Indian polity that knaws at the very roots of our nationalism. A house divided against itself cannot stand. Today, Hinduism is constantly under attack by the anglicized, leftist Hindus, culturally alienated from their soil, roots and heritage. They are a poor caricature of the West and a cruel joke on our national pride. The real challenge to Hinduism comes from them. Hinduism has weathered many storms in its ten millennia existence. But today the threat is from its own people, from apostates within its own flock. Hinduism is well and truly under siege.

Contents

1

Hinduism

The opening truth about Hinduism is that it is not merely a religious construct, but a civilizational undertaking. Technically speaking, there is no such thing as a 'Hindu'. The original word was 'Indu', a term used for centuries by outsiders to describe the people, who lived along and east of the river Indus. Later, due to the inability of the Arabs to pronounce 'Indus' correctly, the word came to be pronounced as 'Hindus', a construct imposed by Western colonizers, which caused disastrous consequences for Indian history and ultimately resulted in the partition of the sub-continent.

Our 'secular' and leftist historians, a pompous know-all breed, do not know the first thing about Hindu genesis. There is no fixed date for the birth of Hinduism. Unlike Christianity, which started a few years after the crucifixion of Jesus Christ in 33 AD, and the birth of Islam after the flight of Prophet Mohammed from Mecca to Madina in 622 AD called 'Hijri' which is the starting point of Muslim calendar, the origin of Hinduism shrouded in obscurity, dates even further back to around 8000 BC. From this date onwards, the indigenous culture and civilizational ethos called '*Sanatan Dharma*' entered the psyche of the people of the Indian sub-continent, continued and metamorphosed in the shape of present-day Hinduism; being a religion with no beginning or end and considered to be eternal, one that time cannot destroy.

It is not easy to define Hinduism, even more difficult to circumscribe it within identifiable contours of thought or benchmarks of religious praxis and rituals. It is neither parochial nor partisan, but eclectic and cosmic in its content. Its diffusiveness and lack of cohesive inter-related literary textual forms often defy simple definitions. Better minds and facile pens have written about Hinduism, and it will be presumptuous to attempt to supersede them. Simply stated, Hinduism is not about claiming proprietary rights on knowledge and truth, nor to prescribe a faith that is superior to others. Its foundations were laid ten millennia ago when most countries did not even exist nor were there any religions around, as we know them today. Since it is difficult for a common mind to fathom its full depth and meaning, Hinduism is often misunderstood, generally distorted and almost always ridiculed by those who seek clarity and definition. A huge corpus of Vedic thought and literature, the profoundest known to mankind, will no doubt be incomprehensible to the uninitiated. Thus to understand Hinduism better, we should start by stating what it is not. It is not rigid, not coercive, not regulatory, not limited, not conclusive, not the last word of God and does not pretend that it is the only religion that leads to God and His kingdom, not the medium of cleansing man's original sin, not prescriptive, not pretentious, not all knowing, not claiming infallibility, nor superiority; but is the largest source of knowledge known to the world.

Hinduism derives its essence from the four Vedas, whose hymns and *richas* (invocations chanted in Sanskrit) convey different symbols. Simple minds, sometimes even the more erudite, have been frustrated by their failure to comprehend the symbolism and imagery of the Vedic 'richas'. On the other hand, it is simplicity itself. Vedas speak of one cosmic reality, a supra universal force, the cause and effect rolled into one, unity of the Creator and the creation, the infinite, the living force in all human beings, the unknown yet present in all living beings, the unborn, undead, eternal, unchanging yet constantly renewing itself in different forms, the invisible, the incomprehensible, and end up by saying "*Neti-Neti*" (Not this, not this). In its simple formulation, Hinduism is a universal thought with space for everyone and every thought and mode of God worship. Its Weltanschauung is 'Fatherhood of God and brotherhood of men'. Its prescriptions for achieving spiritual fulfilment are many. It is not restrictive, but permits dissent and diversity. The Hindu thought of Ramakrishna, Swami Vivekanand, Sri Aurobindo, Tilak and Gandhi is the most tolerant in the world. It neither arrogates superiority over other religions, nor preaches proselytisation like other religions. Thus, there is no stress on conversion. Each thought and path to God has to be respected and there should be no competitive claim on man's mind and body or clash of one religion with the other. It does not say, "Come to me so that you may enter the Kingdom of God, for I am His son." It does not claim special relationship of any human being to God entitling him to declare that "I am the last of His prophets; my word is the revealed religion given by Allah, and only those who believe in me deserve *Jannat* and the rest are doomed to purgatory."

Against this backdrop, inspite of its proverbial spirit of tolerance there are serious limitations to the concept of Hinduism co-existing with other religions. While we shall deal with the activities of some missionaries in Chapter 2 and shall revert to them later in a subsequent chapter, it is pertinent to mention what Sri Aurobindo, the Yogi, the sage and the revolutionary in the fight for freedom, who accepted Lord Krishna's message in *Gita* of *'Karma'* and violence, if necessary, to fight against injustice, with all his catholicity was forced to state in his magnum opus *India's Rebirth*: "You can live with a religion whose principle is toleration. But how is it possible to live peacefully with a religion whose principle is 'I will not tolerate you'. How are you going to have unity with these people? The Hindu is ready to tolerate; he is open to new ideas and his culture has got a wonderful capacity for assimilation, but always provided that India's central truth is recognized." And in September 1899, he stated: "Every action, for instance, which may be objectionable to a number of Mohammedans, is now liable to be forbidden because it is likely to lead to a breach of peace. And one is dimly beginning to wonder whether worship in Hindu temples may be forbidden on that valid ground. The Hindus have discovered that the absolute can be realized or stated through the relative, and the images, crosses, and crescents are simply so many symbols, so many pegs to hang the spiritual ideas on. It is not that this help is necessary for everyone, but those that do not need it have no right to say that it is wrong. Nor is it compulsory in Hinduism."

The problem with Christianity and Islam, which call themselves monotheistic religions sanctified by God or Allah, has always been their intolerance of Hindu idolatry and their God-ordained mission to convert them or kill. This is what Swami Vivekanand had to say about Hindu idolatry:

"One thing I must tell you. Idolatry in India does not mean anything horrible. It is not the mother of harlots. On the other hand, it is the attempt of undeveloped minds to grasp high spiritual truths. The Hindus have their faults, they sometimes have their exceptions; but mark this, they are always for punishing their own bodies, and never for cutting the throats of their neighbours. If the Hindu fanatic burns himself on the pyre, he never lights the fire of inquisition. And even this cannot be laid at the door of his religion any more than the burning of witches can be laid at the door of Christianity."

The pious universality and highly intellectualized spirituality of our sages, not necessarily fully understood and imbibed by the common adherents to this faith, has led to certain vagueness and lack of self-assertion in the Hindu psyche. Buffetted by digital, cybernetic, consumerist and globalization oriented pressure, the modern Hindu has lost sight of the origin, history and role of Hinduism and its essence. Ill-informed and half-baked thoughts have led to a distinct dis-information about Hinduism and the Eternal Religion or the *'Sanatan Dharma'*. Since there are no precise rituals which define the process of being a Hindu, it is little wonder that non-Hindus are as vague about its contours as the poorly informed Hindus themselves. The absence of a single point focus and existence of a large spiritual socio-intellectual spread, which makes Hinduism more universal and capable of encompassing other religions known to mankind, has baffled simplistic definitions to the label seekers. A fierce debate is now raging among the Hindus themselves to circumscribe Hinduism within identifiable parameters without losing its all-pervasiveness and universalism. This is essential to make a Hindu conscious of his identity by defining the paradigms of spiritual and physical existence that he has to undertake. In other words, he should be given a focus for self-assertion and his striving for perfection. The task is not easy but it is being undertaken without injecting any parochialism or narrowness of outlook in its content, which is so diffused and all-pervasive that the fringes and parts are being mistaken for the whole and practised as such by its followers. A conscious effort is also being mounted to enunciate what *'Hindutva'* is all about, moving away from the old benchmark of what it is, to what it is not? Alter this effort to unite the spiritual with the physical, harmonize the semantics with the apparent, practical and recognizable, Hinduism will hold out to the world a more focussed picture of its spiritual yearning and consummate achievement.

In a world of identifiable symbols and benchmarks the Hindu has to redefine himself in visible terms. It need not be in terms of militant fundamentalism but certainly an active assertion is called for so that the devout understands the call and readies himself for his obligations. Since the world perceives a Hindu from the geographical, historiological and philological connotation of River Sindhu; in fact in Saudi Arabia even today an Indian Muslim is called a Hindu, Hinduism will have to be based on an ethnic construct. The Hindus worldwide would then like the Jews, belong to the Hindu Diaspora. This ethnicity need not deprive Hinduism of its wider appeal of transcendental yearning and historic universality. Nor should this bold assertion lead to a narrow religious divide in this country, the staple on which self-serving policy of divide and rule flourishes leading to a lamentable fragmentation of society.

The message of the Vedas and Upanishads, the manifestation of "Brahman" through the quantum view of a relativistic continuum of time and space, and a sense of timelessness of mind and agelessness of body is one of the most logical and scientific, modern and profound systems of thought known to mankind. The Vedas provide a fertile soil for future scientific development and according to some scientists, the more science advances, the nearer it finds itself to the wisdom of the Vedas. Many other religions directly contradict scientific evidence and in their obscurantist zeal have punished those who have denied their basic tenets, teachings and exhortations. The Hindu too, inspite of his profound heritage, has to rise above his inherited atavistic proclivity to senseless totem worship and thought habits to an action and meditation oriented regimen as shown by sages like Ramakrishna Paramhans and Swami Vivekanand. Sitting on a treasure trove of authentic and priceless corpus of knowledge, he can no longer bask in his past glory. He has to recharge his batteries and practise his religion to benefit his fellow beings as articulated by Swami Vivekanand in his clarion call to the Hindus not to wither away in civilizational statism but to rise and act in the present. Hinduism is not atavistic but a thorough understanding of our past is essential to interpret and understand the present and plan for the future. Those who scoff at our constant reiteration of the glories of the Hindu Vedic past must bear in mind what Swami Vivekanand had to say:

"Children of India, I am here to speak to you today about some practical things, and my object in reminding you about the glories of the past is simply this. Many times I have been told that looking into the past only degenerates and leads to nothing, and that we should look to the future. That is true. But out of the past is built the future. Look back, therefore, as far as you can, drink deep of the eternal fountains that are behind, and after that, look forward, march forward and make India brighter, greater, and much higher than she ever was. Our ancestors were great. We must first recall that. We must learn the elements of our being, the blood that courses in our veins; we must have faith in that blood, and what it did in the past; and out of that faith, and consciousness of past greatness, we must build an India yet greater than what she has been. There have been periods of decay and degradation. I do not attach much importance to them; we all know that. Such periods have been necessary. A mighty tree produces a beautiful ripe fruit. That fruit falls on the ground, it decays and rots, and out of that decay springs the root and the future tree, perhaps mightier than the first one. This period of decay through which we have passed was all the more necessary. Out of this decay is coming the India of future; it is sprouting and its first leaves are already out, and a mighty, gigantic tree, the "*Urdhavamumlam*", is here, already beginning to appear, and it is about that I am going to speak to you".

The sweep of the Vedic thought is so vast and all-encompassing, with an incredible depth of perception, that it bewilders the common man, but for this very reason makes its praxis so much easier and so unshackling. The West has only touched the fringes of physical Yoga purely for therapeutic purposes. An important element of Hinduism is '*Karma*', which lays down that a man reaps the fruits of his actions, good or bad, and is born to do good '*Karma*'. The other element of Hindu thought is '*Avatar*'. And finally, the concept of '*Shakti*', the divine energy in the shape of a goddess called by different names. God, the Creator, along with the '*Shakti*', the power to create, has brought into existence the universe as we know it. There are so many sub-cultures and modes of worship such as '*Vaishanavism*', '*Shaivism*', Shakti worship in various forms, such as Kali, Katyayini, Kalyani and the trinity of Lakshmi, Durga and Saraswati; Vaishno Devi, Jwala Devi, various occult rites of Aghories, Tantrik cults, different Akharas, including the '*Nirmohi*' at Ayodhya, '*Nagas*'; '*Dwait*' and '*Adwait Vad*' (Duality and Unity of God) and an unending array of local gods, goddesses and family deities (*Kul Devta*) that can easily confuse the uninitiated.

A word about polytheism. The Muslim invaders and European colonizers have often derided Hinduism on account of what they called its 'pagan character' and 'idol worship'. Nothing could be further from the truth. The Hindus believe in one God, but also believe in innumerable manifestations of the same universal reality. In brief, with its vast variety of god worship from remote antiquity to present times, history has produced the webs and wafts that weave many a delicate web of golden bars and checkered shades on the tapestry that is Hinduism. The Hindus believe in '*Jiva*'—the life moving force of all existence, unfathomable, eternal, indestructible, detached, free and beyond grasp.

Comparing Christianity and Islam with Hinduism, one cannot miss certain fundamental differences. Prophet Mohammed, who borrowed heavily from the Old Testament and portions of the New, recognized the earlier Prophets like Abraham, Moses and Jesus but the last words of God's teachings according to him are the 'Ayats' of *Quran*. These are said to be revealed to him through Gabriel, the messenger of his Allah. His own utterances and actions together with those of his companions and twelve Caliphs that came after him form the bed-rock of Sunnah and Hadis. They lay down prescriptions in Islam for all times to come. In a totalitarian religion like Islam, the spiritual and temporal are indivisible. Islam negates secularism and leaves nothing to human reason or innovation but finds atavistic solution to every small detail of day-to-day living anchored entirely on the sayings and actions of the Prophet and others as stated above and propounded in the Hadith. Not one word can be added or subtracted from these sacred texts. This makes Islam a completely exclusivistic religion driven entirely by past pronouncements and actions with no room for evolution or development in the context of modern science, philosophical thought, art forms and new discoveries. Concentrating entirely on externals with little room for spiritual insight, Islamic injunctions issued through *'Fatwas'* form the corpus of Islamic teachings and their jurisprudence called *'Shariat'* derive their legitimacy from the same sources, dating thirteen centuries back. The *'Fatwas'* are the final word on such petty matters as postures for coitus, urination, wuzu (washing and cleaning), women's rights, marriage, divorce, inheritance, adultery, treatment of non-believers, war against Kafirs, physical actions during Namaz and so on.

Christianity, in comparison, leaves more room for individual actions and interpretations of the religion, though it too suffers from the same insistence on the sayings and deeds of Jesus Christ, the genesis of human race, nature of universe and other temporal matters. Like Islam, it insists to a large degree, on externals, with disregard for inner search and spirituality.

The unique features of Hinduism not shared by other religions are that it never contends that:

i) Man was born of an original sin from which he has to be redeemed;
ii) Man should not enjoy life and remain austere;
iii) Men are not equal; this resonates in the concept of '*Vasudhaiva Kutumbakam*' i.e. fraternity and equality of men.
iv) Men are not free;
v) Death is better than life.

These directive principles place Hinduism in an entirely different mould.

Hinduism attaches great value to the worth of man just as Rabbi Akiba observed that, "Precious is man, since he is created in God's image". The Law of *Manusmriti* ordains that everyone has the right to express his individuality and develop his uniqueness. He is free to express or subsume the thoughts of his mind and the dictates of his soul. In fact, the worth of man is considered even more than that of gods. The gods are immortal but unlike the mortal man they have no freedom of action or *'Karma'*.

Hinduism is the most catholic religion in this world. It has space for dissent, it has prescribed punishment for wrong conduct but not for holding different views. Our religious texts are full of descriptions of heated discourses among learned sages and seers, trying to interpret the teaching of *Vedas* and the *Upanishads*. Even learned women and *Rishi Patnis* took part in these *'Shastrarths'* (interpretation of *Shastras*) and some worsted their male contestants. The name of Gargi and Vidyottama are household words. Coming to more mundane matters, Hinduism has been an extremely liberal thought system. In matters of sex, while it holds sexual promiscuousness culpable, it is more liberal and sensitive to human emotions and corporeal demands. It not only circumscribes sex within the respectability of marital confines but also confers legitimacy on this primal human impulse. The Christian prudery of the Victorian era or the puritanic guilt complex of Islam is laden with sinful implications about any activity connected with sex. In Islamic teachings sex is a forbidden subject for debate or discourse. While it forbids glorification of sex in this world, nonetheless Quranic teachings hold out rewards of co-habitation with the hourries (pretty girls) in heaven for honest and religious deeds in this world. The *'Jehadis'* too have their share of such rewards after their martyrdom. What is not desirable in this world is a pearl of great value in Jannat.

In the praxis of their faith, both Christianity and Islam give almost equal importance to God and His son or the Prophet. In Christianity, unlike Hinduism, no salvation is possible without Jesus, the Son of God. In fact, in Christian theology, Jesus holds the key to the communion of ordinary mortals with God. Similarly, there are more references to Prophet Mohammed in Muslim literature than to God Himself. In every Qawwali, almost the entire emphasis is on Mohammed and Kaba rather than Allah. Even the prescriptive words on the entry permit for conversion to Islam read "*Ya ilah-Lilillah Mohammed Rasul Allah*". (There is but one true God and Mohammed is his prophet.) As opposed to this, Hinduism concentrates directly on God, and the minor gods of Hindu pantheon, merely represent different traits of this God, which are easy to grasp and worship and act as symbols, comprehensible to ordinary people who lack the erudition and yogic power of concentration and the ability thereafter to become one with the cosmic consciousness called *'Nirakar Brahma'*, eternal without beginning or end, all-pervasive, the creator and creation itself. But these gods have not been given the same importance as God nor the key to man's communion with Him. Even salvation is possible by entirely concentrating on the *'Param Brahma'* without the aid of intermediaries. In case of Judaism there is no interlocutor between God and His people. The role of various prophets had been merely to educate the Jews in the path of righteousness and for obeying the dictates of God alone.

To the early Christians, Jesus came first, and it was he who explained the nature of God and His Kingdom to the Jews and the pagans. In the same manner, Mohammed came first and it was he who explained the existence and the nature of a monolithic and shapeless God to the desert tribes who used to worship various local gods and stone idols in and around Mecca and Medina. This is in sharp contrast to Hinduism where God came first and the prophets, sages and seers came later. In a latest effort to pronounce the supra-state of Jesus Christ, the Vatican in one of its annual Diwali greetings sent to India, asserted that Christ is God himself and the ultimate fulfilment of the "human heart's restless searching". This embarrassed even the officials of the Indian Church.

'Hindutva' is the cultural essence of Hinduism and is the end product of three elements: cultural nationalism, intense patriotism and a pride in the collective memory of India's past glory. I have mentioned this subject in brief in my book on Nehru, but the subject bears repetition. The canard about 'Hindutva' as a fundamentalist, misguided Hindu communalism is the worst kind of pamphleteering from the English-speaking so-called 'elite' and half-baked westernized intelligentsia, consistently listing to the Left. They are still willing slaves to their imported Socialistic, Leninist and Marxist thought which has lost its rationale and relevance in the world in general and the country of its origin in particular. This breed nurses a pathological hatred towards anything Indian or indigenous. For the last over 50 years since Independence, under the garb of progressivism, a well-orchestrated campaign has been unleashed to revile the tolerant, mild, liberal and accommodative Hindu religion and the culture and civilization that it has spawned. Through chartered media, dedicated to destroy the self-respect and pride of this ancient civilization, they have spared no pains to traduce everything Indian or Hindu.

Inspite of the risk of incurring the opprobrium of the secularist brigade, a Cartesian dialectic statement about Hinduism can be made without any hesitation. India's ancient ethnic native genius forms the colour and content of its Hindu heritage and there is no reason whatsoever to be apologetic about it. Like Christianity in western countries, Hindus form the majority community and thereby have the right to be called the natural civilizational core of India. They have, and will in future determine the structure and ethos of our civilization and nationality. There is no need to shy away from this reality. The dragon's seeds sown by Nehru, who can be well and truly called the greatest Hindu-baiter, have taken deep roots and his caucus of leftist intellectuals, communists, and their cohorts are simply incapable of facing the fact that Hindu spirit and resurgence is the natural order of the day.

The composite nature of our culture has often been touted by our secularist brigade, and the impossibility of the proposition has been established. Those, who wax eloquent on the multi-cultural, multi-ethnic, pluralistic and composite culture must realise that 95 percent of the minorities, who claim a separate culture are born out of the Hindu stock. They must realize that it is possible to change your religion but not ethnicity. You can change yourself by giving yourself any name but you cannot disown your ancestors or forebears. The genetics and DNA code runs through centuries from generation to generation.

British rulers believed, with some element of truth, that if mental slavery in India is to be perpetuated as a natural corollary to political domination, the first thing to do is to destroy *'Hindutva'*. Unfortunately, they found many Indian collaborators in their grand design. To prove their secular credentials this group finds it necessary to vilify Hindu religion and society. The Supreme Court in its landmark judgement has upheld the proposition that *'Hindutva'* is synonymous with India's culture and is a way of life and has no communal overtones whatsoever. '*Hindutva*' is a product of the geography and history of this landmass called *'Bharat'*, moulded and nurtured through millennia of traditions, thoughts and beliefs, enunciated by our seers and sages. It is through their constant search for truth regarding God, universe, man and earth, and a selfless striving for perfection that they passed down to generation after generation, that the essence of Hindu thought received its natural form. Inimical to none and friendly to all it allows dissent and encourages reasoned argument. Not being a closed system, it is open to constant development and evolution, forever revitalizing itself through assimilating new ideas, while it raises ever-new edifices on the foundations of universal cosmic truths. It is unlike other so-called well-defined religions with their teachings and practices frozen forever in a time-warp of original thought and wisdom, thus denying alternatives as a sequel to new discoveries, and inspite of expanding horizons of human knowledge and perceptions with each passing day. Evolving civilizations, as opposed to the decadent, are not content with "what is", "but strive for what can be". Thus, striving for achieving the highest in achievable is a common running thread in Hinduism. As opposed to this, both Christianity and Islam prohibit any need for readjusting the enjoined sayings and practices mentioned in their holy books. No line written more than thousand years ago can either be questioned or erased, even though their validity and *raison d'etre* is open to scrutiny. Mere material well-being has never been the end all and be all of the Hindu thought. While they accept the need for freedom from want and never frown upon material progress, the ultimate goal however had always been much beyond the satiation of physical needs and a constant striving for perfection, spiritual achievement and even a final search of and immersion into the universal God-head.

A feature unique to Hindu thought is the importance of four *'Ashrams'*. *'Brahmacharya'*, covering the first 25 years, aims at asceticism, scholastic pursuits, building of character, health, acquisition of knowledge and sharpening of skills as a preparation for the life ahead. Thereafter, *'Grahasth'*, which lasts for the next 25 years, means entry into married life in the material world, providing for earthly needs, excellence in profession, utilization of knowledge, efforts at worldly success and raising a family as per the needs of the society and the country's demands, fulfiling the material and worldly obligations. *'Vaanaprastha'*, which commences after 25 years of *'Grahasth'* life seeks something beyond the material and routine, or acquisition of wealth and worldly satisfaction. Social and national service and dedication to the real issues of enrichment of society and the country, exploring the frontiers of knowledge and quest for truth supercede purely material pursuits. In the world and yet outside it, action without desire for rewards, one strives to achieve the state of *'Sthitapragya'*, which means raising oneself above worldly concerns and total detachment from the fruits of endeavour. Serving the world to the best of one's ability, without a desire for personal gain and supreme mental equipoise is the essence of *'Vaanaprastha'*. Finally, man is ordained to achieve *'Sanyaas'*, meaning total renunciation of the world at 75 years. It involves meditation, devotion, '*Yoga*' and the attempt to reach the sublime, by cutting loose from the worldly concerns and aiming to achieve salvation through *'Sadhna'* (intense spiritual striving). With minor adjustment, the system should and can continue in the present world order. Though present longevity is less than hundred years, the time span for each 'Ashram' can be suitably curtailed by devoting the first half of life for self-improvement and family and the second half for impersonal ends. This system is unique and different from all other religions and systems of thought.

The Brahmin, the twice born, who according to Indian mythology came out of the head of the Creator Brahma, was ordained to live the life of an ascetic. His destiny was not the luxury of palaces but to learn, meditate, acquire knowledge, wisdom and disseminate it to all mankind. He was not to think of himself but of others and live for others. To lead and guide men in the ways of God, to prepare them for the ultimate spiritual perfection and salvation. Brahmins were not to earn or store money but depend entirely on alms from the laity and material and protection from the Kshatriya princes. From womb to tomb a Brahmin had to perform *'Anushthans'* (rituals) and *'Sanskaras'* for all Varnas or castes, educate the un-initiated, teach the ignorant and remonstrate with them, to the extent of chastisement of kings to bring them back to the narrow path of virtue and 'Raj Dharma' (the duties of the king). In brief, their duties lay in ushering in to the world the rule of *'Dharma'*, which does not mean a sect. Dharma was a very sacred and emotive word during the times of our proto history. One hears of the splendour of the kings or Kshatriyas; the material wealth of the *Vaish* or the treasury of *'Kuber'*, but the Brahmin is always referred to as ascetic and poor. With the passage of time and the coming of priesthood many evils and covetousness, entered the lifestyle and the conduct of Brahmins.

The early Rishis, who shunned the comforts of cities, lived in jungles and far-off places to carry out their *'Sadhna'* and run the Gurukuls (the family of teacher or a place of learning) and train their disciples in godly pursuits and knowledge of the world. As brought out earlier, these teaching places, or the sanctuaries for the Rishis, almost all of whom came from the Brahmin class, are the greatest assets of our civilizational foundations. Since they did not work for themselves, these Ashrams were maintained by grants released by the kings and princes of Kshatriya class. As pointed out earlier, the priesthood as distinct from Brahmanism entered into our society much later.

The caste system has been the biggest curse of Hindu society. Though initially well meant, with a very sound rationale of equitable division of work and maintenance of an egalitarian social order, the hierarchies of castes, based not on work but birth, got fossilized in a time warp. Being the natural leaders and dispensers of knowledge, the temptation to misuse authority became irresistible and with time the Brahmins forgot their sacred calling and helped in the perpetuation of this abominable system. Though, the other two higher social orders of Kshatriyas and Vaishyas were also responsible to a large extent, being the leaders and lawgivers, the main blame must be taken by the Brahmins. However, having said that, the Brahmins should also be given the credit for keeping their folk together and protecting them from alien tyranny by keeping their faith. The Bhakti movement of Chaitanaya and Tulsidas acted as a shield against forcible conversions to Islam. Later, more subtle attempts were made by the Sufis to inveigle the Hindus into their fold by grafting Hindu mysticism on to Quranic teachings. If not checked by Bhakti movement, this slow and insidious poisoning of Hindu faith would have resulted in the assimilation of the entire Hindu society into Dar-ul-Islam.

Today, venom is being spewed almost everyday and all round against the Brahmins, (read 'Manuvadis'), in perpetuating the much abused caste system. We often tend to ignore their services to the Hindu cause by withstanding centuries of assault and oppression by the foreign invaders and through crises after crises keeping the spirit of Hinduism alive. Even today ridiculed and driven from the public ire the Brahmins have survived adverse situations. Inspite of a highly iniquitous percentage of job reservation arrayed against them and constant social buffeting due to Mandalization, their innate resilience and strength of character has enabled them to dominate the socio-political spectrum. In a recent survey, it was found that inspite of their small number, the Brahmins occupied the largest number of top-slots in all fields of human development. With the free play of market forces, a sequel to economic liberalization and the withdrawal of the state from the market place, the Brahmins, by sheer hard work and gift of education have maintained their superiority over the other castes. Thus, the aim of all human resource development (HRD) and social engineering should be not to bring down the achievements and the merit level of these few, but empower the Dalits and Backwards to reach higher levels of excellence through education and hard work. The levelling process should mean a lifting up of the lower rather than lowering down the upper. Instead of improving our human resource, reservations have divided the Hindu society beyond repair, led to caste conflicts and if unchecked, will reduce Hindu masses to their lowest common denominator of merit.

To unlock the doors of this storehouse and repository of profound learning, the key is to acquire a good knowledge of Sanskrit, which is totally lacking in our present day intelligentsia. Even Hindi, our national language, is derided as a language of country cousins and 'desi behanjis'. It is a crying shame that the postgraduate course in Hindi in Shri Ravi Shankar Shukla University in Madhya Pradesh had once to be cancelled because there were no students opting for the subject. When asked the reason for this, a girl student interviewed by a television reporter replied that if they apply for Hindi, they are made to feel inferior by their own English class colleagues. Returning back to Sanskrit, this is what Swami Vivekanand had to say:

"The attempts of the great Ramanuja and of Chaitanya and of Kabir to raise the lower classes of India, show that marvellous results were attained during the lifetime of those great prophets; yet the later failures have to be explained, and cause shown why the effect of their teachings stopped almost within a century of the passing away of these great Masters. The secret is here. They raised the lower classes; they had all the wish that these should come up, but they did not apply their energies to the spreading of the Sanskrit language among the masses. Even the great Buddha made one false step when he stopped the Sanskrit language from being studied by the masses. He wanted rapid and immediate results, and translated and preached in the language of the day, Pali. That was great, he spoke in the language of the people, and the people understood him. It spread the ideas quickly and made them reach far and wide, but, along with that, Sanskrit ought to have spread. Knowledge came but the prestige was not there, culture was not there. It is culture that withstands shocks, not a simple mass of knowledge. You can put a mass of knowledge into the world, but that will not do it much good. There must come culture into the blood. We all know in modern times, nations, which have masses of knowledge, but what of them? They are like tigers; they are like savages, because culture is not there".

It is hardly surprising that almost all contributions in all branches of knowledge and facets of civilization such as arts and music, architecture, literature, grammar, medicine, astrology, astronomy, mathematics, science and physics, botany and chemistry, human biology and science of health (Ayurveda), all came down from these Sanskrit scribes of Vedic knowledge.

Two greatest sons of India during the late nineteenth and early twentieth centuries were Swami Vivekanand and Mahatma Gandhi. Both were deeply imbued with the spirit of Hinduism and both served Mother India in their own way. While Vivekanand dedicated himself to religion and awakened our people to their greatness and inspired them to greater endeavours, Mahatma Gandhi sacrificed his all to enter politics in order to lead us out of slavery to freedom. Both were deeply conscious of their religiosity and proud of being Hindus. Vivekanand made religion the foundation of a successful temporal world; Gandhiji made spirituality and truth the essence of his political philosophy. Both succeeded beyond measure in their God-ordained mission.

In *'Young India'*, his weekly journal, Mahatma Gandhi wrote that nothing could be further from his thought than that "we (Indians) should become exclusive or erect barriers. But I respectfully contend that an appreciation of other cultures can fitly follow, never precede an appreciation and assimilation of our own". His views on borrowing foreign values were very explicit, and he said, "I do not want my windows to be stuffed. I want the cultures of all lands to be blown about my house, as freely as possible. But I refuse to be blown off my feet".

And then Swami Vivekanand declared: "The old religion said that he was an atheist who did not believe in God. The new religion says that he is an atheist who does not believe in himself. It is the coward and the fool who says this is his fate. But it is the strong man who stands up and says I will make my own fate."

The process of learning never stops. It is amazing to learn how scanty is our knowledge about our urban English speaking elite. On a chat show "We the People" compered by Barkha Dutt on NDTV programme on 21st July, 2002, at 8.00 P.M., every time, the speaker who attempted to speak of Hindu nationalism or tried to put Gujarat riot tragedy in its proper perspective was booed down by the crowd. These youngsters were either totally alienated from our cultural roots or completely under the influence of New Delhi's English chatterati, or what seemed more likely, it was a crowd of camp followers gerrymandered by the NDTV staff. The very mention of the word 'RSS' "Rashtriya Swayamsevak Sangh" or Hindu nationalism was met with sniggers and jeers by some of these social upstarts. Hinduism and the Sangh Parivar were targeted as if they were the social pariahs. To my horror, I realized that what medieval Muslim rulers, Macaulay, Max Müller and Marxists could not achieve in a millennium was accomplished by our own nationalist governments since 1947, their Marxists friends and the English educated elite. Although the medium of discourse in the above show was both Hindi and English, I did not find even by mistake a single speaker except one from the BJP and that too, a Muslim, who could speak a single word of Hindi or express himself in our cultural medium.

Now a look at the strengths and weaknesses of Hindus. The biggest strength is its power of assimilation, open-endedness, continuous evolution and eclectic response to all that is progressive and new. Hinduism can absorb and co-exist with people of any faith as long as they owe allegiance to this mother country. Even a Hindu converted to Islam who shares the same collective memories with the Hindus is welcome in its fold. Hinduism being progressive, the genius of its people can be seen in entrepreneurial skills, business acumen, technological expertise and excellence in all forms of human activities. Unfettered and uncontrolled by a tyrannous state religion, Hinduism encourages self-actualization and abjures acquisitive or imperialistic tendencies.

The weaknesses, though endemic are curable. There is an excessive stress on the individual, which led to a neglect of organized effort and lack of development of social institutions. A complete indifference to collectivism has led to the weakening of our polity and social fabric. The proverbial Hindu tolerance has often verged on cowardice and projected an image of weakness leading to foreign invasions and defeats in battles. Indian history from 700 AD onwards with a few exceptions is a monotonous story of defeats. Inspite of Kautilya's *Arthashastra,* Hindus took little interest in military methods and political sciences. The caste system though well intended at its inception degenerated into a cruel caste divide and led to internal conflict and an enfeeblement of the Hindu nation. To conclude, we can do no better than quote Sri Aurobindo's God-inspired words about Hinduism:

"Something has been shown to you in this year of seclusion; something about which you had your doubts and it is the truth of the Hindu religion. It is this religion that I am raising up before the world, it is this that I have perfected and developed through the *'rishis'*, saints and *'avatars'*, and now it is going forth to do my work among the nations. I am raising this nation to send forth my word.... When, therefore, it is said that India shall rise, it is the *'Sanatan Dharma'* that shall rise. When it is said that India shall be Great, it is the *'Sanatan Dharma'* that shall be Great. But what is the Hindu religion? It is the Hindu religion only, because the Hindu nation has kept it, because in this peninsula it grew up in the seclusion of the sea and the Himalayas, because in this sacred and the ancient land it was given as a charge to the Vedic Aryans to preserve through the ages. That which we call the Hindu religion is really the eternal religion, because it is the universal religion, which embraces all others. If a religion is not universal, it cannot be eternal. A narrow religion, a sectarian religion, an exclusive religion can live only for a limited time and limited purpose.... I say no longer that *'Sanatan Dharma'* is for us nationalism.... *'Sanatan Dharma'* is nationalism."

2

Our Vedic Heritage

No nation on earth can be as proud of its past glory, its cultural roots, civilizational genius maturing into excellence, and the evolution of an ethos unmatched in human history, as India. And the fountainhead of this entire priceless heritage is the early Aryan and the Vedic period dating back to 8000 B.C. But before we take stock of this treasure trove of human achievement, we have to clear the miasma of obfuscation that western historians and the hired script-writers of our British rulers have produced, regarding the origin of the Aryans, the source of all human knowledge and the antiquity of our Vedic efflorescence.

Our first task would be to briefly debunk the so-called Aryan Invasion Theory and set right the facts of ancient history, resurrect the correct chronology, and see what happened, when and why? Let us start at the beginning.

In the long march of Indian civilization, a historiographic disaster overtook our people in the second half of the nineteenth century. Flying in the face of all textual and scientific evidence and for reasons that have more to do with politics than science and scholarship, a colonial missionary construct was foisted on our ancient history to subserve the interests of colonial rule, Christianity and Europe. An Anglo-German, philologist and 'scholar' Frederick Max Muller (1823-1901) worked out a chronology and thesis, unquestioned by the academia till today, and actively supported by the leftist historians, the story of Vedic civilization that was to be retold by these worthies.

A deep study based on a combination of astronomic, literary, philological, ecological, archaeological, mathematical, scientific, geological and meteorological data will establish that the Rig Vedic civilization formed an earlier layer of world civilization that flourished before the rise of the civilizations of Indus Valley, Sumeria and Egypt, and can be dated back to around 8000 Before Christian Era, approximately the date when silver was separated from natural brass casting. Rig Vedic period would be dated even earlier. The theory of Aryan invasion invented by Max Muller has its roots in the nineteenth century political concerns of Germany and the British colonial India. The Aryan theory has its genesis not in India but in Europe. Let us examine the facts. People of North and South India speak languages from different families. The two are derivatives from the Aryan and Dravidian families of languages. We shall soon realize that separating two people on linguistic basis is a gross distortion of facts. Now come back to the motivation of Max Muller's theory in the nineteenth century Europe and the political, racial, religious and nationalistic forces at work in those times. There was no Indus archaeology and there was no known co-relation between Indian and European languages. The two important pillars of the Aryan theory were European racism, mainly anti-Semitism and German nationalism. Comparative linguistics and archaeology did not exist at the time and the fact is that Sanskrit was the source of most European languages. Instead of the 'theory' being the result of archaeology and comparative philology the position is the other way round. Indus archaeology itself contradicts the invasion theory. The invasion of the dark-skinned people by the light-skinned ones was really a replay of the European strategy of colonizing Asia and Africa. Substituting European for Aryan and Asian and African for Dravidian, you have the leit motif of the European colonial campaigns in the two continents. This makes the Aryans a replica of the European colonizers. The archaeological finds of the Indus valley civilization were made to fit the Aryan invasion, which was supposed to have come later and destroyed the former. In fact, the ruins of Harappa and Mohenjo-daro were interpreted as the result of destruction caused by the Aryan invasion. The myth of the invasion was thus invented to corroborate the tautology or a circular argument, as a proof that the Aryans came after the Indus civilization, which they destroyed. This effort totally ignored the fact, as we shall see later, that most of the artifects found in the Indus valley excavations were in use much earlier in the Vedic period. The destruction of the Indus valley civilization was not due to any invasion but the drying up of the river Saraswati, which flowed across the Thar Desert and watered this civilization to prosperity. Later, as the river dried up, the civilisation too came to an end. But this happened much after the Rigveda period.

Certain Shaivic remains found in Harappa with similar finds in Gujarat, and the phallus worship in Dravidian Shaivites led to the belief that the people of Harappa were Dravidian, completely ignoring the fact that the stronghold of Shaivites is not the Dravidian south, but the Himalayan regions of Nepal, Kashmir and the northern parts of the UP and Himachal Pradesh. This was the cradle of the earlier Vedic people whose legacy was passed later to the Harappan Civilization. To quote the famous historian Talageri: "The negative evidence in the form of absence of the horse and rice in the Indus civilization, which was taken as evidence of its Dravidian origin is no more tenable in view of the occurrence of the horse bones and rice at Lothal, Kalibangan, Surkotada and Ropar in India and Mohenjo-daro in Pakistan. On the other hand there is enough positive evidence in support of the religious rites of the Harappans being similar to those of the Vedic Aryans. Their religious motifs, deities and sacrificial altars bespeak of Aryan faith... The word 'Druids' of England sounds strangely like 'Druhyus' who were driven out of India in sustained campaigns and had their Asian origins in the early fourth millennium BCE. Thus, there have been so many Indo-European migrations, and this points to India as the original home of the people speaking the Indo-European dialect, who migrated to the West and North-west in pre-historic times, the exact reverse of the facts of the Aryan invasion theory. I have discussed the subject of the Aryan invasion in some detail in my book *India Betrayed*. The Aryan invasion theory requires negation of a substantial body of literary and archaeological evidence. How could the Aryans, who were basically supposed to be nomads evolve such a refined language as Sanskrit, with its sophisticated texts and generate a vocabulary that spread to the rest of the world, influencing Greek, Latin, Sumerian, and Egyptian languages? The sophistication of Panini's grammar three thousand years ago, the *Ashtadhyayi* and Patanjali's *Mahabhashya* will make one wonder how such a linguistic perfection can be achieved by a nomadic people so late to arrive on the historic scene? This leads to a paradox of a "history" without a "literature" and a "literature" without a "history". The fact of the matter is that "Arya" did not denote a race but was used to address a person of noble origin. There are examples galore in our epics of queens addressing their husband kings as "Aryaputra".

The Harappans of the Indus valley have left vast archaeological evidence over a million square kilometers area from Iran and beyond Afghanistan to Eastern UP and the Tapti valley and yet left absolutely no literary records. The Vedic Aryans and their successors on the other hand have left no archaeological record of their existence. Thus, we have a concrete history and archaeology of thousands of years but no literature, and the ancient Vedic Aryans who left no history nor any archaeological records.

The Harappan society of 3000 BC precedes the Dravidian- Tamil literature by 2000 years, since the latter dates back to first century BC only. Thus, there can be no comparison between Harappans and the Dravidians. The Harappans, we know, were literate but left no literature, while the so-called illiterate Aryans have left a mass of literature behind. There is another hole in the Aryan invasion theory that geometry and astronomy were borrowed by the Indians from the Greeks after Alexander's invasion. A cursory look at the Harappan ruins shows a very well developed art of town planning with straight lines, squares and rectangles, marking streets, houses, courtyards, stables and drainage system. These could not have developed without a thorough knowledge of geometry and mathematics. The late American mathematician and historian of science, Seidenberg, has pointed to certain Vedic sacrificial altars called 'yajnasalas' from the post-Vedic period which contained technical details for their construction. All these are detailed in 'Sulbasutras' the mathematical texts of the Vedic period. The mathematics of 'Sulbasutras' dates back to the period long before 2000 BC. The Egyptian pyramids dating back to 2500 BC, were more likely based on Vedic funeral altars known as the 'smasana-cit'. Seidenberg has conclusively proved that all ancient mathematics is derived from Vedic mathematics or the 'Sulbasutra'. All this preceded Pythagoras, the 'father of Greek geometry'. Thus, there is a paradox that the construction in the supposedly antique Dravidian-Indus sites came earlier, while the instructions for building them are found in the Vedic literature of the supposedly invading Aryans, who came much later. Einstein often said: 'A theory must not contradict empirical facts.' The Aryan invasion theory does precisely that. We will revert to the other mass of compelling evidence against the Aryan invasion theory later, but a mention here should be made that this move had far-reaching consequences on the Indian polity resulting in a skewed and degraded perspective of the past and a permanent Aryan-Dravidian divide. In the '*Amarakosa*' the Sanskrit lexicon dating about 500 AD, an 'Aryan' is '*mahakula-kulinarya-sabhya-sajjana-sadhavah*'. This is unambiguous and means: an *Arya* is one who hails from a noble family, is of gentle behaviour and demeanour, good-natured and of righteous conduct." It has nothing to do with race. Manu, the first man and a seer, much hated by the leftist and today's Dalits, had said that people of all nationalities were Aryan or non-Aryan depending on their culture and conduct. The word 'Aryan' denoted a very high moral code of behaviour and adherence to sacred laws. Manu's list of such people included these from all parts of India, neighbouring countries like China and Persia, Kambojas from the North-East Afghanistan, Yavanas from North-West Afghanistan and beyond. The Dravida probably refers to people of the south-west of India and the South. The following texts occur in an ancient literary text:

- "...*Praja arya jyotiragrah*"

  Children of Arya seek and are led by Jyoti.
- "One who destroys life is never an Arya, and one who desists from taking life is an Arya". – ***Dhammapada 720.***

  This clearly puts the Nazis out of the community of Aryans. Ramayana of Valmiki is not without a message:
- "*Aryah sarva-samascaiva sadaiva priyadarsanah*"

  Arya was one who cared for the equality of all and was dear to everyone. – ***The Ramayana 11.16***

The Holy Bible has two parts – the Old Testament and the New Testament. The Old Testament is a Jewish literary text and deals with ancient times till the emergence of Christianity. To sever its umbilical cord from its Jewish heritage the Christian Europe looked east, mainly towards India to seek its origin from a new race or civilization. This was the time when the word 'Aryan' as a race was invented, sometimes in the middle of nineteenth century. There were two civilisations in the East—Indian and Chinese. The European preferred the Indian Aryans as their forebearers and adopted the word '*Aryan*' to dissect themselves from the rest of the people. With this masterstroke, they adorned themselves with the nobility of birth and a higher civilizational pedigree. Thus anti-Semitism and a colonial drive were the main impulses for the nineteenth century Europe to give themselves an Aryan heritage and invent the theory of the Aryan invasion of India; the logic being of a superior race invading the lesser mortals.

The author of this effort was Frederick Max Müller. The similarity between Sanskrit and European languages prompted the linguists to add their might to the anti-Semitic impulse of Western Europe and give themselves an Aryan heritage based entirely on a pseudo-scientific presumption. Colonel Boden, God bless his soul, established a Professorship of Sanskrit at Oxford University, whose aim, according to Monier-Williams, was "...to promote Sanskrit learning among the English, so as 'to enable his countrymen to proceed in the conversion of the natives of India to the Christian Religion.' Later, prizes were also offered to literary works that undermined Indian tradition.

The first holder of the Boden Professorship was Horace Hyman Wilson (1784-1860). Writing about a series of lectures he gave, Wilson himself noted: "These lectures were written to help candidates, for a prize of £200 given by John Muir, for the best refutation of the Hindu religious system." Frederic Max Müller generally regarded as the greatest Indologist and a Vedic and Sanskrit scholar of his times, (credit he did not deserve), was favoured by circumstances to write extensively on Rigveda with a view to denigrate Hindu religion. Later, challenged by his critics on the inexactitude of his theory, he had to admit: "Whether the Vedic hymns were composed in 1000, 1500 or 2000 or 3000 B.C., no power on earth will ever determine!" Max Muller combined in himself a romantic temper with a Protestant missionary zeal. He wrote in 1868 to the Duke of Argyle, then acting Secretary of State for India: "The ancient religion of India is doomed, and if Christianity does not step in, whose fault will it be?" Another aberration in the so-called "race-science" was the invention of the superiority of the European whites over the blacks which forced the British writer Nancy Stefan to charge that, "On examination it is found that the European whites are at the top and the African blacks at the bottom, with others coming in between." While Max Müller gave credence to the Aryan theory in England and Germany, his friend, E. Renan, popularized the same in France, and Sanskrit thereafter became a popular reading in the nineteenth century Europe, especially in Germany, the home of Indology. However, the credit for the first premise that European languages were a branch of Sanskrit goes to Filippo Sassetti, a Florentine merchant who stayed in Goa between 1583 to 1588.

Now the fortunes turned. Germany had lost its self-esteem after continuous defeats, starting from the Thirty Years' War down to Napoleon's victories and found itself a pawn in the power game of the contemporary great powers of Europe. As a reaction, the unification of Germany began and was completed around 1870, making Germany the greatest European power. The pride in its Aryan ancestry played no mean role in a resurgent Germany's newfound strength. Their over-weaning confidence forced contemporary British to observe, that "a nation has been born out of Sanskrit." The British were already traumatized by the 1857 Revolt in India and were deeply conscious of the reality that if India united under a single leadership, nothing can stop the end of the British Empire. To them the obvious leaders were the Brahmins, who had been respected for generations and traditionally provided all guidance in matters temporal and spiritual. This forced the British Government to remove all Brahminical influence in India and black out past Indian history, by using the missionaries, not only to spread Christianity but to undermine Brahminical influence and denigrate our past. In this effort the greatest contribution came from Thomas Babbington Macaulay (1800-1859), the Education Member of the Governor General's Council, who wrote in 1836, " Our English schools are flourishing wonderfully. The effect of this education on the Hindus is prodigious .... It is our belief that if our plans of education are followed up, there will not be a single idolater among the respectable classes in Bengal thirty years hence. And this will be effected without efforts to proselytize, without the smallest interference with religious liberty, but natural operation of knowledge and reflection. I heartily rejoice in the project." This diabolical plan was aimed to turn the strength of the Brahmins against themselves by using their commitments to scholarship in uprooting their own tradition. The assistance of the Indian educated elite in this regard was most valueable. Macaulay's hired agent in this effort was Max Müller. He, on a stipend of Rupees one lac, a huge sum at that time was asked, as pointed out earlier, to undertake the study of Rigveda and use this knowledge against India's past. With time as the German nationalism and its antagonism to British interest grew, Max Müller had to do a volte face and attempted to wean away Western Europe from their Aryan origins. This was not an easy task, since Max Müller had already made too many bargains with the devil. With the resurgent Germany as the spearhead of the

Aryan race, his own handiwork, and Max Müller being a loyal citizen of England, his own theory became an embarrassment, casting aspersions on his loyalty. He had no recourse but to recant, and refute his own theory of Aryan race and the Aryan invasion of India. Unfortunately, Indian academia and leftist historians are still obsessed with the same old pseudo-scientific version of the race theory.

What are the textual sources that we can search for evidence? It is amazing to note that no author has inscribed his name to any part of the Vedas or *Upanishads* and *Puranas*. The Vedas are important sources of political history for two reasons. First, which is unique, is the incorruptibility of the Vedic text, handed down obligatorily through recital by learned Brahmins who had memorized these with perfect pronunciation. The Vedic Sanskrit differed from the later or classical Sanskrit in that the accent indicated the intended compound. Sanskrit is the mother of all languages with an amazing vocabulary and range of expression. The pulchritudinous rhythm and compactness of its verses runs through the entire Vedic literature, with an almost mathematical exactitude and centripetal binding.

A study of the above literature raises a number of intractable problems if the Aryan invasion theory is to be accepted. The entire mass of Vedic texts has no reference whatsoever to any invasion. Any attempt to justify the Aryan invasion based on Vedic literature is flawed, due to selective references picked up from isolated passages. The nomadic Aryans by no means possessed an organized instrument of war unlike the Mongols who conquered half the known world. And yet, according to Western scholars the nomad Aryans who had no knowledge of the art of war or any worthwhile instruments to wage it are credited with the conquest of the mainland mass from West Anatolia to Babylon to Persia to Afghanistan right upto the Indian heartland. The aggressive trait of the Aryans alone cannot explain this great military achievement. Any invasion or war attributed to the Aryans is only between the Aryan sub-groups or amongst members of the community itself.

In the entire Vedic literature there is not a single reference or any information regarding the place of origin of the invaders themselves. The Vedic too, such as the *Brahmanas*, *Puranas* and other texts are also silent on the subject. An ancient primitive people arriving in scattered waves, through a sub-continental movement, could not have successfully covered up the fact of their arrival from outside, nor suffer from a selective amnesia, and a collective loss of memory of any such odyssey. There also does not exist any such mythology of a central Asian desert or mountain region except that of a riverine and ocean culture in the literary corpus of these people. The oldest texts in Rigveda consist of 1017 hymns and around 10,000 verses; the four Vedas and the related *Brahmanas*, *Aranyakas* and early *Upanishads*, all pre-Buddhist, running into 5000 pages also do not mention any such event. No contemporary civilization or one before the Vedic can boast of such a vast literature. Even if a portion of this was produced outside, how could this be grafted on to a different continent without leaving any trace of its place of origin. The inevitable conclusion, therefore, is that this literature was indigenous to these people in their Aryavarta habitat. The Vedic Sanskrit is a complex poetry with precise metrical forms and an ideal language for computers, because of its lack of ambiguity. To attribute the knowledge of this profound language to primitive invaders is a most unlikely proposition. The primitive invaders matrix just does not gel with the complex traditions of literature and civilization recorded in the language of a highly civilized community. The Vedic people, identified with a high level of civilization and who possessed a profound literature, have been made an instrument of the destruction of the so-called earlier Harappan civilization. This is a bizarre fact of literary history, as pointed out earlier. The highly advanced Harappan culture that had been destroyed has no history or literature, while a much more advanced language is left with no culture to hang on, both occurring in the same part of the world at the same time. Thus, the word Aryan has no racial connotations. Buddha declared his religion as Aryan and when Arjuna refused to pick up arms at the battlefield of Kurukshetra, Lord Krishna accused him of behaving in an un-Aryan or ignoble manner. It was not a racial slur on Arjuna. Cyrus, the first Emperor of Persia, also called himself an Aryan or a noble person. The term *'Aryan'* denoted an elevated or evolved state of man. The battle between light and darkness is well described in various religions as in Vedic texts and denotes a fight between good and evil. It does not have a racial metaphor. There are innumerable myths in Persian, Celtic, Germanic, Egyptian and even Christian religious texts, describing such fights between good and evil, of powers of light and darkness.

Another commonly abused term is '*Varna*'. '*Varna*' does not mean the tint of the epidermis or colour in the racial sense, or caste. A Brahmin is 'white' because of his purity and power of intelligence, '*sattva*'. A Kshatriya, due to his quality of energy, will and action symbolizes 'red'; the Vaisya who deals with trade and commerce is referred to as 'yellow,' while with his quality of ignorance and servitude, the 'Dasyu' or 'Shudra' is termed 'black.' Thus, 'Varna' in the Vedic Aryan lexicon denoted quality of the spiritual level, of light, thought and friendliness, while the Dasyu Varna for the opposite i.e. the quality of darkness, enmity and falsehood.

Manu is the first Vedic seer king as mentioned in '*Satapatha Brahmana*' (1.8.1.) who took shelter in the Himalayas during the great flood. As per Rig Veda (X63.1) he is the original man whose descendants were Pururavas, Ayu, Nahusha and Yayati. Yayati gave birth to five Vedic families called Purus, Ayus, Druhyas, Turvasas and Yadus. Human beings are referred to as '*Manusa*' or '*Manav*'. These five groups of man or '*Panch Manava*' which are generally recorded as the five Aryan tribes, similar to the twelve early Jewish tribes which crossed the river Jordan under Joshua, can be identified in the Puranas as belonging to the Lunar dynasty of kings. The Turvasas related to Southeast Bihar, Bengal and Orissa and were the likely forebearers of Dravidas and Yavanas. The Yadus related to South or South West Gujarat and Rajasthan, traced in the historical times to Mathura, South of Delhi to Dwarka and Somnath. The Ayus related to the North or the Punjab and some parts of Bengal and Bihar too. The Druhyas inhabited the West or Central West including Gandhar, Afghanistan and were later driven to Central Asia, while the Purus were denounced for having sinned against 'Dharma' at various times and the main war involved conflicts between different varnas and Vedic groups as recorded in Puranas, the Yadus, being the most turbulent. Any resemblance to the Yadavas in today's Indian politics is purely accidental. These intra-Aryan wars were conflicts between the virtuous and those who had fallen from grace, and can by no imagination be related to the Aryan-Dravidian divide.

All the four 'Varnas' had their share of the demons and the divine; Brahmins and Kshatriyas included the good, bad and the ugly. There had been many wars within Kshatriyas and also between Brahmins and Kshatriyas. The '*Manu Samhita*', a post-Vedic text, similarly states: 'But in consequence of the omission of sacred rites, and of their not consulting the sages, the following people of the noble class have gradually sunk in this world to the condition of servant – the Paundrakas, Codas, Dravidas, Kambojas, Yavanas, Sakas, Paradas, Pahlavas, Cinas, Kiratas, and Darads. All those peoples in this world, who are excluded from the community of those born from the mouth, arms, thighs and feet of Brahman (the four Vedic classes), are called Dasyus, whether they speak the language of the barbarians or that of the Aryans. - ***Manu Samhita X. 43-45.***

These texts from the Vedas indicate a highly civilized origin of the Aryans and the Dasyus; both being part of the same culture except for their different proclivities. Dasyus even had the same accoutrements of war such as horses and implements as the Aryans.

The Aryans described in the Vedas, had a large number of cities, inconsistent with the nomadic origin attributed to them. The Vedic sages invoked the gods to protect them with cities.

- O fire, protect us with a hundred metal cities.

  - ***RV. VII 3.7.***

- Agni, thus be like a wide unconquerable metal city multiplied a hundred times.

  - ***RV. VII.15.14***

- Protect us with a hundred cities, O Agni.

  - ***RV. VI.48.8***

The Vedic people lived along the great rivers in the land called Saptha Sindhu. Vedic hymns sing glory to the rivers of which the most sacred was Saraswati, frequently mentioned in Vedic literature. Due to climatic and environmental changes, the river dried up leading to the fall of Harappan culture and the movement of Aryans eastward, marking the end of the Vedic age. Dholavira, a port city of the Harappa Mohenjo-daro complex was once a seaport at the mouth of the river Saraswati, which sustained the existing civilisation. As per the present archaeology, it is known that the river Yamuna stopped flowing into Saraswati well before 2300 BC. With the drying up of Saraswati this part of the river basin turned arid and could no more sustain life nor an urban civilisation of the Harappan kind. The site of the great '*Satras*' or sessions by the Brahmin priests were situated along the confluence of the above streams.

Five rivers converged on Saraswati along with their streams. In consequence, Saraswati became five-fold in this region. These five were identified as Drasthavati, Sutudri (Satluj), Chandrabhaga (Chenab), Vipas (Beas) and Eravati (Ravi).

-Sukla Yajur Veda – 34.1

When we add river Yamuna to these, the above rivers became Sapt Sindhu, the highly lauded Saraswati, which became the largest river system of the Vedic times. Gandhar and Afghanistan as brought out earlier were part of the Vedic civilisation and included Shortugai, a Harappaan site located in Balkh or Bactria mentioned in Atharva Veda (V.22.7,14.17). *Attareya Brahman* (VII-34) also mentions the use of camels during the Vedic age. There is also evidence of the existence of lapis lazuli mines near Balkh, the main source of precious stones to the ancient world. The growth of barley (*yava*) and copper (*ayas*) during the Vedic times points to a date earlier than 3000 BCE. The other Vedic lands of Anga and Banga i.e. Bihar and Bengal formed the eastern extremity of the Saraswati region of the Vedic people and was called the land of the unorthodox religious practices.

The Saraswati region lay midway between Balkh and Bengal. The origin of the Rigveda age dates back to the end of the Ice Age, when Saraswati, the heart of the Vedic India, was a mighty stream, which flowed through the desert and had a length of 40 days' journey time on horse back from its origin. This is one basis on which the Aryan invasion theory falls flat on its face and their origin in the Central Asia or Europe suffers the same fate due to the irrefutable evidence of the existence of the perennial stream called Saraswati in Vedic texts. That the westward flow of Yamuna supplied Saraswati with most of its waters, is mentioned not only in Rigveda but in Atharva Veda as well. This single evidence of the change of flow of Yamuna places the chronology of the Vedic period much before the Harappan civilization, which according to accepted dates goes back to approximately 3000 BCE.

The river Ganga where the Vedic people moved after the drying up of Saraswati became the symbol, around which legend and lore were woven without end, and formed the lifeblood of our ancient civilisation. Believed to have descended from the heavens to the head of Lord Shiva, it became the River Divine. However, in more earthy terms, Ganga has a never-ending source of water not only at its origin at

Gangotri from the Gaumukh glacier, but also all the way down up to the sea. For instance, even after the diversion of a large part of its waters into irrigation canals, least of which is at Roorki, Ganga replenishes itself through many hidden sources of subterranean water along its course. Unlike the Saraswati, the Ganga has never dried up nor shall it do so in future. It is a hydrological miracle for the present day marine engineers. If besides the gods, one were to identify one single symbol of Hinduism in our Vedic culture in the past and present civilizational anthology, there shall be only one name—Mother Ganga or Ganga *Mata*.

The Aryan invasion theory received its impetus from the early philologists, as pointed our earlier, who depended entirely on commonality of words between Sanskrit and the Indo-European languages with the movement not from East to West but from West to East. This theory dated the arrival of Aryans at 1500 BCE and the writing of Rigveda around 1200 BCE. For a long time, the linguistics vetoed all scientific and mathematical evidence to the contrary, i.e. the movement of languages from India westwards. As we shall discuss later, the epicentre of the Indus valley civilisation along with Mohenjo-Daro and Harappa was somewhere in the east of river Indus and along the course of the river Saraswati. The Aryan invasion theory creates an improbable hypothesis that the invading Aryans crossed all the six rivers i.e. the Indus and its five tribuataries to establish themselves along a river, which had gone dry almost 500 years earlier.

The relationship between Old Avestan i.e. Zoroastrian (Persian) and Vedic Sanskrit has led to further complications, regarding the relative chronology of the Vedic Aryans vis-à-vis the Persian civilisation. Let us now evaluate the new evidence. David Frawley had noted the mention of a deity named "Himalaya" in the Kassite records of 1750 BCE. The Kassites appeared in history around the time of the final dessication of river Saraswati, when the focus of the Indian civilisation shifted from its basin to Ganga eastward and the political supremacy shifted from the Bharatas on the Saraswati to Magadh on the Ganga. The above facts are well documented in Puranas and other texts. The origin of Kassites is not very clear and they may have possibly originated from the marshlands of southern Babylonia. Some records suggest that the mouth of River Saraswati was near ancient Dwarka known earlier as Kushasthali (Place of Kusha). The Kassites having defeated the Babylonian rulers settled near the Indus site and the Himalayas, under their king named Kastiliashu and are known to have used horses and chariots. Baudhayana, a Vedic scholar, who designed the spoked wheel in his mathematical works is also documented in the Rigveda, thus pointing towards Indian antecedents of the Kassites. The ancient "*Vandianda*" a Persian text, also mentions the "hapta hendu" (Vedic 'Sapta Sindhu') reminiscent of the times, when Saraswati was still flowing. A passage from *Bhavisya Purana* refering to Jarathustra Mag later known by the name "Mag (Shaka)", denotes a semblance to 'Mag-Brahmins'. The words 'Mag' and 'Shaka' also stand for people of Iran as well as India. These two will suggest a linkage westward from India to Iran, which places Indian civilisation much earlier to Iranian Zoroastrianism. The theory of the Aryans moving from an interior land in Eurasia, far from the sea, is further rebutted by countless references to the rivers and the seas so frequent in Rigveda and subsequent texts.

We now return to the mathematical basis for the interpretation of our ancient civilization. The pioneer research in this regard has been carried out by Feuerstein, Kak and Frawley in their book " *In Search of the Cradle of Civilisation*" (1995), which conclusively proves the origin of all Mathematics, Algebra and Geometry to be in ancient India. To this list of authors the most important addition would be A.B. Dutta and A Seidenberg. They repeatedly refer to Vedic texts called the Sulbasutras and its mathematics based on religious rituals. The word 'Sutra' means 'string', and the 'sutra' works were composed in the form of a string of short statements undoubtedly for easy memorization. Panini's masterpiece *'Ashtadhyayi'* with its cryptic statements described as 'aphorisms' by modern scholars, enunciates the principles (formulae) of Algebra and Geometry, while *'Grahayasutra'* could be termed 'principles' for the householder, both sacred and secular. The '*Grahayasutra*' is a mine of useful information on Architecture and Mathematics. The Sulbas of Baudhayana, Apastamba and Katyayana with the mathematics of old Babylonia and Egypt enable us to establish 2000 BCE as the absolute lower limit for the early 'Sutra' literature. Taking this fact along with the astronomical data from *Asvalayana, Grahyasutra* and other works, pushes this date back by another thousand years, the traditional date of Mahabharata War (3102 BCE). Gradually, as the miasma of misdirected linguistics lifted under the glare of scientific evidence, the real source of all mathematics was traced to Sulbasutras and the Vedic texts. The Pythagorean Greek, old Babylonian and Egyptian mathematics came to be derived from a single source or sulbasutra. The credit for this achievement goes entirely to A. Seidenberg, who conclusively proved that instead of being the recipient, Vedic India was the donor of all mathematical science of the ancient world.

Seidenberg's mathematical methods clashed head-on with the contemporary entrenched theory of the Aryan invasion, but he refused to compromise and stated in no uncertain terms that "the elements of ancient geometry found in Egypt and Babylonia stem from a ritual system of the kind observed in the Sulbasutras". From his profound study of Sutra literature containing in the works of Baudhayana, Asvalayana, Apastamba and Katyayana, he concluded that the Sutra Mathematics dated much earlier than the old Babylonian and Egyptian middle kingdom (2050-1800 BC), both deriving from the Sulbas. Ashvalayana's astronomical works too place the Sulba literature to around 3100 to 2600 BC. This was the time when the star Draconis, also called Thuban, in the constellation of Dragon was the pole star, also mentioned in '*Satpatha Brahman*'.

The Sutra literature premises the pre-existence of the four Vedas, which would have been in existence much before. This date agrees with the tradition of Vyasa, who edited the four Vedas and Mahabharata (3102 BCE), a date which is in accordance with ancient mathematical and astronomical data. There are clear connections between the so-called Step-Pyramid or the 'mastaba' (2650 BCE) built by Djoser (2686-2613 BCE) and Samansana-cit (cemetery shaped altar) of Baudhayana dealing with Vedic funerary rituals. The mathematical as well as religious connection between the Vedic altar and the mausoleums called the Pyramids are not accidental. We now come to the Pythagorean theorem. It was Thibaut who first explicitly made out the case that the Pythagorean geometry was derived from Vedic Mathematics. This is rooted in a statement of Baudhayana "that the diagonal of a rectangle produces both squares which its length and breadth produce separately."

He first tried to derive the theorem from the square noting that the diagonal produces an area twice as much as one produced by either side. A common figure in the Vedic altar is given as follows:

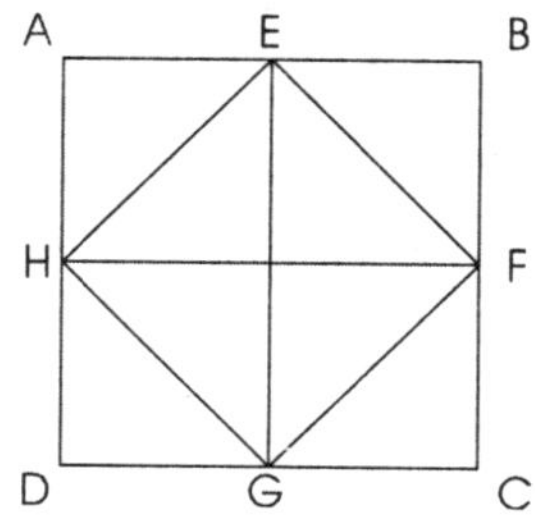

It shall be assumed that the square on GF, i.e. GHEF has an area equal to half of the square ABCD or the total of the square on side FC and CG. Thus, Baudhayana, who derived his theorem from this figure as early as 3000 BCE could legitimately be the father of the theorem of Pythagorus. The Greek followed this much later, in the works of Democritos (440 BCE):

For the Indians and the Greeks geometry was primary, while for the Egyptians and Babylonians it resulted from arithmetic. In Vedic India geometry subserved religion and ritual. In Babylonia and Egypt it has no such religious affiliations.

The unit fraction approximation that frequently appears in the Egyptian and old Babylonian texts can also be traced back to the Sulbas. Consider the following:

$\sqrt{2} = 1+1/3 + 1(3.4) - 1(3.4.34)$

Such unit fractions appear at several places in the Sulbas too. Also the value of π used by Ahmes of Egypt (1550 BCE) is the same as mentioned in the late *Manava Sulbasutra* in precisely the same manner i.e. π=3.160.49=4x(8/9)^2. This conclusively proves that Ahmes and Manava Sulbasutra used the same approximation or the value of π. The two examples given above leave no room for doubt that the Babylonian and Egyptian Mathematics have a common source in Sulbas. We now come to the structure of the Pyramids. The Vedic altars shaped like trapezoidal figures are also found on Egyptian monuments. Two samples from *Histoire de l'art Egyptian d'apres de le monuments'* as given here are also found in the Sulbas.

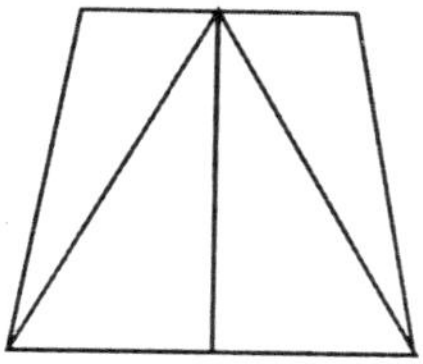 

The trapezoidal shapes and their sub-divisions are noteworthy. The first figure is shown in Sulbasutras and the second dealing with computation of the area and its proofs appear in *Apastamb Sulbasutra*. The trapezoid has connotations to health and wealth, an Indian concern, while in Egypt, they were useful in construction of pyramid.

There is also a mention in Rigveda of large numbers such as the series: 2,4,8,20,30,40,50,60,70,80,90,100 (RV,II.18.4-6). There is also mention of a limited decimal system and terms like *dasa* (10), *sata* (100), *sahasra* (1000), *ayuta* (10,000) and '*parardha*', which stand for trillion (10^{12}) are also mentioned in Yajurveda (17.2). *Trisaptah* which stands for various types of combinations of three and sevens like 3+7=10; 3x7=21; 3+5=8 and others appear in the very first verse of Atharvaveda. The Astronomy and Vedic Mathematics are closely intermingled in Vedic texts. For example, Jupiter being the heaviest of the planets is called *Guru* (heavy), while Saturn, which has the slowest orbital velocity amongst all visible planets, is called *Shani* (slow). The Rigveda also mentions the orbital period of the five major planets as well as the sun and the moon. An interesting feature of geometric algebra of Baudhayana is the construction of the spoked wheel. The chariots with spoked wheels appear in West Asia around 2000 BCE, but in Rigveda they do much earlier. An interesting feature in Baudhayana's Sulbasutra is the ingenious method for designing the chariot wheel using the Pythagorean triples and circulature of the square as illustrated here:

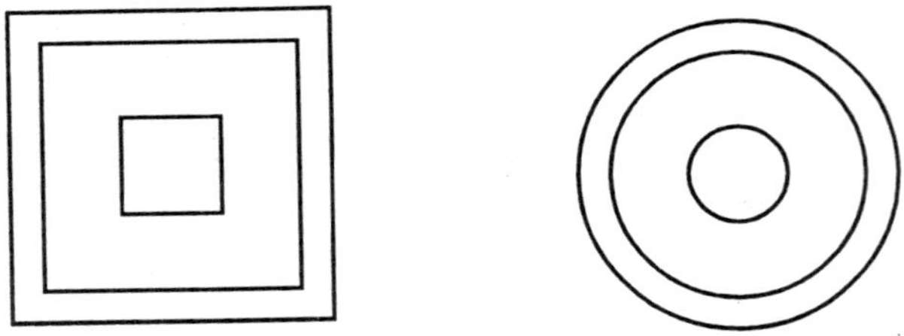

Drawing a 12x12 and 4x4 square and placing them concentrically in a 17x17 square shows that the difference between 289 (17) and 144 (12) covers the felloe of the wheel. By converting the outer (17x17) square into a circle using the Sulba method and then repeating the procedure with the interior 12x12 square and removing it the result makes up the outer and inner boundaries of the felloe. Converting the 4x4 square into a circle makes it the hub. The area left for the spokes became 144-16=128. Since half of 128 is 64 one should place eight spokes in each one of them. Though easy it is an amazing conclusion.

The spoked wheel which played an important role in ancient history will now appear to be born out of the religious mathematics of the Sulba, dealing with the construction of altars and circling of the square. The inverse problem of squaring the circle was a further refinement. Thus, there should be no doubt in the mind of any serious student of ancient history that all mathematics, geometric and algebraic knowledge disseminated from Vedic India westwards.

We should now return to astronomy and its related chronology highlighting some vital chronological landmarks and relate them to archaeological finds, which taking mathematics into account shall help us to arrive at a chronological synthesis. Very few identifiable archaeological remains are available that relate to the Vedic period but the oral evidence is vast and unimpeachable. Frenchman Jean Le Mee, a modern student of Vedic times, states:

" Precious stones or durable materials gold, silver, bronze, marble, onyx or granite— have been used by most ancient people in an attempt to immortalize their achievements. Not so however the Aryans. They turned what may seem the most volatile and insubstantial material of all the spoken word and out of this bubble of air fashioned a monument, which for more than thirty perhaps forty centuries later stands untouched by time or the elements... The pyramids have been eroded by the desert wind, the marble broken by earthquakes, and the gold stolen by robbers, while the Veda is recited daily by an unbroken chain of generations, travelling like a great wave through the living substance of mind".

The Arabs are generally credited with the first knowledge of astronomy. The western thinking on the 'Semitic source' of astronomy is contradicted by a statement of the Spanish Arab astronomer Sa'id Al-Andalusi himself, known also as Qadi-Sa'id (1029-1070 CE), who said...

"Of the Indian astronomical systems, the three that are well known are the Sindhind ... the Arjbadha.... and the Arkand... we have received correct information only about the Sindhind system, which was adopted and further developed by a group of Muslim scientists".

Sindhind is Siddhanta or Surya Siddhanta and Arjbagh appears to be the Arabic distortion of the name of the great astronomer Aryabhatta. The theory propounded by Keith that Indians borrowed their astronomy from the Arabs can again be contradicted on sound technical reasons. The equinoctial position of Western Zodiac is identical to that of Varahmihira (500 CE) but is no longer the same today due to the shift of the equinoxes. However, the Middle Eastern "Tropical" Zodiac of the West remained frozen and did not account for the precession of the equinoxes, while the solstices and equinoxes have regressed by about 23 degrees, a fact known to Hindu astronomers and Panchaang (Calendar). Corrections required in the Indian calendar based on the motion of the sun and moon through the fixed stars are a vital achievement of the Indian astronomy dating back to 4000 BCE. Thus, it would have been impossible to fix the Indian sidereal Zodiac of 27 '*Nakshatras*' by a reverse calculation, since the orientation of the Zodiac requires continued correction for the precession. This effort would require a thorough knowledge of the Law of Gravitation and differential equations. Later day astronomers could not have worked out such a data stretching thousands of years merely by borrowing and super-imposing upon a later zodiacal system.

The Indian Zodiac consists of 27 approximately equal parts, each measuring 13° 20' of arc, and while the solar Zodiac is related to the seasons with respect to a fixed star, the 27 '*Nakshatras*' (constellations or 'lunar mansions') indicate the progress of the lunar month and the movement of the sun along its ecliptic annual solar orbit. The start of a particular season is worked out by the entry of the sun, i.e. noting the sunrise, in a particular constellation. The seventh Mandala of the Rigveda mentions vernal equinox in *'Mrigashira'*, indicating a date near 4000 BCE. A landmark date when the sun entered the constellation *'Krittika'* (Pleiades in Taurus) indicates an era that lasted about a thousand years after 3000 BCE. The *'Satapatha Brahmana'* also specifies *'Krittika'* heralding the vernal equinox, which proves this date to lie between 2900 and 1900 BCE. Both *'Satapatha'* and early *'Sutrakara Asvalayana'* record sighting of a pole star, possibly Dracon is (c.3000 BCE to c.2500 BCE). The three constellations relevant for our purpose with their Indian and modern names are given below:

Mrigashira or the Orion	c. 4500-3500 BCE	Rigveda
Rohini or the Aldebaran	c. 3100 BCE (Transition)	Mahabharata
Krittika or the Pleiades	c.2900-1900 BCE	Sutra and Brahmana

As per tradition Asvalayana was born around 3000-2900 BCE following the five generations after the Mahabharata war, during the *'Krittika'* equinox. The Egyptian mathematics and Sulba point 2000 BCE as a date much later than the Sutra period and thus, there is the convergence between the two evidences. *'Satapatha Brahmana'* also indicates Yajnavalkya's birth about three generations following the Mahabharata war very near to the time of Asvalayana, thereby proving that the Brahmana and the Sutra periods did overlap. This fact receives a confirmation from the observation of the pole star mentioned in *'Satapatha Brahmana'* and *'Asvalayana Grihyasutra'*. "Dhruva star," the ''unmoving" (literally meaning 'certain') is so important that it is shown to a newly married couple to enjoin constancy. The present Ursa Minoris (Polaris), a star of second magnitude that indicates the North Pole today, did not do so in ancient times. Since the orientation of the North Pole moves with the precession of the equinoxes, during much of human history there has not been a pole star. The fact that *Asvalayana* and *Satapatha Brahmana* do mention the pole star, an observable pole star, is a matter of great chronological significance. Our evidence thus far indicates 3000-2500 BCE as the period of the earliest portion of the Sutra literature. This also brings the date of the Mahabharata war to the traditional 3102 BCE. The Greek chroniclers after Alexander's invasion of India were aware of the date of Krishna, the principal figure in Mahabharata. The evidence, however, is confusing when it comes to the identity of Sandrocottos-Chandragupta. Pliny refers to Krishna as Heracles, a word derived from Hari Krishna. He also mentioned that Krishna was held in high esteem by the Sourseni (present 'Suraseni') tribe living around Mathora, now known as Mathura. Sourseni (read Sura) was the father of Vasudeva Krishna or Heracles according to Greek records and is said to have lived 138 generations before the time of Alexander (325 BCE). At a rough estimate of 20 years for each generation, a good average by any standards, this leads to 2760 + 325 i.e. 3058 BCE as the date of Krishna, which tallies with the beginning of Kaliyug from 3102 BCE onwards. While the chronology of the West and leftist Indian historians is based on "a conjecture supported by other conjectures", as Sri Aurbindo puts it, our method has been entirely based on mathematics and science. Thus, the Mahabharata war preceded the Harappan civilization. With so many present day relics, such as Hastinapur, Kurukshetra, Indraprastha and Dwarika it is difficult to believe that the knowledge of cities and town planning was not passed down from the Mahabharata era to the later day Harappan civilization.

Let us now step a little to have a deeper look into the Puranic chronology. The Adiparva of Mahabharata mentions a period of 630 years between Sudas and Arjuna. With a date of 3100 BCE for Mahabharata, according to the method used by Hicks and Anderson in their work, the date for Sudas and the battle of 10 kings would come to 3730 BCE.

The Puranas mention the passage of 31 generations between Rama of Ikshvaku dynasty and son of Dasharatha, upto Brihadabala in Mahabharata records. Brihadabala was slain by Abhimanyu, Arjun's son, at Kurukshetra. Again computing on the basis of 20 years per generation we come to a date of between 3800 and 3700 BCE for Rama. This date is further confirmed by the fact that Vashistha, a senior contemporary of Rama, was also present at the Battle of 10 Kings. To sum up in David Frawley's terms, the chronology of the Vedic age would be as given below:

Proto-Rigvedic Period	Around 8000 BC and before 6000 BCE
Early Rigvedic Period	6000 to 4000 BCE
Later Rigvedic Period	4000 to 2000 BCE
Transitional	2000 to 1000 BCE

Let us now deal with the scientific evidence. Domestication of the horse was perfected in India around 4000 BCE well before it was done in Central Asia and South Russian steppes. Along with the recent findings of S.R. Rao, a marine archaeologist, at the site of Dwarika the above date is further confirmed. There is a mention of gold in Rigveda but not of silver, which should have come after the Rigvedic period. The above facts are in accordance with astronomical and geographical data, particularly the record of vernal equinox in Orian and the perennial Saraswati, both facts being mentioned in the Seventh mandala of the Rigveda. The above together with the evidence of astronomy and the Sulbas and Egyptian mathematics, all independent determinations, indicate the same period of i.e. 4000 BCE for the ending of the Rigvedic age. The archaeological remains found at Mehargarh and other places in Gujarat and elsewhere alongwith the submerged city of Dwarika discovered recently date the earlier Indian civilization as far back as 7000 BCE. With more research in charting the river Saraswati and its desiccation leading to the shift of ancient civilisation from the centre of Saraswati-Drishadvati doab to the south-east, more convincing evidence will emerge on the Rigvedic society and our ancient settlements. The ecological disruptions in the Saraswati basin led to the move of that civilization eastward to the Ganga valley and southwestward into Gujarat and Maharashtra. What further proof of this movement is required than the fact that both Baudhayana and Apsthamba belong to the south? While this dichotomy further explains the Yajurvedic tradition into Vajasaneya and the Taittreya schools, it also proves that the so-called Aryans and Dravidian divide is so much historical humbug. Sethna from his laborious works brings out the fact that cotton was a commodity of daily use in the Harappan times. The Vedas and Brahmanas also mention the making of cloth, and terms like weaving, warp, and weft. The discovery of Indian cotton in Peru during 2500 BCE and even earlier in Mexico accords with the common usage of cotton and its extensive trading abroad and across the seas during the Vedic period. Further findings, tested with calibrated C-14 methods, show that 'the Harappan culture should be dated to the period 2700-2000 BC. This along with the fact of climatic change of 2200 BCE recently discovered, explain the sudden ending of the Accadian Empire and the shift of the Saraswati based civilization to the east and confirms the data brought out thus far. We now come to the question of silver; when did it come to India? It was well known to the Harappans but not the Rigveda. The use of silver in other parts of world goes back to 5000 BCE. This is not a certified fact. Silver as we know is not mined in pure state but is separated from copper after a purification process of the latter. The discovery of the silver ornaments at the Pre-Harappan site of Kunal near Ambala points to a date not later than 2000 BCE. With the application of dendrochronology as practised by European archaeologists such as Colin Renfrew that date could go back to 4000 BCE, several centuries before the Vedic people had learnt to separate silver from copper ore. In 1958, a famous casting known as "Vashistha's head" was discovered by Hary Hicks, an American collector. Subsequent metallurgical tests have shown a high silver content which points to the art of casting of an ancient era. Laboratory tests in California and Zurich on this artifact showed carbon deposits, which according to radiocarbon dating leads to a date between 3800 and 3700 BCE. This conclusively proves that the Vedic age should have ended well before this time. This is also corroborated by Mrigashira vernal equinox, which dates closer to 4000 BCE.

The recent landmark discovery off the Gulf of Cambay by a team of oceanographers followed by the combined efforts of National Institute of Ocean Technology, the Birbal Sahani Institute of Palaeobotany and the National Geophysical Research Institute, has conclusively proved the existence of civilisation in that area much before the Harappan and contemporary civilisations in Egypt, Sumeria and Babylon. Artifects such as construction material, wood with holes and studs, pot shreds, beads and fossil bones, after the process of carbon dating, point to a date around 7500 BCE almost the same as the proto-Vedic civilization that came into existence after the melting of the Ice Cap around 8000 BCE, as discussed earlier.

Professor S.N. Rajguru, former Joint Director and Head of the Department of Archaeology at Deccan College, said, "these collections represent an exciting breakthrough in offshore archaeology. The findings indicate that the entire landscape between Bhavnagar and Hazira was probably connected around 7000 BC". The acoustic images of the area present channel like features, indicating the presence of a river in the region. "Geometrical structures and the antiquities have been discovered in an area only within 200 miles adjoining the channel indicating human activity on the bank of the river that was present at that time." These findings also conclusively prove the existence of river Saraswati in the early Vedic period and its subsequent desiccation. The above effort by the National Institute of Ocean Technology (NIOT), which led to an accidental discovery of this sub-merged township, was further supplemented by the following factoid published in many Indian magazines:

The town lay at a depth of 40 meters below the sea, 30 kilometers off the Gujarat coast and dredging efforts spread to an area of 9 kilometers situated on the mouth of a river with signs of a masonry dam. Geometric forms like those at Harappa in various forms and sizes were found. An Olympic size sunken area with steps going down as for a swimming pool and resembling the great bath of Mohenjo-daro was discovered through photographs and sonar soundings. A rectangular platform 200x5 meters, almost the same size as the Acropolis in Greece, was found as earlier in Harappa. A large granary structure made out of mud 185 meters long could also be seen. As part of this township, rectangular basement resembling remains of homesteads and tiles of a drainage system and mud roads too were found as also 2000 artifects including polished stones, tools, ornaments, figurines, broken pottery, some precious stones, ivory and remains of human vertebra, jaw bone and human tooth. But the clinching evidence of antiquity was provided by a fossilized log of chopped wood that dated back to 7500 BCE. The only other settlement of this antiquity was found earlier at Mehargarh in Baluchistan, which was basically an agricultural settlement in the Bolan river valley.

Saraswati remained a mighty river joined by two other great rivers, the Satluj, and the Yamuna, which followed the course of the dry river Drishadavati. This was the situation around 4000 BCE, when North India was watered by the three major river systems of the Indus, Saraswati, and the Ganga. There was no Thar Desert separating the western and the eastern region as it is today. Astronomically this was the Mrigashira era. Sometime around 3100 BCE, when the great Mahabharata took place, the Yamuna changed its course to empty itself into the Ganga resulting in the diversion of the waters from Saraswati, which gradually dried up. The expanding desert cancerously ate into the fertile land and began to separate the western people and their Sindhu-Sauvira culture from the Kuru heartland around the Ganga.

The desiccation of the Saraswati along with recurring floods resulted in the shift of the heart of the Vedic religious praxis eastward to the Kuru Panchala territory adding to the alienation between the east and the west. These were the times of the rise of the Sumerian civilization and the Sutra period, when the western people were derisively called 'Malecchas' by the orthodox of the Vedic heartland. Subsequently, a centre of Vedic tradition grew up in the Gujarat - Maharashtra region anchored on Taittreya thought led by Baudhayana. While the Yajasaneya school of Yajyavalkya settled in the east, the Yajurvedic tradition as brought out earlier was split into its northern and southern components following the Mahabharata war. The desert continued to encroach on the river Indus and the Harappan civilization, a branch of the main Vedic heartland around Ganga, and along with the drying up of river Saraswati caused the extinction of the Indus valley civilization.

We shall sum up by stating that the entire linguistic, literary, mathematical, scientific, archaeological, metallurgical, radiocarbon, and ecological evidence, which we have listed in some detail points to the indisputable fact that there was no Aryan invasion, which led to an Aryan-Dravidian divide. That Sanskrit was the mother of all Indo-European languages. That all knowledge, mathematical, scientific, astronomical, medical (Ayurvedic) and literary flowed from India westwards and not the other way round. That ancient Vedic civilization, the oldest in the world, had reached a very high level of perfection known to mankind.

Sri Aurobindo, India's Avatar of the Modern Age, as described by Francois Gautier, said in 1926 that the two theorems of modern science have a profound spiritual echo. First, that atoms are masses of swirling structure like the solar system; and second, that all the atoms are constituted of the same element. If followed conscientiously these could lead to profound discoveries. He goes on to say: "our ancient Vedic rishis knew of a triple fire, or Agni which they had named: the ordinary fire – Jada Agni; the electric fire Vidyuta Agni; and the solar fire –Saura Agni. Modern science knows only these first two fires and the fact that the atom is like a solar system could lead them to the third discovery". The third 'saura' fire was rediscovered when the Americans exploded a thermo-nuclear bomb caused due to fusion of four Hydrogen atoms into one Helium atom and the conversion of the remaining surplus mass into an intense solar heat. There are innumerable examples of the prescience of our ancient Vedic sages in almost all fields of human knowledge, which have been discovered later by the Western world. The Vedas, in fact, are the foundation of Indian culture, and the greatest power, which has shaped Hinduism and Hindu culture. David Frawley, one of the greatest of Vedic literature specialists in the west, pronounces, "O Indians, your spiritual tradition, as it is encoded in the Vedas, represents the most precious treasure of the human race. Cherish it, support it, and above all share it with the entire world. For the Vedas are like a sun: in them you will find the key of all light, all life, all love and there is no individual or collective problem which cannot be solved by them. (Arise Arjuna. p. 221)" A. Seindenberg, an American mathematician, has proved that *Sulbasutras*, the ancient Vedic mathematics are the primal source of almost all mathematical developments, which were adopted later by Egyptians, Greeks and the Babylonians. Pythagorean theorem and mathematics, astronomy, value of π, as also the geometry of the Egyptian Pyramids, almost a replica of the funerary altars named 'smasana-cit', have all been derived by the West from *Sulbasutras*. The French historian, Alain Danielou, in early 1947 declared that "the Egyptian myth of Osiris seemed directly inspired from a Shaivaite story of the Puranas and that at any rate, Egyptians of those times considered that Osiris had originally come from India mounted on a bull (nandi), the traditional transport of Shiva". Vedas had also a profound influence on various movements in Greece such as the eleatic, orphic, platonician, stoic, gnostic or neoplatonian. There is a thinking, which has been conclusively proved that there existed some secret links between Hindus and Celts. Thus, the Hindu influence on the Western philosophy continued through almost four millennia. The German philosopher, Frederich Shlegel, was so impressed with the Vedic Sanskrit that he exclaimed that there is no language in the world even Greek, which has the clarity and the philosophical precision of Sanskrit", adding "India is not only at the origin of everything, she is superior in everything, intellectually, religiously or politically – and even the Greek heritage seems to pale in comparison"... The great Schopenhauer agrees with him and writes in the preface to his book, *The World as a Will and as a Representation:* " According to me, the influence of Sanskrit literature on our time will not be lesser than what was in the XVIth century Greece's influence on Renaissance. One day, India's wisdom will flow again on Europe and will totally transform our knowledge and thought". Even Neitzsche having read and admired the Vedas could quote from the law of Manu.

The French Philosopher, Roger Pol Droit, in his famous book, *'L'oubli de l'Inde"* (The Forgetting of India) says that Helleno-centric (Greece centered) education and knowledge is derived from India. He also gives the reason of the ignorance of Vedic source of all knowledge, to the writings of the German philosopher Hegel, who literally created Greek civilisation from a vacuum and gave it all the credit, which was due to the Vedic thought. The same westward look and awe of everything western still haunts the present day elite of our country. Quoting David Frawley again, "everything that then came from the East, took an inferior, or pagan value and if only the West knew that the philosophical and religious framework from which emerged later European science, partakes much more with eastern religions such as Hinduism and Buddhism, than with the Judeo-Christian tradition, they would look at India differently." According to Sri Aurobindo, the West has a proclivity to live from below upwards and from out inwards, thereby allowing the innerself being governed by external factors. Vedic India on the contrary believed in living in a higher spiritual truth and to live from the inner spirit upwards. Thus, whether it is the individual or the Government, the process of discipline and governance emanates from inside outwards. Without ignoring the flesh and the material needs Indians went beyond these towards spiritual achievements.

The early Indian polity was basically clan or tribe based and founded on the equality of all its members. The villages had the "Visah" as their Assembly with only the king above this. Thus, the idea of the republican form of Government is not new to India, or a legacy of the British. India had many republics with democratic assemblies and in some cases even oligarchic senate. The system worked effectively and the civil administration and the armies of these republics worked as the best in the world. And all this happened before the Greek civilisation came into being.

Alexander's invasion of India brought out many weaknesses of these republics, the most pernicious of these being failure to unite against a common enemy. Another misconception about India in the Western mind as also our own intelligentsia, is the fragility and autocracy in our system of governance. As brought out earlier, there were republics and rules with democratic governance. Indian politics though fairly complex allowed considerable communal freedom or self-determination. Just prior to the Muslim invasions the apex of the political structure was occupied by three ruling bodies; the King and his ministerial counsel, which consisted of members from all castes, Metropolitan Assembly, and the General Assembly of the Kingdom. In fact, the entire Indian system worked on a close participation of all classes including even the Shudras. The Metropolitan Civic Assembly in towns or villages too enjoyed enough autonomy. So much so that King Ashoka had to abdicate after his defeat in the power conflict with his Counsels.

The edifice of ancient Indian excellence rests on four outstanding pieces of literary works - the Vedas, the Upanishads, the Ramayana and the Mahabharata. Regarding Upanishads, Sri Aurobindo describes them as " the supreme work of the Indian mind, that of the highest self-expression of genius, its sublime poetry, its greatest creation of the thought and word.... A large flood of spiritual revelation..." (*Foundations of Indian Culture* p.269). The Upanishads, which are a blending of philosophy, religion and poetry are the explanatory treatise on the essence of Vedas, and while the Mahabharata and Ramayana constitute a guide to righteous action, Bhagwad Gita is the most perfect work of spiritual revelation in the entire world.

Since Indian philosophy believes in the extension of the mind materialwards, all the works of literature, sculpture, painting, architecture and other art forms lay emphasis on the spirit of the work and not on its externals, e.g. the beauty of Indian sculpture and painting lie not in their outward form and beauty but the inner spirit which inspired their creation. The Indian painting consists of six organs or elements (sadanga). These are *Rupabheda* i.e. distinction of forms; *Pramana* "proof" arrangement of lines; *Bhava* "depicting emotion or the aesthetic sense", followed by *Lavanya* which stands for beauty and *Sadrsya* the veracity "form", and the last is *Varnika-sanga* i.e. harmony of colours. While the western art emphasizes the *Rupabheda* i.e. external forms, the Indian art goes deeper into the world of intellectual fantasy. The epicentre of these art forms was Kashi, the present day Varanasi, where these arts were developed to their full potential under kingly patronage and even travelled to the south. These art forms are visible even today in Afghanistan and Kashmir, the erstwhile Gandhar. With the blossoming of all these human achievements, early India also produced the greatest scholars on political science and economics. One such figure was Kautilya, the author of *'Arthashastra'*, a text which preceded by two millennia a similar work by Machiavelli *'The Prince'*. *'Arthashastra'* dealt with all aspects of statecraft, science of war, economics and almost all aspects of governance. This legacy of Chandragupta Maurya went down upto the reign of King Harsha Vardhana and was adopted even by the Western nations. Jean Danielou wrote that "King Harsha symbolized all that was right in Hindu monarchy, wielding an absolute power, but each sphere of administration was enjoying a large autonomy and the villages were functioning like small republics". Having reached its apogee during the reign of Harsha Vardhana, this Hindu culture started on its path to decline as a direct sequel to Muslim invasions from 632 A.D. onwards.

In every people or a nation, the power to be great is resident, but not every nation reaches its potential for glory or greatness. A few make the effort, some hesitate, some die, some reach upto the base camp and then give up the final assault on the summit, some turn upon themselves to crush this ephemeral capacity in a rage of self-destruction. But greatness once achieved is never forgotten. The memory never dies, and the history that follows is dictated by how that people use that memory to achieve greatness. No nation on this planet has a history of greatness that lasted over nine millennia. It's time India uses this memory of the great Hindu efflorescence to reach the summit of human achievement yet again.

3

Historical Negationism

Time is a great anodyne. Momentous events of history lie buried under the sands of time. Past hurts are often forgotten to avoid incurring fresh pain. However, this general principle cannot be applied to all forms of historical wrongs, especially those, which shape and mould the character and the psyche of a nation. We in India have an unforgivable propensity, not only to ignore our past glory but also to negate historical wrongs. There is much to learn from both. The past not only inspires and reminds, but also teaches us how not to repeat mistakes. The Israelis have a motto "Past wrongs may be forgiven, but should never be forgotten". They do not forget their Diaspora, their humiliations over most part of their history, and the final holocaust during the Second World War. In fact, it is a tradition for the new entrants to their Armoured Corps to take an oath "Massada shall not fall again". Massada, as we all know, was the last stand taken by the surviving Jewish fighters against the Roman legion, where all the occupants of this fortress, died to the last man as they fell, fighting. There is also a custom that immigrants to "Moshavs" in Israel are first taken to the 'Hall of Horrors' where they are made to listen to the sounds of millions of Jews dying in the gas chambers of Hitler's death camps, 'Lest we forget'.

Our historians since independence, under the influence of Nehru, who spawned a breed of Marxist historians in his eponymous institute, the Jawaharlal Nehru University (JNU), have tried to sweep under the carpet all the cruelties of the medieval Muslim invaders, kings and conquerors. The apologists of these barbarous acts often explain away these brutalities as part of the culture of the times. Such explanations are not only a pernicious perversion of history but also a deliberate attempt to insult human intelligence by putting history on its head.

Let us begin by turning the searchlight on the founder of this "school of scandal" that has fostered this perverted cult of historical negationism; the great Nehru himself. The great "secularist", an amateur, a juvenile history writer and a purblind slave to his Cambridge school of historiography was a pioneer in the field of Hindu bashing. However, before we start on Nehru it would be prudent to state that his ideas were by no means original. This credo of '*suppressio veri* and *sugestio falsie*' had been adumbrated earlier in 1930s by M.N. Roy, a radical humanist and the flag-bearer of International Communism. A member of the Comintern in the pay of the Communist Party of Soviet Russia, he had stated "that Islam has fulfilled a historic mission of equality and abolition of discrimination in India, and that for this, Islam has been welcomed in India by the lower castes. If at all any violence occurred, it was a matter of justified class struggle by the progressive forces against the reactionary forces, meaning the feudal Hindu upper classes." The roadmap laid down by M.N. Roy for historical negationism was followed with a fanatic flavour by our *desi* comrades ruling West Bengal, who, under a state dictat on 28th April, 1989, ordered all adverse references to Muslim rulers to be erased from the history textbooks of the higher secondary school. For detailed information on this the reader is advised to read Arun Shourie's well researched book *Eminent Historians*. Nehru and after him his, legatees, the Congress, the Leftists and the JNU academia founded a theory based not on historical evidence but conjectures and their Marxist predilections that India had never been a nation. It was a conglomerate of feuding provinces, principalities and warlords in the sub-continental geographical space with no pan-Indian national theme. As early as 4000 B.C. we find an invocation to God in Atharvaveda to protect our nation "Twam Rashtrani Rakshati"-*Atharvaveda* 19.30.3 (You are the protector of the nation). RSS today talks of a Hindu Rashtra. They do no more than echo these words of antiquity. This is the example of historical negationism and a trend-setter for post-Independence India.

In a volume written by one of these leftist historians, dealing with the Indian freedom struggle, not only has an unduly large part been devoted to the contribution of Indian communists, inspite of their known treacherous role during the Quit India Movement, but an astounding statement has been made elsewhere that the freedom movement drew its inspiration from Lenin. Now his successor Nehru.

As an example of this perversity of perception and deliberate suppression of truth, nothing can beat the following extracts from *The Discovery of India,* his magnum opus:

"It is thus wrong and misleading to talk of a Muslim invasion of India or of the Muslim period in India, just as it would be wrong to refer to the coming of the British to India as a Christian invasion, or to call the British period in India a Christian period. Islam did not invade India; it had come to India some centuries earlier. There was a Turkish invasion; Mahmud's and an Afghan invasion, and then a Turko-Mongol or Mughal invasion, and of these the two latter were important. The Afghans might well be considered a border Indian group, hardly strangers to India, and the period of their political dominance should be called the Indo-Afghan period. The Mughals were outsiders and strangers to India and yet they fitted into the Indian structure with remarkable speed and began the Indo-Mughal period." And later,....

"Through choice or circumstances or both, the Afghan rulers and those who had come with them, merged into India. Their dynasties became completely Indianized with their roots in India, looking upon India as their homeland, and the rest of the world as foreign. Inspite of political conflict, they were generally considered as such and many even of the Rajput princes accepted them as their over-lords. But there were other Rajput chiefs, who refused to submit and there were fierce conflicts. Feroze Shah, one of the well-known Sultans of Delhi, had a Hindu mother; so had Ghyasud-Din Tughlak. Such marriages between the Afghans, Turkish, and the Hindu nobility were not frequent, but they did take place. In the south, the Muslim ruler of Gulbarga married a Hindu princess of Vijayanagar with great pomp and ceremony."

Nehru has made three points in his observations, the first about the benign nature of the Muslim conquest, the second about the desire of the invaders to make India their home and thirdly, the free intermingling of the two communities. Let us examine the validity of these three propositions. When Nehru talks of a happy mingling of Hindus and Muslims resulting into a composite culture, he conveniently forgets that not only during the period of the Delhi Sultanates, but even during the Mughal rule, the religious life of Muslims was agitated not infrequently by periodic outbursts of puritanism, directed mostly against any tendency that smacked of Hinduising Islam. The two-nation theory later propounded by Jinnah was nothing new. It had its roots even in the early period of our history.

If only Nehru had bothered to read what Will Durrant, one of the greatest scholars of history, had to say in his book *'The Story Of Civilization, Part-I :Our Oriental Heritage'* about the Muslim conquest of India, he would have harboured serious doubts about the benign nature of the Muslim conquest. Sample the following from this book:

"The Mohammedan conquest of India is probably the bloodiest story in history. It is a discouraging tale, for its evident moral is that civilization is a precarious thing, whose delicate complex of order and liberty, culture and peace may at any time be overthrown by barbarians invading from without or multiplying within. The Hindus had allowed their strength to be wasted in internal division and war; they had adopted religions like Buddhism and Jainism, which unnerved them for the tasks of life; they had failed to organize their forces for the protection of their frontiers and their capitals, their wealth and their freedom, from the hordes of Scythians, Huns, Afghans and Turks hovering about India's boundaries and waiting for national weakness to let them in. For four hundred years (600-1000 A.D.) India invited conquest; and at last it came."

Symbiotic to Nehru's leftist thought, and in consonance with JNU historians with whom they keep in constant touch and derive inspiration, there is a prominent school of historic research in France called *National Centre of Social Research (CNRS)*. This august body even outdoes Nehru and the JNU in its efforts to denigrate Hindus and glorify the Muslim conquest. The credit for tutoring young generations in negating Muslim genocide of the Hindus must also be shared to no small extent by Romila Thapar, Harbans Mukhiya and Bipin Chandra, all luminaries of the JNU, the Mecca of negationism and pseudo-secularism. Romila Thapar in her book, *Penguin History of India*, co-authored by Percival Spear makes an astounding discovery that "Aurangzeb's supposed intolerance, is little more than a hostile legend based on isolated acts such as the erection of a mosque on a temple site in Benaras."

Returning back to the CNRS, a group of seven historians in their magnum opus, *Histoire de l'Inde moderne*-(1994, Paris) scatter many pearls of wisdom. Sample just a few: Babur is described as a great poet and humanist and Aurangzeb a Sunni saint. Unfortunately for the authors, Aurangzeb himself made his scribes write down each deed of Hindu slaughter and destruction for posterity to read. It was the kingdom of Vijayanagar that, after centuries of barbaric Muslim conquests, was the precursor of a Hindu renaissance. Two young princes, the founders of this kingdom who were kept prisoners and forced into Islam, soon after their release returned to Hinduism. Their natural and legitimate act was called duplicity and these honourable writers have described the Hindu efflorescence of Vijaynagar as the result of "ambition of Brahmins, who used these two young princes to re-conquer the power that had been lost at the hands of the conquering Muslims".

Now the facts. Alain Danielou, the famous French author of *Histoire de l'Inde* (page 222) has this to say: "From the time when Muslims started arriving, around 632 AD, the history of India becomes a long monotonous series of murders, massacres, spoilations and destructions. It is, as usual, in the name of "a holy war" of their faith, of their sole God, that the barbarians have destroyed civilizations, and wiped out entire races. Mahmud of Ghazni was an early example of Muslim ruthlessness, burning in 1018 A.D. all the temples of Mathura, razing Kannauj to the ground and destroying the famous temple of Somnath, sacred to all Hindus. His successors were as ruthless as Ghazni: in 1038 A.D. the holy city of Benaras was razed to the ground, its marvellous temples destroyed, its magnificent palaces wrecked. Indeed, the Muslim policy vis à vis India, seems to have been a conscious systematic destruction of everything that was beautiful, holy, refined."

Coming back to Will Durant, he described the aim, design and shape of Mahmud of Ghazni's conquest in the following manner: "In the year 997, a Turkish chieftain by the name of Mahmud became Sultan of the little state of Ghazni, in eastern Afghanistan. Mahmud knew that his throne was young and poor, and saw that India, across the border, was old and rich; the conclusion was obvious. Pretending a holy zeal for destroying Hindu idolatry, he swept across the frontier with a force inspired by a pious aspiration for booty. He met the unprepared Hindus at Bhimnagar, slaughtered them, pillaged their cities, destroyed their temples, and carried away the accumulated treasures of centuries. Returning to Ghazni he astonished the ambassadors of foreign powers by displaying "jewels and unbared pearls and rubies shining like sparks, or like wine congealed with ice, and emeralds like fresh springs of myrtle, and diamonds in size and weight like pomegranates". Each winter Mahmud descended into India, filled his treasure chest with spoils, and amused his men with full freedom of pillage and kill; each spring he returned to his capital richer than before. At Mathura (on the Jamuna) he took from the temple its statues of gold encrusted with precious stones, and emptied its coiffeurs of a vast quantity of gold, silver and jewellery; he expressed his admiration for the architecture of the great shrine, judged that its duplication would cost one hundred million dinars and the labour of two hundred years, and then ordered it to be soaked with naphtha and burnt it to the ground. Six years later he sacked another opulent city of northern India, Somnath, killed all its fifty thousand inhabitants, and dragged its wealth to Ghazni. In the end, he became, perhaps, the richest king that history has ever known. Sometimes he spared the population of the ravaged cities, and took them home to be sold as slaves; but so great was the number of such captives that after some years no one could be found to offer more than a few shillings for a slave. Before every important engagement Mahmud knelt in prayer, and asked the blessings of God upon his arms. He reigned for a third of century; and when he died, full of years and honours, Muslim historians ranked him as the greatest monarch of his time, and one of the greatest sovereigns of any age." His grand achievement in temples being destroyed and plundered goes upto one thousand.

The canonization of Ghazni's success inspired other Muslim invaders to follow his example. In 1186 A.D. Mohammed Gouri, a Turkish tribesman of Afghanistan crossed the Hindukush, captured Delhi, destroyed its temples, plundered their treasures and established a sultanate in Delhi, thus, foisting an alien despotism upon Northern India for the next three centuries. His worthy successor, the slave king Qutub-ud-Din Aibak—merciless, fanatical and ferocious—followed in his footprints and destroyed and desecrated 27 temples near the present day Mehrauli, an outskirt of Delhi, to raise Quwwatul Islam, Qutub Minar. More about this later.

To quote Muslim historians, "His gifts were bestowed by hundreds of thousands, and his slaughters likewise were by hundreds of thousands." In one victory of this warrior, who had been purchased as a slave, "fifty thousand men came under the collar of slavery, and the plain became black as pitch with Hindu blood". Another Sultan,

Balban, punished rebels and brigands by casting them under the feet of elephants, or removing their skins, stuffing these with straw, and hanging them from the gates of Delhi. When some Mongol inhabitants who had settled in Delhi, and had been converted to Islam, attempted an uprising, Sultan Alau-d-Din, the conqueror of Chitor, had all the males from fifteen to thirty, thousands of them – slaughtered in one day. Sultan Muhammad Bin Tughlak acquired the throne by murdering his father, became a great scholar and an elegant writer, dabbled in mathematics, physics and Greek philosophy. He surpassed his predecessors in bloodshed and brutality, fed the flesh of a rebel nephew to the rebel's wife and children, ruined the country with reckless inflation, and laid it waste with pillage and murder till the inhabitants fled to the jungle. He killed so many Hindus that, in the words of a Muslim historian, "there was constantly in front of his royal pavilion and his Civil court a mound of dead bodies and a heap of corpses, while the sweepers and executioners were wearied out by their work of dragging the victims and putting them to death in crowds. In order to found a new capital at Daulatabad he drove every inhabitant from Delhi; he ordered them to be dragged from the old to the new capital, so that only a leg remained of the wretch when his last journey was finished". The Sultan complained that the people did not love him, or recognize his undeviating justice. He ruled India for a quarter of a century, and died in bed. His successor, Firoz Shah, invaded Bengal, offered a reward for every Hindu head, paid for 180,000 of them, raided Hindu villages for slaves, and died at the ripe age of eighty. And for these great 'services' to India, one of the important roads in the national metropolis is named after him even today. Sultan Ahmad Shah feasted for three days whenever the number of defenceless Hindus slain in his territories in one day reached twenty thousand.

All of them were armed with a religion, militaristic in operation, but far superior in its stoical monotheism to any of the popular cults of India; they exalted their faith by making the public exercise of the Hindu religion illegal, and thereby driving Islam more deeply into the Hindu soul. Some of these thirsty despots had culture as well as ability; they patronized the arts, and engaged artists and artisans, usually of Hindu origin – to build for them magnificent mosques and tombs; some of them were scholars, and delighted to converse with historians, poets and scientists. One of the greatest scholars of Asia,

Alberuni, accompanied Mahmud of Ghazni to India, and wrote a scientific survey of India comparable to Pliny's *Natural History* and Humboldt's *Cosmos.* The Muslim historians were almost as numerous as the generals, and yielded nothing to the the enjoyment of bloodshed and war. The Sultans drew from the people every rupee of tribute that could be exacted by the ancient art of taxation, as well as by straightforward robbery; but they stayed in India, spent their spoils in India, a matter not of choice but of compulsion. Nevertheless, their terrorism and exploitation advanced the weakening of Hindu physique and morale which had been begun by an exhausting climate, an inadequate diet, political disunity, and pessimistic religions.

To continue this saga of militant Islam and the vandalism of these invaders, this is what Will Durrant says: "The usual policy of the Sultans was clearly sketched by Alau-d-Din, who required his advisers to draw up "rules and regulations for grinding down the Hindus and for depriving them of that wealth and property which fostered disaffection and rebellion". Half of the gross produce of soil was collected by the government; native rulers had taken one-sixth. "No Hindu", says a Muslim historian, "could hold up his head, and in their houses no sign of gold or silver ... or of any superfluity was to be seen.... Blows, confinement in the stocks, imprisonment and chains, were all employed to enforce payment". When one of his own advisers protested against this policy, Alau-d-Din answered; "Oh, Doctor, thou art a learned man, but thou has no experience; I am an unlettered man, but I have a great deal. Be assured, then, that the Hindus will never become submissive and obedient till they are reduced to poverty. I have, therefore, given orders that just sufficient shall be left to them from year to year of corn, milk and curds, but that they shall not be allowed to accumulate hoards and property."

Inspired by the words in Quran, "Oh Prophet, make war upon infidels and unbelievers and treat them with severity", the learned Mullahs sanctified the invasion of India. " Thereupon Taimur crossed the Indus (1398), massacred or enslaved some of the inhabitants as could not flee from him, defeated the forces of Sultan Muhammad Tughlak, occupied Delhi, slew a hundred thousand prisoners in cold blood, plundered the city of all the wealth that the Afghan dynasty had gathered there, and carried off to Samarkand a multitude of women and slaves, leaving anarchy, famine and pestilence in his wake". Later, the Sultans of Delhi, much praised by Nehru, reoccupied their throne and recovered their losses by selective taxation of the Hindus of India.

Coming to the second proposition of Nehru, a historical half-truth verging on negationism is the canard spread by our 'secular' historians that the Mughals came not just to conquer India and establish a kingdom, but to make it their home. Nothing could be farther from truth. Babur, the so-called founder of the Mughal Empire, established his kingdom round Delhi by default. An intrepid fighter and a skilful commander though outnumbered by local forces, thanks to dissension and division within, roundly defeated them at Panipat and Kanwaha. But he was no empire builder, he only came to conquer a limited territory to secure the eastern fringe of his kingdom at Kabul, to plunder, destroy and carry forward the flag of Islam. Being a staunch Sunni, he took upon himself the onerous task of destroying all Hindu temples and raising mosques on their ruins. The Babri Masjid is not the only monument to his Islamic fervour. He had scant respect for human lives as proved by his massacre of Bajau and the cold-blooded murder of prisoners and non-combatants, which he describes with great relish in his memoirs. He rejoiced in the glory of *Jehad*, his God-ordained mission, and the majesty of being a Ghazi, a title he conferred on himself. He never wanted to make Hindustan his home. He disliked its heat and the people and his heart pined to return back to the cooler climes of his beloved native Ferghana valley. It is more due to a fortuitous turn of events rather than a grand design that the Mughal kingdom was established. Babur had to fight one battle after another and had hardly any time to plan a kingdom. Later, his sickness, which he sought from God to cure his ailing son, Humayun, resulted in his death, and this left a tenuous hold of the Mughals on a small territory around Delhi.

Now Nehru's third proposition regarding a happy intermingling of Muslims with Hindus, and marriage of the Muslim ruler of Gulbarga with the Hindu princess of Vijayanagar. Skipping the details that follow later, an unambiguous but a harsh statement has to be made here. Islam does not allow a Muslim male or a female to marry any infidel or *Kafir*. The latter has to convert to Islam before the marriage can be solemnized. There is not a single case in recorded medieval history where a Muslim princess married a Hindu prince or a Muslim prince married a Hindu girl without the Hindu first converting to Islam. It has always been a one way street from the Hindu fold to the Dar-ul-Islam regardless of who marries whom. More on this when we discuss the so-called liberal religious policies of Akbar. Now we come to the greatest tragedy in the memory of Hindu South—the sack of Vijayanagar—to which Nehru refers as the backdrop of this happy marriage. The battle of Talikota fought by the confederation of three Muslim kingdoms of Deccan against the Hindu king of Vijayanagar is a tale of barbarism unparalleled in world history. First the conquest and the vandalism of the battle of Talikota. Again Will Durrant: "The superior number of the attackers prevailed; Rama Raja was captured and beheaded in the sight of his followers, and those, losing courage, fled. Nearly a hundred thousand of them were slain in the retreat, until all the streams were coloured with their blood. The conquering troops plundered the wealthy capital, and found the booty so abundant "that every private man in the allied army became rich in gold, jewels, effects, tents, arms, horses and slaves". For five months the plunder continued: the victors slaughtered the helpless inhabitants in indiscriminate butchery, emptied the stores and shops, smashed the temples and palaces, and laboured at great pains to destroy all the statuary and painting in the city; then they went through the streets with flaming torches, and set fire to all that would burn. When at last they retired, Vijayanagar was as completely ruined as if an earthquake had visited it and had left not a stone upon a stone. It was a destruction ferocious and absolute, typifying that terrible Muslim conquest of India which had begun a thousand years before, and was now complete."

This is what Danielou had to say about the sack of Vijayanagar in his book *Histoire de l'Ind:* "During nearly five months, the Muslims set themselves to the task of destroying everything, the temples, the palaces, the magnificent residences. The scenes of terror and massacre were unparalleled and so much richness in gold, jewels, precious furniture, camels, tents, girls, boys, slaves, weapons, armours, that there was not a single plain soldier who did not depart a rich man. And nothing remained, after their departure, of the most beautiful and prosperous city of that time, but smoking ruins."

The early Muslim conquerors used force to vanquish the Hindu princes in order to establish their kingdom. Having done that they used coercion and sword to convert them into Islam. But the sheer magnitude of the task of conversion was daunting enough to force them to abandon it. The great Akbar, who is touted as the most liberal Mughal, was no less inspired by his Islamic fervor. He realized very early the truth that sword alone cannot convert Hindus, particularly the proud Rajputs to Islam. India was simply too vast and populous.

His father Humayun had received assistance and shelter from the Rajput princes to regain his lost kingdom from Sher Shah Suri, the Pathan warrior. He never forgot the might of the Rajput sword and it was during one of these flights from the enemy in a shelter provided by a Rajput prince at the fort of Amarkot in the pristine desert wilderness, too difficult for the pursuer, that his pregnant queen, Hamida Begum, gave birth to Akbar in 1542. Akbar owed his safe arrival in this world to Rajput chivalry and clemency. He never forgot the might of the Rajputs and was forced, not out of philanthropy, but realpolitic to the conclusion that no empire could survive if the swords of Rajput princes would unite against it. His policy, therefore, rested solely on obtaining Rajput support while keeping them divided, and it paid handsome dividends. It would be too presumptuous to say that he loved the Rajputs; but he made good use of them to build and extend his empire. Rewards were offered and the Rajput loyalty obtained. But, inspite of all the services and sacrifices, the Hindu princes were mainly used for military campaigns in far-off places like Kabul, Kandhar to the North-West and against rulers in South and East. His own trusted Muslim generals were kept nearer at the royal court. Even amongst the Muslim nobles and notables, those who had a Turko-Mughal descent, were given the overlordship of all states and principalities, as well as the command positions in the royal armies. But those Muslims who were India born were kept scrupulously out of the royal favours and privileged ranks. So much for Akbar's love of this land which he intended to rule. The Rajput princes were of course the sons of a lesser God and treated as such. To prove their loyalties, these princes were made to undertake extremely hazardous campaigns and to fight even their own kith and kin. Nehru called Akbar, a great king almost in the same class as Ashoka. The latter too, was no 'secularist' and declared Buddhism, as his state religion. There could be no greater travesty of truth. Akbar was certainly clever but greatness is made of different stuff. He married Rajput princesses to cement friendships and forge alliances in order to expand his rule.

There was not a single known example of a Mughal princess marrying a Rajput prince. It was always a one way street. Col. James Todd had this to say in his book *'Annals and Antiquities of Rajputana'* in the chapter *Annals of Mewar*, regarding the Rajput pride against offering its allegiance to Akbar. In the letter written by Prithi Raj, a Bikaner prince in Akbar's court, he exhorts Rana Pratap thus:

"The hopes of the Hindu rest on the Hindu; yet the Rana forsakes them. But for Pratap, all would be placed on the same level by Akbar; for our chiefs have lost their valour and our females their honour. Akbar is the broker in the market of our race: all has he purchased but the son of Oodoh; he is beyond his price. What true Rajput would part with honour for 'noroza' (nineday festival, indicating shortlived comforts or pleasure); yet how many have bartered it away? Will Cheetore come to this market, when all have disposed of the chief article of the Khetri? Though Putto has squandered away wealth, yet this treasure has he preserved. Despair has driven many to this mart, to witness their dishonour: from such infamy the descendant of Hamir alone has been preserved. The world asks whence the concealed aid of Pratap comes? None but the soul of manliness and his sword: with it, well has he maintained the Khetri's pride. This broker in the market of men will one day be overreached; he cannot live for ever: then will our race come to Pratap, for the seed of the Rajput to sow in our desolate lands. To him all look for its preservation, that its purity may again become resplendent."

"This effusion of the Rathore was equal to ten thousand men; it nerved the drooping mind of Pratap, and roused him into action: for it was a noble incentive to find every eye of his race fixed upon him."

Todd sheds further light on the character of Akbar The Great by describing his 'Noroza' festival.

"The allusion of the princely poet in the phrase, 'bartering their honour on the 'Noroza', requires some explanation. The 'Noroza', or 'New Year's Day', when the sun enters Aries, is one of the great festivity among the Mohammedan princes of the East; but from that alluded to by Prithi Raj we can form an adequate idea from the historian Abul Fuzl".

"It is not New Year's Day, but a festival especially instituted by Akbar, and to which he gave the epithet 'Khooshroz', 'day of pleasure', held on the ninth day (Noroza), following the chief festival of each month. The court assembled, and was attended by all ranks. The queen also had her court, when the wives of the nobles and of the Rajput vassal princes were congregated. But the 'Khooshroz' was chiefly marked by a fair held within the precincts of the court, attended only by females. The merchants' wives exposed the manufactures of every clime, and the ladies of the court were the purchasers'. "His Majesty is also there in disguise, by which means he learns the value of merchandise, and hears what is said of the state of the empire and the character of the officers of government." The ingenuous Abul Fazl thus softens down the unhallowed purpose of this day; but posterity cannot admit that the great Akbar was to obtain these results amidst the Pushto jargon of the dames of Islam, or the mixed Bhaka of the fair of Rajasthan. These 'ninth day fairs' were the markets in which Rajput honour was bartered, and to which the brave Prithi Raj makes allusion".

"It is scarcely to be credited that a statesman like Akbar should have hazarded his popularity or his power, by the introduction of a custom alike appertaining to the Celtic races of Europe as to these, the Goths of Asia, and that he should seek to degrade those whom the chances of war had made his vassals, by conduct so nefarious and repugnant to the keenly cherished feelings of the Rajput. Yet there is not a shadow of doubt that many of the noblest of the race were dishonoured on the 'Noroza' and the chivalrous Prithi Raj was only preserved from being of the number by the high courage and virtue of his wife, a princess of Mewar, and daughter of the founder of the Suktawuts. On one of these celebrations of the 'Khooshroz', the monarch of the Mughals was struck with the beauty of the daughter of Mewar, and he singled her out from amidst the united fair of Hind as the object of his passion. It is not improbable that an ungenerous feeling united with that already impure, to despoil the Seesodias of their honour, through a princess of their house under the protection of the sovereign. On retiring from the fair, she found herself entangled amidst the labyrinth of apartments by which egress was purposely ordained. When Akbar stood before her, she took out her corset, and held it to his breast, dictating, and making him repeat, the oath of renunciation of the infamy to all her race. The anecdote is accompanied in the original with many dramatic circumstances. The guardian goddess of Mewar, the terrific 'Mata', appears on her tiger in the subterranean passage of this palace of pollution, to strengthen her mind by a solemn denunciation, and her hand with a weapon to protect her honour. Rae Singh, the elder brother of the princely bard, had not been so fortunate; his wife, wanting in either courage or virtue to withstand the regal tempter, and she returned to their dwelling in the desert despoiled of her chastity, but loaded with jewels; or as Prithi Raj expresses it: "She returned to her abode, tramping to the tinkling sound of the ornaments of gold and gems on her person; but where, my brother, is the moustache on thy lip?"

Akbar is often described as a magnanimous king and an epitome of chivalry. These were the Rajput virtues, never displayed by the Muslim conquerors. Akbar's attack on Chittor from October to February 1567 amply demonstrates that in moments of victory he could be as cruel as his forebears. The siege of the Fort, heroically defended by a small garrison of brave Rajputs under the command of Jaimal, had already lasted five long months. Ultimately, before the dawn on the 23rd February Jaimal died, while supervising the repairs to the breach in the fortress wall caused by heavy Mughal artillery, shot in the forehead by Akbar himself. The mantle of command now fell on his young nephew Phatta who gallantly fought a losing battle and died. When no one was left to command, the brave Rajput women committed their last rite of *'Jauhar'* by jumping into the fire leaving the men-folk to continue the fight. Early in the morn of 23rd February, Akbar made a triumphal entry into the fortress and ordered a general massacre "which ceased only for lack of victims". Like a gesture in tokenism he got the statue of two elephants installed at the gate in the memory of the brave duo. This was nothing more than a gimmick to consolidate his Rajput support and winning their goodwill.

The Hindus with their proverbial tolerance allowed the Muslim religion and culture to enter Bharat, but the process of Muslim invasion was nothing if not bloody. Today, in the market place of leftist secularism there is no dearth of self-appointed historians who have completely ignored this brutal aspect of Muslim invasions. From nomadic Arabia Islam galloped westwards upto Spain and eastward to India and later South East Asia. The apologists of Islam never tire of saying that Islam which literally means surrender to the "Will of God" can never be a religion of violence. But history speaks otherwise. The weakness of and enmity between princes of India on the east and the decadence of the Byzantine (East Roman) empire on the west enabled the sabre-rattling followers of Mohammed to sweep victoriously to the west in Spain and upto the River Indus in the east. While in the west the tide of the Muslim invasion was finally stemmed at Poitiers in France in 1132 AD by the French King Charles Martel, in the east the Muslim depredations continued and ultimately enveloped a large part of India by the 14th century. Let there be no mistake about the aim of the Muslim invasion. It was pure and simple a desire for annexation of territories, the prospect of the loot of treasures of the Hindu temples and shrines, and equally importantly, the dictates of the Shariat to expand the Dar-ul-Islam by the forced conversion or killing of Hindu infidels *(Kafirs)*. That Islam could succeed in its mission is due not only to the enthusiasm of the nomadic *Jehadis* on horseback and their superior mobility but also to the other worldliness, inherent fatalism, lack of political unity, the Buddhist cult of non-violence and an effete Hindu society through centuries of belief in '*Bhagya'* and *'Karma'*. That this agenda of converting India into Dar-ul-Islam is not yet complete and is the defining credo of Muslim psyche in Pakistan even today, is proved by the fact that their latest long range missiles are named after Ghazni, Gouri and Abdali, the cruelest invaders of India. The list of temples and shrines destroyed is limitless, their atrocities beyond imagination and the terror and massacre inflicted on the Hindus are unparalleled and beyond imagination of any sane human being.

Our revered saints like Kabir, Meera, Tulsidas and Chaitanya sequestered the Hindu masses against Muslim atrocities by driving them into their shells. In their prescription of 'Bhakti' and tolerance they ignored 'Shakti', which is the other face of 'Bhakti'. The nation went into a political anomie as the sword of the tyrant flashed around.

The other example of positive facts about past Hindu glory and nationalism, being negated and trivialized by the "secular" Nehru is the following extract from his '*Discovery of India*':

"It is true that during this period of disruption when Mughal empire was breaking up and main adventurers, Indian and foreign, were trying to carve out principalities for themselves, nationalism in its present sense, was hardly in evidence at all. Each individual adventurer sought to augment his own power, each group fended for itself. Such history as we have only tells us of these adventurers, attaching more importance to them than to the more significant happenings below the surface of events. Yet, there are glimpses to show that it was not all adventurism, though many adventurers held the field."

Nehru describes the resurgence of nationalist feelings in India after Aurangzeb as attempts at personal aggrandizement leading to a confused kaleidoscope of local chieftains fighting each other; calling the Rajputs, the eternal feudals and the Marathas the marauders. These to him were petty fights for limited personal gains and not an effort inspired by a pan-Indian upsurge to shake off the Muslim yoke, and the final signs of a nationalist awakening. Any student of history would know that Shivaji, inspired in his boyhood by the lays of the ancient Hindu gods and goddesses, was a Hindu to the core. And he fought to overthrow Muslim Rule in India. His entreaties to the Mughal king at Delhi and temporary alliance with local Muslim chiefs were merely tactical ploys to gain temporary advantage for the achievement of this ultimate goal, a Hindu Kingdom and Hindu Nationalism, which had in it a place for all minorities, including the Dutch, the Christians, the Portuguese, the English and the Muslims. No wonder, Hindu renaissance and nationalism always started from the soil of Maharashtra. Even Warren Hastings' observations quoted by Nehru (given below) confirm the seeds of this nationalistic fervour planted in the Maratha mind from where it was trying to spread and embrace the whole country in its sweep. This is what he said: "The Marathas, especially, had a wider conception and as they grew in power this conception also grew". He again wrote in 1784: "The Marathas possess, along with all the people of Hindostan and Deccan, a principle of national attachment, which is strongly impressed on the minds of all individuals of the nation, and would probably unite their chiefs into one common cause, if any great danger were to threaten the general state. Probably, this national sentiment of theirs was largely confined to the Marathi-speaking areas. Nevertheless, the Marathas were catholic in their political and military systems as well as in their habits, and there was a certain internal democracy among them. All this gave strength to them. Shivaji, though he fought Aurangzeb, freely employed Muslims". What Nehru, the Indian could not see, Warren Hastings, the foreigner, could see with amazing objectivity and clarity. Removal of Muslim overlordship was one of the essential pillars of this resurgence, which aimed, through Hindu renaissance, to re-establish the Hindu pride. This included, with few exceptions, even the Rajput princes as Col. Todd mentions in his book, *'The Annals and Antiquities of Rajputana'*.

Instead of going into the long and endless saga of destruction and desecration of temples and shrines and their conversion into mosques and Idgahs we shall concentrate only on some outstanding examples of Muslim cruelty. Quawwatul Islam, which means "the might of Islam', has been described earlier. After levelling up 27 temples this mosque was built 700 years ago next to the famous Qutub Minar, the latter named after Qutub-ud-Din Aibak. This was the site of a fort called Quila-e-Raipithora. The construction work started soon after the second battle of Tarain in 1192 AD where Mohammed Gouri defeated and killed Prithviraj Chauhan. This is what one of the enlightened Muslims of 20th century, Sir Syed Ahmed Khan, had to say as translated by Professor Khaleeq Anjum, published in 1990, Volume-I, page 305:

"Quawwatul Islam Masjid, when Qutub-ud-Din, the Commander in Chief of Muizzu'd-Din Sam alias Shihabu'd-Din Ghori, conquered Delhi in AH 587 corresponding to AD 1191 corresponding to 1248 Bikarmi, this idol-house (of Rai Pithora) was converted into a mosque. The idol was taken out of the temple. Some of the images sculptured on wall or doors or pillars were effaced completely, some were partially effaced. But the structure of the idol-house kept standing as before. Materials from twenty seven temples, which were worth five crore and forty lakhs of Dilwals, were used in mosque, and an inscription giving the date of conquest and his own name was installed on the eastern gate....

When Malwah and Ujjain were conquered by Sultan Shamsu'd-Din in AH 631 corresponding to AD 1233, then the idol-house of Mahakal was demolished and its idols as well as the statue of Raja Bikramajit were brought to Delhi, they were strewn in front of the door of the mosque...."

In books of history, this mosque has been described as Masjid-i-dinah and Jama Masjid Delhi, but Masjid Quwwat-al-Islam is mentioned nowhere. It is not known as to when this name was adopted. Obviously, it seems that when this idol-house was captured, and the mosque constructed, it was named Quwwat-al-Islam."

It is not so much the cruelty involved in this episode but the relish with which the founder of Aligarh Muslim University described the incident. And AMU today is a Central University receiving aid from the Government of India and is supposed to be observing the best traditions of cultural pluralism. It is this University which, from its very inception has been the breeding ground of Muslim separatism. It was the nursery that produced the cabal of conspirators, executives and foot soldiers, the flag-bearers and cheer leaders of the movement for the creation of Pakistan, based on religion and the pernicious two-nation theory, which resulted in the partition of India in 1947. Most of these progenitors of Pakistan had moved out to their new Islamic homeland but some among those that remained behind were no less active and made AMU as the dubious distinction of sheltering the largest number of Muslim organizations propagating Muslim separatism, harbouring Pak sympathizers, ISI agents and elements inimical to the integrity and sovereignty of the Indian Republic. One of the leading lights of this University, Prof. Mushirul Hassan, a so-called nationalist Muslim, who retracted on his blasphemous stand after the Muslim clerics had pronounced *a Fatwa of death* on him for opposing the ban on the publication in India of Salman Rushdie's controversial book *"Satanic Verses"*. This same reformist Muslim with redoubled vigour has now taken upon himself the onerous task of inveighing Hindu organizations and spewing venom on them.

The desecration of three conjoint temples at Ajmer, which was carried out as the Quwwatul Islam was being raised is another example of defaced temples converted into a mosque within 60 hours. To enable Mohammed Ghouri to offer prayers, the structure was constructed in a hurry and is called 'Adhai Din Ka Jhopra'. Further embellished with a fabulously carved facade in 1200 AD the structure is full of architectural refinement. But it was the Hindu masons forced into unpaid work, who provided this building "gorgeous prodigality of ornament, beautiful richness of tracery, delicate sharpness of finish, laborious accuracy of workmanship, endless variety of details", as reported by Cunningham, a great historian. Jaunpur was another city where the temple built by Raja Vijaya Chand of Kannauj, the father of Jai Chand, was desecrated by Khwaja Kamal Khan, a deputy of the Sultan of Delhi, and a mosque was constructed in its place by Ibrahim in 1408 AD. This is not the only temple destroyed at Jaunpur. Another shrine in this muster roll of desecration is a temple of rich archeological value at Siddhpur which is a place of worship for departed mothers and is called 'Matrigaya' named after the sacred and famous city of Gaya, where Hindus while performing 'pind dan' offer prayers and worship to their departed ancestors. This famous shrine built by Jai

Singh Solanki (1094-1143 AD) lies buried under a mosque called Jami Masjid. The Hindu timorousness in daring to reclaim their heritage and the silence of the Government and the Archeological Survey of India has resulted in the permanent disappearance of this Hindu relic. One feeble attempt mounted by the ASI to recover the ruins of Siddhpur was stalled on the intervention of Begam Ayesha, an MLA in the Gujarat Government. The National Minorities Commission abetted the intervention and the Siddhpur temple lies buried unremembered and unmourned. This is the type of historical negationism, which is present even today. The next on this short list of vandalized temples is one at Vidisha, a sleepy town in present day Madhya Pradesh, whose grandeur equalled that of Konark and which was finally destroyed by the artillery of Aurangzeb. Here again the salvage and renovation work by the ASI on the ruins of this temple was stopped half way by the Government at Delhi (1991-1994). Gujarat was ravaged by many iconoclasts. Its ruler Bahadur Shah after capturing Vidisha desecrated the Vijaya Mandir in the service of Islam and this glorious deed is recorded in '*Mirat-I-Sikandri*', translated by Fazlullah Faridi of Dharampur, Gujarat. The episode was enacted 200 years earlier under Sultan Alaud-Din Khilzi and Sultan Shamshuddin Iltutmish, one century later. Glorified in '*Tabqat-i-Nasiri*', this temple has the dubious distinction of having been desecrated four times, after being resurrected three times. The desecrations of Mathura, Varanasi and Somnath, which have shaken the conscience of the Hindu world, need no detailed mention. After Ayodhya, the two smouldering embers, which may any day ignite further explosion of religious frenzy, would be Gyanvapi Masjid, next to the Vishwanath Temple at Varanasi, and the mosque raised by Aurangzeb on the ruins of the Keshavadev Temple at Mathura.

The Belgian scholar Koenard Elst calls this negationism in India as a "denial of historical crimes against humanity". In other parts of Asia and Europe, the Islamic sword could easily conquer and convert, but the task against the Hindu India, which was nourished and sustained by a civilization eight millennia old was not an easy one. There was a tremendous resistance all over; and a life and death struggle continued, resulting in untold slaughter and carnage. While the earlier nomadic invaders from the North West after the reign of Harshavardhan from 700 AD onwards, who were pagans with no faith of their own, could easily be assimilated into the vast Hindu land, the Islamic invasion was a different matter. Incidentally, the region of Afghanistan and further west was always a part of the Hindu empire, but the situation changed radically after the birth of Islam. The new invaders not only wanted to conquer territory, plunder, destroy, and slaughter, but also to convert the hated Hindu idolaters to the Allah's preferred and proclaimed religion of Islam. As a prelude to the invasion of Hindu mainland, in 1000 AD, Afghanistan was conquered with the total annihilation of its Hindu population giving a mountain range in this region the name of 'Hindukush,' which means "Hindu slaughter". The process continued upto the Bahmani Sultans of central India, who lived by the rule to kill 1,00,000 Hindus per year. Tamerlane, an ancestor of Babur, slaughtered 1,00,000 Hindus in a single day and carried out the process relentlessly. According to the calculations of some authentic historians of Western origin, between the year 1000 and 1524 AD about 80 million Hindus were killed. This indeed was the biggest holocaust recorded in human history. Islam had utter contempt for the Hindu idolaters, or the *'Kafirs'*, who had only two choices: convert or be killed. But the *'Kafirs'* being too numerous could not all be killed. There were more heads than what the sword could sever, besides, they were needed to plough the land, carry out the menial tasks and produce the wherewithal to meet the expenses of the rulers and their large empire. Sultan Alau-Din Khilzi had the unique distinction of erecting the largest pyramid of human skulls after slaughtering in record time a hundred thousands innocent Hindus on the outskirts of Delhi.

This jehadic fervour continued till the last such Jehad against the Hindus by Tipu Sultan towards the end of the 18th century. And this man is revered as a national hero by our secular historians. In fact, there was a long television serial on this great man titled "The Sword of Tipu Sultan". Colonel Malleson described Tipu Sultan as a Muslim bigot, in sharp contrast to his more liberal father Haider Ali, who was the first Indian ruler to defeat the British East India Company in many small battles. The mass killing of Hindus during the Muslim invasions and rule has been conveniently erased from the records of history. If this is not historical negationism, what is?

We now return to the other features of Muslim invasions. Apart from ravaging the countryside, fire and destruction, the biggest humiliation heaped on a proud people was the desecration of their shrines and places of worship. The driving force behind these desecrations and destruction had many strands of subliminal impulses: greed being the most prominent, flaunting of strength to the subjugated people to compel unquestioned obedience the other; yet another was the dictates of Islam and its iconoclastic fervor and lastly a sadistic pleasure in seeing other people suffer. The most important of course, was to carry the flag of Islam and the expansion of Dar-Ul-Islam (the land of believers) to conquer and assimilate the Dar-ul-Harab (the land of the infidel or land of war)

Let us regurgitate briefly in a chronological order the facts of history. Firozshah Tughlak (1351-1388) personally confirms his iconoclastic zeal in the following words: " on the day of Hindu festival, I went there myself, ordered the execution of all the leaders and practitioners of this abomination; I destroyed their idols, temples and built mosques in their places." Is it a class struggle or a frenetic zeal? Here is the answer as Konared Elst remarks: "Muslim fanatics were merely faithful executors of Quranic injunctions. It is not the Muslims who are guilty but Islam." The dubious glorification of Mahmud of Ghazni and Mohammed Gouri have been described earlier. Travelling down the history lane after the Delhi Sultanate, we now come to the Mughal Dynasty. The great Babur not only ordered the destruction of the Ram temple of Ayodhya to be replaced by a mosque but slaughtered thousands of Hindus alongwith the destruction of another 1000 temples. His successor Sher Shah was no less cruel. He ravaged Punjab and broke his words to the Rajputs of Malwa who had surrendered on an offer of amnesty. They were all massacred after they had killed their women and children fearing the dishonour of their wives and daughters. Humanyun did not enjoy enough power to carry forward the good work of his father. We have dealt with Akbar in great detail earlier and punctured the proposition of his liberalism. His son Jahangir was no less cruel and warped and ordered the killing of Guru Arjun Dev. Shahjahan carried the flag of Islam forward with the same fervour and Aurangzeb (1658-1707) reached the highest point of Mughal cruelty. He ordered the destruction of all temples in North India; chief among them being Kashi Vishwanath where he built a mosque, the birth place of Lord Krishna at Mathura where another mosque was raised, he rebuilt Somnath Temple, the Vishnu Temple above Benaras, replacing it with the Alamgir Mosque, and the Treta-Ka-Thakur temple in Ayodhya. By a modest estimate his achievements in the number of temples destroyed run into five figures according to his own court records. The provincial governors were commanded to destroy all Hindu schools, temples and put an end to all Hindu teachings and practices. His court chronicler mentions: "Hassan Ali Khan came and said that 172 temples in the area had been destroyed… His majesty went to Chittor and 63 temples were destroyed…Abu Tarab, appointed to destroy the idol-temples of Amber, reported that 66 temples had been razed to the ground." And his lasting achievement, of course, was the Jaziya tax, levied on Hindus only, to support Islam. After the death of Aurangzeb, the loss of Mughal power in Delhi, and with the rise of Marathas, this frenzy in Hindu slaughter and temple destruction came to an end. Following this creed of historical negationism of the great Nehru and his followers, after independence, a grateful nation rewarded the bloodshed and cruelties of its Muslim conquerors by naming all the arterial roads in our capital city Delhi after the names of these so-called 'heroes'. Tughlak Road, Firoz Shah Road, Safdar Jung Road, Babar Road, Sher Shah Suri National Highway Number One, Humanyun Road, Akbar Road, Shahjahan Road, Aurangzeb Road. (The name Jahangir has probably been missed out by accident not by design.) This is the humble tribute of a humiliated nation to its tormenters! The first Muslim invader of India, Mohammed Bin Qasim, in the true tradition of Islamic faith who attacked Raja Dahir of Sindh in 712 A.D., ordered massacre of Hindus, destruction of temples, looting of treasures and circumcision of all females and carrying back slaves, came from what is today known as Syria. And how do we honour this rapacious murderer and iconoclast? Rajiv Gandhi on his first visit to Syria as Prime Minister thanked that country for bringing Islam to India. Could a nation degrade itself any more?

While we often read of foreign conquerors and victims of the invaders on our land, we seldom hear what the brave sons of India achieved in foreign lands under unfriendly climes. From the times of the Vedic Aryans till the reign of Chandragupta Maurya and his dynasty and subsequently Samudragupta of the Gupta period, Indian empires stretched upto the River Oxus and included Afghanistan and large parts of Iran and Central Asian republics. Our Marxist secularist historians did not dispute this fact of history since at that time there was neither Christianity nor Islam. However, the anti-Hindu bias never left them. Even when they sang paeans to the nobility of Ashoka who turned into a monk and introduced a theocratic state by declaring Buddhism as the State religion, they did not forget to excoriate the poor Brahmins who according to them did not take kindly to this newly imposed theocracy. Their grievance was a loss of income due to the ban on animal slaughter and other rituals associated with it. We need not contest this indefensible statement, which has been adequately done by other scholars including Arun Shourie in his book, *Eminent Historians*. Tired with the long and monotonous liturgy of Hindu defeats apart from which our secularist historians have nothing else to offer, let us trace the records of later years.

Coming down to the post-Islamic era and the great victories of Hari Singh Nalwa, one of the ablest generals of Maharaja Ranjit Singh, we find that his Afghanistan campaigns have been totally erased from the history books. This great general who defeated one Afghan contingent after another from Attok westward to the very heart of the Afghan Muslim kingdom is a glorious saga of successive Sikh victories. The legend of Hari Singh Nalwa spread far and wide and he was so much dreaded by the Afghans that their women used to put their children to sleep by telling them that if they did not go to sleep Hari Singh Nalwa would come and take them away. The legend still endures in the annals of Sikh history. Another outstanding general Zorawar Singh under Maharaja Gulab Singh, the suzerain of Maharaja Ranjit Singh, led a victorious expedition into the western part of Tibet and defeated successive Tibetan armies. After occupying the whole of Ladakh region stretching westward upto Skardu this intrepid Dogra warrior left a blazing trail of victory in whatever he undertook. The chronicles of Ladakh (original word 'Ladvag') and Tibet are full, and the folklore abounds in the heroic deeds of General Zorawar Singh, and his Dogra warriors (called "Sinpas" in Tibetan). During my stay in Ladakh I had the singular good fortune to come across some original material in Tibetan, Ladakhi and Balti of the famous Dogra wars of Vazir Zorawar Singh, the Dogra version by Basti Ram, vazir of Ladakh from A.D. 1847 to 1861 and Cunnigham's narrative. There were also manuscript folios available in the archives and gompas of Lahaul, Spiti, Rudok, Guge, Zanskar, Skardu and Purig. The present narrative is based on all these sources and attempts to assess the probable course of events, steering clear of speculation and conjecture.

Zorawar advanced to Skardu and laid siege to the fortress. Thirsting for water, Ahmed Shah surrendered the fort after some firing. Zorawar deposed him and reinstated his son Muhammed Shah with a small garrison of trusted soldiers in the river fort. Thus was Baltistan annexed for the Jammu viceroyalty of the Sikh dominions.

Fired with these successes, Zorawar contemplated leading an expedition to Yarkand. Later, however, sobered by the logistics he thought it more feasible to invade the more accessible Tibetan provinces of Ru-thogs (Rudok) and Mnah-ris (Ngari), to which he could base his claims on the old Ladakhi occupation in the times of Singge Namgyal. The monasteries were full of treasures and the country famous for its shawl wool. For this war men and material were mustered from all over Ladakh. It is said that Hemis Gompa (a famous monastery 28 miles southeast of Leh) contributed 12,000 bushels of grain, 300 horseloads and 70 horses. About 6,000 reinforcements and 30 cannons arrived by road from Jammu. More were gathered from Ladakh, Baltistan, Purig and Nubra Valley.

In May 1841, Zorawar, with a force of 5000 soldiers moved along the Indus valley through Byan-la (on road of the Pangong Lake) to the monasteries of Hanle (OY 7894) and Tashigong (OZ 4354) and relieved them of their treasures. The van of his army entered Rudok (OU 5766) and Garo (Sgar, modern Carthog) which fell without resistance. He then passed through the upper reaches of the Indus and established his headquarters at Tirathpuri on the river Satluj in Guge in the district of Mansarover. The whole country was occupied by Dogras and Ladakhi soldiers, Basti Ram being stationed at Takla-khar on the Karnali river near the frontiers of Kumaon and Nepal and Rahim Khan of Chusod at Spiti.

Zorawar built a fort at Garthog (present name Gartok-37 miles southeast of Garzong OZ 7011) and stationed some Dogra soldiers there to give early warning of the enemy advance. The tidings of the invasion reached Lhasa and on the 7th of November, news was received of the advance of a Tibetan army of 300 cavalry and 10,000 foot soldiers. The advanced Dogra detachment of Buran was cut to pieces. The Tibetan army halted there. Eight days later a reinforcement of 500 cavalry and 7000 foot soilders further swelled the ranks of the Tibetans. Basti Ram with 300 soldiers at his forward outpost kept on sending reports of the enemy advance. Zorawar at once sent forward a covering force of 300 men under Nonosunganam to delay the Tibetan advance, but the small force was encircled at Kardan-khar south of Rakas Tal and annihilated. Another party of 600 sent out on the 10th November met the same fate.

Zorawar's army was fighting under heavy odds. The battlefield was over 15,000 feet above the sea level and it was midwinter. The troops, devoid of sheep skin and warming fires, were all frostbitten and many froze to death. The only available fuel was Tibetan "furze". Desperate soldiers burnt the stock ends of their muskets to obtain warmth. On the last day of the battle not more than half the soldiers could bear arms.

The Tibetan army occupied a fort near Do-yo (in Buran south of Mansarover Lake). Zorawar for once made the fatal mistake of under-estimating his enemy. He decided to challenge a Tibetan army 18,000 strong with a force only one-third its size. Advancing from his position at Tirathpuri, he took up a position a little below Do-yo. Five or six great skirmishes took place and the Tibetans being inside the castle suffered little loss. The Dogra casualties were heavy. The final battle lasted from the 8th to the 10th of December, 1841. One morning, it is said the 300-strong Tibetan cavalry with 5000 foot soldiers and archers sallied out of the castle of Stag-La and surrounded the Dogra army. The fighting went on the whole day and the casualties were equal on both sides. When the sun rose again the next day, the Tibetan cavalry and foot soldiers rushed at the Dogra entrenchments while the archers kept up a steady volley of overhead fire. Fierce fighting ensued. Somewhere at noon on the 10th of December Zorawar was hit by a bullet on the shoulder and fell down from his horse. He was immediately surrounded by the Tibetan soldiers. The vazir got up again and began to fight single-handedly with his sword. With failing strength and surrounded by numerous foes, he fought on till a Tibetan executioner cut off his head.

With a ragtag army of Dogra warriors at an altitude above 12,000 ft. where even normal survival is a struggle, under extreme cold, with no winter clothing and short of supplies, he crossed the freezing river Indus and subjugated central Ladakh. A memorial to Zorawar Singh still exists in Tibet near Mansarovar.

We now come to the British conquest of India. There is no dearth of Anglophiles in our country. Starting from Nehru himself, their legacy is the perpetuation of English as the only thriving language in our country. The British did not indulge in the destruction of Hindu shrines and temples but they enslaved the Hindu mind in the most subtle and insidious manner, their missionaries working in tandem with the administration, to smoothen the path of the British rule. Admittedly the knowledge of English is useful in learning modern science, technology and other developments in the fields of arts and humanities, but there are nations such as France, Germany, Russia, China, Japan and South Korea who have achieved pre-eminence in the field of scientific and economic development, some even surpassing the United States and England in technology and competence in manufactured goods and exports. They do not speak English. Seen against this background, the observation of Prof. R.C. Majumdar, a great historian, that the best thing that happened to India was the introduction of English Language, sounds hollow. The British legacy of extensive rail and road network meant to subserve their colonial interests, did unite vast stretches of the country but left us totally enslaved. They destroyed all our local industries and enterprises by carrying away our precious raw material to their mills and dumping the finished goods in our market. The net result was the pauperization of our peasantry, recurring famines, impoverishment of the urban classes and destruction of our national self-respect. Our Anglophile historians have completely negated these aspects of the British Rule. This damage done to the Hindu psyche, the denigration of our glorious past and depriving future generations of a pride in their heritage has been described earlier in Chapter 2, 'Our Vedic Heritage'.

Let us remember what Swami Vivekanand told us about our religion and our past, how we cannot escape it: "We have seen that our vigour, our strength, nay, our national life is in our religion. I am not going to discuss now whether it is right or not, whether it is correct or not, whether it is beneficial or not in the long run, to have this vitality in religion, but for good or evil it is there; you have to stand by it, even if you have not the same faith that I have in our religion. You are bound by it, and if you give it up you are smashed to pieces. That is the life of our race and that must be strengthened. You have withstood the shocks of centuries simply because you took great care of it, you sacrificed everything else for it. Your forefathers underwent everything boldly, even death itself, but preserved their religion. Temple after temple was broken down by the foreign conquerors. But no sooner had the wave passed than the spire of the temple rose up again. Some of these old temples of Southern India, and those like Somnath of Gujarat, will teach you volumes of wisdom, will give you a keener insight into the history of the race than any amount of books. Mark how these temples bear the marks of a hundred attacks and a hundred regenerations, continually destroyed and continually springing up out of the ruins, rejuvenated and strong as ever! That is the national mind, that is the national life-current. Follow it and it leads to glory. Give it up and you die; death will be the only result, annihilation the only effect, the moment you step beyond that life-current."

Indifference, that is the danger. We have suffered in silence for a millennium all the cruelties of the alien invaders who crossed over the Hindukush to kill, to ravage and despoil our sacred land in every possible way. Every shrine desecrated is a crime against humanity.

These stones are not silent. The testimony of these stones is stronger than any evidence that can ever be produced in any court of law in the world. They hold out to us the flame of our past heritage and glory doused a little, but not totally snuffed out and beseech us to carry it forward. And this light will send out its message to generations to come. Shall we be found wanting?

Each year, at Muharram, the Muslims commemorate the sacrifice of Hazarat Ali at Karbala, they mourn his death and vow revenge. Do the Hindus have a similar commemorative mourning for their dead heroes, their holocaust and the destruction of their holy places and vow never to let it happen again? No. It is time they did. A people who negate the past wrongs and forget their humiliations are not worth their salt.

Our answer to the pseudo-secular historical negationists should be: "Hindus shall not be trampled upon again".

4

Neo Secularism

The word 'secular' according to Chamber's Dictionary means, pertaining to the present world or things, not spiritual, civil not ecclesiastical, lay not concerned with religion, not bound by monastic rules. A state is said to be secular if its functions and politics are not concerned with religion or pertain to the present world or things only; if it does not deal with religious matters, does not decide issues on religious basis and shows no bias in dealing with its people professing different religions. While a state can be secular, its citizens, unless one is an agnostic or an atheist, and such people are few, do still live through and express themselves in the idiom and spirit of their religions. All that can be expected from the people is not to allow religion to affect matters of state policy or interest, and while preaching their faith allow the same freedom to others. In other words "*Sarva Dharma Sambhav*". But when a state starts taking sides and tries to protect or shelter a religion or a minority with a different religion than that of the majority, it loses its secular character. The same applies to individuals. When a state law is made for one religion and is not applied to the other religion, that becomes discrimination, and the state loses its secular credentials. Unfortunately, inspite of a constitutional obligation, successive governments in India after Independence have been guilty of this wrongdoing. Starting from Nehru, who instead of condemning communalism, in every religion, declared that majority communalism is more reprehensible and dangerous than minority communalism, that the civil laws and the religious laws applicable to the majority religion will not be applicable to the minority religion. Even the civil and personal codes have been applied in a discriminative manner between the majority and minority communities. In case after case, arbitrated by the Government, there has been a prominently visible minority bias, which has now come to be termed as minority appeasement, or even minorityism. Most of our secularist thinkers and opinion makers drawing on this legacy of Congress rule at the Centre, have by now perfected the art of traducing the majority community, read 'Hindus', and appeasing or even championing the cause of minority communities, read Muslims and Christians.

Inspite of Gandhiji's nobility of character and his saintliness, he in the true Christian spirit, went after the lost sheep and pampered the prodigal son. His constant entreaties to Muslim leaders and masses to co-operate in the freedom struggle had an effect exactly the opposite of what he desired. They became more sullen, aloof and difficult to please. Let us step back a few decades. The more Gandhiji pleaded, the more Muslims thought of themselves as a very special community. Before the partition of India on religious lines, consequent to the two-nation theory and the horrendous blood-bath thereafter, Gandhiji literally begged Jinnah to retract from his demand of a separate Pakistan, by promising him the post of the Prime Minister of an undivided India. Expectedly, Jinnah rebuffed him. The consequences are for everyone to see.

It was expected that after a large section of the Muslim people who demanded and got Pakistan, had moved out of this country, those, who stayed back out of their own choice, and volition, would subscribe to the one-nation theory and live as peaceful citizens of this country without demanding special privileges. This was not to be, and we inherited a long festering sore of a minority, which conscious of a separate identity, perpetually demands special laws and privileges for themselves, while refusing to assimilate into the body politic of the land of their ancestors. The teachings of Quran, Arabic symbols and extraterritorial loyalties have much to do with this phenomenon of the resident non-Indian (RNI) Muslims. Mr. Shahabuddin's semantics that Muslim Indians (Muslim being only an adjective does not detract from their being true Indians) is a better word than Indian Muslims (which means only an Indian qualification to a Muslim) notwithstanding, the distinction of intent is clear. Indian Muslim emphasizes the Indian-ness of Muslim, while Muslim Indian stresses the Muslim identity of the Indian Muslim. This had been the mindset of the Muslims not only in India but in all countries of the world where they are in a minority. Their own countries are of course Islamic and religions of the lesser minorities there do not count, nor even deserve state protection.

Pandering to this privileged minority, there are any number of so-called secularists in this country, who have already made many compromises with the devil to give a new meaning to secularism. Holier than thou, these 'Neo-Secularists' have outdone the purists by losing no opportunity to vilify the majority community for everything that does not please the main minority i.e. Muslims. These two can, at a short notice, muster the support of extraterritorial Pan-Islamism and World Christianity including the Pope himself for the slightest hurt caused to them.

Let us trace the genesis of secularism, the most misused term with nuances that can be used to justify any political skullduggery. The trend to treat the minorities differently from the majority and thus, assuming the halo of a patron saint, with less than noble motives and to treat minorities as a potential votebank is a dangerous undertaking. This trend was unconsciously adopted by Nehru himself but was adumbrated much earlier even before the partition days, by his mentor Mahatma Gandhi. With no intention to cross the Lakshman Rekha that separates true secularism from minority appeasement, it was Mahatma Gandhi, who took the first step in this direction way back in 1905. Gandhiji spoke at the Masonic Temple in Johannesburg during a Theosophical Society function that 'Islam was spread by force and in India a majority of converts to Islam came from the lower classes.' This caused great resentment among the Muslims. Although Gandhi had all the historical facts in his favour and had no reason to apologise, he still regretted the statement in June 1905. Even this he thought was not enough to satisfy the Muslims and he found it necessary to offer a second apology in April 1906 and begged the Muslims' forgiveness for an uncommitted error. A contemporary Hindu observer remarks that "Gandhi had learnt one of the important lessons of his life, and in future he took the utmost care never to hurt the susceptibilities of the Muslims." He never forgot it again. His motto became 'Omit and even altogether forget unpleasant facts about the Muslim minority.' Gandhiji's secularism was the spiritual essence of Hinduism and worthy of angels, but in this mortal world inhabited by those for whom it was meant, this was like holding a candle before the blind. The Muslims just did not reciprocate. While Gandhiji's secularism was blind, that of Nehru was lame, both being driven by a strong minority impulse.

Another example of Gandhiji's weakness for the Muslim community and his attempt to bend over backwards not to hurt their sensibilities came to light when he shocked a grief-stricken Hindu community during the Guwahati Congress Session in 1926 by calling Abdul Rashid, the man who murdered Swami Shradhanand at Delhi on 23rd December 1923 as his brother. To rub more salt into the wound, he went on to say "I do not regard him as guilty of the Swami's murder; guilty indeed are those, who execute the feelings of hatred against each other." To atone for his misconceived outburst, later in March 1927 at the Silver Jubilee function of Gurukul Kangri, Haridwar, he had this to say, "Remember Abdul Rashid did not murder Swamiji, he has made him a martyr." Nehru did nothing more than follow his master and the Congress followed them both in Muslim appeasement and vilification of Hindus. Even as late as 1940 when communal riots broke out in Shikarpur in the Sindh province of undivided India, he advised Hindus to carry out *Hijarat* (to flee) in order to avoid persecution. Was this not a half way acceptance of the principle of partition?

The same saintly naivete and the inability to read the mindset of a scheming villain caused the Mahatma to support the Nizam of Hyderabad in his refusal to merge with the Dominion of India after partition. Here was a Muslim ruler, who was unwilling to sign the instrument of accession. Sardar Patel with his usual farsight could see the consequences of leaving a hostile Pakistan friendly enclave as a permanent ulcer in the soft underbelly of India. Now with hindsight one can empathize with Patel's concerns. An ideal staging ground for subversion by an inimical Pakistan, a shelter and safe haven for cross-border terrorism and a permanent security risk to the integrity of India would have had disastrous political consequences. One shudders to think of Hyderabad sticking out as a Pakistani Muslim outpost in the body politic of India, after a partition that was a sequel to religious bifurcation. Gandhiji was blind to all this. He was adamant and his refusal to abandon his special concern for a Muslim ruler got the better of his concern for national security. The issue was later clinched through a Police action, when the Nizam openly sent emissaries to Pakistan and defied the Indian Government. That was the misplaced concept of secularism by a great man. The same special concern for Muslim subjects of Maharaja Hari Singh of Kashmir, coupled with his visceral hatred of Indian state princes, prompted Nehru to be guided by the leaders of the Muslim majority in the valley to supersede the authority of the Hindu Maharaja and strike his own bargain with Sheikh Abdullah. Of Nehru it was often said "that he was a Brahmin by birth, a European by education and a Muslim by faith." Both Gandhi, the tallest of the freedom fighters, and his anointed numero uno, Nehru, though strongly opposed by Patel, the realist and the Bismark of modern India, suffered from a skewed perspective of secularism leading to dangerous consequences that face the present day India and Hindus.

In the blood-letting that took place during the mass migration of people between India and Pakistan the air was full of rumours of massacre of Hindus and Sikhs in Punjab and Bengal. Most of these were true. This stirred the conscience of even the protagonists of Hindu-Muslim unity. The members of Congress Party felt that while Hindus were being massacred in Pakistan, Nehru was mollycoddling the Muslims in India according to his 'terms of settlement.' This infuriated Nehru and he made fresh efforts to explain the rationale of his policy, anchoring it on long term ideals rather than immediate acts of provocation by Pakistan. His stand was that two wrongs do not make a right. We should not retaliate.

This was an echo of the words and arguments that his 'secular' friend Maulana Azad was prompting Nehru to use in his complaints to Gandhiji against Patel's handling of the situation of Muslims in Delhi, in particular, and against Hindus in general. This further exacerbated the differences between the two. In a series of exchange of letters between Nehru and Patel, Nehru's position as a woolly headed idealist differed drastically from Patel's based on sound ground realities and safety of Hindus. The following conclusion emerges from the above correspondence. That Nehru's idealism and his policy towards Pakistan under the shadow of his concept of secularism was far off from the ground realities. That the Congress Working Committee did not endorse his views. That inspite of Nehru's Rashtriya Swayam-sevak Sangh (RSS) bashing prompted by some of his lieutenants of the so-called 'secularist' mould, the latter was found perfectly innocent of any wrong-doing, when detailed investigations were carried out. That our foreign policy, which Nehru considered his exclusive preserve and of which he considered himself an expert, had been found lacking, since Pakistan did not play ball.

A conference was held at Lucknow towards end-December 1947, organized by Mussaliman-e-Hind consisting of 70,000 Muslims and attended by Maulana Azad. The tone was set by the fiery speeches delivered by Muslim leaders such as Dr. Syed Mahmud of Bihar. Even to the sceptic it was a reiteration of the same logic and arguments that Muslim League had used before August 15. Dr. Syed Mahmud, a Naitonalist Congress Muslim, fumed, "I can tell Hindus and Sikhs that Muslims may be finished in India, but they should know that they also in that case would not survive." Nehru let all this pass.

Patel's secularism differed from that of Gandhiji and Nehru. It was against an unqualified compromise and appeasement of minorities. He did not subscribe to the give-in-to-win policy that amounted to endless concessions to win over the Muslims. He treated Hindus and Muslims alike and believed in plain speaking to both the communities. He told the Hindus "to forget the past, because it is manly virtue to do so. In India every Muslim should feel that he is an Indian citizen and has equal rights as an equal citizen." In the same breath, he could also tell the Muslims, "there is no place here for those who claim separate representation.... For a community to think that its interests are different from that of the country in which it lives is a great mistake." He, therefore, advised them to realize that "the future of a minority – any minority – is to trust the majority," that they should "make friends with others and create a change in the atmosphere. You will then have more than your quota, if you really feel for the country in the same manner as the other people."

Continuing in the same vein, Patel mentioned:

"I am a true friend of the Muslims, although I have been described as their greatest enemy. I believe in plain speaking. I do not know how to mince matters. I want to tell you frankly that mere declaration of loyalty to the Indian Union will not help you at this critical juncture. You must give practical proof of your declarations. I ask you why you do not unequivocally denounce Pakistan for attacking Indian territory with the connivance of Frontier tribesmen? In the recent All India Muslim Conference, why did you not open your mouth on Kashmir?... In the Constituent Assembly, one of the Lucknow Muslim Leaguers pleaded for separate electorates and reservation of seats. I had to open my mouth and say that he could not have it both ways. Now he is in Pakistan." Patel, therefore, advised the Muslims: "Those who want to go to Pakistan can go there and live in peace. Let us live in peace. Let us live here in peace to work for ourselves."

Earlier he had reminisced: "Today, I think of those days when in this city of Lucknow the foundation of the two-nation theory was laid. It was said Muslim culture and tradition were not akin to those of the Hindus. The Muslims were a separate nation." He continued:

"Muslim Leaguers call me their greatest enemy. Formerly they used to call Mahatma Gandhi Enemy Number One. Now they think Gandhi is their friend, and have substituted me in his place. But I too speak the truth.... I want to say a word as friend of the Muslims and it is the duty of a good friend to speak frankly. It is your duty now to sail in the same boat (with the Hindus and others) and sink or swim together. I want to tell you very clearly that you cannot ride on two horses. You select one horse, whichever you like best."

Once those who demanded and got Pakistan left India one would have thought that Muslim separatism was finished once and for all. Those who subscribed to the Two-Nation Theory had left this mainland for good, but that was not to be. Congress still kept alive the apprehensions of the Muslim minority, which stayed back in this country, and in so doing, they purposely painted the Hindu organizations as communal. Thus, the threat from the so-called Hindu communalist was kept alive to keep the electoral arithmetic favourable to the Congress. Nehru and the Congress knew well that the Hindus never vote as Hindus, since they do not think in terms of religion while dealing with political matters. In fact, their's was a true spirit of secularism. While the silent majority of the Muslims also thought on these lines, a few leaders with vested interests with a view to legitimize their leadership assumed the role of their guardians by stoking the fires of separatism and a fear of the majority community. They played into the hands of power seekers, and the Two-Nation Theory in its new incarnation of Muslim appeasement still bedevils our polity. Nehru had no reason to encourage such a trend but he did exactly that and from there all our present problems flowed. It is no one's case that the minorities should not be protected, but there the matter should end.

To those who doubt the secular credentials of the Hindus it should be useful to read what Girilal Jain had to say in his book *The Hindu Phenomenon:* "The dominant concern of Hindus over the last 200 years has been with achievements in the secular realm—education, trade, industry, equality with the British before independence and with the West since independence. The upsurge I have been speaking about, in fact, relates wholly to the secular realm. This does not mean that our spiritual-religious heritage has no place in this scheme. But it does mean that Hindus have recognized once again, as they did in the past, that the secular realm has to be secured if a culture and a civilisation has to flourish. Swami Vivekanand emphasized the importance of secular achievements and so did Sri Aurobindo."

Jain further adds: "It is inconceivable that Nehru was not sensitive to Muslim resistance to modernization and secularization. Indeed, it can safely be assumed that he left them alone in respect of their Personal Law and did not seek to bring them into the orbit of a common civil code precisely because he was aware of the depth of their opposition, though that is clearly an essential part of a modern polity based on the principle of equal citizenship. Perhaps, he expected that their attitude would change in course of time under the pressure of forces unleashed by the spread of education, economic development and the democratic political process. If he ever spelt out his views on how the Muslims would come out of their ghetto psychology after independence, it has still not been made public."

I still remember those dark days of August 1946 when after a call of Direct Action given by Suhrawardy, the Chief Minister of undivided Bengal, communal riots broke out in Bengal and Punjab. News of Muslims' atrocities on Hindus kept pouring in from both sides sparking retaliatory riots in India. One of my sisters, who felt vicariously violated, lashed out at me that, "you Hindus should wear bangles and hide yourselves behind us women folk. Don't you feel ashamed that your Hindu sisters are being paraded naked in the streets of Lahore and subjected to mass rape?" We heard how some brave men from the much-maligned RSS used to risk their lives to rescue Hindus trapped in Muslim localities. There were no Congress men or members of any Congress Sewa Dal present there either to help the Hindus or protect the honour of their women folk, both in Punjab and Bengal. Compared to the mass genocide of Hindus going on in what was to be Pakistan, Delhi riots were merely a side show. Amidst all this slaughter of Hindus, Nehru and Gandhi preached restraint and forbade any reprisal killings. To Nehru a loss of thousands of Hindu lives in Pakistan was a small price to pay to sustain his brand of secularism.

An unusual event occurred in our secular India on 15th January, 1996, at Aligarh where the Mili Parliament, a Muslim body meant to preserve the pristine purity of Islam, passed the following resolutions:

"That the recent secular system cannot ensure the protection of the legitimate political rights of the Muslims; That Muslim MPs of all political hues are lackeys of the Hindus;

"That Muslims should support only those leaders who lead the Namaz in the mosques;

"That Muslim democracy is a constitutional fraud, while secularism and democracy are both un-Islamic and 'Haram'.

"That Muslims should prevent formation of an un-Islamic system of governance;

"That separate electorates for Muslims based on proportionate representation is the need of our hour". This issue had been rejected even in pre-partition India when Gandhiji threatened to go on fast to forestall British deviousness in dividing India on the basis of communities and castes by a demand for separate electorates for Muslims, Sikhs and so on. This very same issue resurfaced during the discussions in the Constituent Assembly, strongly supported by Dr. Ambedkar, but was given a quiet burial after prolonged discussions under Patel, who silenced all opposition.

"That other autonomous States should be formed in the country and that self-defence based security systems be introduced in the country to help only the minorities during riots. (In other words issue arms to the Muslim minorities to protect themselves against the Hindu majority)".

All this happened in everyone's sight and hearing and not a whimper of protest was raised by our so-called secularists who lose no opportunity in castigating Hindu self-assertion as communal. The policy of minority appeasement, started in Nehru's time, has reached its logical climax today.

It was about time that our secularists did some soul searching and tell us why religious freedom has to be one sided. In all Muslim countries from Malaysia to Morocco, the penalty for moving out of Islam is death. While conversion into Islam is welcome, the reverse movement is not permissible. To those who proclaim that Islam is a peaceful religion, it would be wise to know that in many Muslim countries, the non-Muslim citizens have no religious freedom. Whether it is ban on individual religious worship or community celebration of their festivals, in the Saudi Arabia or the United Arab Emirates, the law is the same. Non-Muslims breaking these rules can be punished with death. But the members of the same community in India keep on demanding and do get more and more religious rights at the cost of the majority community. That is secularism for you.

The vast majority of Hindus have their hearts unsullied by religious zealotry or politically motivated collateral calculation, despite a mafia of the fashionable bleeding hearts in the media, their likes in the cocktail-seminar Metro Delhi circuits, and their co-brothers in the Friday club at the India International Centre. The latter species have a blinkered vision, whenever Hindu-Muslim riots take place anywhere in India as they did recently in Gujarat. Before we come to Gujarat riots in detail in a later chapter, one fact is clear that there is far too much politicking in human misery and the first casualty is the truth. One cannot seriously differ from an old statement that "Politics is the last resort of a scoundrel." In India they are the stems coming out of the same rotten political tree, and the irony is that they cannot be wished away. The only light at the end of the tunnel is that people will overcome these mischief-makers and those who trade on the body count of human corpses will be thrown into the dustbin of history. Indian ethos is still strong and cannot be taken in by the pretensions of these power seekers, who chameleon like, change their attire as the occasion demands, unabashedly visit temples and mosques, and offer flowers and 'chaders' at dargahs to pander to their electoral constituency.

Indian Communists are a forlorn community, abandoned by their foster fathers in Russia and China. Not exactly being a tropical flora, suitable for Indian ambience they can only act as a parasite living on the strength of other political formations. Their ideology and Marxian dialectics has long been jettisoned in favour of a dialectical opportunism to survive in any unfavourable weather. Saraswati Vandana in West Bengal is no more a taboo and has been 'secularized'. While in public the Left and the Congress condemned saffronised education, in their own state of West Bengal, the academics and intellectuals are mere party apparatchiks. In a typical Stalinistic fashion, the Congress too, equated its own dynasty with India's historical rulers by the 'divine rights of kings' and stifled any dissent from within and foreclosing other options. For these two high priests of secularism ideological consistency is not a virtue.

An example of the neo-secularist mindset is the pat on the back everyone anywhere in the world, who rails at Hindu nationalist BJP, receives from these worthies. The French author Christophe Jaffarelot mounted a highly vicious attack in his book on the so-called *Hindu Fundamentalism And The BJP's Ineptitude*. When he came to India to release his English translation, the Indian Press corps went overboard feteing him and showered accolades as they filed raving reviews in their newspapers. That is secularism for us. Inspired by the perpetual anti-Hindu theme of our neo-secularist and some left leaning media managers, the United States Commission on International Religious Freedom and the then US Secretary of State Collin Powel demanded that India be included among the "countries of particular concern" under the Religious Freedom Act of 1998. In a demeaning indictment, the Commission stated that "inspite of India's democratic traditions, religious minorities had periodically been subjected to severe violence and the perpetrators were rarely ever held to account." It further stated that "an increase in such violence has coincided with the rise of political influence of groups associated with the Sangh Parivar, a collection of Hindu extremist nationalist organizations that views non-Hindus as foreign to India and hence deserving of attack". It insinuated that due to the rise in power of the BJP, the political wing of the Sangh Parivar "the climate of immunity for the perpetrators of attacks on minorities appears to have strengthened". Citing attacks on minorities like Christians and Muslims, the Commission further observed that "Although the BJP-led Central Government may not be directly responsible for instigating the violence against religious minorities. It is clear that the Government is not doing all that it could do to punish the perpetrators of the attacks and to counteract the prevailing climate of hostility against these minority groups." And it then goes on to remark that "Though the severe violence in Gujarat provided the national government with adequate grounds—under the Constitution and existing laws to counteract communal violence – to invoke Central rule in the state, the BJP Government did not do so, despite many requests and the fact that the killing of Muslims continued on the lesser scale for many weeks". Is this not an echo of what our secularist brigade has been shouting from housetops, literally putting words in the mouth of the accuser. We will soon see in the chapter on Gujarat, what really happened.

Amongst the new converts to the neo-secularist fold, an old RSS hand, Shri Shankar Singh Baghela, a Congress hopeful Chief Minister of Gujarat, during his visit to the USA made an astounding statement that Godhra incident had been the handiwork of BJP. He also declared that if voted to power the Congress would invite a 'probe' in Gujarat massacre by the United States Committee on International Religious Freedom. Rightly, he was criticized for choosing the United States as a venue to make a baseless allegation by propounding a new theory and allowing the real culprits to go scot free under the smokescreen of this controversy. We thought that the days of Jaichands were over. Here was an Indian national opening up his under-belly before a foreign power to diagnose his malaise. In any case, does India need a certification from the United States for its secular credentials and probe into a matter that was entirely an internal concern of a sovereign country. This new brand of secularism derives its rationale from exacerbating the already bruised psyche of the majority community. It has been granted intellectual legitimacy under a manipulable Nehruvian consensus that has plagued this country since independence. This when conflicted with the rise of militant fundamentalist Islam and the fires of Muslim separatism in India not yet quite dead and constantly stoked by a supra-national pan-Islamic libido can be a serious threat to the international security and even the sovereignty of India.

Our psuedo-secularists have arrogated to themselves the authority to hand out labels of 'communal' or 'secular' identity to any party or political formation they deem fit. Anyone even remotely connected with or sympathetic to the Hindu cause is a 'communalist', while even the most rabid fundamentalist and obscurantist Muslim outfits have to be 'secular'. In their lexicon, BJP is a Hindu party and the refrain is picked up by the western writers, who have permanently categorized BJP as a 'Hindu Nationalist Party'. The label givers forget their own past and present actions, and assume a chameleon like pro-Hindu or pro-Muslim stance as dictated by the votebank arithmetic.

Our notable Muslim leaders and professors of secularism do not seem to know the meaning of fundamentalism and fascism that they hurl as their ultimate weapon against the Hindu organizations. Mr.

John T. Scopes of Dayton in Tennessee (U.S.), a teacher of science, was tried and fined a hundred dollars in 1925 for teaching Darwin's theory of 'Origin of Species'. This was a dispute between Darwin's theory and the genesis of *Old Testament* of the Bible. It directly challenged the genesis and caused a raging controversy with those who formed the core of the Christian Church. The conservatives challenged Darwin's theory and were called 'fundamentalists' by the liberals who believed in the evidence of scientific discovery. The conservatives could defend themselves only by an appeal to the Biblical fundamentals. This is the origin of the word fundamentalists. It is possible for a Muslim to be a fundamentalist on account of his blind adherence to the written word of the Holy Quran and Hadith and the consequential perpetuation of outdated customs like '*triple talaq*' and gender inequality. On the other hand, the Sanatan Dharma of Hindus is an ever-evolving religion with room for change, dissent, and the capacity to assimilate all new discoveries and scientific knowledge.

Coming to Fascism, in 1925 Professor Alfredo Rocco, a minister of justice in Mussolini's government, propounded a new ideology stressing that instead of the society existing for the individual, it is the individual who exists for the society. That the interest of the employer and the employed should merge, since economic progress being a social endeavour needs the willing co-operation of all classes of society to achieve high goals of production. In the praxis of this theory there must be a state control over class conflicts; strikes and lockouts be declared illegal and punishable by penalties including imprisonment. To promote the common interest of all classes of society in industries, trade and other professions, all social groups must be organized in syndicated associations. The employers' and employees' associations were required to form unions and a combined guide for ensuring co-ordination and cordiality. In case of disputes, failing collective bargaining, these were to be adjudicated upon by the law courts assisted by experts. Concededly fascism, in essence, stood for class collaboration and had no tyrannical overtones. Thus, we see that the terms fundamentalism and fascism are being applied without proper application of mind to any organization to suit the interests of our neo-secularists.

Another word commonly used and hurled as an abuse at the Hindus is 'communalism.' Communalism is derived from the word 'community', whose meaning, essence and implications are well known to any sociologist. A community which is so large that it accounts for nearly 85 percent of a nation's population, is in no way forced to assert or flaunt its identity. By sheer enormity of its numbers it is under no threat from any community and does not have to protect or announce its identity in the public square. On the other hand, a minority by its very size and a feeling of encirclement develops a marked tendency towards self-assertion and identity symbols. Thus, there is more danger of a minority turning communal than a majority. Added to this is the fact that Hindu India has always been tolerant to foreign immigrants both invaders as well those seeking shelter. Thus, it is not possible for the Hindus to be communal and inward looking, while there is a strong possibility of the minority, specially Muslims, who believe in the superiority of their religion over others and a commitment to convert the world into Dar-ul-Islam, turning communal. Thus, all talk of Hindu communalism is so much trash. The neo-secularists have somehow got the wrong side of the argument by labeling the Hindus as communalists and painting Muslims as innocent victims. In the currency of today's secularists any Hindu who takes pride in his religion is branded as a communalist. But the same is not considered true for the Muslims.

Our neo-secularists rant and fume on Hindu organizations such as RSS, VHP and Bajrang Dal but turn a Nelson's eye to Muslim Jamats like Indian Union Muslim League, MILI, Babri Masjid Action Committee (BMAC), the Madarassas, the Dar-ul-lum of Deoband, and Nadwa centre at Lucknow, all of which spread the message of Islam. In England, a secular country, the Queen is also the head of the Church of England and Christianity is a recognized majority religion to which other minorities pay due respect. And they have to conform to British values. In the United States of America, the Republican Party espouses the traditional American values and the concept of the 'good Christian' conduct. In every important speech that the President makes the last sentence is always 'God bless Us and God Bless America'. If that is so in two secular countries from where the founding fathers of our Constitution have borrowed so many ideas and practices, why can't we, in India, uphold our traditional Hindu values. The growing Hindu awareness verging on belligerence is the inevitable outcome of their long suppression and the encouragement and appeasement of minorities, read compulsive Minorityism.

Like Napoleon, who placed a crown on his head without the Pope's blessings and anointed himself Emperor, our neo-secularists too dispense at will the labels as to "who is communal" and "who is secular". Ordinary people in our country do not wear such badges to gain concessions and oppress others and declare their superior morality. It is this self-proclaimed secularist brigade that has arrogated to itself the authority to declare "what is secularism and how wretched are those who do not subscribe to their dictates."

The political discourse in India is so thoroughly vitiated by double standards of these 'neo-secularist' dispensers of judgement on what is right or wrong that any dispassionate debate on any issue is virtually impossible. At the Goa conclave of Bhartiya Janata Party, the then Prime Minister Atal Bihari Vajpayee made certain observations, which were interpreted as intemperate by these worthies. The secularist brigade bristled up, turned ballistic and accused Mr. Vajpayee, demanding his arrest under POTA (Prevention of Terrorism Activities) Act. Vajpayee, while praising Islam as a peaceful religion had denounced its Jehadi face, which was causing so much trouble and bloodshed in the world. Vouching for India's secular tradition, he declared, "No one should challenge us about India's secularism and no one should teach us about tolerance. We were secular even in early days when Muslims and Christians were not here. We have allowed them to do their prayers and follow their religions." Secular theologists believe that India achieved its unity only after the arrival of the European rulers, but to the cultural nationalists India's unity as a nation existed well before the arrival of even Islam. In a rare moment of candour and possibly a short lapse into a period of soul's awakening Nehru had addressed a majority Muslim audience at the Aligarh Muslim University in 1948 and said, "I have said that I am proud of our inheritance and our ancestors who gave an intellectual and cultural pre-eminence to India. How do you feel about this past? Do you feel that you are also sharers in it and inheritors of it and, therefore, proud of something that belongs to you as much as to me or do you feel alien to it?"

While what Nehru said was completely unobjectionable, did he have to introduce this "you and me" syndrome, implying a difference between Hindus and Muslims? Could he have said the same thing at the convocation of Benaras Hindu University? Like Nehru, Vajpayee did not echo any hegemonistic tendency of the majority community.

But the perception of our neo-secularists is unyieldingly hostile to the Sangh Parivar. None of them, however, denounced Pakistan for calling Vajpayee's speech as bigoted and extremist and they are labeling Vishwa Hindu Parishad (VHP) and RSS as extremist and terrorist Hindu organizations. Is there a silent agreement between Pakistan and our neo-secularists to mouth the same clichés?

The Janus-like legacy of Nehruvian secularism that sees only evil in the assertion of Hindu identity has reaped a bitter harvest of present day 'neo-secularists', whose vision is even more astigmatic. In their exegesis of secularism nothing is sacrosanct except current and visible political interests and a scramble for power.

'Secularism' and 'Minorityism' had been internalized in the Indian polity and under the pretext of protection of minority identities. Reformist efforts such as 'modernization', 'constitutional applicability of personal law and other such issues have come under criticism in India's secularist discussions. The 'Walled city' mentality is defended as progressive and secular. This was the reason that Mr. Kamrul Islam intercepted Vajpayee's speech in the Lok Sabha on May 27, 1996, during the discussion on Uniform Civil Code and said, "I request the Prime Minister not to speak much on this topic. Islamic Law is divine law. Personal Law cannot be brought in this house." What does this logic lead to? Are we to say that polygamy, *'triple Talaq'* and unequal testimonial validity and inheritance based on gender should be immune to criticism because they relate to the minority community? The admissibility of criticism of one community in silence vis-à-vis another amounts to pseudo-secularism and minority appeasement.

The debates in the aftermath of Godhra and its sequel in Gujarat showed the ugly face of our elite intelligentsia and cheer leaders in Parliament, who stalled the House for days together, shouting slogans against the Hindu "extremists", completely ignoring the universalism and cultural thought that is the life blood of Hinduism. India had been under attack from militant Islam from 700 AD onwards and a silent people could do no better than silently suffer. Afflicted by a mentality of slavishness to belligerent Islam and labouring under the illusion of an innovationist and imperialist religion they have lost all sense of proportion and objectivity. Historian H.M. Elliot in his famous book, *History Of India As Told By Its Own Historians* writes, "When the writer is a Hindu then the difficulties increase. In reality we expect him to articulate the longings, feelings, hopes and fears of his community; but he does not write without dictates from some one, and even when he does so, he writes to please his imperialist Muslim master..... In his writings Hindus themselves are the *'Kafirs'* and Muslims are true faithful ... When Hindus die "they are consigned to purgatory but when Muslims die they drink the elixir of martyrdom." These words written in 19th century are as valid today as then. He sums up, "Not a single scribe from this slave community, called Hindus, has written his history with a feeling of self-pride."

After the Muslim imperial affliction it was Macaulay's legacy that took control of the minds of our effete intelligentsia. Pandering to Christian and Muslim minorities, in fact any one but Hindus, has become haute culture. There has been public breast-beating by this class over the death of 800 Muslims in Gujarat but no word of protest over the massacre in 1984, when 3000 Sikhs lost their lives in just three days. No resignations were called for. The camera teams and TV anchors literally flooded the Muslim refugees camps but no one saw the skeletal remains of the Hindu women and children charred at Godhra, or even those Hindus whose bones were interned by the Muslims in inaccessible places. In January 1993, the Muslim backlash of Bombay blasts and arson was quietly explained away as a reaction to Babri demolition. But the same cause and effect theory is not to be applied to Godhra and Gujarat. In 1960s, when the sacred hair of the Prophet was stolen from Hazaratbal shrine, the whole country was consigned to the fires of Armageddon and the cataclysm was dismissed as the typical Newtonian reaction. When Mustafa Kamal under British influence abrogated Caliphate, the slaughter of Hindus by Moplas in Kerala, was dismissed as a natural consequence. What did our secularists say then? There have been riots in 1969 in Godhra, in 1984-85 in Ahmedabad, in 1978, 1980, and 1990 in Aligarh, in 1978, 1979, 1980 and 1981 in Hyderabad, in 1970 at Bhiwandi Chaibasa, and in 1983 in Nelli, Assam. In all these cases, the guilt of the carnage was laid at the doors of the hurt and victimized majority and Hindu organizations. Why do they celebrate Ram Navami or Shivaji Jayanti? Is a Muslim life more precious than that of a Hindu? An ideology born out of a fear psychosis and willing slavery of minority terrorism and their vote-banks, that keeps making a mockery of Hindu texts, testament and traditions, can only lead to disaster. If those who live by the motto of "live and let live" try to teach the same to the minorities, they will find themselves standing in the ranks of *"Kafirs"*.

Muslims have a paranoia about ruling India for 700 years (actually only 400, from 1300 AD to 1707 AD). So they think they are born rulers and this explains their inability to accept Hindu domination and a minority status in a Hindu India. Rome ruled Dalmatia, Byzantium, Turkey, Lebanon, Syria, Egypt, Libya, Tunisia and North Africa for 700 years. But that does not prompt Italy to lay its claim to these territories. India ruled Pak territory, Afghanistan and even parts of Iran and Central Asian Republics for almost 1000 years. Chandragupta Maurya and the subsequent Hindu kings ruled parts of these territories from 320 B.C upto 700 A.D. coinciding with the birth of Islam. Pagan Assyrians, Babylonians and Egyptians ruled Middle East for 500 years. Does that mean they still have claims to the present day Muslim countries?

Let us now turn the flashlight on one organization that is more sinned against than sinning, Rashtriya Swayamsevak Sangh, the bete noire of today's neo-secularists. What is it all about? Ideological pluralism is the lifeblood of any vibrant democracy. After all a free democracy is for free debate and acceptance of dissent. Unfortunately, some of our opinion makers and neo-secularists have, from time to time, pilloried the Rashtriya Swayamsewak Sangh (RSS) and its affiliate organizations, derisively called the 'Sangh Parivar', for having a different perspective on Indian nationalism. These pseudo-secularists have introduced politics in the intra-political discourse with a view to create a totalitarian mindset. In this discursive name-calling their enemy number one is the Sangh Parivar. Earlier, the British were in the habit of accusing the Sangh of being a "communal and fascist" organization, which had refused to co-operate in the war effort during the World War II. Even earlier in 1933, they had tried to ban the RSS, branding it as communal in character. Another grudge they had against the RSS was their participation in the Civil Disobedience Movement. Inspite of their best efforts to suppress the RSS, the British Government was thoroughly humiliated when their circular to ban the RSS was defeated in the Legislative Council of Central Provinces and Berar in the Budget Session of 1934 on a one rupee cut motion against the ban. Further embarrassment to the Government was caused when a Muslim member, M.S. Rehman, challenged the Government to cite even one case of the involvement of RSS in any communal activity or strife.

Till around 1940 the Muslims did not perceive any direct threat from the training carried out in the Shakhas of the RSS and there was no anti-RSS feeling in the literature of the Muslim League, even as late as 21 years after the birth of the RSS. It was only in May 1946 that the *'Dawn'*, the mouthpiece of the Muslim League, in its editorial, called 'Sangh a secret underground organization'. The editor said: "It is undoubtedly true that the Sangh has been long started and, is now already a well organized and trained body; nevertheless, now that details about its object, its modus operandi, and its sinister design are known, it should not be difficult for Muslims to devise counter measures."

In a follow up editorial again on May 31st, 1946, it warned that "it is the duty of every provincial Government to declare the RSS an unlawful organization. We regret to find that Mr. Gandhi, Nehru and other top ranking leaders to whom, we had made an appeal to condemn the ideology and activities of the Sangh continue to maintain strange silence." As a sequel to this anti-RSS diatribe, RSS Shakhas, in Muslim majority areas were attacked and the Home Minister of Hyderabad Khan Bahadur Mir Ghulam Ali Khan categorically said on May 26, 1945, in a Government communiqué: "40 armed Muslims assaulted the RSS men playing in their Shakhas in Hyderabad city". Even after Independence, the later day secularists led by Nehru perceived RSS as a communal organization and Nehru with his lieutenants started a virtual crusade against RSS even without knowing the fundamentals of the organization. After Mahatma Gandhi's death by a Hindu, Nehru again returned to his anti-RSS rhetoric and was proved wrong on the conclusion, of a thorough investigation by Sardar Patel. At this time, the only real study in depth, on the RSS was carried out by an American scholar, J.A. Curran, in 1951. The Sampradayikta Virodhi Committee (SVC) published a booklet *'American Interest in the RSS'* in 1973, saying "and the interest of Mr. J.A.Curran Jr., then Head of the Central Intelligence Agency (CIA) operation in Asia and Africa, is particularly remarkable because he undertook his *Operation Understanding RSS*, when the organization had been banned and when it was not supposed to be a force to be reckoned within Indian politics… the path of the RSS and Americans coincided on the morrow of… Independence." This slanderous propaganda linking the Sangh with CIA got a boost with the threat perceived by Mrs. Indira Gandhi, who presided over the decline and decimation of the Congress during 1977 elections, and her camp followers and pseudo-secularists vilified the Sangh as a militant "revivalist Nazi Movement". A refined understanding of the RSS would reveal that an unconscious ripple effect of this totally apolitical organization has created a political space for an Indian right, not unlike the Christian Democrats in Germany, conservative in its cultural values and yet progressive. There is space for such a political formation in India and to the extent the RSS can, as was the case in Germany, help create it without stretching too far rightwards and causing communal turbulence or hurtling our true secular spirit. It is a welcome development despite all hectoring by our Left-leaning English media.

To the blinkered glasses of our pseudo-secularists RSS is seen as a communal Hindu organization. The word Hindu and communal do not gel. After independence, secularism became a state compulsion to accommodate different religious sensibilities. Further confusion arose when the word 'Dharma' was equated with religion or sect. While religions have led to crusades and Jehads, Dharma has no such history. In fact, there is no equivalent in any other language for this Sanskrit word. While 'Dharma' means ethical and righteous conduct and allows dissent in its praxis, religions enforce uniformity of the sacramental and the intellectual. Thus, while the seeds of conflict are organic to religion, 'Dharma' has no such implications. While religion has sectarian and exclusivistic overtones, 'Dharma' stands for unity of mankind. Secularism is only concerned with the statecraft and cannot enter personal life, since each individual is free to practise his own religion, and man by nature is a religious creature. In this political milieu created by our concept of secularism no one really is free to pursue his religion.

Under this dispensation the Hindu places of worship at Ayodhya, Kashi, and Mathura are out of bounds to them the same way as the Muslims should not practise certain tenets of Quran such as *'Jehad'*, *'Kufr'* and *'Kafir'*. Both Christianity and Islam have their own and only way to salvation denied to others unless they convert. The RSS had foreseen, as early as 1925 that there was no place for violence in religious praxis and religion alone cannot lead to social harmony. Only 'Dharma' and cultural nationalism with a strong patriotic fervour can lead to India's greatness. As such its history, culture and ethos had to be protected. The two deities that the Swayamsevaks bow their heads to in their daily prayers are the Motherland and God. Anyone who believes in these two is welcome to their fold and is a true son of India. It is this dynamo of faith that drives the RSS to unlimited sacrifices and services. In more than 30752 places nearly 6 lac Swayamsevaks, and every week at least 1,12,000 at about 8000 locations, and once each month at 8334 prayer grounds, 1,16,600 of them recite their prayers to Mother India and God and swear to serve the country. Where else can one find an organization of such spartan discipline, so unblemished, with such an ideological clarity and such passion for constructive work at the grassroot levels?

Inspite of the image deficit caused to it by skewed understanding, the RSS has continued to grow and now covers the entire nation in its sweep. The strength of the organization cannot be measured merely in terms of the membership roll, but the conviction and the dedication of its cadres. Napoleon had once remarked that in war moral is to the physical as three is to one. Echoing the truth of this aphorism, G.K. Chesterton similarly stated, "One man with conviction is superior to ten thousand, who have only interests". The Sangh truly epitomizes the above truths. As of now with its strength of dedicated and disciplined cadres in the cause of national service, with a force multiplier or 'Zerbe Momin' as our Muslim friends will like to put it, based on the above mentioned principles the RSS may, to use a military idiom again, outgun and outreach the total firepower of all the political formations in the country.

What is wrong if RSS says that all Hindus are one and should unite? Even Muslims are the brothers of Hindus and as long as they are true to the Indian ethos they are a welcome segment of our society. However, the neo-secularists' talk of cultural pluralism is a dangerous slogan with potential for internal conflicts. Cultural pluralism is a contradiction in terms. Culture may have many strands of thoughts, beliefs and rituals but like subsidiary tributaries these can be assimilated within the one parent and central stream. In fact, an inclusive culture could be a realization of various thought processes. Elaborating this Girilal Jain says: "Culture is indivisible and Indian culture more so. Cultural nationalism can by no means infringe on the freedom of other religions. After all, before the coming of Islam, the Buddhist, Jains, Christians and the Parsis have been living together in peace in Bharat, which they consider as their homeland. Why then should Muslims be placed in a separate social paradigm?" Social coexistence under an overall unified national identity is not only possible but also very desirable. Islam and Christianity transcend national and ethnic boundaries and their adherents look beyond the country of their residence for moral, financial and diplomatic support. Besides this extraterritorial support, the minorities have a permanent and faithful ally in India, even among the majority Hindu fold. These are our neo-secularists and their constant refrain is "down with the Hindu fundamentalists, the Sangh Parivar and their Nazi storm troopers; down with the Fascist Vishwa Hindu Parishad and the Bajrang Dal, the Hitler's and Milosovich's of India; down with saffronization and Hindu terrorism." These are the forces of treason that form the fortifications of an internal siege against the 'Fortress Hinduana'.

Mr. John Dayal, the Secretary General of All India Christian Council, at a conference in Jaipur on March 31, 2002, had demanded that the Minority Commission be reconstituted for its failure to castigate the majority community in Gujarat. Even earlier, during the clashes between Hindus and Christians in Gujarat three years back, he had taken his complaints against the BJP and the RSS to everyone, who would care to listen and that included the US Congress. He probably hoped that the Americans would land rescue forces in Gujarat for the protection of the Christians, and even fondly hoped for an American takeover of the country. Little does he realize that the states of Karnataka, Maharashtra, Tamilnadu and Kerala have Christians of all denominations who have been living peacefully, inspite of the much-maligned Sangh Parivar. He had also accused the BJP of direct involvement in the Staines' murder case in Orissa, that time under a Congress rule. Mr. Dayal dismissed with contempt any idea of a dialogue between the RSS and the Christian youth, feeling this could give credibility to the RSS. A seventy-seven years old organization with a membership of millions does not need a credibility certificate either from Mr. Dayal or his appellate authorities in the West. Hinduism dates back to an antiquity when his patron saints in the West were not even born. If one compares the measly 2.43 percent Christian population in India to the proportionately large number of churches in existence, a simple arithmetic will prove that all the churches cannot be merely for the worship by the laity. The surplus number is obviously meant for use for the harvest of converts or "created Christians".

In one of his articles by our 'secular' friend, Mr. N. Jamal Ansari, he had warned us of strong possibilities of India turning into another Lebanon or Bosnia and so all good men should come to the aid of the party and prevent this catastrophe. However, in the unlikely event of this ever happening the blame will be laid squarely on the shoulders of our neo-secularists and do-gooders like Mr. Ansari and his sympathizers in our arrogant and slanted media and anti-Hindu elite.

Treating Hindu and Hinduism with utter disdain and with a total disregard to their sufferings, they crow only about the riots of Gujarat completely forgetting Godhra, the fuse that sparked off the riots. In concert with this strident Hindu-bashing our worthy MPs from then opposition benches stalled the Parliament proceedings for six days, demanding a debate under Rule 184 but not for providing relief to the riot victims, restore trust, and help the return to normalcy. They never once talked about nearly four lakh Kashmiri Pandits living in miserable conditions as refugees in their own country. Targeting the BJP, RSS and VHP, their refrain was sack Modi, the Chief Minister. This fervour was not for the health of the victims but to score brownie points by traducing the majority community and appeasing the minority for electoral gains. In an interesting column "The Vicious Circle" the famous French writer Francois Gautier wrote, "there is something that I have never understood. Although most of India's intellectual elite is Hindu, the great majority of them are Hindu haters and it sometimes seems that they are ashamed to be Hindus. They always come out with the same clichés on Hindutva, the 'saffron brigade', the 'Hindu fundamentalists' and if you listen to them, you get the impression that India is in the hands of dangerous fundamentalists and that the Christian and Muslim minorities of India are being cruelly persecuted." Pointing to the TV channels for their malicious and negative reporting, maligning India in the international community, all of which was so much admired by Mr. Ansari, Mr. Gautier further says, "This is the vicious circle of journalism in India. The negative goes from the Indian journalist to his western counterpart and comes back to India under the form of unfriendly reporting. The recent Sabaramati burning followed by the rioting in Gujarat showed again the veracity of that phenomenon. When a Graham Staines is burnt alive, all of India's English press goes overboard in condemning his killers, but when 58 Ramasevaks are murdered, they report it without comment.... When will the true India be sincerely portrayed by its own journalists, so that the western press be positively influenced?" Little does Mr. Gautier realize that truth is anathema to our English media and metro elites.

Can a Hindu in Pakistan use such vitriolic language and spew venom on the non-governmental organizations such as Sangh Parivar as Mr. N. Jamal Ansari, a frequent contributor to the English newspapers does? He compares Sangh Parivar with Nazis, using words like Fascism and Fundamentalism. The neo-secularists borrow from the same vocabulary. In fact Muslim authors, who revile Hindu organizations, find tacit moral support from these neo-secularists. They did not dare mention the name of Netaji Subhas Chandra Bose, but did drag the name of Hedgewar and Veer Savarkar. Mr. Ansari scoffs at and derides Shakhas. Not even once does he mention the Madarsas that have mushroomed all over India and are the nodal points of planning subversion against the Indian state, and act as shelters and safe heavens foı ISI-based agents in their nefarious activities.

Can anyone ever dream of an anti-Christian rhetoric even in secular states like the USA, Latin America and European countries, in order to appease their resident minorities? Can one think of the Chinese media and intelligentsia deriding Confucianism to placate Islamic sentiments in Xin Kiang or the Russian Christian secularists vilifying their own Orthodox Church to please the Chechen rebels? But in India all this is passé. Can self-flagellation go further?

Symptomatic of this subliminal impulse of self-contempt in our secularist elite and metro literati is an almost haggiographic admiration of the white foreigner and the suave Pak, read 'Non-Hindu' diplomat. Mr. Jay Bhattacharjee in a satirical piece in *'Pioneer'* datelined February 24, 2002, wrote his farewell ode to one Mr. Ashraf Qazi, one time Pak Ambassador to India, as his aircraft was to "wing its way to Islamabad via some Middle Eastern watering holes, the crumbs from whose Emir's table contributed a healthy percentage of Pakistan GNP." He referred to the very sizeable social circle that Qazi and his wife of Irish descent had cultivated around themselves. In a perfunctory chat during one of these soirees, the name of Tata Group of Industries cropped up and the fact that the Zoroastrian Parsis fleeing religious persecution in Iran, a Muslim country, sought refuge in India and have lived here happily ever after. The Ambassador's lady was not amused. And again when the fact of Harappan and Indus Valley civilizations' pre-Islamic origin and its rightful roots in the Vedic Hindu India, entered the pourparlers, the hosts could barely conceal their displeasure.

Nevertheless, they managed to keep the Capital's greasy hoi polloi nourished on vitamin M and eating out of their hands. The Irish descent of Qazi's wife was a rage, despite the fact that Ireland never really liked their British exploiters and were constantly at war with them. The ingenuity of the Pak foreign office "to let your....Irish blarney make the micky out of the odious 'Hindus'" was for sure a touch of genius. They certainly factored the 'Delhi obligarchy's obsession with the "Whites". The Qazi couple supplemented this white magic with their Urdu, Persian finesse that completely bowled over the "Kabab Kathak Brigade". The 'Irish charm' with a 'Mughal Veneer' made the Indian diplomats look like country cousins and 'jholawalas'. The Qazi's sermon on democracy, peace and secularism, coming from one belonging to a "Mullah Brigadier drug lord state fabric" whose raison d'etre is 'hate India', kept our South Block mandarins spell-bound. This was a clever ploy indeed.

This is just a small pick from the innumerable cocktail circuit tales doing the rounds in metro Delhi. That is mental slavery in its worst form and our neo-secularists are the terminal patients of this incurable disease.

Post- Godhra, the much-hyped Gujarat election results that came proved the obvious. The choice, even before elections, was mainly with a common denominator of development, between Congress and the BJP. Whether the majority community can be permanently ignored, ridiculed and pilloried to appease the Muslim minority. The Congress' plank of Minorityism versus Hindu assertion and nationalism. The five crore people of Gujarat delivered a resounding rebuff to Congress. It is a Hindu obligation, due to their sheer numbers to build this nation, the Hindus will not continue to be treated as unequal, and the Muslims for their votebank will not be pampered as a preferred community. By giving two-thirds majority (126 seats out of a total of 181) to BJP they vindicated the "Gaurav of Gujarat". If the Gujarat elections had been held earlier in May or June 2002 in the aftermath of Gujarat riots in a peaceful state, while the Hindu passions were still inflamed due to Godhra's blazing inferno, the Congress would have been wiped off the map of Gujarat. Even though the elections were postponed by an obliging Chief Election Commissioner, who even went to the extent of crossing his constitutional limits by suggesting that Article 324, empowering him to supervise and superintend free and fair elections, gave him the authority to delay the elections beyond a period of six months, the time lapse between the dissolution of the last assembly and the commencement of the new one, as required under Article 371 of the Constitution. He yet had the good sense to suggest that if Article 371 is to be honoured the assembly can be dissolved and President's Rule imposed under Article 356. In spite of this long period for pro-BJP sentiment to die down the people of Gujarat didnot change their mind. Public memory is proverbially short. But Gujarat did not forget. The die was cast and Gujarat on 12 December 2002 gave its verdict. Nay to Minorityism and Aye to nationalism. It proved that we cannot with impunity push a majority community too far and for too long. Shall traitors like Vaghela be allowed to go abroad and turn against the people of their own state and insult its Hindu masses by blaming them for a so-called Muslim genocide? There shall be no talk of majority or minority. Nehru's shibboleth that majority communalism is more dangerous than minority communalism and so the latter could be accepted has been given a ceremonial burial. Hinduism by its nature and praxis can never be communal. Muslims and Hindus like equal brothers should share the common burden of nation building.

In conclusion, it is useful to remind ourselves that there is need for a consensus on and proper articulation of a theory of secularism that goes with our civilizational ethos and demands of natural justice. It is everyone's duty particularly those, who wish India well to define the limits to which granting privileges to monotheistic religions is to be allowed; without trespassing on the space to which Sanatan Dharma belongs and preventing monotheism from bequeathing a grim legacy of intolerance and violence.

5

Minorityism

Minorityism is an evil that has plagued Indian polity since the rebirth of our state after Independence in 1947. The seeds of this bitter harvest were sown not in our distant historical past, but in the subsequent attitudes, value systems syncretic to the Nehruvian secularist construct, the proverbial Hindu tolerance verging on self-abnegation and competitive populism. It is a phenomenon unique to India that the loudest votaries of minority rights are the Hindus themselves, mainly the metro elites and myrmidons of the leftist secular brigade. We shall deal first with the genesis of minorityism, second the minority mindset with special emphasis on Muslims being the largest minority, third with some of the constitutional safeguards for minorities, and finally bring out some glaring anomalies arising as a direct consequence of minority appeasement.

The problem of minorities has its deep roots in Muslim separatism. It is pertinent to note that Muslim separatism is not a new phenomenon and its abetment by the pseudo-secular Hindus today too is not very original either. During the medieval Muslim rule it was axiomatic that the Muslims would consider themselves as a superior race of conquerors and rulers, and this separated them from their Hindu subjects. This nostalgia had not disappeared altogether during the British rule and though attenuated to some extent, persisted even after Independence. As early as the middle of 19th century, Sir Syed Ahmed Khan had declared that Hindus and Muslims do not belong to the same nation. Later, Dr. Sir Mohammed Iqbal propped up by the Britishers to counter Hindu patriotic nationalism, echoed the same sentiments. That both these high priests of Muslim separatism obtained their Knighthood from a willing Government that practised the policy of 'divide and rule' is no surprise. Iqbal's famous song *"Sare Jahan Se Achha Hindostan Hamara... Majahab Nahin Sikhata*

Apas Main Bair rakhna" (Our India is the best country in the world.... And religion does not teach antagonism), was an early transient thought. He later recanted and unabashedly espoused the cause of a separate homeland for the Muslims. A few in India remember his *Tarana-e-milli*, in which he claims : *"Muslim hain hum, watan hai sara Jahan Hamara."* (We are Muslims and the whole world is ours). M.A. Jinnah, 'the Qaid-e-Azam', merely repeated, what his worthy predecessors had openly declaimed. Ayatollah Khomeni, when interviewed in Iran during 1981, admired the Qaid-e-Azam, the founder of Pakistan, but stopped short of giving him full marks. The reason: Jinnah settled only for two-fifths of India's territory to establish Dar–ul-Islam. Had he waited a bit longer, the whole of India could have been revived as a Muslim Homeland, as it was before the British came. The Hindu resistance, according to him, could be discounted since they did not possess the political will. Maulana Azad concurred with this view and that is the reason he so vehemently opposed partition. Thus, one cannot fault the Muslim minority in India if they relapse into such hallucinations, which create serious limitations to a peaceful co-existence with Hindus. The present day intelligentsia is only too willing to whet this appetite which emerges from this mindset and these were clearly visible even before the partition. Dr. B.R. Ambedkar with his deep insight had said, "the only way to make Hindustan homogenous is to arrange for (an) exchange of population. Until that is done, it must be admitted that even with the creation of Pakistan, the problem of majority (versus) minority will remain in Hindustan as before and will continue to produce disharmony in the body politic." Even earlier Mahatma Gandhi, the noble man that he was, did not fully fathom the implications of co-opting the Ali brothers, Mohammad and Shaukat Ali, to the freedom struggle by supporting their Khilafat movement. This regressive movement for the restoration of Caliphate in Turkey abolished by the British after the first World War, was the first visible symptom of pan-Islamic nationalism and extraterritorial loyalties of the Indian Muslims. The Ali brothers were by no means the protagonists of Hindu-Muslim unity, an ideal that Gandhiji so assiduously worked for and ultimately died for. Almost immediately after this marriage of convenience broke down the Ali brothers boycotted the freedom struggle and had the temerity to say that the noblest and the most learned of the Hindus is worse than the meanest of the Muslims. This is what Mohammed Ali said at that time. "According to my religion and creed, I do hold an adulterous and a fallen Muslim to be better than Mr. Gandhi.... However pure Mr. Gandhi's character may be, he must appear to me from the point of view of religion, inferior to any Muslim, even though he may be without character."

Gandhiji's propensity to bend over backwards to placate Muslims was phenomenal. Some instances have been given earlier. In 1946, as the massacre of Hindu minorities was going on in Bengal at Noakhali, Gandhiji planted a jackfruit sapling in a high school in village Kadhibati and dedicated it to communal harmony. With time the sapling grew into a tree. A few years ago, Muslim fundamentalists cut this tree to make room for a mosque, that too in a school! Salaam Azad narrates the incident in his book, *"Hindu Sampraday Keno Bangladesh Tyag Koriche"*. This is an effort by the Muslims to wipe away their pre-Islamic past. Again it was here that on being asked by a Muslim to remove the party's tricolour from his camp, Gandhiji instantly obliged. These are some of the many incidents that showed how little Gandhiji was able to fathom the Muslim mind. He once toyed with the idea of the Congress functioning from Pakistan even after partition. While he kept genuflecting before Jinnah for Hindu-Muslim unity, to Jinnah he was only a Hindu leader and at best, a 'great' Hindu. Pseudo-secularists who harp on the fact that Gujarat is the state of Gandhi forgot that it was also the home of Jinnah. The lone Muslim state that always voted for Congress, North West Frontier Province (NWFP) of Abdul Gaffar Khan is today the beehive of frenzied Islamic terrorist activities and the operational base of Al-Qaida. It is in Gujarat, Gandhiji's homeland, that Godhra happened. The genes of minorityism lay in Gandhiji whose compulsive Muslim appeasement was the signature tune of his philosophy of Hindu-Muslim unity.

Jinnah was very clear in his mind that partition was not merely a territorial division but was also meant to provide a homeland to all the Muslims of the sub-continent. In pursuance of this objective on November 25, 1946, he demanded a total exchange of populations between India and Pakistan. Earlier on April 8, 1946, Firoz Khan Noon, who later became the Prime Minister of Pakistan, had warned of a repeat of the depredations of Genghez Khan and Halaqu Khan if the exchange of the populations was opposed. In consequence the majority of the Muslims did make it to Pakistan, but those who remained cherished the same dream and even now relapse into this reverie. Before trying to understand the problems created by minority appeasement it will be apt to understand the mindset of Indian Muslims. Apart from a sense of exile from the paradise of Muslim home, the feeling of encirclement by the majority community and the compulsion to subsume their innate violent libido against the newly emergent assertion of Hindu identity has nurtured a feeling of ghettoisation. These feelings get hyped up by foreign media and international concerns regularly exhibited. The Minority Commission of India and the Human Rights Commission further aggravate this hurt complex. An Islamic agency from London had recently raised questions on Muslim security in India. Not to be left behind, our Indian Communists have parroted the same theme. *The Cambridge History of Islam*, Part I, to which Indian communists are no strangers says, "In Russia the Arab script has been banned and the study of Quran and other Muslim texts has become impossible. Village after village have been searched to confiscate the Quran; the Mullas and those who lead the Namaz have been dismissed. From the Volga-Ural region alone, six to seven thousand Muslim clergies and ummahs have been dispatched to the freezing plains of Siberia." Indian Communists should be aware of what Prof. Daniel Pipes says in his book *In The Path Of God.* He says that to deal with fundamentalists and belligerent Islam the Chinese Communists workers in 1962 and 1996 posted stickers demanding the closure of all mosques, and a ban on Quran, religious marriages, female circumcision and closure of all Islamic organizations. All these demands have been accepted by the Communist government of China. The Indian Communists even refuse to accept the realities in Russia and China, the countries of their inspiration and faith. Islamic scholar Dr. Mushirul Haq writes, "while a Muslim believes that he has to spread the command of God in the whole world he cannot view with respect those, whom he considers to be misguided and their religions not true." And further, "any religious thoughts whose source is outside Quran is entirely "Kufr" or "heresy". According to Syed Qutub, another Islamic pedant, those who believe in secularism and comparative study of religions are heretics. So much for the secularist faith of these worthies. To quote Syed Qutub again from his book *Voices of Resurgent Islam,* "for a Muslim there is no nationalism except his faith. It is due to his faith that he is a member of this international Islamic realm or the resident of the house of Islam."

Maulana Madoodi, another Islamic scholar, holds forth that in Islam there is no place for nationalism. He also avers that the meaning attributed to the word nationalism is not consistent with any text of Quran, where 'Kafirs' and the faithful cannot form part of a single nationalism. Prophet Mohammed after his flight from Mecca to Medina found friendship with the Jews expedient. This shortlived truce between the Jews and Muslims to form a shared nationalism can at best be described as a temporary military alliance. After some time this treaty was revoked and the Muslims killed most of the Jews in Medina and drove away the rest. This was not united nationalism. The Muslims and the Jews did not frame joint legislatures and courts that could dispense uniform justice to a united nation. It is the same mindset that prevails among the Muslim Ummah of our country. The desire to form a Muslim homeland within the Indian sub-continent still remains the subliminal impulse of the legatees of Babur. In the book *Meaning of Pakistan,* F.K. Durrani said, "The formation of Pakistan is important in that it can provide a base for the complete assimilation of the remaining India". It is this libidinous thought that prevents the assimilation of Muslims in the Indian mainstream.

The salience of minority interest, mainly Muslims and Christians, in Indian polity is a direct consequence of a misguided and alarmist concern of the great Nehru for their safety against what he perceived, a potential threat from the 'majority communalism'. This trait was manifestly visible in his treatment of Muslims and Christian populations and their concentration in various parts of India such as Kashmir and North Eastern States. Both these are today in a state of turmoil, thanks to the policy laid down by Nehru and followed by the successive Congress governments. Let us deal briefly with the Christians first. It is no secret that under the advice of Dr. Verrier Alwin, his confidante on tribal affairs, Nehru ordered an Inner Line to be drawn in the North Eastern region separating the tribal areas from the valley of Assam. According to this policy, entry into these areas was prohibited to any Hindu religious organization but it was a free land for the Christian Missionaries to preach their gospel and indulge in evangelization. Thus, in all the North Eastern States, Kameng, Subansiri, Siom, Lohit and Tirap districts of Arunanchal Pradesh, the whole of Meghalaya, Nagaland and Mizoram the population is almost entirely Christian. Thus, the Christians, a minority community in the rest of India, are a majority community in these states and cannot claim the status of a minority. Even parts of Assam, Manipur and Tripura are disturbed areas due to tribal insurgencies where the writ of the Indian Government does not run. This is the bitter harvest of Nehru's concept of keeping up the pristine beauty of the tribal culture intact, instead of allowing them to join the national mainstream and benefit from the effects of modernization and economic development. Over the years, many more affirmative provisions have been added to meet the demands of changing times. In fact, India is one of the few countries where minorities instead of being the underdogs, have hogged much more political space than their size would dictate. But like many unilateral conciliatory measures, the demand for concessions feeds on what is granted and grows more strident in proportion to their ever-increasing electoral relevance. The alienation caused by this politically imposed quarantine has led to the creation in the entire North East region of a dangerous border segment of Indian sovereign territory open to secession and poaching by forces inimical to our country. This when seen in the context of Pak encouragement of a similar secessionist struggle in Kashmir lays bare the grand strategy of slicing off the North and North East from the Indian heartland as a prelude to the dismemberment of the country. We shall deal with the activities of the missionaries in these states and the other parts of India later.

Unfortunately, the mass immigration of Muslims from Bangladesh in our Eastern and North Eastern states and a large growth of Christian population due to religious conversions has put a question mark on the distinction between minority and majority communities. For example, in the four north-eastern states, Christians are a majority with an insignificant presence of Hindus, whereas the state of Assam at the present rate of influx of Bangladeshi immigrants, has almost become a Muslim majority state. The same will be the case soon enough with West Bengal. In Kerala, Muslims can hardly be called a minority. Further, in almost all Hindu majority states there are large enclaves of Muslim population resulting in a large number of districts being Muslim majority areas.

Minorityism is a phenomenon unique in India and has come to mean the li=fe-saving drug for our neo-secularists. In Russia, China, Japan and countries of European community, which have secular governments, there is no such currency. In these countries the minorities live, behave and act as normal law abiding citizens. There are no special laws nor disabling clauses or special provisions for the minorities. They have no such organization such as the Minority Commission as we have in India. In other words, the state treats them as common citizens. They neither demand nor are given any special attention or privilege. In short, while they have the freedom to practise and profess their religion, the laws of the land circumscribe this freedom. Freedom of religion or worship does not mean the freedom to convert, except where the person himself is willing to be converted. Among many socio-political systems like Capitalism, Socialism, Communism and Fundamentalism, we have a special brand, Minorityism, in our country. Its raison d'etre is not dialectic but expedient and a calculus of compulsions of populism and electoral arithmetic. One seldom hears of a minority trying to convert members of the majority community in European countries, China or Japan. Has anyone ever heard of French nationals of Muslim origin trying to convert the Christians to Islam or the Chinese Muslims trying to convert the Buddhists or followers of Confucianism to Islam? It is only in India that such things are allowed to happen. In Islamic theocratic states the tiny minorities are too small and insignificant to squeak or even attract notice. They get into the news only when they are charged with blasphemy or killed at will by the faithful after the clergy pronounces their Fatwas. In countries under Islamic rule there are summary trials according to the state religion and swift punishment is meted out as prescribed by the Shariat. The rule of Allah supersedes all temporal authority and the minorities are forced to live subject to the goodwill of the majority Muslim community. However, in countries where Muslims form a sizable minority of the population they demand that the state should declare itself secular and not only treat them at par with the majority community but enact special laws for their safety, special provisions as ordained by Allah for their religious worship, personal laws, laws of inheritance and divorce. Even in matters temporal and not concerned with religion they want special provisions in the administration of state laws and freedom to choose the criminal system by which they wish to be brought to justice.

Our Human Rights activists comprising mostly retired judges and bureaucrats, suffering from ennui, are constantly on the spoor looking for violations of minority rights where none exist and even trying to investigate any case—real or imaginary, regarding excesses by the majority or even security forces. Even when known Muslim terrorists from Pakistan are apprehended by the security forces the priority of protection of their rights goes to the terrorists rather than the forces fighting them, or their victims. It would be pertinent to note what even Nehru was compelled to say regarding the special privileges for the minorities, "if you give special safeguards to a minority, you isolate it. May be you protect it, but at what cost? At the cost of isolating it and keeping it away from the main current in which the majority is going at the cost of forfeiting that inner sympathy and fellow feeling with the majority."

In a recent incident at one of Delhi's posh shopping malls, the Delhi police intercepted and shot dead two Pakistani terrorists on their way to repeat an 'Akshardham', in this crowded complex on Diwali evening. On the unverified statement of a publicity hungry quack doctor with criminal record, that he saw the policemen shoot the drugged 'would be' terrorists in cold blood, our two champions of human rights, Kuldip Nayyar and Praful Bidwai, wrote a letter to the HRC to order the police to investigate the murder and asked them for detailed information. After the forensic reports and autopsy conclusively confirmed that the Pakistani nationals were not drugged and were indeed shot in an encounter, this duo did not have the elementary courtesy to apologize to the Police Commissioner, while our vigilant media did not publish a single apology. All the media hype and 'cry foul' took place because the dead men were Muslims, even though from a hostile neighbour. If this is not minorityism, what is?

A Togadia, who distributes Hindu religious symbol 'Trishul', a non-weapon, is arrested for treason. But, a separatist Kashmiri Hurryiat leader, who boasts of being the biggest Pakistani, can travel abroad on an official passport labeling him as an Indian citizen. He draws pension and has his medical bills paid by the State Government, and signs an affidavit affirming his status as a senior Indian citizen. It is a crying shame that the Muslim underworld is literally holding to ransom Bollywood, one of the biggest industries of the country. Even the Muslim liberals like Kaifi Azmi were not free of this affliction of Hindu baiting. They termed Babri Masjid demolition as the second 'banvas' of Sita, but do not shed a single tear on the countless temples destroyed in Bangladesh, the hounding out of Hindus from their homes in Kashmir and their forcible conversion to refugees in their own land. To these liberals cultural unity demands that Quran be read along with Gita and Guru Granth Sahib at Shanti Van and Vijaya Ghat but only Quran can be read at the tombs of Zakir Hussain and Fakhruddin Ali Ahmed. There is a need to declutter the secular thought and remove from the Muslim mind the hallucinations of an imperialistic past and their obsession with a selective view of the composite culture.

The Muslim rule in Spain lasted almost eight centuries from 711 to 1492 AD. After their being driven out from their last outpost at Granada in Spain, the Christians started converting into churches all mosques, erected on their destroyed shrines, the only exception being Alhambra. In India from 1200 to 1700 AD just five centuries of Muslims rule, the mosques erected on the ruins of temples still exist. One but only one Babri demolition has caused an upheaval. In Europe the Christians from Bulgaria, Balkans and Greece have been exchanged for Muslim population and these countries have been completely purged of any Muslim presence. Why did we not cleanse Indian Muslims as demanded by Jinnah and remove the festering sore? Muslim homes provide shelters to ISI agents and are the nodal points for recruiting and sending Indian Muslims to Pakistan for terrorist training and then return to India to attack Hindu leaders and our holy shrines. Haren Pandya's murder and a number of terrorist strikes elsewhere in the country have exposed the existence of such Muslim terrorist modules in India. With four million Muslim Serbs and Turks resident in the country, Germany does not grant citizenship to the migrant Muslims. It does not permit sacrificing animals on Id-ul-Zuha except in mosques. In India all this is passé.

In one of the letters to the Editor of an English Daily, one contributor makes a candid confession, stating his reasons for leaving Islam. In addition to the usual syndrome of Dar-ul-Islam (The House of Islam) and Dur-ul-Herb (The House of War) and the obligation on the former to destroy or assimilate the latter within its fold, he says,

"Muslims are not permitted to make peace with a non-Muslim country until its inhabitants surrender to Islam. They can agree to a cease-fire for a certain period of time, but not to peace." Islam is the 'active form of *Salaam*–peace or surrender. Muslims view their religion as a peace- making force that can use weaponry, sacrifice, intrigue, coercion and every other means to secure its goal. According to them, true peace can exist only where the *Shariat* rules and controls all matters of state. He converted because he personally believed that unjust peace is better than a just war. Anwar Sadat of Egypt, compelled by the former US President Jimmy Carter to arrive at a partial peace with Israel, paid the price with his life for agreeing to an unhallowed pact.

The grand Mufti of Cairo in Egypt when interviewed and asked to comment on Muslim terrorism post 9/11 not only exonerated Osama Bin Laden and his Al-Qaida of all wrongdoing but also retorted, "of course there are some Muslim terrorists, but that is true of all religions. Look at Ireland, Chechnya and Bosnia where Muslims have been massacred by Christians." According to a western assessment the Muslims perceive themselves as the persecuted and despised underdogs: 90 percent suffer from low morale and live in fear of the future. Imam Abdul Jalil Sajid, a British Muslim of note, says, "Islam is the victim. 90 percent of the trouble spots in the world are Muslim and 90 percent of onslaughts are against Muslims; be it Palestine, Chechnya, Iraq, Gujarat, Bosnia, Kosovo, Somalia or Libya."

Even Egyptians who represent the moderate face of Islam take pride in the University of Al-Azar, a religious institution where a student has to recite by heart the entire Quran consisting of 114 chapters and 6000 verses. True enough, 70 percent of the Egyptians go to the mosque on Friday and offer namaz while thousands who cannot be accommodated inside kneel in prayers outside the city wall daring the cold, rain, traffic and noise. In Damascus too at Salaheddin mosque, the sight is the same; the decibel level of the sermon booming from the loudspeakers is about 20 times that of the common Anglican Church, all this to demonstrate that 'every thing in Islam is clear'. To the faithful, God's revelations starting from the Old Testament to the New Testament end in the Quran; their's is the final truth. The old ones are redundant. Quran is the last and the only true gospel and there is nothing more to add and no more questioning. To the rational this dogmatic certitude may seem fanatical but to them this is the final truth. Indian Muslims think no different.

Mr. Franacois Gautier, a French journalist who has made India his home, visited Kashmir to gauge public sentiment after the State Assembly elections. He was told by a lady he met at Srinagar that "we feel safer with Pakistan". This observation belies the euphoria of success of the democratic process, when the popular sentiment runs as follows, "Whatever the Indian Government says, whatever some of the opinion polls may state, non-Arab Muslims all over the world often feel that their first allegiance is to Islam, and not the country of their birth. This is not only true in Kashmir, but frequently so even amongst lower and middle class Indian Muslims. It is not that they are more unfaithful than any other person; it is just that their religion teaches them to look up to another country, Saudi Arabia, where the Mecca is situated; to read a scripture, the Quran, which is composed in a language alien to their own land of birth; and on top of it all, a scripture that was written some 15 centuries ago for a people who were not Indians, and which have never adapted to modern times." And later he quotes Sri Aurobindos's words uttered in 1947 in the aftermath of partition: "The old communal division into Hindu and Muslim seems to have hardened into the figure of a permanent division of the country. It is hoped that the Congress and the nation will not accept the settled fact as forever settled, or as anything more than a temporary expedient. For if it lasts India may be seriously weakened, even crippled. Civil strife may remain always possible, possible even a new invasion and foreign conquest. The Partition of the country must go."

In post-Independence India, Nehru's thought outlived the man. A man with the clouded vision, in a rare moment of self-revelation uttered the truth about himself, "I have become a queer mixture of East and West, Out of place everywhere, at home nowhere." Be that as it may,. Nehru disliked what he called Hindu religious mumbo-jumbo and his romance with socialism drove him to the Left of the political spectrum. His agnosticism was the perfect alter ego that the communists were looking for. This marriage somehow could not consummate. His daughter, however, had no love lost for Communism. Dictatorial and imperious like her grandfather she had learnt her statecraft lessons well. It was she, who got the first elected Communist government of Kerala in early 1950's dismissed for less than honourable reasons and became their arch enemy. Then came the Congress split of 1969. Again for reasons more personal than ideological, as the rump Congress (later called Congress I) became a minority government, she needed outside support. Thus, driven entirely by political expediency to retain a majority, she had to embrace the Communists and share power with the Left. It was then that she declared her socialist programme including bank nationalization, abolition of privy purses and other socialist jargons. Once in power the Communists had tasted blood and made sure that from then onwards they shall not only ride piggyback on the Congress but swarm out into all political and academic fields like the Indian Council of Historical Research (ICHR), National Council for Educational Research and Training (NCERT), JNU and others. This was the beginning of the ignoble alliance between the Congress and the Left. And they have never looked back thereafter. But their common minimum programme was Hindu baiting and pampering Muslim minority. Since then inspite of all talk of liberalization, free market forces, privatization, and globalization, at heart the Communists and Congress carried their anti-Hindu agenda to perfection. In the process there developed a morphic resonance between the Congress and the Left against their common target–Hinduism. Her lieutenant and able disciple and a quick learner in the science of electoral calculus, Hemvati Nandan Bahuguna, once Chief Minister of Uttar Pradesh (UP), did one better. He assiduously nursed his Muslim Constituency so much so that when he became the Minister of Petroleum and Chemicals at the centre in the Janata Party government he got all the name plates in Shastri Bhawan embossed in Urdu script and inducted a large number of Muslim bureaucrats in his ministry. Ever since Independence, minority appeasement has never really left the public square in all matters political and social.

The Constitution of India provides enough safeguards for the religious and linguistic minorities as enshrined in the Articles 25 to 30. These are listed at Appendix A. This is all in order but is contrary to the egalitarian spirit of the Constitution and has set an unhealthy trend. The distinction between the majority and the minority communities and discrimination thereof, is an act of communalism amounting to minority appeasement. This, as pointed out earlier, is violative of the principles of secularism, one of the fundamental features of our Constitution. The clarificatory note to Article 25 states that while Section 25 guarantees the freedom to an individual to profess, practise and propagate his religion this freedom is circumscribed by clause (2) (a). To profess a religion means the right to declare freely and openly one's faith. It should, however, be noted that while the individual may propagate freely his religious views or the edification of others, this freedom does not include conversion, least of all conversion by inducement, fraud and force. Further, the freedom to practise one's religion is subject to public order, morality and health. Any practice, which hurts the feelings of another community, cannot be covered under the freedom of worship. In the case Qureshi v. State of Bihar, the question was whether the prohibition of cow slaughter violated the freedom of religion of the Mohammedans. It was contended that the sacrifice of cow on the Bakrid, was enjoined by the Quran and, therefore, the practice was an integral part of the religion. The court, after review of evidence, held that the practice was not an essential part of the Mohammedan religion and could, therefore, be regulated under clause (2)(a) of Article 25.

In its hearings of Articles 29 and 30 consequent to a number of petitions from the beneficiaries of the minority rights, the Supreme Court decided to examine in detail ten salient points on the minority rights. These included inter-alia the definition of the term "religion", the problem of communities with majority and minority status in different states and the degree of independence conferred by the Constitution regarding administration of minority institutions and implications thereto. Unfortunately, there was no senior advocate to represent the national view and the voice of the silent Hindu majority, against whom these minority rights are directed. To ensure full justice to the deliberation under Article 142(1), certain facts have to be kept in mind before a final decision is taken.

There is nothing in the Constitution to define the "majority" and the "minority" communities. The Arya Samajis, members of Ramakrishna Mission in West Bengal, Lingayats in Karnataka, Jains and the Buddhists, had in the past to discard their Hindu label to claim a minority status in order to avoid state interference into their internal matters. Articles 29 and 30 cannot supersede the Fundamental Rights under Article 14, which offers equality before law to all citizens of the country. The minorities cannot enjoy a higher status than the majority. According to the Constitution, the term 'minority' includes only those 'non-dominant groups in a population, which possess and wish to preserve stable ethnic, religious or linguistic traditions or characteristics markedly different from those of the rest of the population. Such minorities should properly include a number of persons sufficient by themselves to develop such characteristics and the members of such minorities must be loyal to the State of which they are nationals. The unqualified loyalty of each minority community or group to the state is a pre-condition for the grant of a minority status. During the freedom struggle the Congress in the constitutional battle against the British was a combined force, inclusive of divergent religions, in other words a secularist combine. On the other hand, Muslim League harped on Muslim separatism and the tyranny of the Hindu majority. Having conceded partition to avoid a civil war, the Congress should have stuck to its position of a citizenship not based on religion. Overwhelmingly, a large majority of Muslims subscribed to the two-nation theory and a large portion who stayed back in India did the same. Therefore, having rejected the two-nation theory there should have been no need for special statutory provisions for the minorities based on religion, which is a dangerous concept and has the potential of ranging the minority community against the majority. The segregation of people for special rights can only be called a blunder and failure to learn from history. Further, such provisions are in contravention to the criteria laid down by the United Nations.

The implications of Article 30(1) also impinge on the spirit of Articles 15,16 and 19, which declare unequivocally that there will be no discrimination in any field on the basis of religion and language. When the first communist government in Kerala in the 1950s tried to exercise some governmental control on all educational institutions, the Christian institutions frustrated the government efforts behind the shield of Article 30(1). The controversy on the rules of admission to the minorities institutions totally financed by the government or given a grant has been finally laid to rest by the recent Supreme Court judgement, wherein the states have been empowered to regulate the percentage of the admission of other communities to these minority institutions. As far as the property rights belonging to the minority community are concerned Article 30(1A) also discriminates between the majority and the minority communities. The statement "In making any law providing for compulsory acquisition of any property of an educational institution established and administered by a minority referred to in clause (1), the State shall ensure that the amount fixed by or determined under such law for the acquisition of such property is such as would not restrict or abrogate the right guaranteed under the clause." It is obvious that the construction material for the property whether belonging to the majority or minority is the same. Should then there be a special provision for assessment of compensation to the property belonging to the minority community? This discrimination is not only unfair but bad in law. Hearing a petition before it, the Supreme Court has averred that since the fundamental rights include freedom of religion, equality before law, right to property, freedom to choose one's occupation, etc. Article 30 loses its locus standi. After all the Human Rights Commission is meant to ensure the availability of such rights.

Coming now to the issue of Wakf property administered by the Muslim community. Little information is available on such properties in India. The trickle of facts coming out from the mutawallis (Wakf managers) is at best a matter of conjecture. The Wakf lands generally exceed the land ceiling limits fixed by the law. More than half the land in Jaunpur is in the possession of Wakfs as also all land in the hillocks in Kannauj. Wakf occupies a large percentage of the total land in various towns; about 13 percent in Ahmedabad, more than 5 percent in Kolkata and about 8 percent in Patna and recently laid claim of ownership of monuments like Taj Mahal. According to the Muslim view, "Wakf is a permanent foundation for a religious or pious object; the corpus belongs to God and cannot be consumed." The word 'Wakf' stands for 'Detain or the dead hand'. There is so much confusion and corruption in the administration of Wakf lands that the state governments have not yet woken up to the need of regulating these huge properties. The entire authority for decision making regarding use, hiring and appropriations of Wakf property lies in the hands of Allah. In other word the administrators' word is supreme with no temporal checks and balances. It is worth mention that other Muslim countries such as Egypt, Turkey, Algeria and Morocco have abolished their Wakfs long ago. In a secular state to allow a community to hold land in the name of God is another rather expensive form of minority appeasement. Wakf is not a historical legacy and can be abolished and controlled by the state. The Christians, Parsis or the Jews have not been given any such privilege. Why so for the Muslims? Is it not a case of inter-communal discrimination? Not only the Wakf but also Dargah Khwaja Saheb Act (1995) also grants enormous privileges to the functionaries of the Dargah. While Wakf is immune to state interference, the Hindu shrines at Tirupati and Vaishno Devi are being managed by their respective state governments.

The Muslim Wakf properties have been exempted from the provisions of the Rent Act, thereby depriving thousands of tenants the protection offered by this Act. The same is not true in the case of properties of Hindu charitable trusts. The government has thus far sanctioned crores of rupees from the taxpayer's money to the Muslim Wakf Board for payment of monthly salaries to the mullahs and maulvis at mosques but the pandits who teach Sanskrit in temples remain debarred from this largesse. The government had granted Rs. 5.28 crores to the Central Waqf Council of Muslims for the development of urban Waqf lands while the same government ordered Lord Venkateshwara Temple at Tirupati to pay Rs. 20 crores as tax on sale of *prasadam* in 1975.

Wakf is the biggest landlord in India. According to Joseph Schacht, an authority on Islamic law, "the Wakf has one of its roots in the contribution to the holy wars which Mohammed incessantly demanded from his followers in Medina. The Wakf property is the outcome of conquest and thousands of temples turned mosques provide the proof. The conflict over temples thus extends to Wakf itself. The Privy Council judgement in late 19th century on the Wakf dispute described it as "a property of the worst and most pernicious kind". The Wakf properties are the living monuments of the medieval Muslim conquests. These silent reminders of temples turned mosques are the bitter harvest of loot and plunder and vitiate communal harmony. The sooner this institution is scrapped the better.

Let us look at the other inequities between the two communities as a direct result of minority appeasement. While polygamy leading to incremental population is permitted to the Muslims, the same is not the case with the Hindus who are exhorted to keep the family size to two children. While the laws have been framed to regulate Hindu personal and family affairs, under Article 44 the same uniform civil code has not yet been applied to the Muslims. In various cities under different states the Hindu *'Maha Aarties'* and the use of loud speakers after 10 PM has been banned, but in Kolkata the Communist West Bengal government has not been able to prohibit the high decibel blaring out of namaz from the mosques. At the Dumdum airport of Kolkata there is a mosque close to the runway, which is a flight hazard. The Communist government has till date not been able to muster enough courage to get the mosque removed to an alternate site. In metropolitan Delhi itself a large number of mosques along with the adjoining madarsas have sprung up at unauthorized places. There have been any number of encroachments on government (NDMC, MCD and DDA) lands all over Delhi. Of particular concern is the one near Jama Masjid, where unauthorized construction of shops has defied all High Court orders. The Delhi Police and the DDA seem helpless, as the Central and the State Governments look the other way. The Shahi Imam of Jama Masjid had once made a speech for which he was charged with treason, but the punishment is yet to come. While there is a government subsidy paid by the taxpayer for Haj pilgrims amounting to Rs one hundred crores there are strict regulations, demand for medical fitness certificates, and advance deposit of about Rupees 30,000/-from each pilgrim to Kailash Mansarovar. Mr. Shahabbuddin and his ilk often repeat the Congress accusation that the majority community has no right to question the loyalty of the Muslims, nor do they need any certification from anyone on this score. All this is fine and taken as read. But can one point out a single instance when Shahabuddin himself has asked the religious and political leaders of his community to mount a popular movement from the mosques/ madrasa centres and others to unequivocally ask their co-religionists not to shelter radical Islamic terrorists? Have these madarsas ever been asked to proclaim tolerance and respect for all religions or for that matter has any single Muslim leader asked his community not to shelter Pakistani terrorists and enemies of the state?

The non-application of the uniform civil code has been discussed earlier. As mentioned, the subsidy from the public exchequer to the Haj pilgrims is passé, the same is not available to Kailash Mansarovar

Yatris. In another blatant act of minorityism in January 1977, a Muslim judge of the Supreme Court Mirza Hamiddulah Beg was promoted as Chief Justice of the Supreme Court by superseding a senior Hindu judge Hans Raj Khanna. Does it not amount to the violation of the fundamental principle of secularism? The provisions of Article 370 are even more pernicious. This has been given in some detail in my earlier book on Nehru and is common knowledge. Another secular PM of India, VP Singh ordered Prophet Mohammad's birthday to be observed as a national holiday to appease his Muslim constituency. The parliament passed a bill to confer a special Muslim status on Aligarh Muslim University. There is no such case elsewhere of a Hindu University. BHU has no comparable privileges as the AMU. From 1990 onwards, the complete expenditure of the Muslim majority state of J&K was borne by the central government, 90 percent as grant and 10 percent as loan. The same is not the case with any other state government. In view of the existence of a human rights commission, is there a need in a secular country for setting up a minority commission and minority cells?

Another PM of 'secular' India, officially declared 40 Muslim districts as 'Muslim intensive population' districts with special officers appointed in the banks to grant loans to the Muslims, and others as liaison officers to monitor the recruitment of minority members in banking services. As of now, there are at least 20 lakh illegal Bangladeshi immigrants in Delhi alone. In addition, another two crore have infiltrated into the states of West Bengal, Assam, Nagaland, Bihar, Orissa and Uttar Pradesh. As the record goes, there are no plans to detect and deport these aliens to their country. Due to the indifference of the government to act on this burning issue Assam has almost become a Muslim majority state. If all this is not minority appeasement, what is?

In a recent effort to rationalize and review the Constitution, central government formed a National Commission to Review the Working of the Constitution (NCRWC), and submit its findings. This report is now lying in cold storage. The Commission, while dealing with Articles 14 to 16, has stated that "it is open to the State to make reservation" for minorities if it is of the opinion that such reservation is necessary and justified." Such a recommendation would only encourage further demands for reservation on the grounds of religion and is likely to further widen the divide between the majority and minority community.

Though legally 150 million Muslims of India, numerically equal to the population of Western Europe, claim to be a minority, does this large number justify any safety provisions? In fact, their numbers added to those of their highly vocal sympathizers amongst our neo-secularists, members of the Congress and Left combine, and the English media, make up for their numerical deficiency. All this added to the votebank factor makes the Muslim community a formidable force. In fact, Sardar Patel was forced to state that "a minority that can cause the partition of a country is no longer a minority." With the potential for such a political if not territorial divide they do not need the crutches of constitutional safeguards. In fact, there is a strong case for the disbandment of the Minority Commission and its replacement by a Human Rights Commission. Our arm chair intellectuals and secularists, who daily sermonize on tolerance and syncretism should make their stand absolutely clear. As it is the Hindus, have in the past sacrificed their lives in large numbers to uphold their civilizational ethos and cultural values. But they shall not accept an aggravated assault on their legacy without cost to the culprit. It is about time that the myth of syncretism is nailed down once and for all, the Nehruvian vulgarity of secularism rejected outright, and the limitation of a genuine synthesis of Muslims in the body politic of India exposed to public gaze in its full implications. Syncretism is not a Hindu cul-de-sac, forcing them to accept alien values with no reciprocal responsibility to be borne by the Muslims. Minority appeasement should go and the monster of minorityism given a ceremonial burial.

It is pertinent here to make an un-ambiguous statement that while the majority of the Indian Muslims are innocent of any wrong doing and generally wish to live peacefully in this country with their Hindu neighbours there are a large number of strident voices emanating from their self-appointed leaders, religious ummas, opinion makers and religious bigots, often with proven extra-territorial instigation and support. The potential of harm due to their divisive activities and religious extremism leading to dismemberment of India cannot be ignored. Let us put on record some of the statements of these "Hon'ble personalities".

"Waging Jehad against India is an Islamic duty of the Muslim world. Kashmir issue cannot be resolved by any means other than Jehad."

-Osama Bin Laden

"Osama Bin Laden is not a terrorist, and neither is Jammu and Kashmir an integral part of India."

Sardar Nagouri, General Secretary of "Students Islamic Movement of India" (SIMI), an outlawed organization.

"Muslims should have ruled India after the departure of the British, and not the Hindus. Population growth helped Muslims to annex a large part of India for creating a separate Islamic State of Pakistan. Such efforts on the part of the Muslims should be continued to gradually convert the rest of India into Dar-ul-Islam (land of the Muslims)."

- Syed Shahabuddin

"India is the greatest Muslim country in the world....The Muslim demand for the creation of a Muslim India within India is, therefore, perfectly justified.

- Allama Mohammed Iqbal

Hakim Ajmal Khan, who was President of the Congress in 1921, while addressing the same Khilafat Conference in presence of Gandhiji said:

"India on the one side and Asia Minor on the other, are but two extreme links in a chain of future Islamic federation, which are gradually but surely joining together all intermediate states in one great system."

A senior leader of the National Conference of Kashmir, and former minister and Deputy Speaker of Kashmir said:

" I am first a Muslim and then an Indian..... As for the question of conversion of all to Islam, it is the fundamental duty of a Muslim to strive for conversion and any Muslim, who does not remember this duty, does not deserve to be called a Muslim."

Abusslam, the Supremo of Hizb-e-Mughalistan, published a map of Mughalistan stretching from Kandhar to Bangladesh, including all Indian territories within. He also advocated the carving out of Dalitistan for the Indian Dalits. His declaration "Mughalistan will be a part of worldwide Islamistan. Muslims are more than one-third of the population of the world. Hence there should be separate Islamistan. The Muslims, who constitute 70 percent of the population in South Asia, should be called Mughal-Muslims. The national language of Mughalistan will be Urdu. In addition to Muslims, those who renounced their religion and embraced Islam can live in this new country called Mughalistan. The Muslims, who speak in Hindi i.e. Ajlaph, can be citizens of this new Islamic state." And for good measure he shows a map of the Mughalistan covering the whole of North India.

Declaring that there is no place for secularism and nationalism in Islam, the following eminent Muslims in a language, which leaves no room for doubt in the minds of those who wish India well, declaim this – a writing on the wall to those who wish to indulge in minority appeasement.

"Secularism has no place in Islam. Propagation of Islam is the first duty of Muslims. Muslim youths will propagate Islam with swords in their hands."

- Syed Abdullah Bukhari

"Islam can never be secular".

- General Zial-ul-Haq

"Nationalism is incompatible with Islam.... The Quran has explicitly rejected the basis of nationalism. ...the concept of a 'nationalist Muslim' is as absurd as that of a 'religious Communist' or 'capitalist Marxist'. ...when the ideology of Islam expands, nationalism is destroyed, and when nationalism grows, Islam is annihilated

-Dr. Ali Mohammed Naqvi (of the Deoband School of Islamic Ideology.)

"Islam has been born to turn the whole world into Islamic. We have to change this secular rule in Bharat, and establish Islamic rule in its place. To achieve this great objective all the Muslims must organize themselves. ... The idea of secular rule is itself a contradiction of Islam. We have, therefore, to slowly work for the establishment of the sovereignty of Islam here."

-Syed Ahmed Hussain, leader of Jama'at-I-Islam.

"The ideologies of democracy, secularism and nationalism have replaced the objects of worship of the past. It is our duty to demolish these ideologies and establish the Caliphate as enjoined upon us by Allah."

- Magazine of 'Student Islamic Movement of India (SIMI)

Let us now turn to the teachings of the holy Quran. Concededly certain portions of Quran do enjoin forbearance and forgiveness. But a larger part speaks in intolerant notes. First the message for forbearance:

> "I do not worship
> What you worship,
> Nor do you worship
> What I worship,
> I will not worship,
> What you worship
> Nor will you worship
> What I worship,
> To you, your religion
> And to me, mine."

-Holy Quran, Sura 109, Ayats 2-6

> "The recompense for an injury
> Is an injury equal thereto
> (In degree); but if a person
> Forgives and makes reconciliation
> His reward is due from Allah
> For (Allah) loveth not those
> Who are cruel and do wrong."

-Holy Quran, Sura 42, Ayat 40

That is where the forbearance ends. Let us now come to the other parts which teach only hatred and Jehad. Hatred is a stronger emotion than love. For a people to be united there must be a common enemy, a target of hate. Love is defused, while hate is a focussed assault on an identifiable enemy. Here is the sermon of hate:

> O believers! Wage war against the infidels,
> Who dwell around you,
> Let them find harshness in you."

-Holy Quran, Sura 9, Ayat 123

"And slay them (unbelievers)
Wherever you catch them
For blasphemy (persecution) is worse
Than slaughter."

-Holy Quran, Sura 2, Ayat 191

"I will instill terror
Into the hearts of the unbelievers;
Smite ye above their necks
And smite all their
Finger-tips off them"

-Holy Quran, Sura 8, Ayat 12

"And fight them on
Until there is no more persecution,
And religion becomes
Allah's in its entirety."

-Holy Quran, Sura 8, Ayat 39

"Whether unarmed or well-equipped
March on and fight
For the cause of Allah
With your wealth and your persons
This will be best for you
If you but knew it."

-Holy Quran, Sura 9, Ayat 41

"They (unbelievers) shall abide in Hell
For ever, and drink boiling water
Which will tear their bowels
Into pieces."

-Holy Quran, Sura 47, Ayat 15

"O Prophet! Exhort the believers
To fight; if there are
Twenty steadfast men among you,
They will vanquish two hundred,
If there are a hundred."

- "Fight against those who believe not
  In Allah, nor the Last Day,
  Nor hold that forbidden
  Which hath been forbidden
  By Allah and His Messenger,
  Nor acknowledge the Religion
  Of Truth from among
  The people of the Book,
  Until they pay the *Jizya*
  With willing submission,
  And feel themselves subdued."

  -Holy Quran, Sura 9, Ayat 29

- "Mohammed is Allah's Prophet
  Those who follow him
  Are ruthless to the unbelievers
  But merciful to one another."

  -Holy Quran, Sura 48, Ayat 29

- "Ye seize him, and bind him (unbeliever)
  And ye burn him
  In the Blazing Fire.
  Then fasten him with a chain
  Having length of 70 cubits!
  For he did not believe
  In Allah, the Most High."

  -Holy Quran, Sura 69, Ayats 30-33

- "Nor hath he (infidel) any food
  Except the foul pus
  From the washing of wounds."

  -Holy Quran, Sura 69, Ayat 36

With such religious injunctions with the faithful from their holy Quran, is it any wonder that the history of Islam is splashed with blood. To state that Islam is a religion of peace is wishful idealism that has been followed more in its breach than compliance. To ignore this fact is the surest way to encourage minorityism. These teachings embedded in the book of faith are the last word of wisdom to which not one word can be added nor any line erased. Thus, any effort to assimilate Muslims in the mainsteam of Indian polity appears to be a daunting task.

In order to grasp the futility and danger of encouraging minorities in India one must comprehend the defining feature of India and by implication Hinduism. In its long history of ten millennia this land has absorbed and assimilated a huge corpus of faith of those that came from outside. It has sheltered and embraced fugitives from countries all over the world. Its tolerance is limitless. India has allowed diverse ideologies to prosper within its fold including Communism which does not even have any commitments to national sovereignty, which looks beyond national boundaries for its source of inspiration, subsuming Nationalism for international Communism. The principal minorities have never been under threat from the 850 million Hindu majority. Besides the constitutional safeguards, the very nature of Hinduism is accommodative and not exclusivistic. It does not encourage a dichotomy of believers and non-believers; the faithful and the infidel, monotheistic correct and the pantheistic incorrect. A recent UNESCO report revealed that out of 128 countries, where the Jews lived before the State of Israel came into being, it was only in India that they were allowed to practise their faith peacefully. Before the Gujarat election, the English media screamed that Hindu fundamentalists went on a rampage. But did they care to find out why this happened? This is what Francois Gautier says, "But what if Gujarat was the first sign that good, peaceful, non-violent, middle-class and even lower class Hindus have had it and that they are tired of being made fun of, attacked, bombed, burnt, killed, their women raped, their temples destroyed? What if, rightly or wrongly, it is the portent of things to come, that the next time innocent Hindu women and children are targeted, Hindus might be tempted to take an eye for an eye, a tooth for a tooth, the way Israel does at the official level? You may argue that it is a hateful , mad and blind violence, but it is also true that Hindus have been at the receiving end of Christians' and Muslims' attacks for centuries, that even today 400,000 of them have been made to flee from their ancestral homes in the valley of Kashmir."

The Indian Muslims should realize that every attack on Hindu temples, bomb explosion, sabotage, derailment of trains causes loss of innocent lives. Bombay blast, Coimbatore blast, the blast at U.S. Centre at Kolkata, Akshardham and Raghunath temples, attack on Parliament on 12/13 were engineered from a base of operations in India. ISI sponsored terrorists need a foothold to establish their terrorist modules and where did they find them? Who helps them? Is it not Indian Muslims?

The same way our Christian brothers should realize that Syrian Christians came to this country and settled down in Kerala centuries ago and have lived there all these years in complete peace and harmony with their Hindu neighbours. The problem arose only when Christian missionaries tried to bring the kingdom of Christ by dubious means and work for destabilization of this country. The fringe Hindu, Lord be praised, is not a fundamentalist and the fanatic Hindu does not take offence unless provoked. Minorities in India are safe and it is about time that the evil of minorityism is given a quiet burial once and for all.

There are a few Muslim brothers who have broken ranks with their co-religionists and come to acknowledge and appreciate their pre-Islamic past. Having drawn the elixir from the limitless font of culture they do recognize that all that preceded Islam was not an area of darkness that has to be disowned.

Our neo-secularists, instead of purging Indian polity of Muslim separatism, have added fuel to the fire by resorting to the worst form of minority appeasement completely out of sync with a liberal progressive and holistic development of national identity. Instead they deride the Hindu organizations for fissures in the Indian society.

The worst example of minorityism resulting in humiliation, indignity and injustice heaped on the Hindus in India is the festering sore of the Ram Mandir dispute at Ayodhya, which has been allowed to turn into a gangrenous outcrop. In a Hindu majority country, a government in an inglorious retreat from its obligations, finds itself incapable of allowing the construction of the Ram Temple at the so-called disputed site, solely because a pampered minority refuses to withdraw its claim at the ruins of a non-mosque structure, raised by a Muslim conqueror at the very site where once a temple of their most revered God, Lord Ram, stood. Firstly, the construction of the mosque after the destruction of the temple was an act of vandalism and a crime against Hindu

India. Secondly, opposition to rectify the four and a half centuries of historical shame on a proud people, on the specious ground of legality of land ownership of the undisputed land around, to delay and deliberately sabotage the process of temple construction is untenable. Matters of faith cannot be arbitrated in courts of law. Here is the centre of faith of 900 million Hindus and the issue is being trivialized and deliberately put through a slow moving legal process to aggravate the passions of an injured people. Babri Masjid was no Mecca or Medina. It was a structure with only three domes and no minarets. It has no association with Allah or Mohammed but for the Hindus, it is the holy birthplace of their most revered incarnation of God.

There is more than a grain of truth in the statement that matters of faith are not justiciable. Take the example of El-Aqsa, the mosque at Jerusalem that is located right above the very spot called Mount Moriah in Jewish lore, where the Bible speaks of Abraham making an altar to offer his son as a sacrifice to his Lord. Later, on this holy shrine, David built the famous Temple of his Lord, Jehovah. This was long before Islam and its prophet were born. Later, on a belief unsupported by historical evidence, that Mohammed undertook his journey to heaven on his steed al-Burak from that very spot. Suleiman, the Caliph of Kurdish origin, built a mosque there to commemorate this holy event. If Mohammed travelled to heaven in real life, he could not have lived later to die in Medina. But if this was merely a dream, was there any logic to destroy the sacred Jewish temple to build a mosque there? Are dreams more important than Biblical facts corroborated by archaeological evidence? According to some historians, the Arabs are masters in building on ruins of other faiths. In a thousand years, they have built only one town in Palestine. Muslims all over the world have emulated this propensity to destroy and build. India is no exception. The early impression that Akbar, the great secularist, built an entirely new township at Fatehpur Sikri is negated by the discovery during recent excavations of ruins of Hindu temples in that area.

Purely on points of evidence regarding the existence of a temple, immediately after the demolition on December 6, 1992, more than 265 pieces of artifacts with authentic Hindu transcriptions and figurines embedded in the walls of the structure were recovered, a typical Islamic practice of using the temple material for the construction of mosques. The clinching evidence in the form of a stone slab, 5ft x 2 ft was proof enough of a Sanskrit record speaking of the construction of a magnificent gold domed temple of Vishnu Hari. The texts also speak of Lord Ram who destroyed the evil Dashanana (Ravana) and the dating of the temple built by King Nayachandra and Ayushchandra during the reign of Emperor Govindchand Gahadwal goes back to 1114-1154 AD.

Let us look at the ground facts as of date. The area of the demolished structure with a core of 33 acres along with the precincts of 60ft x 40 ft amounts to 2.77 acres. P.V. Narasimha Rao's Congress government further acquired the surrounding land of 67 acres in 1993 from its owners VHP and Ram Janma Bhoomi Nyasa, inspite of Hindu protests, ostensibly to safeguard the disputed site, as also to provide facilities for pilgrims such as shelters, library and so on. In October 1994, a five-member Bench of the Supreme Court upheld the acquisition with a caveat that "it would be not merely permissible but also that the superfluous excess area is reverted to its earlier owner", a fairly clear-cut order. Government consulted the VHP and All India Muslim Personal Law Board (AIMPLB), to agree to the settlement, wherein 67 acres of land belonging to the VHP and the Nyasa be handed over to them and the court verdict awaited on the disputed 2.77 acres of land. AIMPLB refused to comply. Later in February and March 2002, thousands of *Kar Sevaks* assembled at Ayodhya to carry out *Shila Pujan* at the usurped land. But the *Shila Pujan* was stopped in consequence of a petition from Mohammed Aslam Bhure of Delhi to the Supreme Court. A three-member bench of the Supreme Court forbade "religious activity of any nature" on this 67 acre land and thus fused the 'disputed' with the 'undisputed' land. The Government in February 2003 woke up to its responsibility and asked the Supreme Court to allow the undisputed 67 acres of land to be transferred to its rightful owners. This government petition sought to crease out two main anomalies. Firstly, the apparent mismatch between the 1994 and 2002 orders since the former sought the status quo only on the 2.77 acres of land while the latter on a further 67 acres as well. Secondly, can a three-member bench overrule the earlier five-member bench? Even though the judiciary can never be second guessed, the VHP and the government were hopeful of a favourable verdict, but the Supreme Court refused to expedite the hearing before 15 February, 2003, notwithstanding VHP's resolution to hold on 22 February *dharma sansad* (a religious parliament) in Delhi. This convention of preachers and gurus, Hindutva's collective papacy, was to deliberate on the timing and other details of the construction project.

The case first filed by Mahant Ram Chandra in 1949 is still pending in the court though the attempt to recover the site by Hindus dates back to 1885, when Mahant Raghubir Das filed a petition in Faizabad district court. A British judge turned down the petition, but he did mention that though the mosque was built under order of King Babur, the land had a strong reverential association with the Hindus. No namaz has been offered at the place since 1936, while the worship of Lord Rama's idol placed inside the mosque has been going on since 1949, when the district judge of Faizabad opened the gates of the mosque. For Hindus, the temple is revered as a dwelling place for God, while in Islam a mosque like a Jewish synagogue is just a place of worship that can be shifted. There are numerous examples of such displacements of mosques in orthodox Islamic countries. The antagonism of Indian Muslims, most of whom are Hindu converts, to yielding space to the Hindus is driven by a subliminal urge to disown their pre-Islamic past. Sir V.S. Naipaul was dead right when he mentioned in his book, *Beyond Belief* that a converted Muslim's memory anywhere outside Saudi Arabia is limited to the time of the Prophet's birth and wipes out any ethnic past preceding that date. Indian history before 700 A.D. does not belong to Indian Muslims. Dr Ambedkar in his book, *Thoughts on Pakistan* (1940) echoes the same views. Ram being pre-Islamic is a divided legacy.

Regarding the temple construction and the present situation today is far different from that prevailing in February-March 2002, when 58 Kar Sevaks returning from Ayodhya were burnt alive in the Sabarmati Express at Godhra on 27 February, 2002. The conditions now are more peaceful and there should be no reason for the legal delay in returning back to VHP what belongs to it. Legal quibbling and political expediency apart, Hindus have every right to claim their religious shrine and rectify centuries of national shame. No nation worth its name can suffer vandalization of the holiest place of its worship. To quote Menachim Begin, an earlier Prime Minister of

Israel, "What our ancestors refused to tolerate from their ancient oppressors, even at the cost of their lives and freedom, is tolerated by the generation of Jews, which described itself as the last of oppression and the first of redemption. A people that does not defend its holy places and that does not even try to defend them, is not free, however, much it may babble about freedom. People that permit the holiest spot of their country and their most sacred feelings to be trampled underfoot, are slaves in spirit. And we determined there and then that when the time came we would cleanse our people of this shame, and if we should have the strength we would not permit the oppressor's myrmidons to violate our Holy place, disturb our prayers and desecrate our Festival."

It will be an eye - opener to read Dr. Ambedkar's book *Thoughts on Pakistan*. Contrary to popular belief that Ambedkar favoured the Muslim minority ("a friend in need of the dalits"), ranged against caste Hindus in achieving Pakistan, the facts speak just the opposite. He knew the Muslim paranoia for ruling India inspite of their small numbers. He knew that they could force our 'secularists' to concede any demand they will make. After all, did not Gandhiji promise to make Jinnah the Prime Minster of undivided India? They would impose the Shariat and enact anti-blasphemy laws. They had earlier burnt the bookshop of a Hindu, Rajpal, in Lahore in April 1929 for a scurrilous book on the Prophet Mohammed titled *'Rangila Rasool'*, in response to an earlier outrageous pamphlet by a Muslim agent provocateur titled *'Sita ka Chinala'*, vilifying Sita, the wife of Lord Rama, as a woman of loose morals. Would they ever co-exist peacefully with Hindus in an undivided India? Their Khilafat movement, that started on October 27, 1919, did not support Gandhiji's civil disobedience movement that came after 10 months. It was Gandhiji who co-opted the Muslims against the abolition of the Caliphate by the British to his cause. It was his movement that supported Khilafat not vice-versa. When Bhagat Singh and his two comrades in arms were executed on 23rd March, 1931, all Hindus at Kanpur observed a hartal (bandh is a recent invention) by closing down all shops in the town. The Muslims refused to co-operate and down the shutters. Instead, they looted Hindu shops in the town. Even the armed forces that had a Muslim content out of all proportion to their share of population would have been subverted and with their pan-Islamic friends abroad, could have severely eroded the sovereignty of India. Instead of allowing a Muslim minority rule in India, Ambedkar thought it better to let the Muslims leave and stay in Pakistan. Recently, with a population of just 9.6 percent in Maharashtra if they can cause a riot in Sholapur, when an American Catholic priest, Jerry Falwell, makes some unpalatable remarks, force Hindu shops to close down and resort to violence if refused; what would the harvest have been if they were to stay in India with 33 percent population?

After Ayodhya, the other issue where the Government has buckled under minority pressure is the singing of our national song, *Vande Mataram.* There is no other country in the world except India which has two national songs: *Jana Gana Mana* as the national anthem and *Vande Mataram* as the additional national song. *Vande Mataram* is the most emotive song of our freedom struggle, when thousands of sons of India embraced the gallows singing these famous lines written by Bankim Chandra Chatterjee. Maharshi Aurobindo mentioned this song in his writings in 1907, referring to its birth around 1874-1875, well before the famous novel *Anand Math* was written by the same author. In the second session of the Congress in 1886, at Calcutta, Hem Chandra Bandopadhyaya first sang a few stanzas of this song along with his own composition. This was the first recitation of *Vande Mataram* in a Congress session. Later, in the Congress session of 1896, Rabindra Nath Tagore gave voice to this song. From 1907 onwards, every Congress session opened with this song and it received a position of national honour, during the Bengal partition movement. The original theme of this song by Bankim Babu was confined to Bengal only when the total population of India stood at about 30 crore. With increase in the song's popularity and as the contours of new India emerged, the word '*saptkoti*' was replaced by *trinshkoti*. In 1906, with the foundation of the Muslim League, began the opposition to the song. In 1925, in the Congress session at Kakinada, Maulana Mohammed Ali declared that the song was un-Islamic and should not be sung during the Congress session. Despite his opposition, Pandit Vishnu Digambar Paluskar defied him on the ground that the Congress session was not a mosque, and sang the full song in a full throated mellifluous voice all his own. Muslim League's objections continued and later even Muslim members of the Congress were ill at ease with the song and Muslim majority schools in East Bengal strongly opposed it.

Later, the Congress Working Committee under Jawaharlal Nehru, Maulana Azad, Subhas Chandra Bose and Narendra Deo formed a sub-committee, to which Tagore was invited only as a special nominee, to deliberate on the issue. The committee decided that only the first two stanzas of the song need be sung in public meetings, thus accepting only nine lines out of a total of 26. The succeeding lines incorporating references to Saraswati, Durga and Lakshmi were to be deleted. Again in 1936, in the correspondence between Nehru and Jinnah, the latter reasserted that the song is un-Islamic since it mentions Hindu goddesses and promotes idol worship, and further, that the song was culled from the novel '*Anand Math*', a novel that was based on an anti-Muslim struggle and had anti-Muslim overtones. Based on this correspondence, the decision to retain only the two opening stanzas became final. The association of Tagore with this decision raised many eyebrows and he had to defend himself saying, "The discussion on the song *Vande Mataram* should be closed as this has given rise to enough controversy. It is very sad. While expressing my views on the subject I remember that during the lifetime of the father of this song, I was the man who was fortunate enough to give music to his words. The first part of the song is full of noble thoughts and faith in our values and is the most vivid description of the beauty of our motherland. All this completely enthralled me. Inspite of being brought up in the praxis of my faith in the unity of God, I have full sympathy for all parts of the song." In 1948, Nehru declared in the Lok Sabha that "*Vande Matram*' is clearly and without question the foremost national song of the country and is a great national heritage. It has been closely associated with our freedom struggle." Thus, on 24th January, 1950, *Vande Mataram* was accepted as the prayer song to be sung at the opening of each session of the Parliament. On the other hand, the motivation for *Jana Gana Mana,* many discerning historians believe, was to honour George V on his arrival to India, thus giving it the colour of colonial slavery. This may not entirely be true. Also, *Jana Gana Mana* suffers from the inexactitude of including *Sindh* in present day India. But the downgrading of *Vande Mataram* and its unacceptability on the ground of Muslim angst is untenable. The fog must be cleared. In any case, no single song in the Indian struggle for freedom is more emotive and full of national pride and glory as *Vande Mataram.*

The recent example of a mini Ayodhya conundrum in the making came to light when public attention was focused on a disputed shrine in the township of Dhar in Madhya Pradesh. The Bhojshala cum Kamal Moula mosque, a protected monument under Archaeological Survey of India (ASI), a Hindu shrine also claimed by the Muslims conjointly, for whom it is open for prayers every Friday, but for the Hindus only once a year on Basant Panchami.... The state Government's partisan stand was clearly visible this year. The VHP protested at this inequity and demanded that the restriction on Hindu worship be removed. To prevent breach of peace, the state government made elaborate security arrangements including deployment of Rapid Action Force (RAF) for Saraswati puja on Basant Panchami on February 6, 2003. The Hindus were chafing at this invidious discriminative justice. This is a potential trouble spot and unless the state government takes a reasonable stand, Hindu passions are likely to be inflamed. On 19th February, 2003, there was an open confrontation by the Hindu Jagaran Manch (HJM) and VHP activists leading a procession of devotees to offer their prayers at the Bhojshala. The district administration ordered police firing and lathi charge wherein many worshippers, including many women were wounded as some police personnel received injuries as well. The cauldron was on the boil. The entire Malwa region with five major cities, including Indore and Dewas, was under a curfew, as the state government obfuscated the issue by claiming that it is waiting for a clearance from the centre for regular Hindu worship. The movement gained momentum. The Hindus demand that since the Muslims are allowed a regular Friday prayer, they too must be allowed free access to the shrine instead of one day in a year on Basant Panchami.

Let us step back a little into history. The building of Bhojshala, a temple for Saraswati worship, was constructed in 1034 AD and finds a mention in the Jain scripture *Prabandh Chintamani.* Dedicated to the goddess of learning the temple became a residential university and the centre of Hindu philosophy and Sanskrit studies. At one time it employed 1400 theologians, scholars and poets. Magha, Banbhatta, Kalidasa, Bhavbhooti, and Bhaskar Bhatt, were some of the luminaries, who got patronage at the university where famous scriptures such as *'Avni Koormshalam'*, *'Saraswati Kanthbharana'*, *'Tithisarnika'* and *'Rajamarrtand'* were scripted. According to Dhar District gazetteer, the Bhojshala was a great centre of learning for most religions of India of those times. A magnificent crystal stone statue for Saraswati was installed in the Bhojshala in 1035 AD accompanied by a 14-day festival commencing on Basant Panchami, believed to be the birthday of the goddess. After a *Maha Saraswati Mahayagna* performed on the occasion and attended by thousands of the devotees from all parts of the country, the *Maa Saraswati Yagna* became a regular feature. A part of this Bhojshala was destroyed by Dilawar Khan Gori after his conquest of Malwa in 1401 AD. Later during an attack by Mahmood Shah Khilji in 1514 AD, 1200 scholars of the Bhojshala were slaughtered and some put to work at cleaning the toilets of the victors. A dargah was subsequently built here. Despite the partial destruction of the Bhojshala, for 100 years no Namaz was offered at the shrine. In 1930, Muslim efforts to offer Namaz were strongly resisted by the Hindus and the ruler of Dhar State adjudicated the issue. In 1935, the local administration upheld the Muslim claim to hold Namaz on each Friday, denying any such privilege to the Hindus. After communal riots broke out in 1944, the Archeological Survey of India (ASI) took over the shrine in 1952.The decree by the ruler of Dhar state laid no restriction on Hindu visits throughout the year. The same year in 1952, Maharaja Bhoj Smriti Basantotsava was held. This was the sequel to an earlier visit to the town in 1951 by Padmashree Dr. Visnu Shreedhar Vakanankar, an archeologist of international fame, also a RSS pracharak, to see the Saraswati statue there. He discussed the issue with Nehru, who agreed that the statue be brought back to the country. In 1997, the VHP put Bhojshala on its agenda of reclaiming Hindu shrines. On May 12, 1997, Madhya Pradesh Government sent for approval to the centre the request of the Hindus to allow unrestricted access to the shrine and pooja once a year on Basant Panchami. The then Prime Minister Deve Gowda issued an order to the ASI that the Bhojshala be closed to all communities till July 31, 1997. The Madhya Pradesh Government defied the centre's orders and continued with the restrictions on Hindus even after July 31,1997. Thus, the present crisis was the handiwork of Congress Government of Madhya Pradesh. Consequent to a repeat of communal riots in 1984 and observation of Shaurya Diwas by RSS activists in 1994; the Bhojshala was declared a restricted area. The ASI formulated the present invidious and discriminatory practice in 1998 leading to a Satyagrah by the Hindu Jagaran Manch (HJM) in 2002.

The disturbances had spread over large parts of Malwa and south-east Madhya Pradesh. There were six districts under curfew with reports pouring in of mounting casualties and increasing tension. With a Chief Minister allowing only a weekly visit on Tuesday to Hindus and Friday Namaz to Muslims, the matter was still not closed despite the centre's directions to allow unfettered access to Hindus. Ultimately the writ of the Central Government prevailed.

The most pernicious provision pandering to minorityism and out of sync with national interests and dictates of sovereignty and integrity of the land, but aimed at a minuscule minority in Kashmir is Article 370. Conceived in secrecy and of unholy parentage, this constitutional provision though of a temporary nature has acquired a permanence all its own and vitiated the national political scene. This single piece of legislation has acquired the status of a holy cow and is the biggest threat to the security of our country. Let us begin at the beginning.

Article 370 was a stratagem to clothe the Centre's incapacity to do its duty in the garb of pompous principles. This Article, it was emphasized, was the umbilical cord, which bound Kashmir with India and through which provisions of the Indian Constitution could be extended to the territory of Kashmir. It was the link to serve a temporary purpose till the State is totally integrated within the Indian Union. That the Article is a temporary provision is evident from its very title which reads: "Article 370—Temporary provision with respect to the State of J & K." Remember that such an important matter concerning Home was being handled not by the Home Minister, Sardar Patel, but by N. Gopalswamy Ayyangar, an earlier Prime Minister of J&K for six years with effect from 1937. Subsequently an aide to Nehru, he was later promoted to the rank of a Minister, dealing with the delicate problem of J & K. The discussions on Article 370 in the Constituent Assembly are revealing. When on October 17,1949, two years after the invasion of Kashmir, Ayyangar moved Article 306 A (since then repealed), a member asked, "why this discrimination please?" Nehru had no answer. Later, he prevaricated and said, "Till a Constituent Assembly comes into being, only an interim arrangement is possible and not an arrangement which could not at once be brought into line with the arrangement which exists in the case of other states". And then he went on to say, "Now if you remember the viewpoints that I have mentioned," he summed up, "It is an inevitable conclusion that, at the present moment, we could establish only an interim system. Article 306 is an attempt to establish such a system." And he elaborated that just as Defence, External Affairs and Communications, subjects which are Centre's responsibility in other States can be extended to Kashmir through the concurrence of the State Government, the other parts of the Constitution can also be similarly extended. The State Government in either case had the veto power to accept or reject the introduction of these provisions within their territory. This was a patently undemocratic action to single out a State in this manner. But Gopalaswamy Ayyangar kept on harping on the nature of the provisions of Article 306 A and Article 370.

The Sardar had reluctantly acquiesced to the usurpation of Kashmir portfolio by Nehru, a subject legitimately falling under the Department of States of the Ministry of Home Affairs. He did this to avoid unpleasantness. However, he did feel concerned when without consulting him Nehru brought in Gopalaswamy Ayyangar as a minister without portfolio to help him in dealing with Kashmir and the duo started muddling up things. He mentioned the same to Nehru without mincing words. Nehru flared up and replied on December 23, 1947: "Gopalaswamy Ayyangar has been especially asked to help in Kashmir matters. Both for this reason and because of his intimate knowledge and experience of Kashmir he had to be given full latitude. I really do not see where the States' Ministry (the Sardar's Ministry that is) comes into the picture except that it should be kept informed of the steps taken...."

"All this was done at my instance and I do not propose to abdicate my functions in regard to matters for which I consider myself responsible. May I say that the manner of approach to Gopalaswamy was hardly in keeping with the courtesy due to a colleague?" From the records kept by V. Shankar, ICS, Personal Secretary to Patel, and the *Correspondence of Sardar Patel*, published by Durga Dass, it is clear that Nehru had finalized the draft of Article 370 in collusion with Sheikh Abdullah without even consulting Patel and then proceeded abroad leaving Ayyangar to hold the baby during his absence through debates in the Constituent Assembly. In an earlier exchange of letters, Nehru had shown his irritation with Patel over their differences on 23 December, 1947. And yet Nehru was using the same colleague with whom he differed so much and often quarrelled, to get his draft passed in Parliament. Shankar records in *My Reminiscences of Sardar Patel, Vol 11, pages 61-64:* "In the Congress Party, there was a strong body of opinion which looked askance at any suggestion of discrimination between the Jammu and Kashmir State and other states as members of the future Indian Union and was not prepared to go beyond certain limits in providing for the special position of Jammu and Kashmir. Sardar was himself fully in accord with this opinion, but due to his usual policy of not standing in the way of Pandit Nehru and Gopalaswamy Ayyangar who sorted out problems in their own light, he had kept his own views in the background. In fact, he had not taken any part in framing the draft proposals with the result that he heard the proposals only when Gopalaswamy Ayyangar announced them to the Congress Party... The announcement was followed by a storm of angry protests from all sides and Gopalaswamy Ayyangar found himself a lone defender, with Maulana Abul Kalam Azad an ineffective supporter. Metaphorically, the situation may be succinctly described by saying that both Gopalaswamy Ayyangar and his proposal were torn to pieces by the Party".

"Later in the evening Sardar received a telephone call from Gopalaswamy Ayyangar explaining the genesis of the proposals he had put before the Party and describing the scenes that he had painfully witnessed. He felt that only Sardar could intervene to save the situation and appealed to him to come to his rescue. Sardar heard him and lapsed into silence." Loyal to his absent colleague, Sardar tried to defend what he himself was convinced was indefensible. He convened a meeting of the Congress Executive. As Shankar recalls:

"The meeting was one of the stormiest I have ever witnessed, barring the Party meeting which discussed the proposition relating to Rajaji becoming the first President of Indian Republic. The opinion in opposition to Gopalaswamy's formula was forcefully and even militantly expressed and the issue even brought in of the sovereignty of the Constituent Assembly to draw up the Constitution without being tied down to the apron-strings of the Kashmir State Constituent

Assembly. In such a situation even Maulana Azad was shouted down. Barely two years later on 24 July, 1952, after the Sardar's death, Nehru made a detailed statement on Kashmir in Parliament dealing with all the issues including the slow progress of integration of the State of Kashmir and mentioned "Sardar Patel was all the time dealing with these matters". Stressing again the temporary nature of Article 370, he obfuscated the issue and involved the Sardar in the decision-making, the very man who opposed it tooth and nail. He said: "This came to an end in November, I think of 1949, when we were designing our Constitution in the Constituent Assembly. Well, we could not leave everything quite vague and fluid there. Something had to be stated in our Constitution about Jammu and Kashmir State. That problem had to be faced by Sardar Patel. Now, he did not wish to say very much, he wanted to leave it, we all wanted to leave it in a fluid condition because of these various factors, and gradually to develop those relations. As a result of this, a rather unusual provision was made in our Constitution relating to Jammu and Kashmir. That provision is now in Article 370." Later referring to this speech of Nehru, Shankar remarked, "When I was working as his (Ayyangar's) Joint Secretary in July 1952, the self-same Article came in for criticism in the Lok Sabha. In defence, Pandit Nehru took the stand that the Article was dealt with by Sardar in his absence and he was not responsible for it. I met Gopalaswamy the same evening as he was walking on the lawn of his residence. I questioned the bonafide of Pandit Nehru's stand. Gopalaswamy's reaction was one of anger and he said, "it is an ill-return to Sardar for the magnanimity he had shown in accepting Panditji's point of view against his better judgement." He added, "I have told Jawaharlal this already." A year later on 8th August, 1953, Nehru realized his earlier blunder and ordered the arrest of Sheikh Abdullah. *"Jawaharlal Royega"* were the prophetic last words of the Sardar and the chicken came home to roost.

Article 370 midwifed by Nehru and Sheikh Abdullah did not really secure the integration of Kashmir with the Indian Union but encouraged the Sheikh to carve out an independent fiefdom for himself. It did not allow the benefits of equality, liberty and freedom from feudal oppression and economic development to reach the people of Kashmir but kept them in a permanent state of serfdom under their feudal lords. The fruits of economic aid and enormous resources poured into the State were cornered by a few self-seeking politicians, while the people remained poor, illiterate and steeped in misery. The discontent kept simmering. The rigged elections of the National Conference and Indian National Congress coalition in 1987 proved to be the proverbial last straw, and the youth of Kashmir, frustrated, unemployed, long suffering from inequities, while their feudal rulers prospered, said "enough is enough". The cult of the Kalashnikov was the inevitable consequence. The seeds of alienation of Kashmir were sown as early as July 1952, when Nehru announced in the Union Parliament the Delhi Agreement leading to the incorporation of Article 370 in the Constitution of India. The root cause of alienation of the Kashmiri people and separatist trends in the politics of that unhappy State is the continued presence of Article 370 in the Constitution of India which ensures a special status for the State as against the other States of the Indian Union. The tremors of this historical act of Nehru have shaken the historical, social, economic and political foundations of the State and dealt a deadly blow to the unity of India while leading to deleterious effects on our polity. The consequences, if the Article is not abrogated, may be even more far reaching. There is little doubt that vested interests of the Sheikh and his successors have been the prime beneficiaries as also the *raison d'etre* of this Article. The isolation of the State from the rest of Indian polity was not for its good health but to create a territory where the laws of natural justice, development and fair play would not prevail. In consequence, the few power elites and their brokers have filled their coffers and kept the poor poorer. The beneficial laws of our Constitution such as the Wealth tax, Gift tax, Urban Land Ceiling Act, the right to buy property and intermarry with other Indian nationals has not been allowed to operate in Kashmir. The Central Government under this Article can, besides Defence, Communication and Foreign Affairs, make laws even on items featuring in the Union and the Concurrent List. But these can be applied only with the concurrence of the State. This amounts virtually to granting the State a veto on what it wishes to be introduced in its territory. The position is not the same in regard to the other states where the Union Parliament is free to make laws in respect of any State within the Indian Union. However, under fair weather and with adroit political handling, some provisions of the Indian Constitution have been extended to the State from time to time. The process started after the Delhi Agreement of 1952, which enabled such an exercise. Some of these worth mention are Article 356 and the jurisdiction of the Supreme Court, Central Election Commission and the Comptroller and Auditor General. But there are still large areas mentioned in the Concurrent List and the residuary powers that have been left untouched in the State. One of these is Article 352, which gives the President the power to declare national emergency, and another one, Article 360 regarding financial emergency, which cannot be imposed in Kashmir, just as Article 356 enabling the President to suspend constitution of the State is not similarly applicable. Kashmir has its own Constitution by virtue of Article 370, unlike other states which have a uniform Constitution as enshrined in Part IV of the Indian Constitution. Inevitably, a number of discrepancies and avoidable problems, such as the right to hold property, citizenship and freedom of settlement for the Indian citizens, have arisen. An Indian national has no right to settle or buy property in this State. While an average citizen of India can claim only one citizenship, the one in Jammu & Kashmir can have two citizenships, citizenship of India and that of the State. Those outside Kashmir cannot vote. What is most galling is that a woman of Jammu & Kashmir origin if married to an Indian who is a non-citizen of the State loses claims to property, both her own as well as that inherited from her parents. Such unreasonable, archaic and legally unsound laws, which are incompatible with the fundamental principles of our Constitution, have a field day in Kashmir. The State has its own flag and emblem, unknown in any other state of India. Many financial frauds have been perpetrated in the State in the absence of a close scrutiny by the Central Constitutional authority. Considerable wheeling dealing which started from the time of Sheikh Abdullah continued till the times of his worthy successor Dr. Farooq Abdullah where the State laws on property sale and purchase were flouted with impunity, with no checks and balances available to monitor the happenings within the State. In the case of renewal of lease to Nedous Hotel in March 1988 and the Karal Sangri Hill in 1985, according to Jagmohan, ex-Governor of the State, the State exchequer was defrauded of crores of rupees, which belonged to the public. Corruption and nepotism were rampant and selective patronage to persons, plants and projects had a free run in the valley with total disregard to financial probity and public interest. The Urban Land (Ceiling and Regulation) Act, 1976, prevalent in India has not till now been extended to Jammu and Kashmir. It beats human intelligence as to how such a provision could detract from the special status of Jammu and Kashmir. The under- lying motive for non-extension of the above provision could only be less than noble intention of the ruling class, to perpetuate a politically corrupt oligarchy under shelter of Article 370. The Anti Defection Act was not extended nor adopted fully in the State. It is the Leader of the Legislature Party and not the Speaker who can adjudicate on matters of defection. The situation is virtually tantamount to all powers of governance, political activities, distribution of party tickets and nomination of Ministers being centered in the party chief who heads the Government. It is he who takes decisions on the propriety of his own acts or those of a Minister in the Government or a Member of his Legislature Party. The 18th Amendment Act 1987, enacted such a provision in the Constitution of Jammu & Kashmir. It stipulates, "If any question arises as to whether a member of the House has become subject to disqualification under this schedule, the question shall be referred for decision to the Leader of the Legislature Party to which such member belongs and his decision shall be final". If this is not constitutional dictatorship what else is? The infirmity imposed on a woman citizen of Jammu & Kashmir after her marriage to an Indian citizen can have serious implications. Not only does she lose her property rights as mentioned above, but also suffers certain other disabilities, such as admission to Government aided colleges – Medical or Engineering. It is a mockery of justice when a person who is a citizen of India, by virtue of being a citizen and permanent resident in Jammu and Kashmir, forfeits his or her rights for admission to the Medical College funded by the Union Government, after marriage with an Indian citizen. The case of migrants from West Pakistan after the partition who have been settled in Jammu and Kashmir for more than the last four decades and have still not been granted the basic human rights is something to which our so-called conscience-keepers and custodians of human rights such as the PUCL have turned a Nelson's eye. These unfortunates cannot cast their vote in the panchayat, municipality or the state elections, nor get admission to State colleges or secure state loans. These are the 'nowhere' people residing in our country, who have left their homes for no fault of theirs and are unable to secure even elementary justice in their new homeland. It is not incidental that most of these people are Hindus. The plight of these unfortunates is the hidden sting of the infamous Article 370 and its consequences.

An argument that has often been touted for the retention of Article 370 is the need to maintain a special identity for Kashmir and its people and to preserve its cultural heritage. Is such a plea not applicable to the remaining states of our country, such as Andhra Pradesh, Tamil Nadu, Gujarat, Maharashtra, Punjab, and West Bengal, Sikkim, Nagaland, Meghalaya, Tripura, Rajasthan, to mention just a few. These have their own clear and distinctive culture and history. Why then Article 370 has not been applied to these States? How is it that Article 370 finds its rationale in the one and only one Muslim majority State of Kashmir? Jinnah had raised the ghost of two-nation theory. Does this Article then not amount to a shameful homage to Jinnah's theory and an effort to validate it? Jawaharlal Nehru along with Gandhiji and Patel denounced the two-nation theory during the pre-partition days, what 'compelled' Nehru to perpetuate it in Kashmir by introducing Article 370 and ensuring its existence against all opposition in the rest of the country?

Article 356, a provision under which President's rule can be imposed in any State within the Indian Union, cannot be enforced in the State of Jammu and Kashmir without the consent of the Governor who himself is an appointee of the President. In other words, the President has to seek the permission of his own appointee to order what he considers right in national interest. Take another instance. If the Governor of Jammu and Kashmir decides to become a 'Sadar-e-Riyasat', then again Article 356 cannot be introduced without his consent. The situation really boils down to the fact that the elected Government of Jammu and Kashmir can defy the President of India should it so desire, virtually placing the State Government in a position superior to the head of the Indian State. Defence is a subject under the Union but the State of Jammu and Kashmir can refuse the building of a cantonment at any site or refuse to allot land for Defence purposes if that becomes necessary, and defy the needs of national security. In other words, a subject as important as Defence can be subverted by a recalcitrant State Government which wishes to obstruct the plan of the Government of India in respect of any concrete measure that it may deem necessary for the defence of the State. Kashmir, through Article 370, usually forgets that the State is not a homogeneous entity. There are Buddhists in Ladakh, as different from the Muslims of the Valley and the Hindus of Jammu. The nomad Gujjars, Bakarwals and the Muslims of Kargil as also Nubra valley are likewise vastly different from the valley people. The Nubraites are of a different Aryan Afghan Turkoman blood, distinct from the ethnic group in Srinagar Valley.

Now we come to a very anomalous position regarding electoral representation at the level of the State Assembly and the Parliament. The total area of Jammu and the remaining parts of Jammu and Kashmir excluding the Valley is 70%, larger than the Valley, which represents only 40% of the total State population. While one million people in the valley elect one Member for the Parliament, it is 1.4 million people from Jammu who have the same privilege. In other words per unit of population in Jammu sends less number of Members of Parliament than the valley. Similarly, out of a total of 76 seats for the State Assembly, 42 come from Valley while Jammu provides only 32 seats. This position is due to the fact that while in Jammu 90,000 people elect one M.L.A. to the State Assembly, in Kashmir only 73,000 people elect one—again a gross distortion of voting rights between Jammu and the Kashmir Valley. To accommodate the aspirations of the Valley people three new districts were created in 1979, on an ad-hoc basis, while three districts recommended by Wazir Commission (1981-83) for Jammu have not been created till date. With such a step-motherly treatment against Jammu and favouring the Valley, let us have a look at the distribution of Plan funds to the two parts. While Jammu with its two million tourists, mainly to the Vaishno Devi shrine contributes the lion's share to the State exchequer, only half a million tourists visit the valley contributing almost one-fourth of the share of Jammu's contribution to the State resources. As against this, huge funds amounting to 90% of the total allocation to the tourist sector, goes to the Valley alone. Huge expenses on project such as a cable car at Gulmarg and the Srinagar Golf Course have gobbled up Rs. 50 crores. But their poor cousin, the

Dogri Art Gallery in Jammu with its rich collection of antiques, paintings and museum pieces, gets nothing. The injustice does not end here. Jammu with a total area of 26,293 sq. kms. has only 3,500 kms. of roads while the Valley with an area of only 15853 sq. kms. has been gifted with 4900 kms. of road network. This leads to a situation in which Jammu has only 18% of its area covered by roads, while the Valley has 40% of its area so covered. The situation of Ladakh is even worse than Jammu. That is the treatment under the State control, and sheltered from the Centre's eye, thanks to Article 370 that has been bestowed selectively by the State Government! Privileges, pelf, resources and funds have flowed into the Valley out of all proportions to its size and population and against the stronger and better justified demands of Jammu and Ladakh. That is where Article 370, midwifed by Nehru and Sheikh Abdullah and nursed by Farooq Abdullah and his successors, under the approving eye of Nehru and his successors has taken the State today. Could there be a bigger mockery of justice, fair play and constitutional propriety? Nehru sired and midwifed Article 370 and nursed it advancing specious arguments for its retention inside and outside the Parliament, till the hand of fate removed him from the political scene, a sad and weary man. His successors perpetuated the blunder. The neo-secularists, blind to the integrity of the nation, have created a festering sore on the body politic of the nation. Even after the relatively free and fair elections in Jammu & Kashmir, the ground situation is far from normal. Before we close this chapter, let us remind ourselves in brief of the gravamen of minorityism leveled against that great apostle of Hindu-Muslim unity Mahatma Gandhi himself and then follow up with the blunders of his followers in Congress. Here it goes:

- Gandhiji's one-sided concept of non-violence and Hindu-Muslim unity was mainly aimed at Hindus, which made them effete while it encouraged Muslim aggressiveness.
- In his confused reading of non-violence he mistook righteous fight for violence, and glorified surrender before killers as non-violence, thereby emasculating Hindu spirit further.
- While he abhorred violence he had no moral compunctions in recruiting Indian soldiers for the British during the World War I.

- He refused to support the court case against Gen. Dyer, the author of the Jallianwala Bagh massacre.
- He even forbade the use of force for self-defence when he advised the Hindus to willingly die at the hands of the murderers.
- He even labeled the soldiers as murderers and those spinning yarn as the saviours of mankind.
- On 6th May, 1946, while addressing the Socialist Workers he said, "then we can pitch our camp of non-violence amidst the violence of the Muslim League and succeed in reaching an agreement with them." He thereby blunted Hindu reason by making him prefer death to resistance.
- When the revolutionaries succeeded in inspiring Indian troops stationed in India and Thailand to mutiny, the British Government panicked and sought Gandhiji's help, which he willingly offered.
- His obsession for Hindu-Muslim unity prompted Gandhiji to support a regressive Khilafat movement of which the end result was the Mopla mutiny of 1921 in Kerala. The Mopla Muslims converted and slaughtered thousands of Hindus, burning their homes, abducted and mass-raped their women, forcing the rest to jump into the wells to save their honour. Instead of condemning their barbarism and killing spree, Gandhji praised them as *"Khuda ke Bahadur Bande"* (Brave Soldiers of God).
- In an article in *Young India,* he exhorted Hindus to shout *'Allaho Akbar'* and sing Muslim songs and went to the extent of advising them to recite Arabic words. But he never told the Muslims to chant "Om".
- He echoed the sentiments of the fundamentalist Muslims of Khilafat movement inviting the Amir of Afghanistan to attack India.
- To appease orthodox Muslims he even declared national heroes like Maharana Pratap, Shivaji, Guru Gobind Singh as misguided patriots.
- He even advised Maharaja Hari Singh of Kashmir to uphold the majority Muslim interests of the Valley, abdicate and do penance at Kashi; but he did not advise the same to Nizam of Hyderabad and Nawab of Bhopal, both ruling Hindu majorities.

- He denounced the word 'Shuddhi' (Re-conversion) to Hinduism as anti-national and prejudicial to Hindu-Muslim unity.
- He even praised the Muslims for converting his own son, Hira Lal as Abdullah holding Islam to be as true a religion as Hinduism.
- He was even prepared to issue a blank cheque to the Muslims to negotiate on behalf of India during the Second Round Table Conference.
- It was Gandhiji, who honoured Jinnah with the title of Qaid-e Azam.
- He refused to lend support to the mass movement against the tyranny of Nizam of Hyderabad declaring his misrule as an internal matter of the State. Contrast this with his advice to Maharaja Hari Singh. He was even prepared to hand over to the Nizam the kingdom of India calling it 'Home Rule'. Veer Savarkar strongly opposed him saying that even the tyrannical rule of Alauddin and Aurangzeb was Home Rule though Hindus gave their lives to fight against it.
- While asking the British to quit India, he was prepared to keep the British Army in India.
- When Muslim League threatened violence to achieve an Islamic State, he requested them to rule the whole of India, since to him Islamic rule was still a Swadeshi rule!
- Completely under the spell of Maulana Azad, he gave him a carte blanche to negotiate India's freedom on behalf of not only the Congress but all Hindus. These were his words – "I heartily support the proposal given by Maulana Saheb to the British that India can be transferred to any community. If this right is given to the Muslims even then I will not have the least regret."
- Explaining his creed of truth and equality, Gandhiji said, "Being a Hindu I should know that if in each decisive province the seats earmarked for the majority go to the Muslims, I would suffer no loss. Under the Communal Award, Gandhiji upheld as fully justified, democratic and truly national the principle of one vote for five Hindus and five votes for each Muslim.
- He visited Jinnah's palatial residence at Mount Pleasant Road 19 times but Jinnah did not return the courtesy even once.

- In a duly authorized letter Gandhiji wrote to Jinnah, "Congress shall have no objection if the British Government transfers all its existing rights and the whole of India including the so-called "Bhartiya Bharti" to Muslim League.
- Within first three years of his declaring the demand for Pakistan sinful, he secretly, through Rajagopalachari proposed, to offer Pakistan to Jinnah. He even arrived at a secret understanding with Liaqat Ali Khan through Bhulabhai Desai in the first fortnight of 1945.
- He bulldozed his way for the acceptance of partition by the AICC against their reasoned judgement. He even went to the extent of suggesting the conversion of whole of India into Pakistan if that was in public interest.
- In a dictatorial edict Gandhiji announced that the Muslim majority areas can declare themselves as Pakistan but the remaining larger part of India should not call itself Hindustan since it means a Hindu land.
- He rejected the sensible suggestion of Jinnah :
  - (i) Not to support Khilafat Movement, and
  - (ii) Allow transfer of population as a sequel to the partition.

  If the latter proposal had been accepted there would have been no bloodbath and later no minority problem.
- The cabinet on the request of Sardar Patel agreed to renovate the Somanth Temple on State expense. Gandhiji got this decision overturned. But later on 13th January, 1948, he went on a fast unto death to force Patel and Nehru to renovate the Jama Masjid at Government expense. Gandhiji was not even a member of the Congress or a part of the Cabinet.
- The Hindu refugees returning from Pakistan seeking shelter in evacuated unclaimed mosques were thrown out on the streets to shiver and die in the cold under Gandhiji's direction.
- The case of releasing Rs. 55 crores due to Pakistan from the Consolidated Fund of India, led to strong differences and acrimony between Patel and Nehru. Gandhiji's insistence on its release to Pakistan, engaged in the Kashmir war against India, was the last straw, which led to his assassination by a Hindu fanatic.

- The other blunders of Gandhiji on minorityism are listed below:
  - (i) The seeds of partition sown in the Lahore Pact.
  - (ii) Principle of representation to Muslims on the basis of religion was granted and Muslim League recognized as the representative body for all Muslims.
  - (iii) Though opposing the two-nation theory in principle, in practice the Congress gave its approval.
  - (iv) The three leaders chosen to negotiate with the members of Cripps Mission, on behalf of India were three staunch Muslims—Jinnah of Muslim League for Indian Muslims, Nawab of Bhopal for princely states, majority of whom were Hindu states and Maulana Azad representative of all Hindus.

Now the Congress culpa:

- The Congress fought the decisive election of 1946 on a platform of United India but agreed to partition. Savarkar asked them to resign since they had shamefully betrayed the electorate. They should either have resigned or sought fresh mandate or held a plebiscite for partition.
- According to Leonard Mosle, the Congress was too exhausted to fight the obdurate Jinnah. Nehru even confessed that it was due to his old age, weakness, fatigue and disappointment that he had no further stomach for fight against partition.
- Was partition the only way to avert riots? Even after partition, there have been riots. The reason, refusal to accept population transfer.
- In the 1946 elections almost all of the 23% of Indian Muslims voted for Pakistan. But a hefty 30% of Indian territory was given to Pakistan out of proportion to their population. Congress had boycotted the 1931 and 1941 Census, which was rigged in favour of the Muslims by the British, bloating their numbers. But surprisingly, they accepted these figures as the basis of partition and even the non-Muslim majority parts were also given to Pakistan.
- Was it a mere coincidence that they accepted as chairman of the Boundary Commission, Cyril Radcliff, who was a junior associate of Jinnah during his practice in London? The debt was repaid when Lahore, Tharparkar district of Sindh, Chittagong hill tracts and Khulna district of Bengal were awarded to Pakistan.

- Thanks to the ineptitude of the Congress 44% population of Hindus of undivided Bengal got only 33% share in the new territory of West Bengal. 56% Muslim got the lion's share of 70% in East Pakistan. The Chittagong hill tracts, comprising 98% Buddhists, and the Hindu majority area of Khulna were awarded to Pakistan and Congress remained silent.
- While the voice of the Hindus of district Tharparkar being 94% of total population of Sindh province was suppressed on the plea that partition cannot be on the basis of districts, the voice of Muslims in the Sylhet district of Assam who had only 51% share of the population was heard and the district handed over to Pakistan.
- Under Israel's "Law of Return" every Jew has a right to return to Israel and obtain mandatory citizenship, but our secular Government does not grant this right to Hindus, traumatized after partition and suffering indignities in Bangladesh and Pakistan, seeking to return.
- During partition the Congress Government gave repeated assurances of preserving human rights to Hindus, left behind in Pakistan. But the dictatorial Nehru reneged on his words. After Nehru-Liaqat Pact of April 8, 1950, Bengali Hindu refugees attempting to escape torture from Muslim religious bigots were forcibly sent back to die at the hands of their Muslim tormenters.
- In April 1950 Nehru went to the extent of arresting Veer Savarkar, the great freedom fighter, under Protective Security Act to please Liaquat Ali Khan.
- If the Indian Government can move the UN for a separate homeland for one million Palestinians what prevents it from demanding the same for two million Hindus and Buddhists living in hell in Bangladesh?
- As per the 1958 Nehru-Noon Pact, 17 square miles of Angaopeta and Dahgram area which being an enclave in its territory was to be transferred to India, but the Congress Government in 1992 instead of raising this demand handed over Teen Bigha area to Bangladesh on a 999 years lease to be administered by that Government.
- On a demand from Muslim League the Communist Government of Kerala, restructured three districts of Trichur, Palghat and Calicat to form a Muslim majority district of Mallapuram.

Appendix A

Article 25

Freedom of conscience and free profession, practice and propagation of religion – (1) Subject to public order, morality and health and to the other provisions of the Part, all persons are equally entitled to freedom of conscience and the right freely to profess, practise and propagate religion.

(2) Nothing in this article shall affect the operation of any existing law or prevent the State from making any law-

(a) Regulating or restricting any economic, financial, political or other secular activity which may be associated with religious practice;

(b) Providing for social welfare and reform or the throwing open of Hindu religious institutions of a public character to all classes and sections of Hindus.

Explanation 1 – The wearing and carrying of kirpans shall be deemed to be included in the profession of the Sikh religion.

Explanation II – In sub-Clause (b) of Clause (2), the reference to Hindu shall be construed as including a reference to persons professing the Sikh, Jain or Buddhist religion, and the reference to Hindu religious institutions shall be construed accordingly.

Article 26

Freedom to manage religious affairs – Subject to public order, morality and health, every religious denomination or any section thereof shall have the right-

7(a) to establish and maintain institutions for religious and charitable purposes;

(b) to manage its own affairs in matters of religion;

(c) to own and acquire movable and immovable property; and

(d) to administer such property in accordance with law.

Article 27

Freedom as to payment of taxes for promotion of any particular religion—No person shall be compelled to pay any taxes, the proceeds

of which are specifically appropriated in payment of expenses for the promotion or maintenance of any particular religion or religious denomination.

Article 28

Freedom as to attendance at religious instruction or religious worship in certain educational institutions –(I) No religious instruction shall be provided in any educational institution wholly maintained out of State funds.

(2) Nothing in Clause (1) shall apply to an educational institution which is administered by the State but has been established under any endowment or trust which require that religious instruction shall be imparted in such institution.

(3) No person attending any educational institution recognized by the State or receiving aid out of State funds shall be required to take part in any religious instruction that may be imparted in such institution or to attend any religious worship that may be conducted in such institution or in any premises attached thereto unless such person or, if such person is a minor, his guardian has given his consent thereto.

Article 29

Protection of interests of minorities-(1) Any section of the citizens residing in the territory of India or any part thereof having a distinct language, script or culture of its own shall have the right to conserve the same.

(2) No citizen shall be denied admission into any educational institution maintained by the State or receiving aid out of State funds on grounds only of religion, race, caste, language or any of them.

Article 30

Right of minorities to establish and administer educational institutions –

(1) All minorities, whether based on religion or language, shall have the right to establish and administer educational institutions of their choice.

(2) In making any law providing for the compulsory acquisition of any property of an educational institution established and administered by a minority, referred to in Clause (1), the State shall ensure that the amount fixed by or determined under such law for the acquisition of such property is such as would not restrict or abrogate the right guaranteed under that clause.

(3) The State shall not, in granting aid to educational institutions, discriminate against any educational institution on the ground that it is under the management of a minority, whether based on religion or language.

6

Religious Conversions

In its tortuous history of the last millennium, India has suffered from a severe ulcer in its body politic, not only through physical subjugation by foreign invaders and conquerors, but also through never ending assaults on its cultural values and religion through an unending saga of conversions by the two inveterate proselytising religions of the world—Islam and Christianity. The process is still on in a more subtle and insidious manner, thanks to the callousness and cynicism of our secular elite. As pointed out earlier, the missionaries' assault on the Hindu pagan doomed to destruction was their noble way of putting him on the path to salvation through Jesus Christ. The Islamic conversions have also been covered and we will deal with them here only briefly. However, the religious conversion by the missionaries needs to be discussed in some detail. First, Jesus, during his preaching had exhorted his pupils to go out and spread his gospel. Islam later followed the tenets of Quran and the actions of their prophet, whose life was spent in conquering new lands and countries. Their conversions involved violence and thereby outdid the followers of Jesus Christ. However in India, Islam came first leading to conversions, but Christianity, which had set the precedent was not too far behind and its aim was to spread the gospel in a far more subtle and insidious manner. Though Christianity predated Islam, in India it was Islam which came first with its sword of conquest and conversion.

The conversion to Islam is continuing even today. Let us look at the facts. As per the census reports the Hindu population in India between 1951 to 1991 has decreased from a percentage of 84.98 to 82.41 i.e. a decrease of 2.57 percent. Assuming that this fall continued for the next decade i.e. 1991 to 2001, the percentage in 2001 comes to 82.41 – 2.57% of 82.41 i.e. 81.71 or a loss of 3.27 percent. Thus, the total decrease of the Hindu population for a billion people would amount to three crore and twenty-seven lakh. During the same period Muslim population rose from a percentage of 9.91 to 11.67; adding further increase in the next decade this would amount to more than 2 percent, i.e. about 2,00,25,000. This increase would be due to a differential growth rate of the Muslims mainly due to conversions. Between 1981 and 1991, the decadal growth rate of the Hindus had been 2.78 percent against 32.76 percent of the Muslims. The conclusion is obvious. In 1991, the Hindus were in a minority in seven out of thirty two states and union territories of India. These include Jammu and Kashmir, Punjab, Arunachal Pradesh, Nagaland, Mizoram, Meghalaya, and Lakshdweep. In Mizoram and Lakshdweep the Hindus form less than 10 percent of the population. In the rest of India out of 356 districts, in 38 districts Muslims form more than 50 percent of the population and in 9 districts Christian population is more than 50%. In 1990, the entire Hindu population of 2.5 lakh was driven away from the Kashmir valley by the depredations of the terrorists and local insurgents. Nagaland, Meghalaya and Mizoram are Christian majority states, whereas, in Manipur, Kerala, Andaman and Nicobar islands, Goa, Daman and Diu, they comprise more than 20 percent of the population. Looking now at the after-effects of the partition, the Hindu population from a 40 percent of the total population of undivided Bengal fell to 7 percent after the partition. In Pakistan the population of Hindus, which formed 25 percent of the total before the partition came down to one percent after the partition. In Kerala alone the number of Hindus from a percentage of 66.63 in 1911 came down to 57.28 percent in 1991. For the same period the population of the Christians rose from 15.41 percent to 19.32, while the number of Muslims rose from 12.68 percent to 23.33 percent. The conclusions are obvious. That there has been a consistent increase in the Muslim population in India at the cost of the Hindus and a marked increase of the Christians in the seven states of the Union, and in a large number of districts in India, the Muslims outnumber the Hindus. It is evident that there has been a mass exodus of the Hindus from our two neighbouring Islamic states and also a sharp reduction in the population percentage in their own country. That the accretion to the Muslim and Christian population is not merely due to a natural demographic increase due to birth rate but largely on account of conversion of Hindus into these faiths.

India in its long and tortuous history from 700 AD onwards was perpetually under attack. Movements of races took place with migrations from North West and North East, notwithstanding the impenetrable Himalayas. The influx from North East was gradual and peaceful and the migrants, mainly the Shan and Trans Burman tribes, quietly settled down in their new found home, assimilated themselves in the local culture and ethnicity and produced a heady mix of local colour and foreign flavour resulting in an explosion of cultural outpouring. But the North West had a different story of convulsive clashes. A series of invaders, Greeks, Scythians, Sakas and Huns came to conquer but were conquered in turn by the rich Indian culture. The Mongols barely brushed our North Western borders and left a transient impact. Being pagans themselves, they had no religion of their own and were easily absorbed in the all pervading Hindu religious order and culture. Then came Islam with its horrendous consequences. The rest is history. Unlike the others who crossed the Hindukush, through the Khyber Pass, Islam came to conquer and convert. We have discussed at some length the nature of Muslim conquest of India and the furious proselytizing zeal of the conquerors. Being a revealed religion Islam claimed an exclusiveness and finality that left no room for co-existence with the non-believers. The Kafir had only two choices to make—convert or be killed. But the task was simply daunting. There were limitations to the power of the sword. It could cut only limited swathes in a sea of Hindu humanity that was India, but it could not fell them all. The power of their faith was too strong. The much-maligned Brahmins kept the faith and the Hindu folk together by infusing new vigour through the Bhakti movement. Having failed to convert by force the Muslim rulers used a more acceptable opiate, a mix of Hindu mysticism and the moderate teachings of Islam "Sufism". This soft and persuasive approach was more successful, the central idea remaining the same, enlarging the Muslim brotherhood. Having taken all this as read, we shall deal here with the more insidious type of conversion by the other revealed religion, Christianity, through their missionaries.

As pointed out earlier the shift from Islamic proselytisation to that of Christianity gave no relief to the Hindu stock, as one form of conversion was to replace another, a more effective and all-pervasive. Enough literature exists on the subject and we shall confine overselves to some lesser-known aspects of these crusades against Hinduism.

The fundamental driving force for evangelisation lies in the self-imposed responsibility of all Christians as stated by Charles Trevelyan, a member of the Governor General's Counsel., "...as the Christian religion is the only one capable of correcting the disorders caused by the passions of mankind, and of gradually leading on the world to a state of perfection, it must be of divine origin, and we are bound to promote its universal diffusion in obedience to its founder, Jesus Christ...." To this assertion of faith Fredric Maxmüller adds his might, "As to our own religion, its very soul is missionary, progressive, world-embracing: it would cease to exist if it disregarded the parting words of its founder: 'Go ye therefore and teach all nations...' The missionary spirit is what has marked Christianity from the time when as yet it counted no more than twelve apostles, and which lays on every one that calls himself a Christian the duty of avowing his convictions, whatever they may be, and gaining others to embrace the truth. In that sense every true Christian is a missionary. And added to this religious obligation of all Christians there was the God-sent opportunity of using all the might and resources of the British empire ruling colonies so vast that 'the sun never set on the British empire'." Monier Williams, another luminary proclaimed, "for what purpose then has this enormous territory been committed to England? Not to be the 'corpus vile' of political, social, or military experiments; not for the benefit of our commerce, or the increase of our wealth – but that every man, woman and child, from Cape Comorin to the Himalayan mountains, may be elevated, enlightened, Christened." T.B. Macaulay declared, "Every young Brahmin.... who learns geography in our colleges, learns to smile at the Hindu mythology...".

To these divinely anointed sons of Christianity who had drunk deep at the font of theosophical knowledge, Hinduism was an abomination, a religion of pagans of weird practices, almost Baalic in nature and doomed to damnation. Again Trevelyan: "The Grammar and spelling book suffice to destroy the Hindu religion..." "It is so destitute of any thing like evidence, and is identified with so many gross immoralities and absurdities, that it gives way at once before the light of European science..." "....It is sufficient to prove that the world does not rest on the back of a tortoise, or is not composed of concentric circles of wine and cake and milk, and so forth, and their religion is gone...". But the damnation will not be allowed to continue and the great missionaries, who, like Lilliputian knights in armour had given unto themselves the onerous task of reforming and remoulding the oldest religion known to mankind believed in 'never say die'. The family of Macaulay, Maxmüller and missionaries tilting at the windmills of the great Vedic culture had reason to be satisfied with their efforts. Trevelyan remarked: "A generation is growing up which repudiates idols. A young Hindu, who had received a liberal English education, was forced by his family to attend the shrine of Kali, upon which he took off his cap to 'Madam Kali', made her a low bow, and hoped her ladyship was well...". Richard Temple observed, "Hinduism is gradually breaking up, like the clouds before the rising sun.... Hinduism is still the religion of the millions, but only of the uneducated millions. It is no longer the religion of the educated Hindu. It is no longer the religion of those who have either theoretical enlightenment or practical knowledge. It is being gradually dissipated, like the mist, before the science of the nineteenth century - that science which is being freely distributed amongst the people through the agency of Government..." And finally, Maxmüller, the Sanskrit scholar commissioned to revile and vilify Hinduism as pointed out earlier, wallows in self-congratulation for the rewards of his strenuous efforts and glories in his hour of triumph. "But the ancient religion is doomed, and if Christianity does not step in, whose fault will it be?" "That religion (Hinduism) is still professed by at least 110,000,000 of human souls... and yet I do not shrink from saying that their religion is dying of decay.... The worship of Siva, of Vishnu, and the other popular deities... belongs to a stratum of thought which is long buried beneath our feet: it may live on, like the lion and the tiger, but the mere air of free thought and civilised life will extinguish it... ask any Hindu who can read and write and think, whether these are the gods he believes in and he will smile at your credulity...". So did Charles Trevelyan, who was satisfied at India's march to the baptismal font "...Multitudes, quite outside the missionary communities, have accepted Christianity in principle... No doubt you have heard of Ram Mohun Roy, Devendranath Thakur, and Keshab Chandar Sen, the leaders of a vast secession from Hinduism, which has already advanced more than halfway to Christianity...." "...many of them (the Brahmo Samaj leaders) are almost persuaded to be Christians. Some of their ministers actually preach sermons from texts taken from the Bible, and they have declared that the British government may be the secular ruler of England, but the supreme ruler is no less than Christ the Lord..." And then the cruelest cut from T.B. Macaulay, of whom we have spoken earlier, the abetter of Aryan invasion theory, turned the Brahmins into Maxmüller robots to use them to destroy Hinduism.

Charles Grant (1746-1823), Chairman of East India Company, reviled Hindus in no less humiliating terms. "We cannot avoid recognising in the people of Hindustan a race of men lamentably degenerate and base, governed by malevolent and licentious passions, and sunk in misery by their vices." Claudious Bucchanan, the company's chaplain, went even further to say, "Neither truth, nor honesty, honour, gratitude, nor charity, is to be found in the breast of a Hindoo!" And Lord Hastings, Governor General of India, noted in his diary on October 2, 1813: "The Hindoo appears as being nearly limited to mere animal functions, with no higher intellect than a dog or an elephant, or a monkey..." Till as late as 1858, the South Indian Missionary Conference laid down the agenda of education in India : "The object of all missionary labour should not be primarily the civilisation, BUT the evangelisation of the heathen....schools may be regarded as converting agencies and their value estimated by the number who are led to renounce idolatry and make an open profession of Christianity..." Maxmüller had great expectations from the reforming zeal of this trio of Raja Ram Mohun Roy, Keshab Chandra Sen and Devendranath Thakur. He fondly hoped that Brahmanism, the final enemy of Christianity, the sole custodian and cementing force that had kept Sanatan Dharma going for eight millennia and held the Hindu folk together, is like a ripe fruit about to fall, and the efforts of Brahmo Samaj will be crowned with success. But to his horror Swami Vivekanand was shaking the conscience of the western nations at the International Parliament of Religions in Chicago and splashing a refulgent Hinduism across the sky in its colourful splendour. He had denounced the missionaries in such blistering words:

"If we Hindus dig out all the dirt from the bottom of the Pacific Ocean and throw it in your faces, it will be but a speck compared to what the missionaries have done to our religion and culture." Later sobering down a little, Swami Vivekanand told the missionaries that a starving people needed no sermons from them.

"Christians must always be ready for good criticism, and I hardly think that you will mind if I make a little criticism. You Christians, who are so fond of sending your missionaries to save the soul of the heathens – why do you not try to save their bodies from starvation? In India during the terrible famines, thousands died from hunger, yet you Christians did nothing. You erect churches all through India, but the crying evil in the East is not religion—they have religion enough—but it is bread that the suffering millions of burning India cry out for with parched throats. They ask us for bread but we give them stones. It is an insult to a starving people to offer them religion; it is an insult to a starving man to teach him metaphysics. In India a priest that preached for money would lose caste and be spat upon by the people. I came here to seek aid for my impoverished people, and I fully realised how difficult it was to get help for heathens from Christians in the Christian land".

"But they should understand that ours is a different mission." " We do not go there to afford them simple medical relief or a knowledge of the three R's; our going to them is a small proof of our repentance and our assurance to them that we will not exploit them any more. I should never think of opening a hospital where there is already one; but if there is a Mission school, I should not mind opening another for Harijan children, and I would even encourage them to prefer our school to the other. Let us frankly understand the position. If the object is purely humanitarian, purely that of carrying education where there is none, they (the missionaries) should be thankful that someone whose obvious duty is to put his own house in order wakes up to a sense of his duty. But my trouble is that the Missionary friends do not bring to bear on their work a purely humanitarian spirit. Their object is to add more members to their fold, and that is why they are disturbed. The complaint which I have been making all these years is more than justified by what you say".

A fire fighting operation had to be mounted to undo the damage done to the efforts of Christian missionaries, and who could be the best person to vilify the great saint? None else than the new admirer of Christianity. So Keshab Chandra Sen was sent to rebut and denounce his own countrymen. The evangelisation of India was to reinforce the monumental effort mounted for the colonisation of India, and the consolidation of the British Rule, by the enslavement of the minds of their subjects to the British values, culture and institutions and making them willing partners in the task of their own cultural retraction and a denial of their glorious past. That they succeeded beyond their wildest imagination is there for everyone to see.

Unfortunately, the frontal assault of conversion did not yield the success as was planned for in the 19th century. This called for a new strategy. First, there was a need to develop a new architecture of education by dismantling the old one. Whatever was left after the Muslim depredation and destruction of schools, places of worship, irrigation facilities and industry was to be swept off to be filled by the British system and values, all in the name of elevating their subjects from ignorance to enlightenment and second, thereby to destroy the sense of national unity and respect of their own culture, value and tradition. The starting point in this process was to be education, and the introduction of English as lingua franca for the country. During the earlier rule of the British East India Company over the territories, conquered by them, the missionaries were not allowed to operate. But the missionaries and the Church zealots had made the strong case for themselves by painting India and its culture black. Some sane elements in the administration opposed this view and one of them even stated, "indeed, when I turn my eyes either to the present condition or ancient grandeur of the country; when I contemplate the magnificence of her structure, her spacious reservoirs, constructed at an immense expense, pouring fertility and plenty over the land, the monuments of a benevolence expanding its cares over remote ages; when I survey the solid embellished architecture of her temples, the elaborate and exquisite skill of her manufactures and fabrics, her literature sacred and profane, her gaudy and enamelled pottery on which a vile and prodigal fancy has lavished all its opulence; when I turn to the philosophers, lawyers and moralists who have left the oracles of political and ethical wisdom to restrain the passions and to awe the vices which disturb the commonwealth; when I look at the peaceful and harmonious alliances of families, guarded and secured by the household virtues; when I see amongst a cheerful and well-ordered society, the benignant and softening influence of religion and morality, a system of manners founded on a mild and polished obeissance, and preserving, hear without surprise, mingled with horror, of sending out Baptists and Anabaptists to civilize or convert such a people at the hazard of disturbing or deforming institutions which appear to have hitherto been the means ordained by Providence of making them virtuous and happy."

Despite this the missionaries won and began to establish schools of their own to re-educate India, 'The Dark Sub-continent'. The British rulers having in the first place destroyed India's economy to subserve their colonial commercial interests, the third arm of this triad, the missionaries stepped in to redeem India. Pandit Sunderlal in his famous book *Bharat Mein Angrezee Raj* written in 1920 reminds us that Keir Harde, a British Parliamentarian of repute, in his book *India* quotes: "MaxMüller, on the strength of official documents and a missionary report concerning education in Bengal prior to the British occupation, asserts that there were then 80,000 native schools in Bengal, or one for every 400 of the population. Ludlow, in his *History of British India* says that in every Hindoo village which has retained its old form I am assured that the children generally are able to read, write, and cipher, but where we have swept away the village system as in Bengal there the village school has also disappeared."

Horace Hayman, a professor at Oxford, the Oriental visitor to Haileyburg and a member secretary of the Committee of Public Instructions, opposed this policy of the Macaulay-Trevelyan-Bentink trinity and insisted for the continuation of Sanskrit as the medium of instruction, which he said was the most suitable language, with a vast countrywide base, and maximum commonality of vocabulary with the native languages. He was overruled; although his ultimate objective was no different from that of the trinity, i.e. alienating Indians from their past culture and implant British values in their place. His only difference was that the use of Sanskrit would be more practical than the imposition of English, an altogether new language that few could speak or understand. He was questioned, " The substance of your evidence is that you think more attention should be paid to obtaining a class of well educated schoolmasters, and that Sanskrit for the purpose should be made the basis of their instructions?" To this Wilson replied in the affirmative and elaborated further, "We want to have at our command a well educated class of natives from among those who are considered by their countrymen as learned; it is not that I want to make schoolmasters the Pandits of the colleges, but if we send into the country a number of men possessing the greatest influence among their countrymen, even men possessing the knowledge without being bound to teach it, we raise ourselves in the estimation of the people. We shall have a useful class of the people at our command,

and the influence they may exercise will be beneficial to the people in proportion to their proficiency in those acquirements which we can encourage them to obtain."

The object was the same enslavement of the Indian, read 'Hindu' mind that would help religious conversions. To those who today deride Sanskrit, the life breath of Hinduism, as a dead language it is pertinent to note what this Englishman had to say during his interrogation by the Committee about Sanskrit, "A man will easily become a good vernacular scholar if he is a good Sanskrit scholar, or a good Arabic scholar." And further, "the system of learning Bengali among the natives has not been the study of the Bengali grammar; they never had Bengali grammars till we gave it to them; their notion of learning Bengali was by learning Sanskrit. If you make a man a good Sanskrit scholar he will be able to write Bengali with perfect accuracy and elegance." When asked about the extent of commonality of Sanskrit words in other Indian languages, he replied, "It is well known, that Bengali is the language most akin to Sanskrit. I have taken pains to ascertain the proportion of Sanskrit in the first 500 words of '*Shakespeare's Hindustanee Dictionary,*' and they amount to 305. In the Bengali *Hitopadesh*, which is a class-book, in which the students are examined in the college, out of the first 147 words, there are only five, which are not Sanskrit; so that a young man knowing Sanskrit would find in that book, which is the first book given to him when he arrives in India, that he already knows 142 words out of 147." Someone asked, "I have supposed the relation between Sanskrit and Hindustanee and the vernacular languages to be something like the relation which subsists between Greek and English, is that the case?" The answer was that Sanskrit forms the very basis of most dialects spoken in North India, and Wilson further confirmed, "Though it is not so essentially a part of the languages of Southern India, yet it enters so largely into the composition of even the language of Malabar, that four-fifths of the words are Sanskrit."

And so it came to pass that Sanskrit was declared a dead language, its users were denounced as exploiters and rapacious, the Hindu practices covering the entire sub-continent of Bharat damned as superstitious; that India had never been a united entity and that there never was anything like an Indian nation or a Hindu India. I do not have many regrets in life. But the one and only one lifelong regret and remorse that I nurse is my ignorance of Sanskrit. I say nursed not out of a desire to turn against myself in a spirit of self-destruction but to sedulously keep alive the embers of the fire of a paradise lost; to exhort myself to greater efforts in order to rejuvenate my cultural pride and the sense of Hinduism. Sanskrit, a pearl of great price, is the umbilical cord that ties Hinduism with its precious Vedic heritage. English translations of the sacred Vedic texts are totally inadequate to convey the sublimity, sweep, and substance of our scriptures and the summit of our spiritual achievements. In Israel Jews converging from all corners of the world, speaking different dialects and languages decided to adopt Hebrew, the language of their sacred religious texts, the Bible the *'Torah'*, the *'Talmud'* and the *'Mishna'* as their national language. Today every Jew speaks Hebrew. This is not to suggest that they do not know and study other languages. Most Jews speak Arabic, English, Spanish, German, French and Russian with as much ease as Hebrew, besides speaking different dialects of their Diaspora, the Ladino and the Yiddish. Even in a family the husband and wife when quarrelling and shouting at each other relapse into Yidish, Ladino or the language of their exile. But to a man every Jew speaks Hebrew as a mark of national pride and Yahweh's gift to the seed of Abraham. How many Hindus can claim such devotion to their motherland and the language of their ancestors of a distant past. It is a crying shame that we Hindus despise our own "*Deva Bhasha*" the celestial language, and run after English the language of our oppressors. If this is not religious conversion of another kind what is? During my last visit to America I was agreeably surprised to listen to my granddaughter, a US born citizen, recite Sanskrit verses with the same ease, exactitude, pronunciation and accent as she did her colloquial Yankee tongue. She knows more about *Panchtantra* than many students of Public Schools in Delhi. The moral is clear: learn, as many foreign languages as you wish and broaden your knowledge and vision, but do not despise your mother tongue and language. The same is true of Hindi our national language. Is it not the same language that our present day elite and Leftist ventriloquists scoff at while deriding Sanskrit.

Some time ago Father Vermeil of Jeshpur Roman Catholic mission informed his superiors that some members of the Servants of India Society, allegedly sent by the then Prime Minister, came to nearly destroy their newly established mission of the Norbertine Father at

Mandla in district Jabalpur. And he reassured them that "they dare not do so since we are prepared well in advance and we are doing all we can, including protest meetings to defeat their nefarious designs. Their aim is to prevent us from carrying out conversions and caring for the weaker sections of society. They have even established state schools, 40 of them for Adivasis and one in a village where we had a school running for the last 30 years. We are ready and we shall prevent them from withdrawing the children from our schools." If their aim and purpose is only philanthropy and uplift of the poor and uneducated why should they object to Hindu organisations, which have government approval, from carrying out the same good work. The conclusion is obvious. All this philanthropy is a cover for religious conversions. Over the decades, the Church in India and their reaction to the Hindu attempts to ameliorate the conditions of the backwards and the tribals is as sharp and strident as it was before. They even suspected Gandhiji's intentions on the removal of untouchability, which they claim was stealing away the popularity of the missionaries and causing disturbance to their activities. To this Gandhiji replied : "I see what you mean," and " But I do not know why it should disturb them. We are not traders treading on one another's province. If it is a matter of serving oneself, I should understand their attitude, but when it is entirely a matter of serving others, it should not worry them or me as to who serves them." The spokesman for the missionaries retorted, "But perhaps, the authorities in charge of a Mission hospital would rightly feel worried if you sent your people to go and open a hospital in the same place". Gandhiji's reply was simple and typical of the man and his acute prescience: "But they should understand that ours is a different mission. We do not go there to afford them simple medical relief or a knowledge of the three R's; our going to them is a small proof of our repentance and our assurance to them that we will not exploit them any more. I should never think of opening a hospital where there is already one; but if there is a Mission school, I should not mind opening another for Harijan children, and I would even encourage them to prefer our school to the other. Let us frankly understand the position. If the object is purely humanitarian, purely that of carrying education where there is none, they (the missionaries) should be thankful that someone whose obvious duty it is to put his own house in order wakes up to a sense of his duty. But my trouble is that the missionary friends do not bring to bear on their work a purely humanitarian spirit. Their object is to add more members to their fold, and that is why they are disturbed. The complaint which I have been making all these years is more than justified by what you say...."

While on the one hand the Church talks of an egalitarian Christian society they still cry for reservation of their so-called 'lower order'. Failure to prevent the government organisations from carrying forward their efforts to empower and educate the deprived makes them more schizophrenic. Obstructed from their self-proclaimed turf, they discredit such efforts and even those of non-government organisations (NGOs) in their conversion activities. Defeated on this front the missionaries then turned their attention to carve out Christian majority states in the North East, thereby further endangering the cultural and political unity of India. In the North Eastern States this is a real cause for concern as it puts extra pressure on the already heavily burdened and overstretched security forces to prevent secessionist forces, abetted by the missionaries, from fulfilling their agenda.

The fact that the church has been able to carry out its systematic campaign of conversion behind a facade of philanthropy, inspite of public opposition and government restrictions, is due to a huge inflow of unaccounted foreign funds. Like the Islamic groups in India, the trans-nationality of the church makes this inflow easy but difficult to detect. Another reason is the double standards of our secularists and the timorousness of the local administration which prefers to look the other way as the mass of converts move out of the Hindu fold, and put the entire blame for this relentless exodus on the Hindu caste system. In the North East the administration is too supine to stop this trend that threatens the security and sovereignty of India. It is a known fact that in Nagaland and Manipur the insurgents regularly collect taxes and ransom money from the public and the government servants alike to run a parallel government. They even declare the total revenue and the expenses from their budget on various items such as arm purchase, guerrilla training and the establishment of new centres of subversion. The Arunachal Pradesh Freedom of Religion Act 1978 prohibiting conversion by force, inducement or fraudulent means is a mere scrap of paper, as the missionaries simply mock at this legal provision and have, in fact, mounted a counter campaign for its removal, to allow them a free play to dismember the country. Similar laws are in existence in the states of Madhya Pradesh and Orissa, but have been totally ineffective in preventing mass conversions of the Hindus to Christianity and Islam. The ordinance issued by Ms. J. Jayalalithaa, the Chief Minister of Tamilnadu, to the same effect caused such convulsions amongst our secularist brigade that they have turned ballistic and have started hurling missiles at the lady of Poes Garden and her sympathisers amongst the Hindu masses. A debate is still raging on this issue, with battlelines sharply drawn for and against this ordinance. Long back Gandhiji had rejected the theory that no salvation is possible outside the Church and after a long and protracted debate and state intervention, Vatican at last accepted this possibility. Inspite of considerable Indianisation of the Church the ultimate aim of salvation through conversion still remains its leit motif. At last the Catholic Bishop Conference of India (CBCI) condescended to state that "Those also can attain everlasting salvation who through no fault of their own, do not know the Gospel of Christ and his Church, yet sincerely seek God, and moved by grace, strive by their deeds to do his will as it is known to them through the dictates of their conscience."

Realising the futility of a head-on collision with the forces of Hindutva, the CBCI has cleverly deflected criticism though a process of Indianisation of the Church as mentioned above. This is in sharp contrast to the separatist approach of Islamic movement beginning from the Tabligh movement, Shah Waliullah and Maulana Maudoodi to the present day fundamentalists who attempt to segregate the Muslims by purging Islam of all syncretic practices with insistence on adherence to a separatist agenda. With the process of Indianisation, the Church intends to become, more relevant to India's current needs, inspite of facing many dilemmas and unsettling facts. Nevertheless, the efforts at evangelisation in a more acceptable form like the Sufi movement in Islam is on and the church is constantly looking for issues of concern, such as environment, women lib, etc. In sum, the Church instead of deviating from its direction of evangelisation, has kept its steering wheel steady and on course while merely changing gears to adopt a new face of acceptability by shifting the emphasis from calumny to empathy for the would be converts, renouncing its exclusive claims on salvation, truth and ecumenism, and finally moving away from uniformity to contextualisation. But the libel at the foundations of

Hinduism continues and that still remains their fundamental aim and 'raison d'etre'. Many of our intelligentsia repeat the arguments articulated lately by Bishop Partric D'Souza of Varanasi: "I have a comment, more than a question." "I know that Gandhiji said those things about the motives behind missionary services like education, medical services, etc. But schools and hospitals set up by Christian missionaries are everywhere. If there were any truth in this view, all of India would by now have become Christian. This has not happened. Is not the accusation itself motivated?"

The answer is very simple. Most of the people who take advantage of these services come from reasonably well-placed families and can make a conscious choice. They cannot be easily inveigled into Christianity by threat, inducement or fraud. If the number of Christians has not increased in proportion to the services rendered, it is more because of the strength and staying power of Hinduism than for any lack of trying on behalf of the Church and its functionaries. In any case according to the Church's own proclamation that salvation is possible in each religion, where then is the need for religious conversions. Once a missionary told Gandhiji that since his mission as ordained by Jesus is to spread the gospel, he has no recourse but to preach and what was the effectiveness of preaching? Gandhiji's reply is something that all our pseudo-secularists and Hindus must pay heed to. He said "To live the gospel is the most effective way. Most effective in the beginning, in the middle and in the end. Preaching jars on me and makes no appeal to me. And I get suspicious of missionaries who preach. But I love those who never preach but live the life according to their lights. Their lives are silent yet most effective testimonies. Therefore, I cannot say what to preach, but I can say that a life of service and uttermost simplicity is the best preaching. If, therefore, you go on serving people and ask them also to serve, they would understand. But you quote instead John 3, 16 and ask them to believe it. That has no appeal to me, and I am sure people will not understand it. Where there has been acceptance of the gospel through preaching, my complaint is that there has been some motive."

With the growth of prosperity in the west after the Second World War, the huge funds available were injected worldwide for carrying out evangelisation for the perpetuation of colonialism by other means.

Conversion is not only another form of denouncing the validity of other religions of would be converts, but also a denial of its co-existence; the establishment of superiority of one above the other and to offer a choice to select the best. That is wrong. In a true secular society, the secular religious continuum is a reality with no dividing cracks. The movement out from Hindu Dharma to a monotheistic religion causes a loss of common culture and a shared past of millennia. Recently, there have been bizarre cases of the clergy of one religion teaching in a secular educational institution, attempting to denigrate other religions. To replace qualified teachers with the clergy is entirely unconscionable, especially when the institutions receive government aid. The vast network of madarsas flush with foreign funds, mainly from Saudi Arabia and other Middle Eastern Muslim countries, are nothing but breeding grounds of proselytization. In South India even Government employees of a particular religious persuasion are openly indulging in conversion activities. And what about the faith of those converted? Far from having a sense of exultation, they feel the loss of sympathy from their erstwhile co-religionists and with the incision of the umbilical cord tying them to their cultural ethnicity, find themselves trapped in a cultural *'cul de sac'*.

A news item appeared recently in one of the English dailies that Father Marian Zelazak, God bless his soul, who had been working with a devout fervour treating lepers in Orissa and ministering to their souls to achieve salvation through Christ, is being considered for the award of a Nobel Prize for peace. A similar Nobel Prize was earlier awarded to Mother Teresa of Calcutta slums fame, who, in addition to caring for and treating the neglected poor and the dying on the streets of Calcutta, assured them of a glorious hereafter in the company of saints in the kingdom of God by converting them to Christianity. While efforts for her deification by the Vatican are still on, and her anointment to sainthood a foregone conclusion, some uneasy questions refuse to die. Of those treated and offered salvation, almost all were converted to Christianity. Her gigantic efforts spreading over the entire world, the Missionaries of Charity, a Christian organisation, received enormous funds from all over the world. In fact the funds outpace the expense programme and were kept a cleverly guarded secret. While the living quarters, kitchens, dispensaries and hospitals of this organisation bore an humble look and an inexpensive visage, the whereabouts of billions of dollars donated by the world remain a mystery. Although it is not the intention here to carry out an audit of all the funds received, it can safely be stated that the Missionaries of Charity were more than amply rewarded in material terms for their labours to convert the sick and the dying, the neglected children and the poor of India. So much for charity. Indeed Mother Teresa in the true Christian spirit of charity helped the poorest of the poor, whom their own rich Hindu brothers had abandoned and left to die. With few exceptions like the members of Ramakrishna and Vivekanand missions, the Art of Living and the RSS, few Hindu organisations participated in this noble effort. The field was thus left free for Christian missionaries to move in and sure enough they did. But with all her benevolence and spirit of service, Mother Teresa did not forget two things. First, projecting a negative image of India to the outside world and second, reaping the rich harvest of faith from those who had no choice to decide, most of them too poor to think of religion and to the others nearing death, it made very little difference whether they died as Hindus or Christians. In her entire life as a citizen of India and an Indian in spirit, she never once defended her own country; worse she made it an object of pity to the world that was shown only one side of the picture, the suffering, sick and the dying. Is that all that India is about? With all her piety and Christian values, did she ever care to understand the deep spirituality of our country, the glory of our past culture and the abiding faith of our people in our ethnic values? Or did she think that we are still a nation of heathen people needing redemption through adoption of Christianity?

In some late developments in the Vatican, Mother Teresa has been put on the fast track towards canonization in view of some miracles to her credit, such as curing a woman, Monica Basera labelled an animist by the Missionaries of Charity, of cancer on the streets of Calcutta, notwithstanding the fact that many doctors who treated her have challenged this claim. Many believe Mother Teresa's imminent anointment to sainthood is yet another mission of the Church towards aggrandizement. The work of the Missionaries of Charity was now mired in controversy on account of the criticism of Vatican's criteria for conferring sainthood and a simultaneous Nobel Prize Award already bestowed upon her. The evangelical zeal of the Church to substitute alien systems of belief and worship with its own icons is now being questioned.

Another view expressed is that inspite of its liberal pretensions, the Missionaries of Charity are engaged in aggressive evangelization against autochthonous traditions in countries like India. It also seems strange that all the Nobel Prize aspirants including the obscure Father Zelazek, who is deeply involved in conversion activities are Christian missionaries. Much against local resistance in Orissa and riding roughshod over native sentiments, they are not working in their own society. Mother Teresa did the same. Walter Wullenweber, a Calcutta born, raised some questions on the so-called charitable actions. He claims that Mother Teresa was created by Malcolm Muggeridge in 1969 and thereafter promoted and magnified larger than life by the world's rich and mighty and was a monumental fraud on the gullible in India.

In a debate published in an English daily some time ago, two reverend officials of the Indian Church gave out their divergent views on the controversial canonisation of Mother Teresa. K.T. Francis, President of Poor Christian Liberation Movement, was unhappy at the indecent haste shown by Pope Paul in his fast track canonisation of the Mother, thus, depriving her of her very Indianness and her noble work among the Indian poor and sick. He bemoaned that in so doing she will become another totem for the Roman Catholic Church, bring material gains in huge donations from the rich of the Catholic Christian world to their Church establishment. He asked P.B. Lomeo a question as to what the hand of the infallible parson in Rome is going to achieve. He averred that Mother Teresa's sainthood will suffer the humiliation of standing in a line and toeing the grand Roman tradition of sainthood. This is what hurts the innate religious sense of the Indian people the most: Rome virtually dethroning the Mother and giving her over to the Roman Catholic Church. She will now remain only Teresa Pvt Ltd., while she deserved to be crowned as *"Rashtra Mata"*. On the other hand John Dayal, the spokesperson of the All India Christian Council, held that these apprehensions were churlish and entirely unfounded and that the Roman Catholic Church and its other myriad organisations will not gain financially. That Indian Church was a vibrant organisation, two thousand years old. Mother Teresa's canonization is merely to put a stamp of sainthood on the *"Rashtra Mata"*. Any Indian with a little self-respect will completely agree with the idea of reverend K.T Francis, as far as the national susceptibilities are concerned with valid reservations on the canonisation issue. Now the facts. Christianity in India or anywhere is not 2000 years old. Even Jesus died in 33 A.D. and Christianity in its present form was born much later. Secondly, both the luminaries have thought it proper to completely ignore the basic point that all her nobility was aimed at proselytisation, and that by any means, and lastly, do Indians not have a large galaxy of their own saints– Tulsidas, Kabir, Tukaram, Chaitanya, Narayana Swamy, and of course the whole array of Vedic seers—that they now need an Albania-born foisted on them as yet another saint. If Mother Teresa's charity work were not accompanied by mandatory conversions, she would have perhaps received the eternal gratefulness of a nation and achieved a permanent place of honour among Indian saints.

After a repeat of mass conversion at Madurai in Tamil Nadu, the state government realized that if unchecked the process is going to cause unmanageable problems and forced the hands of the State Chief Minister, J. Jayalalithaa, as mentioned earlier, to promulgate an ordinance barring conversions by force, allurement and fraudulent means. But the State Congress Party cried foul and had the gumption to brand this as a draconian curb on the fundamental religious freedom, attributing political motives to the act. The Vice Chancellor of the Mahatma Gandhi University, Kottayam, Professor Cyrus Thomas, in his Metropolitan Memorial Lecture 2002 at Delhi stated: "These days the issue of conversion has also become a controversy – conversion in its positive concept is a right bestowed by the Constitution on every one of us. But it should be conversion without coercion. Conversion has a meaning before God or men, if only it is a voluntary act on the basis of one's conviction. It is wrong to prompt anyone to change their faith through temporary temptations of money, job or anything of that sort. True conversion should signify a change in the philosophy of one's life. Mass conversions can be dangerous and justifiably provocative in an otherwise peaceful society."

One has to remember that conversions are providing a terrible asymmetry in our social structure by bringing about a change in the mentality of the converts and by alienation, focussing their loyalties at extraterritorial centres of religious praxis. V.S. Naipaul in his book *Beyond Belief* mentions the phenomenon of new converts disowning their early ethnic past and their memory being restricted to the beginning of Islam. All the past before Islam is deliberately obliterated. Swami

Vivekanand has expressed the same view: "Every man going out of the Hindu pale is not only a man less, but an enemy more." Mahatma Gandhi was equally forthright in his expression: "If I had power and could legislate, I should certainly stop all proselytising." Justice Niyogi's report, inter alia, mentioned. "Evangelisation in India appears to be part of the uniform world policy to revive Christiandom for re-establishing Western supremacy and is not prompted by spiritual motives. The mass conversion of a considerable section of Adivasis with this ulterior motive is fraught with danger to the security of the State. The Christian missions were making a deliberate and determined attempt to alienate the Indian Christian community from their nation. The Church in India was not independent but accountable to those who paid for its upkeep.

The incorrigible communalist Syed Shahabuddin sings a different tune amounting to treason. In any other country, he would have been put behind the bars. But it is only in our secular India that such anti-national writers go unchallenged with no fear of retributive state justice. This is what he wrote in an English weekly in 1983: "Muslims should have ruled India after the departure of the British, and not the Hindus. Population growth helped Muslims to annex a large part of India for creating a separate Islamic State. Such efforts on part of the Muslims should be continued to gradually convert the rest of India into Dar-ul-Islam (land of the Muslims);" and the means? Mass conversion?

To the Christian zealots who are still intent to convert the Hindu 'infidels' to save them from damnation and hell fire, it is worthwhile to note what David Frawley wrote in *Path of Divinity:* "Today, throughout the world, and in the United States, with very little exception, there is no *Sarvadharma Samabhava* thought in religion. It is something I never encountered in my Christian education in the West. We were taught that Hinduism was a religion of idolatry. It was a religion of polytheism and superstition and that there was no place for Hindus in heaven. Even a great Hindu like Mahatma Gandhi might be revered on a certain level, but he was not given the type of religious credit that he would have been given had he been a Christian. These attitudes still exist throughout the world and India does not exist in isolation. And Hindus in India are, and India as a whole is, still being targeted for conversion. Why is this so? If all the religions teach the same thing, why is it that certain religions are seeking to convert the members of other religions to their beliefs?" Emphasizing that Hinduism is a pluralistic tradition he stated, "The average Christian throughout the world has been taught to believe that only Christians gain salvation. The idea has been projected as an eternal heaven for the Christians and an eternal hell for the non-Christians, particularly for idol-worshipping Hindu...."

"To date, there is no major Christian leader, or a Moslem leader, in the world, who is saying that Hinduism is as good as Christianity or Islam. I do not know of any Christian leaders in the West who would say that a Rama or a Krishna is equal to the Jesus." And finally, "I want to read a statement from *The Coming of the Third Millennium*, which was issued very recently by the Pope, in relation to the situation in Asia: 'The Asia synod will deal with the challenge for evangelisation posed by the encounter with ancient religions such as Buddhism and Hinduism. While expressing esteem for the elements of truth in these religions, the Church must make it clear that Christ is the one mediator between God and man and the sole Redeemer of humanity.' That is a statement of exclusivism and it is my contention that such exclusivism is going to breed intolerance. And such intolerance is going to end up causing conflict, division, disharmony and poor communication."

On October 27, 2002, some 80 Hindus were reported to have embraced Buddhism as a protest against the lynching of 5 dalits by some hoodlums at Daliana in Haryana on 17 October on the mistaken crime of having skinned a live cow. That the SHO of the police station happened to be a Muslim may be entirely a coincidence. After much sound and fury, most of the converts recanted and reverted back to Hinduism, spiting Udit Raj, the prime mover behind the conversion ceremony. During the period of intense media heat after the event, Kanshi Ram shouted that anyone who had seen the massacre would exhort all dalits to join Buddhism. Admittedly it was a macabre incident, condemnable by all, that resulted in conversions. But is conversion the answer to this problem? Does the lot of converts improve in the process? In villages the middle class and the OBCs still look down with disdain on the genuine dalits and their converted brothers alike. Even when a dalit becomes a Christian and enters a Church in Tamil Nadu, he has a separate pew to sit, duly marked as a segregated area. The dignity of equality promised does not materialize. On the other hand the unsettling effect of mass conversion can be dangerous and it is time that the proselytizers draw a fine dividing line between preaching and conversion. The legal position under Articles 25 and 26 has been explained earlier that propagation does not mean conversion by inducement, fear and fraud. Further while individual conversion may pass scrutiny, mass conversions not only vitiate the social atmosphere, particularly in the countryside, but create ripples and reactions amongst the Hindus all over, who counter such conversions by their 'Shuddhi' ceremony to readmit the converted dalits or tribals back into the Hindu fold. Mass conversions far from solving the problem sharpen the social divide and hurt the sentiments of the helpless non-proselytizing Hindus on whom abuses are hurled, castigating their caste system and rubbing in the fact of inequality of faiths. Affirmative action of integration and empowerment of dalits should be the shield against this self-serving evil of mass conversion.

Never say die. Yet again in its issue of *Pioneer* dated 26 October, 2002, a Delhi reader through the *Letters to the Editor* column expressed his disgust with some alleged attempts to devalue the Saint of Kolkata. He seemed to have studied in a Catholic school in Karachi with Mr L.K. Advani and gave a clear certificate to his teachers cum priests who were not guilty of any attempt at conversion. I too have many examples of my sons and grandchildren studying in Convents and Christian schools to quote where there is no visible effort at conversion. But can it be denied that they have a compulsory subject Moral Science teaching nothing but glorification of Jesus and the virtue of Christianity? Can such an effort by Hindu religious teachers be accepted in our schools today? As it is, there is heavy criticism by our secular brigade of the new NCERT textbooks in History and Civics and those dealing with our religion. Further, what has filthy roads, garbage tins and dirty waters of Yamuna got to do with Hinduism or Delhi. He does not have to tell us that caste system is an evil. But which religion in its praxis has not suffered from ritualistic extremes and distortions? The case of King Rinchen who was refused admission to Hindu fold by Kashmiri Pandits seems to be on his approval list. To him Father Damien and Albert Schwteitzer are greater than any Hindu saints. He grieves over the killing of Staines and promises help from Americans and Europeans for the poor of Kolkata; and driving the last nail into the coffin of Hinduism, he quotes Vivekanand chiding Hindus for their caste system, which has encouraged conversion to other faiths. He conveniently forgets the facts that dalit Christians and Muslims are still segregated and looked down upon in their new religion. Their being dalits does not ameliorate their cause after conversion. Why do the two egalitarian religions practise discrimination on caste basis, even after admitting them to their faith? Not very smart. The charade replayed on the Star TV in its programme *The Big Fight* on Saturday 26 October, 2002, at 8.00 PM had some interesting moments. Anchored by Rajdeep Sardesai, the panelists comprised Mr. B.P. Singhal from VHP (Vishwa Hindu Parishad), Jayanti Natrajan of Congress and a Christian father. The debate was centred on Ms. J. Jayalalithaa's ordinance banning forcible conversions in Tamil Nadu. The Christian father was fire and brimstone, blaming Hindus for their caste system and holding the Christians completely free of any wrong doing for their conversion activities. Quoting Article 25 of the Constitution that defines Religious Freedom he completely forgot the Supreme Court judgement that clearly stated that the freedom to propagate one's religion does not mean conversion. Natarajan vehemently opposed the spirit of the apex court's judgement and pilloried Mr. Singhal for all the evils she could find in the Hindu religion. Thus, hectored by our secularist media friends and blamed for conversions out of the Hindu fold, he had to suffer all the criticism for all the atrocities real or imaginary committed on the dalits by caste Hindus. He repudiated all charges successfully and pinned down his tormentors on the single issue that conversion to Christianity or Islam brings no relief to the dalits since they are still treated as dalits and inferior species from their new co-religionists. The secularists cried in chorus that the "Lunatic fringe of Hindus" was manufacturing the issue of conversion for political ends. Sardesai could not agree more. There was no one to support the Hindu stand. Outnumbered three to one Singhal had a tough task on hand. He made a valid point that conversion by educated people in full knowledge of the consequences of the act poses no problem, but the mass conversion by fraudulent means of those who cannot make an informed choice is not fair. Admittedly, there was a need for reform in Hinduism as it is in all religions. Hindus alone cannot be singled out for the tyranny of the caste system. Natarajan went to the extent of saying that Hindus also proselytized in South East Asia through means not always above board. In the process she exposed her ignorance of history. Hinduism did not move out of India to convert. It was Buddhism that did so. The little Hindu influence that is found in Jawa and the Island of Bali was a cultural rub off from great Hindu kings of India, who were great maritime leaders and during their rule foreign trade prospered. Inevitably, some Hindu totems and symbols were internalized in some pockets of these lands. But by and large the whole of South East Asia remained predominantly Buddhist or Muslim. Some even pointed out that Ambedkar, who led the mass conversions into Buddhism, could also then be branded a criminal. The fact of history is that Ambedkar did not convert forcibly. Even he himself cherished the old age Hindu values and to him Buddhism was nothing if not reformed Hinduism. Some speakers with a chip on their shoulders found it too humiliating to leave the matter of use of force or inducement in conversion to be decided by the local collector. To them this basic pillar of administration was a non-entity before the mighty politician and should not have any power to decide on the nature of conversion. From the beginning to the end the debate had a pre-written script, 'Anti Hinduism'. The questions were loaded and the arguments all having political overtones. Natarajan conveniently forgot that the ordinance that Jayalalithaa issued was already a law in existence in the Congress-ruled states of Madhya Pradesh and Orissa. What is good for Congress-ruled states is not good for non-Congress states. Such is the perversity of our secular mind.

After the conclusion of the Indo-Pak war in 1971, sometimes in January, 1972, Mother Teresa visited the Advanced Headquarters of Indian Eastern Command in Dhaka, where I was serving as a Senior Staff Officer for the Civil Affairs Organisation to resettle the country, after the ravages of war and the wanton destruction of all civil facilities under the 'scotched earth policy' of the retreating Pak forces. There were thousands of Bangladeshi women raped by their co-religionists, who had become pregnant. This posed a serious human problem. Mother Teresa's ostensible aim was to extend a helping hand in their rehabilitation. For reasons not known, the Muslims clerics and local leaders did not take kindly to her overtures and she had to return empty handed. That was the first time I saw her. Bangladesh with all its misery was not India and the Muslims were in no mood to allow social service as a cloak for proselytisation and barter conversion for services rendered. In India the case would have been entirely different. For every rehabilitated woman there would have been five more converts to Christianity as happened in Haryana recently.

It is no wonder that a majority of Hindus, except the westernized elite, feel that there has been little or no change in the attitudes of Catholic or Protestant Christians in trying to save the pagan Hindu from perdition by conversion. Inspite of all her dedication Mother Teresa was at heart a Christian Missionary. With the present day elite who send their children to the Christian schools for a supposedly better education it is not difficult to find a huge crowd of admirers in our metropolitan cocktail circuit.

On balance, Mother Teresa presented such a negative image of India to the West that her services and charity cannot wash the damage. Another would be Nobel laureate, who puts the ugly face of leprosy along with her Christian 'Healing Touch' is bound to send even stronger negative signals to the world. The Vir Singhvis and Navin Chawlas, the biographers of Mother Teresa, having moonshine in their eyes, may not appreciate the immense harm done to Hindus and India by such anointed saints, but they cannot stop the West from being the condescending neo-colonials to us. One wonders if these authors ever use the power at their elbows to write something about Indians, who have done much more for the poor and the dying. But that won't be the done thing for our English scribes. The real motive of the missionary run schools and the intensity of their desire to convert can be seen by the simple fact that in Tamil Nadu the Roman Catholic Christian fathers have threatened to close down 5000 schools run by them if the ordinance against religious conversion is not revoked. Is education then a quid pro quo for the change of religion?

Dr. Joseph Pulikunnel, the Director of the Indian Institute of Christian Studies (IICS), declared: " The entire Christian wealth of India belongs to Pope. This is nothing but colonialism. Bishops are being appointed by the Pope, not elected by the believers. There is an increasing opposition to this. India had a Swadeshi Church, which was broken by the Portuguese who made it Westernised. The Pope should have control only over moral and spiritual issues and not over Christian property in India." This was a voice of sanity.

Vincent A. Smith in the *Oxford History of India* 1996 mentions: "The Muslim historian was 'indifferent to distinctions among idolaters' and thus claimed 'the majority of inhabitants were shorn-headed Brahmins who were all put to the sword'. These victims were Buddhist monks, whose places of learning and libraries were destroyed; The ashes of Buddhist sanctuaries at Sarnath near Benaras still bear witness to the rage of the image breakers. Many noble monuments... were wrecked in the course of the early Muslim invasions."

We shall conclude this chapter on religious conversion by simply quoting the phenomenon in Chhattisgarh that was changing the face of the tribal belt. Here The BJP Rajya Sabha member, Dalip Singh Ju Dev, the erstwhile ruler of Jeshpur, Chhatisgarh, was the moving force behind the "*Ghar Wapasi Abhiyan*" (Home Coming Movement) aimed at assimilation of Christian tribals back into the Hindu fold, by the hundreds. Some excerpts from his interview:

Q. Does the *Ghar Vapasi* Programme target other non-Hindus, apart from Christian tribals, and in other parts of India?

Ans. I come from a tribal land. Lakhs of people there are tribals. First, I'll see to my own area. Twenty-eight generations ago, the *'Adivasis'* there accepted my ancestors, and made one Maharaja. So, there is a special obligation (towards them).

Q. Isn't it somewhat controversial to try and reconvert people who left the Hindu fold?

Ans. I am a well read person and a well travelled man. I did my graduation from a mission school. I know this hanky panky very well.

Q. Why should there be conversion?

Ans. Because of poverty and promised economic benefits, one assumes.

Q. If there is poverty, why aren't these Christians going and converting Muslims in say, Pakistan, in Afghanistan?

Ans. I don't think the governments of those countries permit, whereas our government permits.

Q. Why are they not allowing? If the government allows, it doesn't mean that we should suffer it. What I am saying is that there should be no trade-off in the name of social service. Why aren't they (missionaries) going to western countries? The churches are empty. Why are they coming here?

Ans. ?????

Q. There is a view that tribals, who engage in animism, etc., don't really belong to the Hindu mainstream?

Ans. This is an international conspiracy. You have heard of divide and rule. It's everywhere. Tribals have surnames like Ganesh, Ram, etc. They practise Dharma, no doubt. All know that those who live in Hindustan are Hindus. Even Christian and Muslims here have Hindu blood. There have been conversions.

Q For instance, a Muslim of many generations, now has different *'samskaras'* (proclivities). How can you expect him to become a Hindu?

Ans. It has happened. In Kashmir, many who had converted out of compulsion, came to the Maharaja and told him they wanted to return. But the Brahmins objected on the grounds that these people had eaten beef. And the plan fizzled out. What I and my group do is go and wash their feet. We are the first to have begun this practice in India. The message that goes out is that the son of the Maharaja is washing our feet. We are stopping the cultural and religious assault on them. And I can proudly say that we are advancing in the face of this diabolical conspiracy, devised across the seas.

Q. How many tribals have you reconverted?

Ans. About 6 lakh.

Q. How do you identify those who want to reconvert?

Ans. They come to us. We distribute literature. Two books need to be mentioned. One is HV Seshadari's *Aur Est But Gaya.* The another is Tasleema Nasreen's *Lajja.*

Q. How does one ascertain that no force is used?

Ans. Our workers tell them that Western glamour has lured them away from traditional puja of, say, Hanumanji. They have also got economic benefits and education. Money is not God, but it seems not to be less than God.

Q. Is there any economic rehabilitation programme for those who reconvert?

Ans. Those who should be co-operating, raise objections. There are two kinds of work, one can either help create history, or get entangled in daily routine. I know that we are creating history. Those forces have very wide reach, as they have enveloped entire continents. The church has finished North America and South America, the aborigines of Australia, South Africa, where the Whites have huge land holdings. It's a clear case of exploitation. There are about 150 Christian countries. They should be satisfied with this. Leave us alone! We know our problems.

Q. In the West, people who embrace other faiths, usually do so out of conviction. Here, it is the deprived, who normally convert. How do you propose to remedy this?

Ans. I can't answer this question. Christians may be a mere 3 percent in India. But there are pockets, as in my region, where they are 30 percent. In Bihar and Orissa, they are 40 percent. In the North-East, they are over 90 percent. These people have left our society because of the temptation held out by the West. We are doing for them whatever one brother can do for another. I've learnt that they are afraid of my group. According to the law of the land, no non-tribal can purchase land from a tribal. All institutions whether it's VHP, or Jamaat-e-Islami, or Holy Cross, come in the non-tribal category. All their land should be returned to the original people.

Q. Have you faced any threat on account of your work?

Ans. They killed 10 of my men. I have been attacked. We say "*Dum nikle is desh ke khatir, bus itna arman. Dum nikla Hindu dharma ke khatir bus itna armaan hai. Kyonki ek baar is raah main chalna sau janmon ke samaan hai. Dekh ke veeron ki qurbani, apna dil hai dola, Rang de Basanti Chola.*"

According to a report an estimated $45 billion are spent every year to support global Christian activities. There are 4 million full time workers in the service of the Church who run 13000 major libraries, publish 4 billion texts, in addition to running 1500 universities, 930 research centres and 800 Christian TV and radio stations, and over 400 institutions to train a quarter of a million foreign missionaries.

Mother Teresa may come and go, but the proselytizing drive of the two monotheistic religions that has fuelled much violence in the past is not likely to be checked unless very strong counter-measures are taken, preferably by the state. A secular state that believes in equidistancing itself from all religions must not allow one to poach on the other. As in the past so in the present, forcible religious conversion poses a great threat by promoting cultural alienation, disorientation and disharmony.

Hindutva just cannot be wished away. The refulgent mass of knowledge, wisdom and truth and its weltanschauung of syncretic ecumenism bequeathed by our Vedic sages has lightened mankind its way through long period of darkness in human history. To quote Mark Twain, "India is the cradle of human race, the birthplace of human speech, the mother of history, the grandmother of legend and the great grandmother of tradition. Our most valuable and most instructive materials in the history of man are treasured up in India."

7

The Independence Movement

The saga of the Independence struggle is a story told and retold many times by the dramatis personae themselves, contemporary observers and pen wielders with the wisdom of hindsight. The main credit for sufferings and sacrifices undoubtedly goes to the leaders and followers of the early erstwhile Indian National Congress, and they have been more than fully rewarded for their exertions. Largesse, ministerial offices, power and pelf to them and their dependents more than compensated for their labours. Even their families are entitled to freedom fighter pensions and the requirement to gain such privilege is merely a certificate from a jailer even if the confinement was for one day. In a gross trivialization of the services rendered in the freedom struggle, Indira Gandhi started her famous scheme of offering *Tamra Patra* which was refused by the genuine freedom fighters and ridiculed by no less a person than Acharya Kripalani. For all those rewards offered to the Congress and its foster organizations, one thing stands out in stark contrast. The total erasure from public memory of the other noble souls, who did even more for the freedom of our country. Many illustrious sons of India who suffered the worst tortures and incarceration are not even known, let alone remembered. They did not crave for rewards but a grateful nation should not forget the services rendered by these unsung heroes, whose only fault was that they belonged to a different political ideology or volition.

In a volume written by the leftist historians, dealing with the Indian freedom struggle, not only has an unduly large part been devoted to the contribution of Indian Communists (inspite of their known treacherous role during the Quit India Movement), but an astounding statement has been made elsewhere that the freedom movement drew its inspiration from Lenin. Brushing aside these ridiculous distortions and half-truths so routinely peddled by our Leftist historians and present day Communists, we shall look at the picture clear of the miasma of ideological predilections and prejudices. The Indian Communists inspired by the dogma of dictatorship of the International Proletariat, which transcended national boundaries had no love for nationalism, least of all Hindu nationalism. Russia had rejected God and religion and their Indian counterparts followed their example not only in being irreligious, but had no time for a narrow national struggle of freedom. Barring a few exceptions, the freedom struggle as we have seen was mainly a Hindu effort. There was very little contribution from the Muslim community. We have earlier discussed Gandhiji's efforts to solicit Muslim support, arising out of their angst against the British due to the abolition of the, Caliphate after the liquidation of the Ottoman Empire. The Khilafat movement was a temporary expedient, which failed miserably, and the damage done was much more than their contribution towards communal harmony.

It would be highly disingenuous on anyone's part to reassess Mahatma Gandhi and his role in the freedom struggle. Besides the countless accolades showered on him and the ultimate epithet of the 'Father of the Nation' so richly deserved, one of the other qualities not so well-known and often little understood was his capacity to identify himself with the common Indian, read Hindu. He understood the idiom of Hinduism and its symbols. Unlike Nehru whose head was always in the clouds and feet nowhere, Gandhi had his ears on the ground and fingers on the pulse of the nation. His *Ram Dhun*, invocation of Ram and Rahim, movement for the removal of untouchability, wearing of Khadi, his half-naked body like that of a Hindu saint symbolizing his identification with the poorest of the poor, instantly struck a chord in the Hindu mind and they followed this pied piper blindly. In the parlance of modern management, he was the most effective manager and a leader of men who was wholly dedicated to the cause and who led from the front. His efforts to enlist the support of the Muslim masses were only partially successful. There was an inherent perception among the Muslim masses that after the British left, the power to rule will pass into Hindu hands and they shall merely pass from one kind of slavery to another. In a Hindu majority state, they will lose the preferred status of a pampered minority, which the Britishers had conferred upon them pursuant to their policy of divide and rule. The

Britishers knew that the threat to their rule would come not from the minority Muslims who could be pampered and cajoled, but from the majority Hindu community. Hence, their encouragement of Muslim separatism and a stress on their minority identity. During the 1857 freedom struggle, wrongly described by Britishers as a sepoy's mutiny, the Muslims freshly deprived of their status as rulers, were eager to throw out the Britishers or the *'Firangee.'* But after a lapse of seventy years, when memory tends to fade, their ardour died and the fear of Hindu domination replaced the hatred of the Britishers. During the freedom struggle, the choice before the Muslims, as they saw it, was either to be ruled by the Britishers with the status of a favoured minority or pass into the bondage of a Hindu majority rule. With few exceptions all Muslims, moved by an anti-Hindu impulse kept themselves away from the freedom struggle and secretly wished for a separate Islamic homeland after independence. The seeds of the Two-Nation Theory inherent in Islamic philosophy and the tenets of Quran dormant from the times of Muslim invasion had been lying buried for a long time. They needed a fresh impulse to sprout. Mr. Jinnah sold them the dream of a separate homeland for Muslims, and promised Dar-ul-Islam. Mahatma Gandhi completely misread the Muslim mind. He was too noble to suspect this base instinct in a fraternal community. The shortlived Hindu-Muslim unity during the *Khilafat Movement* was due to a fortuitous turn of events which invoked Muslim loyalties to the cause of the Caliphate in Turkey after the collapse of the Ottoman empire, as a sequel to the British victory over the Turks in the First World War. This was the only time that Muslims made a common cause with the Hindus against the Britishers in the struggle for Independence. But this honeymoon between the Hindus and Muslims was merely a flicker, which lasted for a very short time.

While Gandhi's moral authority, his body language, his saintly simplicity and use of Hindu symbols united the Hindus and endeared him to the common man, these very same symbolisms put suspicion into the Muslim mind, whose memories of Islam lay in Mecca and Arabian desert. After all, the language of Quran was Arabic and Gandhi spoke pure Hindi. Thus, the freedom struggle was reduced to a majority Hindu movement against the British rule, the very same thing that Macaulay feared so much and tried to forestall by enslaving the Hindu mind in every possible way through his hired agents, the missionaries, MaxMüller and the Marxists. With a few honourable exceptions, where some of our enlightened Muslim brothers, unshackled by the limitations of a regressive Muslim impulse and the dictates of the Ulemas, made some sacrifices, the struggle for freedom was basically a Hindu phenomenon. The names that will be written in letters of gold include Ashfaq Ullah, the revolutionary, and some Congress leaders like Maulana Azad, Rafi Ahmad Kidwai and Khan Abdul Gaffar Khan. They all rendered commendable services to the cause of freedom. But these were the few exceptions. The majority played at the most a marginal and sometimes even a negative role.

While Gandhiji's faith in truth and non-violence as the main weapon of the freedom struggle had many merits and it will be highly churlish to deny its effectiveness, a strong case can equally be made for the noble efforts and effectiveness of the method of the revolutionaries who believed in an armed struggle. After all, no nation in history has ever gained its freedom without the use of force. It could also be said with an element of truth that the Civil Disobedience Movement alone did not help us gain freedom. The activities of the Indian National Army (INA), US President Roosevelt's pressure on Churchill and the simmering discontent within the Armed Forces, which erupted into the Naval Mutiny of 1946, made the British realize that a nation cannot be held captive without its consent. The Second World War and the events that followed along with the international situation made even a hard boiled realist General A.P. Wavell, the then Viceroy of India, recommend to His Majesty's Government to wind up the British rule in India. After all many other British colonies also gained independence after India. They had no Gandhi to lead them. This is not to belittle Gandhi, but to emphasize that his cult of non-violence imposed on a nation, already under a heavy dose of excessive tolerance, lead to a sense of complacency among its people and a refusal to be aggressive when the need arose. Except for the Armed Forces, which carried their tradition of valour, our leadership and masses became effete, believing more in rhetoric than action. India became a soft state and the political leadership turned puissant. Unlike nations like the United States, Italy, Germany and France, which fought for their freedom and retained their national vigour, we became meek and submissive. It is no one's case that we should turn aggressive, but our leadership should deliver on their brave words. "Our patience should not be unlimited', our leadership thunders, and draws a line on the sand. After another attack on India's sovereignty, whether it is the J & K Assembly, the Indian Parliament, Kaluchuk, or Akshardham, the leaders carried out this ritual, and then slank away to their cosy retreats. It is no surprise that USA and Pakistan do not take India's repeated warnings of the "*Aar Paar Ki Larai*" (fight to the finish) seriously. Freedom is not won by words. Viewed against this background, one is forced to the inevitable conclusion that our highly publicized face of non-violence, as practised during the freedom movement was not an unmixed blessing. It left our polity highly anaemic and incapable of handing out retributive justice to the aggressor.

Enough credit has been given to Mahatma Gandhi, but before the last word is said on this politician and saint, a few qualificatory observations will not be out of place. Gandhi was tall because he stood on the shoulders of the great Titan of our freedom struggle, Lokmanya Balgangadhar Tilak. It was Tilak, who took the activities of a petition seeking Congress out of the confines of the cozy drawing rooms and transformed the freedom struggle into a mass movement. It was he who created the infrastructure of this forbiding national undertaking by machining the tools of cultural nationalism, from the raw material of Hindu religious fervour by synergising the Ganesh and Shivaji festivals with this endeavour, thereby touching the very soul of the Hindu majority. He desired amity and cooperation with Muslims but was astute enough to realize that Muslim separatism would always be a big hurdle in homogenizing the movement. He could see, as later Hedgewar and Golwolkar did, that the large Hindu population and their ethnic civilizational strength would form the hardcore substance of the Indian nation. It was he who uttered the immortal words "Freedom is my birthright and I shall have it," in a court of law in complete defiance of British colonialism. It was he who gave impetus to the philosophy of Swadeshi and boycott of British and foreign goods. Gandhi was the natural legatee to Tilak's heritage; but later changed course and drifted away from Tilak's radicalism to Gokhale's pacifism and finally his own mantra of truth and non-violence. To make a crude analogy, Tilak was the Mazzini of India while Gandhi a non-violent Garibaldi. Tilak fostered a generation of radicals and revolutionaries that can be the pride of any nation, while Gandhi produced a breed of pacifist and armchair constitutional defence counsels using verbal pyrotechnics in place of real bombs.

Gandhi's followers were the beneficiaries of the rewards of freedom, while Tilak's fighters sacrificed their lives, suffered privations, long jail sentences and transportation for life and with a few exceptions, died unremembered, unwept and unmourned. Tilak had more prescience than Gandhi in reading the Muslim mind and did not believe in the artificial parity and forced equivalence between Hindus and Muslims. The freedom fight was to be a predominantly Hindu undertaking with or without any help from the Muslims, certainly not by cajoling and entreating them for their co-operation. The Khilafat movement has been described earlier. To Gandhiji, means were as important as the end and the end had to be an ideological construct, as also the means. But by co-opting Muslim support and justifying Khilafat, an obscurantist movement, Gandhiji not only defiled his end that was far from being ideologically correct, but laid the foundations of soliciting support from the most orthodox and regressive elements of the Muslim community. His Congress flagbearers have continued the trend even till today. A V.P. Singh genuflecting before the Shahi Imam, Sonia Gandhi seeking fatwa from a Muslim cleric for electoral support from Muslims are a few examples that point to a perpetuation of the same precedent. We have discussed how Gandhiji misread the Muslim mind and the disastrous consequences that followed, leading to partition on the basis of religion and the creation of Pakistan, the very thing that Gandhiji fought against all his life. Muslim appeasement knew no limits. From the early atrocities on Hindus during the Mopla riots, when Gandhiji tried to justify their anger, to the mass massacre of Hindus during partition Gandhiji's only concern appeared to be Muslim safety and Muslim feelings. All great men have their blind spots. Gandhiji had his share – extreme Muslim appeasement, blind faith in Nehru, contempt for the revolutionary and a blind adherence to non-violence; not merely as a justified practical ploy but as a philosophy of life that has resulted in excessive Hindu tolerance to a fault, an effette nationalism and reactive leadership. There is a saying that 'leaders are born and chalk out their mission'. In India we have a mission ready; making India strong, but waiting for a leader. How can we find a leader who can be proactive when all we have learnt is to petition, to cry foul, to appeal to the international community for help and praying others to fight our battles.

We go back to Tilak, may his tribe increase, a well known name in the trinity of the leaders of the freedom struggle along with Lala Lajpat Rai and Bipin Chandra Pal—the three Bal, Pal and Lal. We shall highlight in the following pages, the achievements of this forgotten brigade of radicals and revolutionaries, who too served this nation with blood and toil and received no recompense. Let us turn the searchlight on the most prominent of these. This was Sri Aurobindo.

This titan amongst the freedom fighters, who worked harder than any individual for the liberation of Mother India, was the true visionary of an independent India, a yogi, a saint, almost an avtar ignored by history. Born on 15 August, 1872, in Calcutta, he grew to be five years at Rangpur (now in Bangladesh), sent thereafter to Loreto Convent School in Darjeeling and then packed off to England for a western education by his father, and entered Saint Paul School in London in 1884. Later, he attended King's College, Cambridge, in 1890, and a brilliant student that he was, passed the I.C.S., but gave it up by refusing to appear for the riding test. Having spent 13 years in England and South Africa, he returned to India on 6 February, 1893, twenty years of age. He worked in the Baroda State Service from 1897 to early 1906, taught French and English at Baroda College and became its principal. It is here that he started his public life by writing articles, 'New Lamps for Old', in the *Indu Prakash,* a Maratha English daily, published from Bombay. A piece of his earlier writings: "I say of the Congress that its aims are mistaken, that the spirit in which it is proceeding is not a spirit of sincerity and whole-heartedness and that the methods it has chosen are not right. It does not have the right sort of men to be leaders. In brief that we are at present the blind led, if not by the blind, at least by the one-eyed." As early as 1890, he did not subscribe to the Congress philosophy of constitutional agitation and passive resistance. A true believer in the Gita, he was convinced that violence can sometimes be the only recourse to fight for Dharma against injustice. Swimming against the tide of Congress opinion and that of the moderates, he declared, "There is a certain section of India, which regards Nationalism as madness and they say nationalism will ruin the country. They are men who live in the pure intellect and they look at things purely from the intellectual point of view. What does the intellect think? Here is a work that you have undertaken, a work so gigantic, so stupendous, the means of which are so poor, the resistance to which will be so strong, so organized, so disciplined, so well equipped with all the weapons that science can supply, with all the strength that human power and authority can give". Again he reaffirmed in his work, *India's Rebirth*, "Politics is the work of the Kshatriya and it is virtues of the Kshatriya we must develop if we are to be morally fit for freedom." "What India needs at the moment is the aggressive virtues, the spirit of soaring idealism, bold creation, fearless resistance, courageous attack."

While the moderates dismissed him as a mystic, Lord Minto, the Viceroy of India, knew better and described him as "the most dangerous man we have to deal with at present". Aurobindo's views on Nehru were candid and forthright and were similar to those of Alain Danieleu. "Nehru was the perfect replica of a certain type of Englishman. He often uses the expression 'continental people', with an amused and sarcastic manner, to designate French or Italians. He despised non-anglicised Indians and had a very superficial and partial knowledge of India. His ideal was the romantic socialism of 19th century Britain. But this type of socialism was totally unfit for India, where there was no class struggle and where the conditions were totally different from 19th century Europe." On Hindu-Muslim unity his views were clear: "I am sorry they are making a fetish of Hindu-Muslim unity. It is no use ignoring facts; some day the Hindus may have to fight the Muslims and they must be prepared for it. Hindu-Muslim unity should not mean the subjection of the Hindus. Every time the mildness of the Hindu has given way. The best solution would be to allow the Hindus to organize themselves and the Hindu-Muslim unity would take care of itself, it would automatically solve the problem. Otherwise we are lulled into a false sense of satisfaction that we have solved a difficult problem, when in fact we have only shelved it." For suspicion of being linked to his brother's secret society involved in the assassination attempt on a British judge, he was sentenced to a one-year imprisonment.

If we readjust our looking glasses, re-align the optical prism and have a look at the events before and after independence an altogether new picture will emerge. Most of the Congress men with the exception of Gandhiji were western educated and anglicised in mind and thought, and their liberalism was peppered with socialism in the British labour style. They were the inevitable product of a constitutional reformist's approach to create a class of westernised elite, cut off from their Indian roots to serve as on intermediary hierarchy, with a 'moderate face' and act as the link between the master and the slaves. They had little of the soul and glory of India, Hinduism and the India of the average people. They slowly and independently started the process of de-Hinduising India. The provincial Congress Governments in 1938 in a large number of provinces modelled Indian education on the British system. As Danieleu remarks, "the teaching of philosophy, art and science, which constituted the prestigious Indian cultural tradition became more and more ignored and survived thanks to the Brahmins without any help whatsoever from the state. When the Hindu Mahasabha, a cultural, social and political movement aimed at defending India's true heritage took the field, it was openly maligned by the Congress leaders. Its attempt to counter the vicious propaganda of Muslims was simply sneered at. That great monk Swami Karpatriji leading the much-reviled Ramrajya Parishad was ridiculed by the Congress, who exaggerated the problems of caste untouchablity and cow slaughter like their western masters. Indian nationalism could draw nourishment only from its innate genius and rich spiritual heritage. In a way with the noblest of intentions even Gandhiji fell prey to Muslim appeasement. Our present institutions are rooted in foreign soil." To quote Francious Gautier in his book *Arise Again O India:*

"Indians are so proud of their judicial system; but isn't it a carbon copy of the British one, with a consequence, a flurry of problems, whether it is the political interference in the naming of judges, the incredible backlog of pending cases, or the overcrowding of jails? Again, the Indian judiciary relies for its judgments on western values, on European jurisprudence, which are totally unfit for India. Once more, it is proud of its "secular" values and often comes down heavily on the fanatical bigots, meaning the Hindus. In education, Nehru carried on with the British policy of imposing a westernised English system; more and more the universities and schools of India, many of them run by Christians missions, produced a generation of English speaking diploma holders, who did not belong any more to Hindu society, but only to a fake bureaucratic society with westernised manners."

"I think, therefore, I am". That is what Descartes had said long ago. Israelis echoed this sentiment in their struggle for freedom somewhat differently: "I fight, therefore, I am." Ras Bihari Bose was the epitome of this creed. "I was a fighter/ one fight more/ the last and the best." That was his credo, exuding tremendous enthusiasm to die fighting for India. Born on 25 May, 1885, the arch-type revolutionary escaped from India in 1905 in the aftermath of the Ghadar uprising. As the Japanese entered World War II in their pursuit of The Great South East Asia, Ras Bihari Bose appeared from nowhere in 1943 when Subhas Bose became the founder and Supreme Commander of the Indian National Army (INA) in South East Asia. In a life marked by dramatic escapes and deceptions he spent the last 30 years of his life in Japan never to set forth on Indian soil again. Ras Bihari Bose is the only revolutionary, constantly on the move, who has never been caught dead or alive, in or outside India.

An exceptional revolutionary and a great Hindu, he was reviled and denounced by his own people, the Military Wing of the Indian National Acadamy as the Japanese stooge, while others held him as the predecessor of Subhas Chandra Bose. He is still remembered in Japan as the most revered Indian after Gautam Buddha. Veer Savarkar after his exile and incarceration of more than a quarter of a century was subsequently elected as the President of the Hindu Mahasabha in 1937. Ras Bihari Bose kept in constant touch with him, exchanged secret missives through wandering Buddhist monks and founded a Branch of the Hindu Mahasabha in Japan. Completely under the spell of Veer Savarkar, like many before him, he expressed these feelings in an address from Radio Tokyo on 21 March, 1942: "It is now no secret that it was Savarkar who first suggested the idea of the "Great Escape" to Subhas Bose when they met in Bombay at Savarkar Sadan on 21 June, 1940." Even earlier, in a secret letter that was intercepted by the British intelligence and never reached its destination, he had suggested to Subhas, after his election as the Congress President in 1938, to work on a twofold strategy– control of the armed forces and Hindu unity. In his actions and thoughts, Subhas Bose was also greatly inspired by Ras Bihari Bose, suggesting an almost morphic resonance between Ras Bihari Bose and Savarkar. Ras Bihari Bose met Subhas Bose alias Matsudo during the latter's stay at the Imperial Hotel in Tokyo after an 88 days submarine odyssey. He, on 21 October, 1943, in a crowded ceremony at Cathay Hall in Singapore, introduced Subhas Chandra Bose as the leader of India, in South East Asia, in their fight for freedom. Soon after, Subhas Chandra Bose declared the formation of the Provisional Government of Azad Hind and Ras Bihari

Bose was appointed its adviser. He had many close brushes with the police, but due to his disguise he would hoodwink his pursuers. While still outwardly a faithful subordinate of the British Officers serving in the Forest Dept. of Dehra Doon, he kept his revolutionary fervour alive. He masterminded the bombing of Lord Hardinge in Delhi in 1912 for which Master Amichand, Bhai Bal Mukund, Abadh Bihari and Vasant Kumar Biswas were hanged. Before the British could get wise on him he fled to Lahore incognito with a reward of Rs. 5,000/- on his head, a big amount in those days. He now travelled extensively to instigate uprisings in the army cantonments from Peshawar to Singapore in close collaboration with the Ghadar Party, but before D-Day of 21st June, 1915, the plot was aborted by a traitor, Amrit Singh, at Lahore. In this famous Lahore conspiracy case, Kartar Singh Sarabha, just 15 years old, was hanged. Ras Bihari Bose under an alias Pronath Tagore, a relative of late Rabindra Nath Tagore, had to flee by sea to Japan.

In Japan he was the protégé and a closely sheltered guest of Mitsuru Toyama, "the unknown man of Japan", the Chief of Black Dragon Society, who was a friend to all foreign Indian revolutionaries. Ras Bihari Bose went underground, married a Japanese girl and set out to translate Hindu scriptures like the *Gita*, *Ramayana* and *Mahabharata* in Japanese. He raised the cry of de-colonisation followed by a call "Asia for Asians" from a guest house "Asia Lodge". Embodying this spirit of denial of access to Westerners, and befriended by Sun Yat Sen, he helped finance the freedom struggle, both in India and Japan. His family life was a tragedy – an estranged wife, a son dead in the Japanese army and a daughter 'Niguchi' who lived long enough to visit India. Ras Bihari, the eternal revolutionary, died on 23 January, 1944, about three years after Pearl Harbour and his funeral was attended by a huge crowd of dignitaries and commoners alike. The Japanese Prime Minister Koki Hirota himself chaired the Funeral Committee. His last relics lie unremembered and unsought in Japan. Unlike the ashes of Subhas Chandra Bose diligently trailed like the holy grail after his mysterious death in an air crash, our Government did not deem it fit to honour this forgotten, great son of India who lived only for his country and died in a foreign land unwept, unhonoured and unsung.

Much has been written about Subhas Chandra Bose, duly awarded a Bharat Ratna, posthumously. However, we shall quote some of his famous words.

Thus spake Subhas:

(Echoes from Abroad)

- The enemy that has drawn the sword, must be fought with the sword. Civil disobedience must develop into armed struggle and only when the Indian people receive the baptism of fire on a large scale will they qualify for their freedom.
- Friends! We have a grim fight before us—for the enemy is powerful, unscrupulous and ruthless. In this final march to freedom you will have to face hunger, thirst, privation, forced marches and death. Only when you pass this test, will freedom be yours.
- When France declared war against Germany in 1939, there was one cry, which rose from the lips of German soldiers – "To Paris! "When the brave soldiers of Nippon set out on their march in December 1941, there was but one cry which rose from their lips. "To Singapore, to Singapore!" Comrades! My soldiers, let your battle cry be – "To Delhi, to Delhi!"
- I have always felt that though India is otherwise ripe for Independence in every way, she has lacked one thing – namely an army of liberation. George Washington of America could fight to win freedom, because he had his army. Garibaldi could liberate Italy, because he had his armed volunteers behind him. It is our privilege and honour to be the first to come forward and organize India's National Army. By doing so we have removed the last obstacle in our path to freedom. Then, when India is free, we will have to organize the permanent army of Free India whose task it will be to preserve our liberty at all times.
- I assure you that I shall be with you in darkness and in sunshine, in sorrow and in big joy, in suffering and in victory. It does not matter who among us will live to see India free. It is enough that India shall be free and that we shall give our all to make her free. May God bless our army and grant us victory in the coming fight!

INQUILAB ZINDABAD!

INQUILAB ZINDABAD!

Now we open a new chapter in the annals of the revolutionary movement. The name that springs to mind, the greatest of the revolutionaries and a legend in his lifetime, is Swatantrya Veer Savarkar. Vinayak Damodar Savarkar was born on 28 May, 1883, in a Chitopavan Brahmin family at Bhagur, a holy city in Maharashtra. By the time he was 22 years he had obtained a BA degree from Fergusson College, Bombay University. He was imbued from his childhood with the spirit of liberating his motherland with whatever sacrifices it demanded. He was only 16 when in May 1899, three Chapekar brothers were hanged for shooting two cruel British officers in Pune on 22 June, 1897. On reading the news in Tilak's paper *Kesri*, already suffering from fever the boy trembled with rage and took a solemn oath before Goddess Asthbhuja Durga to avenge the martyrdom of these gallant fighters for freedom, just as his hero Shivaji had taken a similar oath in the temple of Rohideshwar. His other role models were Mazzini and Tilak. Fired with the spirit of liberating his motherland Savarkar left India and sailed for England on 9 June, 1906, less for further study but more for continuing his revolutionary activities of Nasik and Poona, his "Jerusalem and Rome" in India. Later, he was to disclose on 14 November, 1913, at Dadar that a hidden agenda for his five years stay in England was to learn the art of bomb making, the only possible way according to him to meet "Gun with guns, pistol with pistol and bomb with bomb". The recent victory of Japan over Russia had punctured the baloon of the white man's invincibility, and Asia was in ferment.

He found his lodging at 65 Cromwell Avenue near Hampton Heath High Gate, London, on a weekly rent of Rs. 16, capable of accommodating 25 to 30 persons. The place called "India House" or Bharat Bhawan was founded by Shyamji Krishna Verma, the founder of India Home Rule Society and a monthly journal *Indian Sociologist*. Lokmanya Tilak too had recommended him in strong words to Shyamji. Admitted to Grays Inn on 26 July, 1906, when only 23 years of age Savarkar became an active member of India House activities and out-did all his peers. The Society comprising 10 active members held regular meetings to discuss political problems and their answers. Savarkar's role during these meetings is vividly described by C. Rajagopalachari in his English biography of Savarkar, written in 1926 under the pen name of Chitragupta. The book was immediately banned.

While at Bharat Bhavan, Savarkar came in contact with certain other radical members engaged in furthering the cause of the freedom struggle. This illustrious galaxy included Bhai Parmanand. Bhai Parmanand, then 28, was the first Arya Samaji teacher, who came to

England and on his sea voyage via South Africa, met Gandhiji at Durban. A brilliant scholar he later wrote a thesis for his M.A. degree from London University, titled *Rise of British Power in India.* The thesis was rejected due to its anti-British overtones. On his return to Lahore in 1908, he wrote some more books and worked in close association with another revolutionary, Lala Hardayal. After a degree in San Francisco University in 1913, he returned home and was arrested for his suspected anti-British activities and tried on some trivial and trumped up charges such as Delhi Conspiracy Case (1912), Lahore Conspiracy Case (1914) and Cama Gata Maru Case and transported for life to Andamans, where he gave good company to Savarkar for five years.

Lala Hardayal, younger to Savarkar by one year, educated at Saint Stephens College, M.A. (English) in 1904, topped from Punjab University and remained a topper in all his examinations. He finally joined Saint John's College, London, on the scholarship of 200 pounds to finish his History (Honours) and later like Shyamji became a Boden scholar in Sanskrit at Oxford in 1907. A staunch Hindu and a living encyclopedia, gifted with a photogenic memory, he could simultaneously play chess, count the strokes of the ball, recite verses in Latin and Arabic and solve arithmetic problems. One of his letters in the 1906 issue of *Indian Sociologist* rocketed him to fame and a permanent place on the political landscape. But again his anti-British outbursts made him give up his scholarship and leave Oxford, the latter poorer due to this loss of talent. He returned to India in 1908, went back to England to fight for the national cause, taught at Garcia and Stanford University and fired by his patriotic fervour resigned and founded the International Radical Club, A Fraternity of the Red Flag, later metamorphosed into Ghadar Party, a staunch anti-British outfit abroad.

Pandurang Mahadev, popularly called Senapati Bapat, landed in England on a Sir Mongal Dass scholarship for engineering studies at Edinburgh and was swept off by the waves of nationalism. He churned out a revolutionary pamphlet, *The British Rule in India* that sent shock waves all around the British Isles. Completely under Savarkar's spell he abandoned his academic plans and toyed with the idea of going to France to learn how to make a bomb. He believed in Savarkar's maxim "murder committed to meet justice is fair and just." His scholarship was withdrawn and he was mentioned in glowing terms in Tilak's *Kesri* in 1931. He visited Savarkar in Ratnagiri Jail and gave fiery speeches defending V.B. Gogte, who shot JEB Hotson on 20 July 1931 and in consequence was sentenced to seven years rigorous imprisonment.

Virendranath Chattopadhyaya of Hyderabad, brother of Sarojini Naidu and the poet actor Harindranath Chattopadhyaya son of scholar poet Pt. Aghorenath, a graduate from Calcutta University, came to England to join the I.C.S (Indian Civil Services) but entered instead the Middle Temple Inn to study law. He, too, with all the academic prospects beckoning him, was inspired by Savarkar and joined his group believing that "all is fair in fighting for freedom". Treading the thorny path to freedom under a pall of intense suffering and misery, he started a paper *Talwar*. He kept up his friendship with Savarkar, visited him 15 times in Brixton Jail. Nehru in his autobiography spoke of him in glowing words. During World War I, he fled to Germany and planned a military expedition carrying soldiers and munitions of war via Afghanistan and Baluchistan to spark off a military uprising in India. Affectionately called Chattu, his end like the death of Subhas Chandra Bose is shrouded in mystery.

Another active member of this group, J.C. Mukherjee popularly called "Dada" for his age, was a great writer contributing a weekly column *'London Letter'* for *The London Opinion* since 1905. But it was the alchemy of Savarkar's influence that he changed his earlier pacifist mode into a highly charged revolutionary writing. Gyan Chand Verma, a law student, later Secretary of the *Free India Society,* was a tireless worker, of strong will and enormous energy, and totally devoted to the nationalist cause. Another prominent member of this circle, Sardarsingh Revabhai Rana came from a princely family of Saurashtra. Savarkar's elder by five years, a graduate from Bombay University and called to bar in London, he went over to France to continue his revolutionary activities there. He financed *The Abhinav Bharat,* a Savarkar publication, and got the second edition of *The Indian War of Independence 1857* published in this magazine. Another colourful personality of this group was Harnam Singh, a 21 year old Sikh, who travelled to London in the same ship with Savarkar; more on him later. But the most radiant and glittering star of this galaxy was Madam Bhikaji Rustom K.R. Cama, leader of the India nationalists in Paris, was called the "Mother of the Indian Revolution", the moving spirit behind the revolutionary activities in Paris, who later came to be called the "Indian Joan of Arc". Born on 24 September 1861, she was a frontline fighter for Savarkar's society. Lecturing on Indian politics at London's Hyde Park, disseminating revolutionary literature, she inspired many an Indian to join the freedom struggle, while she published *Bande Mataram,* a paper with wide circulation in the USA. There were many other great patriots working in this group, from "the house of mystery" alias "the house of terror" which was the command headquarters of revolutionary activities.

There was a historic meeting between Gandhiji and Savarkar in London in 1906, when Gandhiji left Johannesburg to visit London to assess for himself the activities of these young Indian revolutionaries. Here is a face-off between two diametrically opposite ideologies both aimed to achieve India's freedom. A London correspondent described this meeting of Mr. Gandhi "with his intellectual face, a low but intense voice and dedication to his cause with Savarkar, a multi-faceted genius – journalist, historian, thinker, poet and critic, a fiery orator and inspired patriot". Tapan Ghosh describing Savarkar's "irresistible impact" said, "The effect of his gospel was so comprehensive and so general in its sweep that it was difficult, rather impossible to assess his personal ability for the effect Savarkarism happened to produce on a certain individual, or a group of individuals." M.P.T. Acharya once said of "Savarkar" that his personal charm and a mere handshake could transform even strong personalities like Hardayal and V.B.S. Aiyar and make them give out their best. David Garnett, a notable writer, an admirer of Hinduism and a friend to the revolutionaries, mentioned in his autobiographical work *The Golden Echo,* Savarkar's eloquence and his appearance as "small, slight in built, with broad cheekbones, sensitive refined mouth and an extremely pale skin, which was almost as pale as ivory on the forehead and cheekbones but darker in the hollows."

Savarkar's magnum opus *The Indian War of Independence* was secretly printed a few months later. Deeply inspired by the two great Italian fighters for liberation, G. Mazzini (1805-72), and G. Garibaldi (1807-82), Savarkar also translated into Marathi, Mazzini's autobiography, which broke all sale records. As to his Italian heroes, the liberation of his country was to Savarkar a matter of deep religious faith, establishing an indivisibility between politics and religion. Later

Savarkar was to write, "Politics and religion are inter-dependent". As religion teaches tolerance but not surrender, similarly politics means freedom and not subservience. It is this freedom, which has been hailed even in the Bible and sung by all poets. "Better to rule in Hell than serve in Heaven." The voracious reader and writer that he was, Savarkar sought the help of Harnam Singh, Bhai Parmanand and Madan Lal Dhingra to learn Gurumukhi to be able to read classics such as *'Adigranth'*, *'Panth Prakash'*, *'Surya Prakash'*, *'Vichitra Natak'*. He thereafter issued a pamphlet *Khalsa* in Gurumukhi, that roused the feelings of Sikh soldiers of the Indian Army. He also wrote the history of Sikhs, started in 1907 in England and completed in Paris in 1910. The British intelligence got wise to this publication and spread out a dragnet to confiscate this book. To save it from falling into British hands the book was consigned to the sea. To the parapsychologists it would be an interesting exercise to study the phenomenon of Garibaldi, Mazzini and Savarkar as a case of reincarnation or *'Punarjanma'* according to Hindu belief. Savarkar's association with places like Bhagur, his birth place, Nasik, Poona, Ratnagiri and Bombay, where he was born, educated, confined and died respectively are sacred shrines and heritage sites for the revolutionary tribe of India.

On 1 May, 1907, the British Government decided to celebrate a "Special Thanks Giving Day" to commemorate their ruthless suppression of the Indian mutiny of 1857. The Indian students of Oxford and Cambridge deliberately pinned on their coat lapels an insignia carrying the word "Honour to the martyrs of 1857". Madan Lal Dhingra, an engineering student, exhibited this badge as a "college colour" despite angry exchanges with his college mates and scuffles with the Bobbies. Harnam Singh even clashed with his professor, who asked him to remove the badge with the following words, "One who dies fighting for his motherland is always a martyr, everywhere in the world. I do not know what is he in your country. While a murderer is he ..." He was not allowed to complete the sentence. Dr. Richard Congreve, an Honorary Fellow of Wadham College, Oxford, and the founder of the Positivist community in London, strongly protested against the Thanks Giving Order, took up the Indian cause, and challenged the contention of the English Victory, saying that the narration of historical facts had completely warped the real essence of the Indian mutiny. He ended his declamation by the following words:

"Men must reap the things they sow;
Force from force must ever flow,
Or worse..."

To those who still believed in the theory of "a superior race", Richard Congreve appealed to ponder over what Edmund Burke had to say on India. "This multitude of men does not consist of an abject and barbarous populace, much less of gangs of savages like Guaranties and Chiquitas, who wander on waste borders of Amazon or the Plate; but a people for ages civilized and cultivated; cultivated by all the arts of polished life, whilst we were yet in woods. There have been princes once of great dignity, authority and opulence. There are to be found chiefs of tribes and nations. There is to be found an ancient venerable priesthood the repository of their laws, learning and history, the guides of the people whilst living their consolation in death; in nobility of great antiquity and renown; a multitude of cities that exceeds in population and trade those of the first class in Europe; merchants and bankers, individuals, houses of whom have once vied in capital with the Bank of England, whose credit has often supported a tottering state and preserved their government in the midst of war and desolation; millions of ingenious manufacturers and mechanics; millions of the more diligent, and the least intelligent tillers of the earth. There are to be found almost all the religions professed by men, the Brahminical, the Muselman, the Eastern and Western Christian."

As the fortunes of Free India Society rose, on 23 February, 1907, Shyamji, with a donation of Rs.10,000/-during the annual meeting of the Indian Home Rule Society in London, announced the establishment of an organization of political missionaries in India. He sought the advice of Bal, Pal and Lal (Balgangadhar Tilak, Bipin Chandra Pal and Lala Lajpat Rai) who promptly endorsed the project and their opinions were published as an article in the May issue of the *Indian Sociologists* titled "A stunning appeal", "a highly distinguished Master of Arts at an Indian University... now fitting himself for the duties of a political missionary by studying history and politics and by acquiring collateral culture in Europe". He was none other than Lala Hardayal, who, in the words of Lala Lajpat Rai "came to Oxford to believe that the English were undermining Hindu character; that their educational policy and methods had been designed to destroy Hinduism and to perpetuate the political bondage of the Hindu by destroying their social consciousness and their national individuality." Lala Hardayal added the might of his pen in the following words: "the ideal of a free and united India has been intellectually appreciated by a large majority of our countrymen. But the moral force which is necessary for embodying it in actual movements and institutions is wanting .... What sort of men do we want for this Society of Political Missionaries? ...They should love nothing more than the cause. It should be, for them in the place of father, mother, brother and friend. They should reject the counsels of timid prudence, anathematized by Burke, even if they come from the nearest and the dearest relatives. They should undertake the task in a religious spirit; earnestness and self-denial should be their guiding principles. They should grieve like Commander Hirose of Japan, that they have only one life to give to their country. If such men appeal to the downtrodden masses of India, they would conquer the hearts of the multitude of our people, who pay sincere homage to genuine character, but are not moved by mere rhetoric..."

The plan being completed, now was the time for execution. The first step was to learn the art of bomb making. After some extensive collection of information from everywhere and trials, a bomb manual was prepared by Harish Chandra Das and Senapati Bapat and was widely circulated. One copy was even given to Bal Gangadhar Tilak. Das was a voracious reader and a disciple of Swami Vivekanand, jovial in nature and fond of music and folk songs. So was Paramanandji, his collaborator in the bomb manual, who on hearing the death sentence pronounced on him burst into one of Ghalib's ghazal.

As Shyamji's revolutionary activities drew the attention of British authorities, he was forced to flee London to France. Madam Cama already stationed at Paris and known by now, as the "Mother of Indian Revolutionaries and the Indian "Joan of Arc" was pursuing her Paris activities as assiduously as Savarkar and Shyamji in London. She made a moving appeal to Indians at home and abroad in such inspiring words: "I was shocked to hear that one of us, Mr. Lajpat Rai, a true patriot, was snatched away from his hearth and home and become a prisoner. Do not depend upon the promises of foreign rulers, because they are in India not for the purpose of aiding you but they are there for fleecing you... Youths of India, you stand between the past and the future, work up for the cause and the principles, though it may not be our destiny to reach the promised land, but only to hail it in dying and from far off. Remember, FREEDOM IS A CONQUEST AND NEVER A BEQUEST. Open your eyes, I beseech you to open your eyes! Listen to the cry of the millions eager to advance. Glory be to those brave men, who have put their all, their very life, on the altar of Motherland" and she concluded by saying "May Indians unite and rise to the occasion through the inspiration of VANDE MATARAM."

In his never ending campaign to organize and speed up foreign propaganda, Savarkar never lost a chance to use any public forum of consequence. He took part in the International Socialist Congress at Stuttgart, Germany on 22 August, 1907, attended among others, by 123 British delegates sponsored by H.M. Hyndman of the Socialist Democratic Federation, who himself presented his celeberated report *The Ruin of India by The British Rule*. It was here that Madam Cama supported by delegates from Germany and France passed a resolution on Indian freedom and unfurled a "Flag of Free India". The flag had three horizontal stripes of equal width in red, white and blue colour. Other sources point out that the colours from top were green, sacred for Muslims, the centre saffron, sacred for Buddhists and Sikhs and the lower stripe Hindu red with "Vande Mataram" in Sanskrit script embroidered in gold. Unfurling the Indian flag, Madam Cama made a historic speech whose ending stirred the conscience of the world. And as she held it in her hand she uttered the following words: "this flag is of India's independence. Behold, it is born; it is already sanctified by the blood of martyred Indian youth; I call upon you, gentlemen, to rise and salute the flag of Indian independence. In the name of this flag I appeal to lovers of freedom all over the world to cooperate with this flag in freeing one-fifth of the human race."

While all this was happening Savarkar laboured and made out his programme for the liberation of the motherland encapsulating the following main points:

- Teaching of Swadeshi, boycott of foreign goods and national training.
- Acquisition of weapons from the neighbouring countries and smuggling them to India.
- Operating small factories, to manufacture arms and ammunition.
- Use of guerrilla tactics, where possible carrying the message of freedom into Indian Armed Forces, and inciting them to revolt at the opportune moment.

Dr. D. Keer in his book *Savarkar and His Times* describes the momentous events of the year 1908 when India saw a series of upheavals and stirring. "A new spirit was rising everywhere. The country was at the dawn of a new epoch. It was a time of violent repression, profound discontent and fierce antagonism. New hopes, new desires, new measures and new thoughts were in the air. Love of freedom, hatred of slavery and hope for a great future captivated the young and the old alike. Poets and patriots blossomed forth. Youth vied with one another in making the purest and greatest sacrifices on the altar of freedom. Even revellers left their revelry and revolted. India drifted from the policy of petition to the policy of pressure under Tilak and from the politics of pressure to the potency of power under Savarkar". Senapati Bapat, another remarkable revolutionary in collaboration with his Bengali patriots such as Birendranath Ghosh, Profulla Chakarborti and Narendra Gosain, threw a bomb on 30 April, 1908, at Kingsford, the Chief Presidency Magistrate of Alipore, notorious for his floggings of freedom fighters during the Bengal partition. Khudi Ram Bose, sentenced to death, gladly embraced the gallows on the 11 August with the "Geeta" in his hands. Another bomb exploded at Grey Street, Calcutta on 15th May followed by four more explosions around the station and at railway carriages. Swami Vivekanand's brother Bhupendera Nath Dutt, editor of *Jugantar,* Aurobindo Ghosh, editor of *Bande Mataram,* Bhaskar Vishnu Phadke, editor of *Vihari* (Bombay), Pritvigeer Harigeer, editor of *Harikishore* (Yeotmal), Shivrampant Pranjpe, editor of *Kal* (Poona), and above all, Lokmanya Bal Gangadhar Tilak, editor of *Kesri* and Savarkar's hero, wielded the weapon of their pen. Tilak's crime was to write an article on Khudiram in the *Kesri* on June 22, and he was sentenced to transportation for six years to the Mandalay jail in Burma, just on the eve of his 51th birthday. *Manchester Guardian* on hearing the news of Tilak's sentence wrote: "The nature of the sentence passed upon Mr. Tilak will be interpreted throughout India as a proof that the Government had resolved by hook or by crook to remove him from their path. He has been condemned on his "general record" – which being interpreted means that he has been punished because he can and does stir up higher things and emotions of a multitude that understands him."

There was another anniversary of the Indian National Uprising of 1857 on 10th May, 1908, at India House organized by Madam Cama where Savarkar gave out his vision in the following words:

"O' Martyrs
The battle of freedom once begun
And handed down from sire to son.
Though often lost is ever won..." and ends by saying, "No, by Hindustan, No." "The historical continuity of the Indian nation is not cut off. The War begun on the 10th of May 1857 is not over on the 10th of May 1908, nor shall it ever cease till a 10th of May to come sees the destiny accomplished, sees the beautiful India crowned, either with the lustre of victory or with the halo of Martyrdom. It was on this day that the war cry *Maro Firungee Ko* was raised by the throats of thousands. The Sepoys of Meerut, having risen in a terrible uprising, marched down to Delhi, saw the waters of Jamuna glittering in the sunshine, caught one of those historical moments which closes a past epoch to introduce a new one, and had found, in a moment, a leader, a flag, and a cause, and converted the mutiny into a national and a religious war. You may hang me today, you may hang such as me every day, but thousands will still rise in my place – your object will never be gained. Indians, these words must be fulfilled. Your blood, O' Martyrs! shall be avenged."

This is the time when Savarkar was engaged in writing his famous book *Indian War of Independence of 1857* searching every possible source–history, diaries, travelogues, on the spot accounts, army dispatches, eyewitness records, letters, treaties, confidential documents of friendship, records of war, of surrender, maps, photographs and clippings of contemporary papers, specially the trials, punishments and parliament proceedings. At the end of the year he had consulted 1500 references for his would be magnum opus. Originally written in Marathi in 1908, when Savarkar was just 24 years, branded as explosive and treasonous, the book was sought after by the British authorities for confiscation and surprise raids were conducted on some prominent printing presses of Maharashtra. The book was also printed in Germany, and an English translation printed in Holland was smuggled into India in thousands by ingenious devices. The '*Indian War of Independence of 1857*' today stands as a monument to Savarkar's patriotic fervour and literary genius. There were many English editions to follow, the fifth one in the hands of the Indian National Army (INA) and the last sixth edition was published as a challenge to the ban on the book. The book became the Bible of Indian revolutionaries and paid our national debt to the memory of the warriors of 1857. Savarkar intended the book not only to highlight the annals of the past, but also to act as a source of inspiration and guide to the future struggle of independence. Vidya Sagar Anand described the reactions of the British authorities in England and India as follows: "*The Indian War of Independence* stood for nearly half a century as the Indian revolutionary's handbook or gospel. It is almost impossible to exaggerate the wide and profound influence exercised by its militant propaganda for future Indian freedom. It is scarcely surprising that the book was banned throughout India; and even in that sanctuary of liberal culture – the British Museum Library, where Karl Marx wrote *Das Kapital*." The book was suppressed from the General Catalogue and not until India's independence, in 1947, was it included, a singular compliment to be paid by the British both to Savarkar and the potency of his revolutionary influence, particularly, when we consider that even in the hey-day of the Russian revolution, the works of Marx were never similarly banned.

On 1 July, 1909, young Madan Lal Dhingra, a co-revolutionary with Savarkar shot dead Sir Curzon Wylle and the British Press flashed the news stating that the Indian student has been arrested. He was tried at Old Bailey and sentenced to death on 23 July to be executed on 17 August. Before Dhingra climbed the gallows he threw a challenge, which read as follows : "I admit, the other day I attempted to shed English blood as a humble revenge for the inhuman hangings and deportations of patriotic Indian youths. In this attempt I have consulted none but my own conscience; I have conspired with none but my own duty. I believe that a nation held in bondage with the help of foreign bayonets is in a perpetual state of war. Since open battle is rendered impossible to a disarmed race, I attacked by surprise; since guns were denied to me, I drew forth my pistol and fired. As a Hindu, I feel that a wrong done to my country is an insult to God. Poor in health and intellect, a son like myself has nothing else to offer to the Mother but his own blood, and so I have sacrificed the same on her altar. Her cause is the cause of Shri Rama. Her services are the services of Shri Krishna. This War of Independence will continue between India and England so long as the Hindu and the English races last, if this present unnatural relation does not cease. The only lesson required in India at present is to learn how to die and the only way to teach it is by dying ourselves. Therefore, I die and glory in my martyrdom. My only prayer to God is: may I be reborn of the same Mother nay may I re-die in the same sacred cause till the cause is successful and she stands free for the good of humanity and the glory of God. VANDE MATARAM"

Dhingra embraced the gallows singing :

Yeh na thi hamari kismat ke visale yaar hota
Agar aur jeete rahte, yahi intizaar hota

(Alas! I was not destined to see my beloved (freedom). And had I lived more, I would have still waited for my beloved (motherland) all the more.) Before he could finish another voice joined him. This was Bhai Parmanand, who could recite *Shlokas* of *'Geeta'* under the infernal conditions of his incarceration in the Andamans. Savarkar's philosophy of revolution founded on reason, action, and will was the quintessence of the teachings of Lord Rama and Krishna, Chandragupta Maurya, Chanakaya, Mazzini and Garibaldi and finally President Thomas Massaryk, who believed that "revolution is a moral act when it is the only means left for the defence of Liberty and Justice." To Herbert Spencer, "Peaceful evolution has meaning and sense, peaceful revolution has none."

Dhingra's martyrdom sent tremors far and wide. His statement was widely acclaimed all over England and Winston Churchill even compared him with "Plutarch's immortal heroes", but Gandhiji described it as "mere childish". Castigating Savarkar, he said, "those who instigated him to do this act will be called to account in God's court and are also guilty in the eyes of the world and deserve to be punished." But a Britisher W.S. Blunt observed that if there were five hundred Indians like Dhingra, India would be free. Gandhiji persisted. Contradicting Blunt's observation, Gandhiji prophesied: "I must say that those who believe and argue that such murders may do good to India are ignorant men indeed. No act of treachery can ever profit a nation." Note that what was even to the greatest British diplomat, Churchill, "a fine example of patriotism", was to Gandhi, the Indian leader, "an act of treachery". Gandhiji continued: "Should the Britishers leave in consequence of such murderous acts, who will rule in their place? The only answer is the murderers. Who will then be happy? I am afraid some Indians will commend the murder. I believe, they will be guilty of a human sin. India can gain nothing from the rule of murderers

– no matter they are black or white." Gandhiji had a habit of calling all revolutionaries, murderers. If the assassin happened to be a Muslim he became a brother, but the assassins of British officers, Khudi Ram Bose, Dhingra, Kanhare, Bhagat Singh and Udham Singh were cowards, sinners and at best "misguided patriots." Dhingra's last wish was to be reborn in India and die again in consonance with the dictum that "he who will seek to save it shall lose it'. He recalled the saying, "Revolution is a moral act when it is the only means left for the defence of Liberty and Justice." Emil Herfferick, a German patriot involved in the Indian movement of Independence, had observed: "The path of freedom for India was long and arduous, and the end—which brought freedom and partition of India—seems as tragic as the destiny of Savarkar himself. For, it will be recalled, although he played a major role in the liberation, when the goal had been achieved, he was deprived of his own freedom on the grounds of complicity in the death of Gandhi." And to quote Anand, "Fearful of Savarkar's great popularity, Nehru's government did not stop at merely detaining him but proceeded to implicate him in Gandhi's murder. It is impossible to conceive of a more heinous crime against patriotism than this".

Nehru went one step further. He was reported to have torn non-violently, the "Release Savarkar Memorandum" to pieces. And all this happened before Savarkar had joined the Hindu Mahasabha as a political party in opposition to the Congress. Coming events cast their shadows before. Let history record this fact which is stranger than fiction. After Savarkar's release, in a function in 1937, Gandhiji introduced him. Later, Savarkar gave out a small piece of his glimpse: "Hindus are the heart of Hindustan. Nevertheless, just as the beauty of the rainbow is not impaired but enhanced by its varied hues, so also Hindustan will look all the more beautiful across the sky of future by assimilating all the best from the Muslim, Parsee, Jewish and other civilizations." Asaf Ali, who was also there later described Savarkar "fragile as an anaemic girl, restless as a mountain torrent, and keen as the edge of a torpedo blade. Nor is it an exaggeration to say Savarkar is one of the few really effective speakers I have known and heard, and there is hardly an orator of the first rank either here or in England whom I have not had the privilege of hearing excepting Mr. Eardly Norton, of whom I have read so much that I should be almost reluctant to avail myself of the opportunity of hearing him speak lest I should be disappointed."

On 22 December, 1909, Savarkar heard that a 16 year old boy Anand Kanhare, a Chitapovan Brahmin of Nasik shot dead the district magistrate of Nasik in a theatre and the murder was linked to Savarkar because of his old association with the Chitapovan brothers. The murder weapon, a 21 Browning pistol was sent by Savarkar through a courier. English newspapers screamed punishment for Savarkar, who by now had become synonymous with sedition and England's public enemy Number One, to be crushed at any cost, to bury the very legend of Savarkar. As things became hot in London, Savarkar had to cross over the channel to reach Paris. There he was arrested from the ship by the Marseillies police under a warrant granted by Bow Street Court London, on 22 February, 1910, on five charges of sedition, including one of conspiracy against His Majesty the King of Britain. Savarkar, a chained prisoner, arrived at the Victoria Station, London on 13 March, 1910. The court convicted him and directed that he be sent back to India on 12 May, 1910, to stand trial.

Many rescue plans were prepared by his friends but none could succeed against the strict security cordon. Locked at Bristol gaol, Savarkar awaited his fate, still hoping for a miracle. Hand-cuffed and heavily guarded Savarkar sailed off from London on Orient Liner "S.S. Maurya" used for carrying His Majesty's mail. Before the ship could touch Marseillies on the 7th evening of his journey, Savarkar decided to escape. The next morning on July 8, he dodged his two police guards, and entered the toilet and threw away his dressing gown. Thinly built as he was, he squeezed himself through the porthole, virtually naked and shivering and dived into the sea. Chased by two marine guards he outpaced them and reached the steep side, off the harbour and clambered up exhausted and cold. As he ran, the guards cried 'thief' and raised a public alarm as the French Police closed in on him. This derring do astonished the onlookers. There were many versions to this daring escape, stranger than fiction or drama. A semi-nude Indian on French soil challenging the might of the British empire to escape. Myths were woven round this episode and Savarkar became a hero overnight, being compared to Napoleon Bonaparte at Elba. Despite the International Law on grant of asylum to a political fugitive, the French Government played foul. Savarkar continued his journey to India upto Aden where he was transferred from "S.S. Maurya" to "S.S. Sasti" and continued to stay in a cage like cabin with only four feet space to sit or stand, heavily guarded from outside. The ship reached Bombay on 22 July, 1910. Handcuffed, bilboed and under an armed guard, he was lodged in Yarvada jail. He stood three trials; every rule in the law book was twisted and natural justice mutilated to punish this man; special provisions were used; a special tribunal of three British judges tried him, while three British prosecutors bayed for his blood. There were four defence counsels, three Indian and one Christian. For this mockery of a trial which began on 15 September, 1910, Savarkar was moved from Yarvada jail to Dongri as 50 armed policeman guarded the Bombay High Court. All defence objections were overruled. On 23 December, 1910, the day of the Saturn, the sentence was pronounced 'transportation for life and confiscation of all property'. The British Government had a paralytic fright of Savarkar; what if he returns again after 25 years? So another trial took place and the special tribunal sentenced the same 'Special Savarkar' the same punishment; another transportation for life.' Keer recorded the general reaction to this unparalleled verdict:-

Two transportations! Unsurpassable, unheard of! Release after half century? A unique record and a landmark in the political history of the world! It is significant that the judgments of these famous trials have not been reported in the law reports. Was Savarkar shocked at the savage sentences passed upon him? Not, in the least. He had entered the sacrificial conflagration with an iron will and a divine devotion. Nothing conquered his invincible spirit, for nature had given him the stout heart of his age that could not be crushed by adversity or peril. He felt that a cause for which Nanasahib died, Tatya Tope fell and the glorious Maharani Laxmi Bai gave her life on the battlefield was worth dying for. The punishment inflicted upon Savarkar was titanic, but his indomitable spirit was an iceberg. He was aged twenty-seven years, eight months and three days when government laid him in his veritable watery grave. India and the world shook to its foundations. Fifty-year sentence! But Savarkar was unfazed, oozing confidence. When one cussed British jailer asked him, "Do you think you will survive these 50 years of imprisonment and return alive?" Savarkar shot back, "and do you think that this barbaric and brutish British rule will stay in India for 50 years?" Prophetic words! Well before the date for the completion of 50 years of sentence the British left India in 1947! And Savarkar lived upto 1961 to see his motherland liberated, a decade before his term could end.

Savarkar endured an exile of 26 years, even though he was actually sentenced for 50 years with the successive sentences of 25 years each. He spent 11 years of his exile in the Andamans undergoing rigorous punishment – "more hellish than hell". His wife Yamunabai, like Sita, suffered the separation for her husband for 20 years. (1906 to 1926). Married in 1901, she was left alone in 1906, knowing conjugal happiness only for five years till she was reunited with her husband when the latter was interned in Ratnagiri. During their ten years of stay together in the same Cellular Jail (1911-1921), they met only two or three times. Yamunabai wept and waited for 10 years to meet her husband suffering extreme poverty, loneliness, discord and even insanity and died just a few days before she was permitted to meet her husband in the Andaman Cellular Jail. In the entire history of India's struggle for independence, there is not one example of such heroism, sacrifice and suffering. Savarkar, the patriot, will endure forever.

A true Hindu, Gandhiji was a great devotee and follower of Rama, his *'Maryadapurushottam'* and *'Adarsh Purush'*, who killed Ravan the epitome of evil. But when Savarkar and his followers planned to kill the British tyrants, such as Curzon Wylle, Jackson Rain, Saunders and O Dwyer, he and his comrades Dhingra, Kanhare, Bhagat Singh, Udham Singh etc., were condemned by Gandhiji. With all their faults, the British, though they wished to liquidate "Savarkar the patriot", they had nothing but admiration for his genius as a poet, scholar and historian. But his own country has erased from its history the literary genius of this very revolutionary. After his return from exile, instead of being welcomed as a hero like Nelson Mandela, who spent even less number of years in the prison, Savarkar received not adulation or expression of gratefulness from his country but suspicion, criticism, neglect, humiliation, torture, trials, and utter indifference. Gandhiji speaking of Savarkar once mentioned: 'I am very proud to have the honour of sitting by the side of Savarkar' and that 'India would reap the fruits of Savarkar's sacrifices and patriotism.' India did reap the fruits but Savarkar was not destined to taste them. Besides being sentenced to two life sentences totaling 50 years he also suffered the loss of his entire property, his complete works banned and he was released a long time after independence!

On 18 July, 1935, a committee called Savarkar's Restrictions Removal Committee was set up in Bombay under the chairmanship of Doctor M.B. Valkar in response to over one million signatures for the release of Savarkar, who had already suffered 25 years of imprisonment. When approached for his recommendation, Gandhiji prevaricated, feigning ignorance of such a move. When reminded that he had met him in London and Ratnagiri Jail, he further queried! Savarkar seemed to have been an anathema to Gandhiji—the high priest of non-violence. This antipathy was further confirmed when on his release Savarkar was felicitated by Nehru, Subhas and Ambedkar; Gandhiji preferred silence (maun). A chained titan breaking his fetters had burst forth on the national scene. Was Gandhiji afraid of losing his pre-eminence? Even great men have their Achilles heel. Nehru, his disciple, even outdid his master. In Keer's words, "Savarkar on his Vijayadashmi's speech talked of Rama and Ramrajya but did not forget to state that the consummation of Navratri is the slaying of the demon Ravan on the tenth day".

Asaf Ali, who listened to Savarkar's speech in rapt attention, had this to say…

"The tremendous impact of this speech could be assessed by a remark by Padmanabhan in his biography of V.V.S. Aiyer. "The India House inmates felt that if Gandhiji was exposed to a few more speeches of Savarkar he would have given up his Ahimsa and joined him."

While Gandhiji and Nehru went to study in England not on academic merit, but being sons of affluent parents, the group of revolutionaries, each one of them, went on a merit scholarship. These great souls were no ordinary homegrown country cousins but were, all without exception, men of great learning who had obtained degrees from prestigious universities in England and America and would have received great academic honour, if they had not sacrificed their careers and comforts for the motherland. Everyone of them was a great scholar, and academician who could put to shame most of the leaders of the Congress and also other national parties by sheer intellectual brilliance and sweep of their thought. Some of them like Savarkar were great poets of substance. These great sons of Mother India were household names in the 20s and 30s of the last century. How many young minds in the present generation remember them? The life and times of these great revolutionaries are a saga of unending courage, patriotism and sacrifices that should be a compulsory reading for our youth. Lest we forget.

In a scurrilous article, "Celebrating Hindu Rashtra" in *The Indian Express,* an English daily, Mr. Mani Shankar Aiyer tried his best not only to trivialize Savarkar, but viciously by innuendoes, half-truths and quotes out of context, denigrate the greatest freedom fighter that the country has known. Savarkar's fault; he did not subscribe to the Congress ideology of non-violence, read 'comfortable jail terms with nourishing food available to political prisoners'. The first man at present to vilify Savarkar, Mr. Aiyer has got his Cambridge or whatever University he attended, background all mixed up with his love for Muslims and a visceral hatred for Hindus and Hinduism. Instead of wasting words in rebutting him on ideological grounds post-Gujarat, which state he decries as the epicentre of pogrom, we shall confine our critique to some substantive points on facts raised by him. That Savarkar asked for mercy is the biggest Goebbelean lie. He, in the spirit of Shivaji, was adept in foiling his captors to engineer an escape, as he did at Marseilles. As a true revolutionary, he had a few tricks up his sleeve, like feigning death to put his pursuers off his spoor. The so-called mercy petition, wrongly quoted, was merely a ploy for escape. Being a dangerous prisoner, the British authorities wanted to take no chances with Savarkar and allow another escape. Hence the extra guards and handcuffs. This is precisely what Savarkar wanted to achieve, slackness in his guards and relaxation of rules so that he could affect an escape, while pleading loyalty to the British and lulling them into a false sense of complacency. The Home Member of the Governor General's Council, Sir Reginald H. Craddock, after inspecting the Penal settlement, in October/ November 1913, had observed, "In the case of Savarkar, it is quite impossible to give him any liberty here, and I think he would escape from any Indian jail. So important a leader is he that the European section of the Indian anarchists would plot for his escape which would before long be organized. If he were allowed outside the Cellular Jail in the Andamans, his escape would be certain. His friends could easily charter a steamer to lie off one of the islands and a little money distributed locally would do the rest" (P.221, *Penal Settlement in Andamans*, by R.C. Mazumdar, Publications Division, GOI-1975).

Aiyer at least could not deny the facts of his torture, his prison life at the Andamans and the life sentence of 25 years redoubled. Aiyer also concedes that Savarkar was a dangerious prisoner and was strictly guarded, but he castigates Savarkar for his book, *Hindutva*, written in 1924. Does Mr. Aiyer know how the book was written in a cell, 8 feet by 8 feet with no writing material and no books to consult, as Nehru had for his *Discovery of India;* a library, a garden to walk in, a comfortable room to live in and good food? If he had not been a revolutionary, Savarkar's muse or poesy alone would have put him among the world's greatest poets. And how did he write his verse confined in a cell? He had no paper to write on, except the bare walls of his cell crowding in on him. He had no pen or ink. He used his nails, thorns or pebbles to scratch his poetry. Between physical torture and great mental anguish, he used the infernal Bastille where he had to spend two life terms, as his retreat to complete some of the best parts of his vast poetic literature. After scratching the lines on the walls, he used to memorize them and wipe the surface clean to write new lines of his poetry. During these long years (1911-21), before he was brought to Ratnagiri jail, he had written and memorized 6,000 lines of his finest poetry that he finally put to paper at Ratnagiri. Is there any such example in the entire literary world, of poetry being written under such conditions? How much more can the flesh suffer and the heart endure? No wonder the legend of Savarkar refuses to die!

It seems Aiyer even grudges Savarkar his ripe old age of 81. He lived so long because he was physically and mentally tough, a fast swimmer who could swim miles in the sea, and a man with an iron will. Perhaps Aiyer does not know that Savarkar when young challenged an Englishman, a great swimmer himself, to take any length of handicap and having swam that distance wave to Savarkar to start. This he did incredulously after about half a mile. Savarkar overtook him in no time and swam past. Besides his physical prowess, his other literary achievements have been totally lost on Mr. Aiyer just because he differed from Gandhi and the Congress. This scriptwriter of Congress leaders from Rajiv Gandhi to Sonia Gandhi may write any amount of polemics or speeches but his knowledge of facts and conclusions are jejune and juvenile. He should realize that Mr. Vasant Sathe, Minister for Information and Broadcasting in Indira Gandhi's government, had mooted similar proposals to what Mr. L.K. Advani did. Even Mrs. Gandhi had termed Savarkar as 'one of the greatest patriots of India.' To prove one's loyalty to a family, one need not stoop so low. It is only such Congress pygmies who will attempt to show a candle to the sun. Savarkar needs no certificates from the likes of Aiyer to prove his greatness. History has judged him like so many western authors and Indian luminaries did. Mr. Aiyer grudgingly accepts some facts about Savarkar like his jail term and escape attempt at Marseillies, but also mentions Godse's visit to him. Was it a crime to meet an Indian, who by all means, had till then been a great patriot? In any case, Savarkar was acquitted of the charge of the conspiracy of assassination of Gandhi by judge Atma Charan. Even Nehru fault-footed on this score when after the inquiry ordered by Sardar Patel, the R.S.S. and Savarkar were found not guilty of any wrongdoing. Where does it place Mr. Aiyer? A propagandist after the event? We need not waste any further space on the merits or otherwise of a Hindu Rashtra.

If anything, the act of Mr. L.K. Advani's dedication of the airport at Port Blair to the nation after Veer Savarkar is a rectification of a half-century of history's shame. Long after the breed of pseudo-secularist pen-pushers is consigned to the dustbin of contemporary news, leave alone history, the legend of Savarkar shall endure. To refresh memory, Savarkar in 1907, when just 24 years old had undertaken the humongous task of writing his famous work, '*Indian War of Independence*' on the day of commemoration of fifty years of this momentous event in the history of India. A bestseller of the times, the book was immediately proscribed. As a teenager at Karachi, Mr. Advani was given the book for Rs. 27, a large sum those days, by his friend from a bookshop in Lahore that sold proscribed books. Mr. Advani was so moved on reading this book that when he came to India after partition, the one place he wished to visit first was 'Savarkar Sadan' in Bombay. The great hero left an indelible stamp not only on young Advani, but also on a Congress stalwart, Mr. Vasant Sathe, (no arm chair patriot) who had taken an active part in the Quit India movement at the tender age of 17 and later became a Lok Sabha member from Wardha constituency. On taking over as Minister for I&B in 1980, he ordered a documentary film to be made on this great patriot. When Indira Gandhi was the Prime Minister, she observed *'Amrit Mahottsva'* to celebrate the 75th birthday of Savarkar. Subsequently, a postal stamp was also issued in 1970. In 1980, Mrs.

Gandhi donated Rs.11000 to Savarkar Nyas Trust. On 4 May, 2002, at 4pm Savarkar was remembered at Port Blair. It was left to Mr. Advani of the BJP-led coalition to reinstate this great Hindu hero in the pantheon of the greatest of the greats. The unveiling of the portrait of Savarkar on 26 February, 2003, in the Central Hall of the Parliament was not without its irony. The opposition led by the Congress who had accepted the proposal on 6 December, 2002, suddenly made a U-turn and staged a walk out in protest against honouring what they called a supporter of the two-nation theory, an ideologue of the Hindu Rashtra, a supplicant for mercy from the British, and accused of Gandhi's assassination. The charges deserve to be condemned with the contempt they deserve. Ranjit Savarkar, the grandson of Savarkar's younger brother Narayan Savarkar, admonished a rebuke. Said he, "I doubt whether Sonia Gandhi ever heard the name before", her memory of India being limited to the date of her marriage to the son of India's Prime Minister. The then speaker, Mr. Manohar Joshi, invited Ranjit's parents to New Delhi. Rubbishing the mercy petition canard as ridiculous, he counter-questioned: "Who's talking about this? Ram Manohar Lohia brought a resolution in Parliament to pay homage to Savarkar. Indira Gandhi had said Savarkar's name is synonymous with nationalism, sacrifice and courage. But now her daughter-in-law terms him an anti-national." He called the Congress bluff by demanding suo moto action by the Supreme Court against those who accused Savarkar for Gandhi's assassination saying that since the court had already acquitted him, to raise the issue now would amount to a contempt of the judiciary. And then he fumed, "How can people who do not know the first thing about the Independence movement talk in such an irresponsible manner and betray the trust of the country?" Finally brandishing a photograph of a plaque installed in 1985 by the Greater London Council in commemoration of Savarkar as "an Indian patriot and philosopher", he questioned that if the British could do it, why not our own Parliament? The walk out of the secularist brigade amounts to political distortion of history. Ideological plurality is the lifeblood of a democracy. Savarkar is too big to need any certificate of patriotism from those who collaborated with the British during our struggle for Independence or those who defy their own political idols, nor from those fair weather Congress leaders who wish to hijack the credit of the freedom movement entirely on the basis of free tickets obtained from a dynasty whose last two generations never saw the in side of a jail. The story of our revolutionaries in the freedom struggle shall remain our valued possession and a priceless heritage in the days to come.

Menachim Begin described the spirit that fired the souls of the Jewish freedom fighters in the following manner: "They went to concentration camps, were thrown into dark cellars, starved, beaten, and maligned yet not one ever broke his solemn undertaking not to retaliate on his tormentors. I saw them in their anguish and I was tormented with them. But I also saw them in their greatness and I was proud of them. Discipline? What is military discipline, discipline in action, compared with this discipline of inaction, when your whole soul cries out for retaliation and retribution? A human "order" would have been of no avail here. The order came from "somewhere", from the depths of Jewish history; and it was obeyed. We were spared the catastrophe of catastrophes. And before many months went by the revolt embraced the whole people. The persecutors and persecuted of yesterday went out to battle together, to a common battle for our people and our country..." Indian revolutionaries were no different, particularly those, who were incarcerated for long prison terms. Each one of them is a shining star in this galaxy of revolutionaries.

It is worthwhile remembering the following stirring echoes from the Andamans where this great son of India was incarcerated. Fittingly, his portrait was unveiled in the Central Hall of Parliament by President APJ Abdul Kalam on 26 February, 2003, as a fitting tribute to this great man.

Thus spake Savarkar:

> Many a flower is born and blooms and withers. Who have even numbered or noted them! But behold the flower that was plucked by that mighty elephant to affect his deliverance and was offered at the feet of the Lord stands immortalized by bards. The garden that sheds all its flowers for the garland of the God is in blossom forever. Jails have a great sustaining power. They corrode but they do not kill. They petrify, but they preserve.
>
> Just think, is suffering no work? Who worked more for humanity? They who suffered in silence and unknown or they who worked? Surely both, they who work for a good cause outside, work

much ... but they who suffer for it in prisons and fields work more. At bottom work, if true, is suffering; and suffering, if true, is work. Suffering is the motor, the power that moves and goads and propels a people. Unless the best amongst them suffer, the rest cannot work. The worker is great for he puts stone upon stone and chisels and moulds; but then the cement of the Church is the sufferer! The martyr that bleeds!!

Although it is true that prisoners are not free to do or say what they will; but it is also true that one is free to dream what he likes. And I take the fullest advantage of this concession. Almost every night, I break jail and move out by dale and down and by tower and town, go on romping till I find someone: someone close to my bosom. Every night I do it but my beneficent jailor takes no notice of it. You have only to wake in the jail, that is all they say.

"We dedicated to thee our thoughts; our speech and our eloquence we dedicated to thee, Oh Mother Land! My lyric sang of thee alone: my pen wrote of thee alone Oh Mother! It was on thy altar that I sacrificed my health and my wealth. Neither the longing looks of my young wife vainly waiting for my return, nor the peals of laughter of dear children nor the helplessness of sister-in-law stranded and left to starve could hold me back at the call of thy trumpet."

8

Media: The New Caesars

Little could the founding fathers of the Constitution have imagined that the freedom of speech, expression, press and the media, which was being enshrined amongst the fundamental rights, would be used as a weapon of terror and intimidation. That instead of acting as a check on the other three organs of the State, the legislature, the executive and the judiciary, the fourth estate will fall from its high pedestal of impartiality and objectivity into a morass of sycophancy, motivated slander and even abuse. However, at the very outset it should be made clear that all the media does not qualify for the above criticism. Most have an agenda of their own in purveying vested interests, political or otherwise. Before this truth can be put on record there are some honourable exceptions to this malaise. In general the English media cannot pride itself on having many such honest, upright, fearless and objective media managers. The role of the media is to inform and some times present a view, clearly defining and separating one from the other. Today our media, especially English print and visual, has succumbed to the lure of openly purveying vested interests, personal bias, exaggeration, sensationalism, and unconfirmed and often concocted facts. The picture painted is entirely different from what the facts reveal. It is a dangerous undertaking to criticize the media; since anyone be it a politician or a freelance writer has always burnt his fingers while doing so. Let us therefore, concentrate on hard facts and not opinions and be impartial in our scrutiny.

One should not be naïve and ignore the basic fact that media is big business and has to make profit; that media managers are no saints but career-driven individuals like ordinary mortals. But there are some rules of the game and as long as they play by the rules one cannot blow the whistle on them. Just as for a business corporation the success or failure of the CEO depends on the market value of the company's share, the salary value of an Editor-in-Chief is measured in terms of the circulation of his publication. So from the lofty heights of its noble ideals the media has come to the market place to sell; and sensationalism sells just as yellow journalism sells. Keyhole reporting is the stuff that paparazzi thrives on. Even the editor of a very respectable newspaper had to admit that they have to include glitz and glamour in the last page just to keep the paper afloat. Serious articles do not pay. Just as in own our Bollywood, box office success is the buzzword and in the process decency and good taste can go to blazes. Whatever the public wants is served and we end up with the lowest level of trash. Even so-called intellectuals and whiskey-swilling old hands are not free from this virus. The film-maker zeroes on what will be appreciated by the lowest and the largest denominator of the viewers' sense of entertainment: tantalizing, obscene, aimless and puerile. In this world of permissive and captive viewers anything goes, as the Bollywood serves ad nauseun repeats of gore, sex, smut, semi-nude females, provocative visuals; in fact anything that titillates. So also with the media. The cash coffers must be kept ringing and information and education be damned. With the globalization and ingress of western values the situation is going to get worse. It was so distressing to observe the entire English media with one honourable exception suppressing facts, peddling half-truths and by innuendos and chicanery indulging in the worst form of Hindu-bashing. To them there seems to be nothing right in the praxis of Hinduism and whatever positives exist, lie outside the pale of media nihilism. Broadly speaking, as per popular perception, the print media with the exception of *The Pioneer* generally serves an anti-Hindu fare. The *Statesman* with its colonial origin is staid and above low level politics but distinctly anti-Hindu. And surprisingly *Hindu* is the most virulent critic of Hinduism. *Hindustan Times* owned by the Birlas from the days of the independence movement was and seems to be the Congress' pocketborough and a captive newspaper. *Times of India* with all its pretensions of objectivity still remains anti-Hindu. While the *Indian Express* criticizes all and sundry under the sun, its favourite whipping boy being the Hindu.

We shall now focus on the specific shortcomings observed in the recent past and the damage caused there upon to the national polity, social fabric and even national security. Such journalism is not a sacred obligation to the readers to know the truth and form an informed opinion. The leading lights of this band of journalism are not the uneducated amateurs. The Indian elite of today and their media managers, the so- called opinion makers are a breed apart, born out of wedlock of a decaying West and a somnolent East and completely out of sync with the real India that lies beyond their metro world and the cocktail circuit.

Before we look at the ills plaguing our media let us examine the structure of self-restraint and play by the rule that exists to rein in the delinquent among the media. Press Council of India is one such organization headed by a retired judge of unimpeachable integrity and good sense. The constitutional safeguards against suppression of free thought guaranteed under Article 19 of the Constitution have degenerated into license. By circumscribing this Article by placing reasonable restrictions in the interests of sovereignty and integrity of India, security of the state and public order, decency or morality the founding fathers did not expect this freedom to be used for defamation and incitement to offence. If we observe the performance of the media since 27 February, 2002, till recent times, it has not only used this freedom as a license to defame and calumnise but cross all limits of restraint. A simple example should do. The *Indian Express* in the aftermath of Godhra and Gujarat riots had a front-page column titled Modi Meter, in which many unverified facts were mentioned as if there was a war on and it was a war correspondent reporting from the front. More on this in the chapter on Gujarat. Next, innuendoes, insinuations and even open declaration by some papers that the Godhra incident was the handiwork of the BJP-VHP combine to draw political mileage, and was the inevitable reaction to inflaming communal passion over Ayodhya's Ram temple. Again more on this in the chapter on Godhra. And then the Goebbelean big lie that Gujarat riots were nothing short of a Muslim genocide. More on this later where we shall try to enlighten our media friends on the true meaning and substance of a genocide, taking a leaf from a not too distant past.

Some perceptive observers have even remarked that thanks to our English media an emergency like situation surrounded the then BJP Prime Minister. Around that time Iftikhar Geelani, a correspondent of *Kashmir Times* and the Pakistan English Daily *Friday Times,* was arrested in Delhi on a tip off from intelligence agencies for acting as a conduit for transferring illegal Hawala backed money into Srinagar to help the insurgents. The intelligence agency intercepted a conversation between a London based ISI agent Thakkur and Hurriyat leader Geelani, the father-in-law of Iftikhar. Mr. Geelani, the Hurriyat leader's income tax return showed only an annual income of rupees seventy thousand, while in an IT raid carried out on his premises the officials seized Rupees eleven lakh and ten thousand US dollars in cash, one ambassador car, one Tata Sumo and also found that he owns a number of flats in Srinagar and Delhi. He had 14 servants and his estimated monthly expenditure was Rs. 1.5 lakh. Where did all this slush money come from? Leads on senior Geelani's criminal activities led to his linkages with Iftikhar Geelani. A raid at Iftikhar's residence led to the discovery of many defence related secret documents and information besides clues to many other unlawful activities. The Indian journalists as usual cried foul, even in this case of anti-national activity stating that the material was already published but forgot to mention that the publication was in Pakistan not India. Intelligence agencies then discovered that the source of Iftikhar's secret information was not from published sources. Indian Press called this arrest harassment and attack on the freedom of the press. Again they challenged the Income Tax (IT) raids on the Mumbai industrialist owner of *Outlook Weekly*. The money involved was so large that the owner was prepared to pay huge sums to IT sleuths to drop the case. But the press again went ballistic, defending one of their ilk, even though he was cheating the national exchequer. Does the ownership of a periodical grant immunity before law and permit tax evasion? Again in the case of the correspondent of *Al-Jazeera,* a known mouthpiece of international terrorist Osama Bin Laden, the press was caught on the wrong foot, when Government of India did not permit him to open shop in India. The *Tehelka* again showed that the media manager and his staff can be guilty of other punishable offences and are not above law. Use of liquor, concealed cameras, call girls and laying money traps are the new weapons in the information technology of another kind. Again FERA violations are actionable offences and media is not above law. A journalist or a reporter is as much punishable as an ordinary citizen and cannot be granted immunity against law on activities not connected with freedom of expression.

In the Star T.V. serial *Hotline* telecast at 7.30 PM on May 17, 2002 the anchor virtually asked the enemy that we are contemplating strong action against you and what do you have to say? This was during the discussion on Indian response to the latest Pakistani violence in killing 30 Hindu men, women and children, army family members at Kalu Chek in Jammu by three Pak terrorists on May 14, 2002. The subject had already been discussed in the Parliament and there was unanimous agreement to take retaliatory action against Pakistan. The invitees to this discussion were General Roy Chowdhary, Ex Chief of Army Staff, Mr. Kuldeep Nayyar and a member of National Conference of J & K.. The anchor asked Mr. Rashid Khan, the Pak spokesman of his country, what his views on the subject were. A very visible tendency in our visual media is an effort at trivialization of cross-border terrorism. In the aftermath of Thursday, September 24, 2002, Akshardham Temple, Star TV discussed the event in its serial *'The Big Fight'* on September 28, 2002, at 8.00 PM. The subject of the discussion was 'Has terrorism become a political slogan?' In the US, the whole country united against the Al-Qaida attack on the WTC and the Pentagon building. No pictures of mangled bodies were splashed on the TV screen. The destruction of the twin towers was shown followed by a national consolidation to fight against the evil of terrorism. There was no debate even on *Larry King Live.* No one in the country talked in partisan terms. I was in the US on 9/11, 2001, and saw every inch of the footage on all TV channels. How different it is in India that the media should sermonize restraint in order not to inflame passions or cause panic in public. Some speakers even criticized the late arrival of National Security Guard Commandos (NSG) commandos by 8 hours. They completely ignored the fact that it takes time to fly troops deployed on the international border at far off places and formulate a plan of attack in darkness using tree cover, and that the people locked in the sanctum sanctorum constrained the actions of the NSG. They waited till dawn to avoid unnecessary casualties and in the morning killed all the terrorists and freed the pilgrims. Even this wise action came under criticism.

There seems a distinct anti-BJP bias in our English print and visual media. The investigative journalism selectively targets BJP and most often indulges in blind criticism. Dissent is unobjectionable in a democracy like ours, but to play with facts is not cricket. Our media often falls a victim to this temptation. In the much publicized Petrol Pump scam a process of selection was applied but the public was informed that all the beneficiaries were from the ruling party, completely suppressing the names of other party men and their loyalists. The same fact can be put in different words giving a different emphasis. Mr. Praful Goradia quoted an example from the cold war days regarding the outcome of a sports match between the US and the USSR, wherein the US defeated the Soviet team. The US media reported that the Americans had defeated the Soviets, to which Soviet media retorted that 'we secured the second position, while the US was the last but one'. How completely contradictory the pictures are though the facts are the same? Then, there were headlines carrying stories of a land-scam highlighting land allotment to RSS and its affiliates, completely ignoring the fact that successive Congress governments during their tenure in the past made a large number of similar allotments to their chosen ones for ideological and not so noble reasons, specifically, excluding BJP and RSS. What was routine for Congress could not be so for the BJP government. It so happens that the BJP was the only party that did not have a building of its own in Delhi. The Communist Party occupies the large Ajoy Bhawan on Bahadur Shah Zafar Marg area and the CPI (M) a well-furnished building at Gole Market in the prime land of metro Delhi. Both occupy a pint sized political space in the country. Why then this hue and cry about the RSS, the hither-to political pariah? And despite the fact that land price for such institutions is always lower than the market rates just as was the case with Congress, CPI, CPM or the Rajiv Gandhi Foundation or the newspaper offices in the prime land of Bahadur Shah Zafar Marg. Some of these newspapers have rented out for commercial purposes almost all parts of the accommodation allotted to them, and have only token press activities therein. What was passe so far became objectionable now, since the beneficiaries happened to be BJP and RSS affiliates. Does the media ever visit Qutub Institutional Area, the den of many such bogus organizations of doubtful activates? The Constitution does not stipulate any ideology whose purveyors have a special privilege in land allotment. If Leftists and Islamic institutions can get land, why bellyache about the RSS? The issue of government allotment of land so much below the market rate to institutions per se can be questioned, but can the Congress led INTUC, Rajiv Gandhi Foundation, All India Women's Conference, UNI, PTI, and the Press Club of India afford the market price? Can one question who was the original allottee of the land where Rajiv Gandhi Foundation today stands? How was a place allotted and advertised as Congress Headquarters pass to a private trust? The Congress and its allied organizations are occupying a large number of government buildings, not to speak of costly heritage buildings. When the building opposite Shastri Bhawan in prime metro land is allotted to Congress and becomes a family run trust, the media looks the other way, but hell is let loose if an allotment is made to BJP or RSS? Are these not double standards? Do Congress and the Left have a monopoly on both ideology and material largesse to the exclusion of the so-called not so right political formations? The media has many things to answer for, this is just one of them.

On June 26, 2002, on the *Indian Express* editorial page Mr. Mushirul Hassan, a luminary of Aligarh Muslim University, had suggested to the newly appointed President Dr. APJ Abdul Kalam to put VHP President Ashok Singhal behind the bars for his statement that Gujarat symbolized the first positive response of Hindus to Muslim fundamentalism in 1000 years and implored the Home Ministry to wake up to the realities in Gujarat. Angry with a relief fund not reaching the victims of what he called 'genocide', he doubted whether Kalam's election as President will bring comfort to those thousands languishing in the camps. A one sided picture of Gujarat again with the usual accused – BJP-VHP. Trivializing the external threat of Pak sponsored cross-border terrorism and magnifying and caviling at a political party's overzealousness and even encouraging partisan postures for political gains, they score brownie points against each other. This was the game that media played, instead of standing united against the enemies' undeclared war. History repeats itself. This has been the story of our country for the last thousand years. Invaders were knocking on our doors and we were a house divided, involved in petty rivalries and pulling each other down.

Not content with prejudging the issue of Godhra and Gujarat violence, The *Indian Express* in its February 27 issue published a dispatch from its correspondent Ayesha Khan from Nadiad, Gujarat, in a column dedicated to the investigation of the Gujarat riots. The report was on expected lines, conforming to the newspaper's policy of editorializing news. She alleged that on interrogation, the witnesses were reluctant to depose before the judicial commission out of a sense of fear. They had no complaint against the Police, who they mentioned even rescued some victims from houses on fire. All this before Justice G.T. Nanavati and Justice K.G. Shah. Yunus Kapadia of Naveranda and Musa Vohra of Kalgaon gave the State Police a clean chit. However, one Valiuddin Mistry of Nadiad did say that instead of the compensation of Rs. 8 lakh announced by the government he had received only Rs. 50,000. Ahmed Vohra of Dumral sounded confused. What a pity? The witnesses do not seem to be saying what *The Indian Express* would like them to. One wonders whether with such agencies that seem to know all and can act the Daniel, is there a need to institute a judicial probe? The newspaper seems to have arrogated to itself the role of the accuser and the judge. It is precisely for this reason that the Lucknow Bench of the U.P. High Court had warned the media not to publish day-to-day proceedings of the Ayodhya case and refrain from giving out any information that may prejudice a fair investigation. Again dissatisfied with the Gujarat verdict, some of our media pundits are blaming the people who, they moan unlike the customers are not always correct. They sermonize that people have elected a Hitler and will rue their choice sooner than later. By nitpicking that the Congress also had polled nearly 50% of the total votes, the BJP victory is no cause for celebration. What has happened is wrong.

Our English media is so pre-occupied with its anti-Hindu tirade that it forgets to take up even important social issues. Sometime back, Patna was rocked for a long time by the scandal of a daylight abduction of a beautiful married woman, Mrs. Kanchan Mishra, by a notorious gangster, Sultan Mia. After the subsequent forceful marriage in a mosque in the Manipura locality of Patna, the issue came up before the National Commission for Women (NCW). The Imam denied the marriage. But the lady, legally married to another man and not yet divorced, deposed that she feared for the fate of her family and herself. The worst part of this murky episode is the fact that the *nikah* was blessed by the RJD member, Ejazul Haq, who hosted a reception attended by the local bigwigs and police top brass. NCW sources allege that the police and the administration are not pursuing the matter since Sultan Mia is a protege of the infamous RJD MP from Siwan, Mohammed Shahabuddin. Despite NCW's directive to arrest and prosecute Sultan Mia and produce Mrs. Kanchan Mishra before the commission, the lady remained in illegal custody in clear defiance of the directive. All national dailies steered clear of the episode so as not to hurt the feelings of RJD chief Laloo Prasad Yadav and his wife Rabri Devi, the self-proclaimed messiahs of 'social justice', and incur the displeasure of the Muslim MP and his community!

The defeat by a narrow margin of Jean–Merri-Le Pan described as a Fascist in France has worried our English media at home. What if he could manage to win? Fascism again! After Gandhiji's death in India, fascism they say lay low, but is again staging a comeback after 50 years as the BJP and RSS fascists return to power. God help India! Scared at the prospect of BJP and the Right occupying centrestage in Indian politics, Amulya Ganguli screamed on the editorial page of *Hindustan Times* May 22, 2002, '*Hitler Rides Again,* and in good measure not to leave any doubts about identities juxtaposed a picture of Modi against Hitler.

Enormous funds have been flowing in for decades into India from Saudi Arabia for madarsas all over the country, the worst type of terrorism, but Indian Press kept quiet. Foreign Christian organizations pour billions of dollars and convert innocent Harijans and tribals by inducement and turn them against their own culture. The media keeps quiet. But when a service centric Hindu organization like Ekal Vidyalaya does a commendable job for tribal children the media cries foul, dubbing them as fundamentalists. Taking a leaf from our own English media, some the US based Christian and Muslim organizations and a Maryland based publication in particular, called *The Campaign to Stop Funding Hate,* has pilloried the India Development and Relief Fund (IDRF) for allegedly raising millions of dollars from NRIs and US corporations to fund a 'hate campaign in India'. Synchronously the Federation of India American Christian Organization of North America (FIACONA), Javed Anand's Sabrang Communications and one Teesta Setalvad have demanded a probe by the US Congress into the activities of IDRF, blacklist it and cancel its Income Tax exemptions. Biju Mathew, the President of FIACONA, a non-descript organization, has in its 91-page report charged the IDRF with:

- Pumping millions of dollars for the use of violent sectarian Hindu supremacist organizations.
- Funding relief, natural disaster management and anti-communal violence measures, which discriminate against Muslims and other minorities.

- Funding divisive forces to communalize Indian polity.
- And claimed that " In recent times, the organization has raised funds for Bangladeshi Hindu victims of communal violence, Kashmiri Hindu victims of terrorism, and relief efforts following the September 11 attack in the US."
- While "In contrast to date, IDRF has not announced any relief for the victims of communal riots in Gujarat in February and March 2002."
- Using a network of professional Indians working for large US corporations in the Silicon Valley chiefly Cysco son, Oracle and Hewelett Packard employees and the use of RSS Swayam sewaks to "push" the IDRF agenda and collect funds from the gullible for relief and development work in India and even for RSS itself.

The IDRF rebutted this slander for what it was worth and stated, "The report is a string of allegations manipulated skillfully. By piecing together information available on IDRF website and further that the allegations do not stand up to any rational scrutiny. Donors to IDRF are among the most well-informed of the donors to any South Asian non-profit charitable organizations operating in the US. IDRF questioned the creditability, motives and the political agenda of these splintered and virtually unknown groups that have launched the Hate Campaign against them. IDRF does not subscribe to any religious, political or sectarian agendas. Further, IDRF does not discriminate against any religion, sect or race in either the collection or distribution of funds." Consequences of this mischief. The SUN Microsystems followed by CISCO put on hold all current donations pending clearance from Internal Revenue Service (IRS). The IDRF is not on the IRS list of agencies supporting terrorism. It declared: "Any non-profit and non-proprietary organization that has been granted 501 (c) (3) tax exempt and public charity status is eligible to receive matching gifts from Sun Microsystems." However, CISCO employees clarified that all money went to good causes in India such as Orissa cyclone of 1999 and was duly reported to IRS. One NRI Mr. Rangnathan said, "IDRF seems to be gathering more money than others, because people are aware of the good work done by IDRF and so money is sure to go into right causes and not because people are duped". Palleti concurred and said,

"The word duped is insulting to employees who build innovative networking products and because of whom we can communicate with ease. I don't think the articles published in the Indian Press cause anybody to reduce their help to IDRF, but only incense them to think that their own media is not India-friendly."

My son who works for a multinational corporation in the US echoes the same sentiments and once remarked that when Hindu's Raghunath Temple in Jammu is attacked and innocent civilians, the families of Army Jawans, killed in Kaluchek, the Indian English media merely mentions but never condemns the heinous acts. Following the Muslim practice of excoriating Hindus, the British condemn anything to do with Hindu or Hinduism. Our English media is no different. For our media, times have changed since the days of "facts are sacred, comment is free". TV with its worldwide reach and instantaneity can show 'televised war on screen nets' but its incredible speed cannot compensate for lack of perspective which is essential. The print media is better placed on this score, and its fast courier role is not exactly a disadvantage since it allows the time and opportunity to analyze and comment. An example of how the *Tehelka* TV exposes adversely hit our defence preparedness can be gauged by the fact that for almost a year and a half the entire defence procurement agencies went into a state of frightened paralysis, seriously jeopardizing the national defence and security. And the much touted slush payoff did not exceed a few lakh rupees. In comparison the Rs. 80 crore of Bofors scam and Rs. one thousand crore of security scam is described with a straight face by Manmohan Singh of the Congress as a systemic failure. Besides the petrol pump scam, urea scam, fodder scam, the list is endless. Where is the sense of proportion? TV can be a dangerous weapon in the hands of irresponsible, sensation-seeking reporters. Personal bias has coloured all the TV debates ranging from Godhra, Gujarat, madarsas, POTA, *Tehelka* tapes, Minorities in Bangladesh.

Arundhati Roy of Booker Prize fame in an article *Democracy; who is she, where she is at home* (May 16, 2002), gave a fictional but explicit description of the 'stripping and burning' of the so-called daughters of a Congress MP, late Ahsaan Jaffri, by members of the VHP during the riots in Ahmedabad, almost posing as an eyewitness. Now, the facts. The MP's son T.A. Jaffri in an interview to *The Asian Age* categorically stated that his only sister and brother are settled in the US. To those who may not have read junior Jaffri's interview Roy's facts disguised as fiction are a lie, so glibly peddled by this woman. Roy the 'enfant terrible' of Indian literary tabloid born in the ambience of the International Communist thought and India baiting, has perfected the art of showing India in the blackest colours possible. One thought that the days of Ms. Mayo were over. Ms. Mayo, it may be recalled had brought out the worst face of India in her book *Mother India,* which Gandhiji so aptly described as the report of a sanitary inspector. Ms. Roy has not only specialized in gutter journalism but has created images of Hindu India far removed from reality. Publicity hungry Roy of *'Narmada Bachao Andolan'* had no compunction in making a scene outside the Tihar Jail passing derogatory comments against the judiciary. While she was putting across her histrionic talents to good use our secular media lapped it all up. Our media was too glad to oblige Ms. Roy with all the publicity, she sought. The likes of Ms. Roy are no respectors of truth. And it is precisely such writings that the western press is constantly on the prowl to pick up to denigrate India in the less than 4% space it allows for South Asia coverage. While Phoolan Devi's election campaign in 1996 and Medha Patkar-Roy's anti-Narmada Dam agitation in 1999-2000 hogged the headlines the mass-exodus of Hindus from Bangladesh is muzzled up and dismissed by the secularists as "Social Trouble". When karsevaks at Ayodhya present a huge stone relic of an ancient Ram Temple with authenticity to prove its existence, *Hindustan Times* in an article by Purnima Joshi on April 7, derisively captioned the events and the photo as *Kar-sevak archeologists.* This is the tyranny of our English media.

The Ansal Plaza case has been mentioned earlier. The bleeding hearts for the human rights of the terrorists did not even bother to verify the authenticity of the evidence of Dr. Harikrishna, the so-called 'eyewitness' till *The Pioneer* came out with complete facts about the man and his testimony. The furore raised is the repeat of what happened at Chhattisingh Pura, when innocent Sikhs were massacred in Kashmir, during President Clinton's visit to India, by the terrorists and the blame was sought to be passed on to the security forces. Mr. Praful Bidwai, Mr. Kuldeep Nayyar and Mr. Colin Gonzalves took the Delhi Police to task while Mr. Gonzalves went public on Star TV. The TV anchor did not even question Mr. Gonzalves on his statement that contradicted the versions of other people whose cars were damaged in the cross fire, till a Hindi news channel came out with all the details, the same night. While *The Pioneer* showed up Dr. Dubious in great details the English TV channel decided to ignore the unpleasant facts. Driven by their hate of the so-called Hindu Government the media went berserk in putting down the Delhi Police and playing against national interests. Quacks are heroes and mascots of human rights and the darlings of our sensation hungry media.

The visceral hatred of the English media against the BJP led NDA government was so deep that according to them whatever the government did could not be right. Instead of giving credit for handling Akshardham Temple attack and subsequent prevention of communal clashes, the media went to town saying why could the same not be done in Gujarat by calling the Army in time? Why were the Mumbai riots after Babri demolition not controlled in time by calling the Army forgetting that the Government during the Mumbai riots and Babri demolition was from the Congress Party. Narasimha Rao was the Prime Minister, who mysteriously disappeared to surface again after the moment for crucial action had passed. The facts about Gujarat riots will be discussed later, but a mention here can be made that Army units were mobilized within 72 hours by pulling them out from their operational positions on sensitive borders from different places. The time and space factors were daunting enough, but the Army did it in record time. So what is the grouse? One of *The Pionee*r columnists was quite fond of calling BJP, Bhartiya Mangata Parti. Mr. Siddhartha Bhatia, a frequent contributor t*o Pioneer*, added his might to denounce Amitabh Bacchan for being apologetic on not taking off his shoes before reciting Gayatri Mantra in a film. He wanted him to take up communal causes a la Dilip Kumar, who had no compunctions in accepting a reward from Pakistan, an enemy country. Artistic freedom should be the law. The sentiments of Hindus be damned! Inspite of hard evidence a TV channel had the gall to suggest that the torching of Sabarmati Express was an inside job, read "Hindu engineered", thus totally absolving Pak terrorists and their Indian collaborators of any wrong-doing. Immediately after Akshardham, anticipating a Hindu backlash, a TV reporter visited the narrow lanes of Naroda Patia, a Muslim locality and threw loaded questions at the dwellers to add to communal mistrust and literally prompted them to express their fears of a reprisal. The reporter might have felt sorry that nothing really happened and a human tragedy could not be sensationalized. And this incident takes the cake. During the second round of J&K elections, a correspondent visited a Hurriyat stronghold where for obvious reasons no voting took place. Sure enough the Pak TV, and PTI reproduced the same clipping to show that Kashmir did not participate in the polls and Musharraf had rightly declared the elections to be a farce. Many readers in their letters to the editor expressed their boredom over such antics of the media and expected them to be more honest and impartial and abstain from their pseudo-secularist activities and Hindu baiting.

The Western media, especially the US, delights in serving back whatever fare is sent to them by our very own secular English media reporters and most of this is derogatory and biased. Mr. Francois Gautier writes, "two weeks ago, the *Boston Globe,* one of the most venerable US papers, published a piece by M. Greenway, an ex-foreign editor and a regular columnist, which basically said that the US should be more wary of Hindu fundamentalism than Islamic militancy! You cannot write something more fallacious than this, but it was probably based on the input that Greenway gets from the *New York Times* correspondent (The *Globe* belongs to the NYT Group). Being in Boston and having met the previous day the *Globe's* foreign editor, James Smith, I immediately called him and said that as a French journalist having covered India and South Asia during 20 years for prestigious European newspapers, I would write a rejoinder. Will he please forward it to the Open page editor? He did, but the rejoinder was never published." He again quotes from *Houston Chronicle* (4,00,000 readership) an article *Living together*, the story of a Muslim in Gujarat betrayed by his Hindu friend during the 'pogrom' of Muslims by Hindu fundamentalists and "Right at the end of the piece, the writer mentioned, in passing, that "a little before the riots 58 Hindu militants coming from Ayodhya—where a mosque was razed earlier by Hindu fanatics – were killed by a Muslim mob." The blame was put on their being 'aggressive' and there was not a single mention of the 54 innocent women and children who were burnt. Now, another story. The lady who did this piece for the *Houston Chronicle* was in India, and in Gujarat. And she had ample time to get her facts straight. But probably, she intentionally decided to omit the fact that the cold blooded Godhra massacre triggered the riots against Muslims in Gujarat.

Again in a White House press briefing a lady with the Director of National Security Council in typical double speak on India and Pakistan had only a pat for India for her restrained response, but a double pat for Musharraf, their ally in their war against terrorism. No Indian journalist except Chandan Mitra, Editor of *Pioneer*, took the US reporter Alex Perry to task for ridiculing Atal Bihari Vajpayee on his piece *Asleep at the wheel.* Could the US reporter do the same to Chinese Prime Minister Jiang Zemin? Our English newspapers, primarily the purveyors of personal prejudices, past hurts and bruised ego, present views rather than news. The *Indian Express* editor with a crown that shows signs of wisdom and wealth surpasses other newspapers in sensationalism and the cult of paparazzi. In investigative journalism the facts are mixed with prejudices to make them appear plausible. The *Hindustan Times* as pointed out earlier is a one-sided reporter for Congress, while the *Times Of India* still carries the British India anti-Hindu baggage and dubiously secular credentials. Same for *Hindu*. But the *Indian Express* takes the lead following in the footprints of *Blitz* a yesteryears publication purveying sensationalism, screaming headlines and much ado about nothing, criticizing one and all except Nehru. The *Indian Express* hits both Congress and the BJP alike but is generally anti-government and works on the premise that any government can never do anything right. I remember during my days as an instructor at Defence Services Staff College at Wellington, one of my colleagues mentioning to me that after reading his morning *Indian Express* newspaper he lost all appetite for breakfast. It seems there was nothing right with India. Once its editor remarked to me in a chance meeting when he found that I did not subscribe to his paper, that my education has been neglected. Presumptuous, arrogant, mister know all who can pontificate on almost anything under the sun, his coverage of Gujarat was in tune with his predilections. In a front page daily column titled *ModiMeter*, he zeroed in on one individual and churned out reams of paper, using words like 'holocaust' and 'pogrom' and never refrained from calling Sangh Parivar fascist and fundamentalist, not knowing the first thing about these words. We have already discussed these two words earlier in our chapter on Hinduism. If abuse, calling names and sitting on judgment is journalism, what about information, facts and putting across news items. Views if printed must be annotated as belonging to a certain correspondent and his ideology. Slavishness to western values and mocking Indian culture and denigrating Hindus and Hinduism cannot be the staple of good journalism.

To the Cassandras and soothsayers of doom and the media who see nothing positive in our country these lines from our President APJ Abdul Kalam must be compulsory reading. They must regurgitate every sentence, every syllable thrice a day when criticizing our country. "My second vision for India is DEVELOPMENT. For 50 years we have been a developing nation. It is time we see ourselves as a developed nation. We are among top 5 nations of the world in terms of GDP. We have 10 percent growth rate in most areas. Our poverty levels are falling, our achievements are being globally recognized today. Yet, we lack the self-confidence to see ourselves as a developed nation, self-reliant and self-assured. I have a third vision. I believe that unless India stands up to the world, no one will respect us. Only strength respects strength. We must be strong not only as a military power but also as an economic power. Both must go hand in hand."

Why are we in India so embarrassed to recognize our own strength, our achievements? We are such a great nation. We have so many amazing success stories but we refuse to acknowledge them. Why? We are the second largest producer of wheat and rice in the world. We are the first in milk production. We are number one in remote sensing satellites. Look at Dr. Sudharshan. He has transformed a tribal village into a self-sustaining, self-driving unit. There are millions of such achievements but our media is only obsessed with the bad news. One of my friends in Tel Aviv was reading the Israeli newspaper. It was the day after a lot of attacks and deaths had taken place. The Hamas had struck. But the front page of the newspaper had the picture of a Jewish gentleman who in five years had transformed his desert land into an orchid and a granary. It is this inspiring picture that everyone woke up to. The gory details of bombardments, deaths, were inside in the newspaper, buried among other news. Also, why are we, as a nation so obsessed with foreign things? We want foreign TVs, shirts, and technology. Do we not realize that self-respect comes with self-reliance? As an amendment read that India occupies number one position in the export of rice, wheat and milk.

The allergy of our English media, in this case the *Indian Express* with anything to do with the Hindus or Saffron is so strong that even a progressive effort on the economic front is an anathema and a subject for derision. In a news item dated September 18, 2002, by some reporter they made a snide heading *Green ethanol gets a saffron signal.* Ethanol is a byproduct of the sugar industry and has been used in many foreign countries as transport fuel for almost 50 years. When I was serving the army as Deputy General Officer Commanding Andhra, Tamilnadu, Kerala and Karnataka Area headquartered at Madras (Chennai) in 1983, Shakti Sugar Management with their plant at Coimbatore had come out with this discovery. It was only a question of time when the product was to be put to commercial use. In the two-day conference organized by the Centre for Bharatiya Marketing Development (CBMD), a part of Swadeshi Jagaran Foundation (SJF), the latter highlighted the utility of ethanol blended petrol and biodiesel in the presence of technocrats from Indian Institute of Technology (IIT), Indian Institute of Sciences (IIS), Indian Institute of Petroleum (IIP), staff of important sugar mills, farmers and IOC and BPCL. The then Deputy Prime Minister LK Advani happened to be present at the conference alongwith some other politicians. The very association and encouragement shown by the Sangh Parivar to the SJF for this laudable product was cause enough for our secular media to make a snide reference to something which can solve the problem of an oil hungry country. Such is the deep prejudice against Hindutva, Swadeshi and anything they sponsor.

In a news item published on 17th June, 2002, the *Time* magazine of the United States came out with a startling revelation that Atal Bihari Vajpayee, the then Prime Minister of India, was incapable of exercising control over the nuclear weapons and his Goa speech was a license to keep the violence going in Gujarat and that the Indian Government in order to extract sympathy from the U.S. was claiming to be a victim of terrorism. All in all, the magazine graded India as more unreliable than Pakistan and at least equally culpable if not more for the prevailing tensions in the South Asian sub-continent. This is nothing new. The *Time* has always followed a policy in the international fora of holding India responsible for turbulence in the region. Inspite of all this, the intellectuals and media have ignored this injustice and insult done to the then Prime Minister. Earlier, in its 27th May news item of five lines only, the magazine had branded India as the culprit for the massacre of 34 innocent civilians at Kaluchek to discredit India's protest against terrorism. It is time that we recognize that western news media only peddle their countries' concerns and interests without getting sentimental about international concerns, impartiality, justice and democratic values. It is only in India that our media managers keep busy painting their own country black behind the mask of 'secularism' and public interest with scant regard for truth, thus helping powers hostile to India. Our English media is totally westernized in its language, lifestyle, idiom and vocabulary. The *Time, Newsweek, CNN,* and *BBC* have an identical approach driven entirely by their national interests and concerns. To them China is important and deserves respect and should be empathized with; Russia is a crumbling edifice; poor Japan is riddled with problems and an ineffective leadership; Saudi Arabia should be looked after and is useful for oil; Pakistan is useful and should be helped financially, using carrot and stick; India is a peculiar case full of problems and uncertainties, tries to imitate the West and should be shown its place and so on. Purveying national interest, the *Time* magazine mentioned India only once on its first page in 2002 and China six times, while on the inner pages there were twelve news items for India, all negative. Its 14th February, 2002, issue on Orissa, was full of accusations of ill-treatment of cyclone victims while the 21st February issue carried Godse's interview debunking Gandhiji's idealism; 13th March – the subject was Tiger poaching; 20th March dealt with irresponsible conduct of India-Pakistan on mutual tension and 3rd April, mocking at President Clinton's feel good response during his India's visit; 10th April, deriding the inflated sense of patriotism in India after Kargil victory; 29th May – miserable conditions of Indian cows and need for animal care; 12th June – Pepsi Cola war; 10th July, whole of village Mandi in U.P. called 'thief pocketing buried wealth four thousand years old;' 4th August kidnapping of Raj Kumar by Veerappan; 18th September, illustrations of eunuchs in India. This is the negative fare served by the *Time* in the whole year of 2002.

Newsweek is the same. When Musharraf dethroned Nawaz Sharif, *Newsweek* of 25th October, 1999, cried foul but made a U-turn in its Ist November issue. The role of U.S. media immediately after the bombing of WTC and Pentagon building on 11 September, 2001, stands in sharp contrast with our own Indian media. The U.S. media fully co-operated with the Government and did not create internal unrest. The anger was carefully focussed and directed against the forces of international terrorism. There were no bickerings about lack of security or criticism of Government on failure of intelligence. Not once during my stay there those days did I see a discordant note struck anywhere. The nation was one, solidly behind the President. In fact, in no time the rating of George Bush soared high with no special effort on his part. The scene in India in March 2002 was entirely different. There was an attempt to put blame on the Government. The electronic media in India failed its crucial test. Sensationalism, cheap popularity and viewer rating got the better of national interest and communal harmony, and Pakistan laughed its heart out at this self-flagellation. Unbridled power is dangerous. The media should use its immense power and reach with restraint and discretion. A constructive role towards social harmony should be the prime concern. There is an instantaneity about the visual reporting and during times of communal turmoil this can be disastrous. The more scenes of horror and gore are flashed on the TV screen, the longer the violence will last. It becomes a vicious circle. Violence feeds on rumours; how much would be the damage if in place of verbal tales the same is dramatized before the eyes. Restraint does not mean suppression of facts. Along with the macabre deeds of humanity those of communal amity should also be presented in the visuals. If Gujarat riots have a lesson for us, it is to avoid excessive media activism and visual extremism.

Coming back to Arundhati Roy, whose sole mission in life is scavenging and serving putrid gutter material from Indian society to please her western readers and admirers. She does one better than the golden retriever, who scents dirt, runs up to the pothole, scavenges the gutter, picks up the scum and serves the cadaver, bones, rotten flesh and all, and returns back to her masters in the west, who have put the collar of Booker prize round her neck. All this is music to the western ears. Comparing Modi with Hitler, she reports that six hundred Muslims against only fifty Hindus died in the rioting in Gujarat amounting to a 'mass genocide'. If only she could remember that six million Jews died in the gas chambers of the Nazi occupied Europe. Did any German die in Jewish retaliation? How our secular media loses all perspective and gets carried away by its own rhetoric thus mixing facts with fiction. The BBC and the foreign media replicate the version of our English media since they have no knowledge of Hindi and cannot read Hindi newspapers, in any case not available across the seas, and serve us the same putrid dish of information and news and analysis sent to them. Are there no limits to national shame?

Some never say die. The diehard secularist media managers refuse to accept the facts that the media had gotten it all wrong in the case of Gujarat elections and that it is time to separate news from opinion. In a discussion organised at Indian Women's Press Corps on "*Gujarat: Why the media got it wrong*", various views were expressed on the complete failure of the English media to read what was obvious to the meanest intelligence. Veteran columnist Pran Chopra remarked, " We are doomed to continue misreporting if we stick to editorializing news reports. Predictably the associate editor of the *Hindu* was not convinced that the media had indeed gone wrong. Far from being chastened he trashed such remarks as mischievous and malicious. The editor of *Outlook* equivocated, but Mr. Swapan Das Gupta of *India Today* opined that "the media coverage in Gujarat since February 28, 2002, and campaign and slogans raised against Mr. Modi and BJP also helped the ruling party in Gujarat elections." The psephologists and their opinion polls, which went completely off the mark, also came for some criticism. While the NDTV special correspondent Barkha Dutt had the grace to admit failure, she found no need to apologize to Mr. Modi, but quietly forgot how one of her colleagues had been asking Mr Modi loaded questions in a manner that was almost inquisitorial. He was duly snubbed by Modi who shot back whether he was asking questions, supplying answers, or holding a trial by media. Chandan Mitra, editor of *Pioneer,* was nearer the truth when he said, "A lot of Gujaratis were hurt by the way a campaign was launched against Mr. Modi and it only went to boost his electoral prospects." And further, he stated that there was a need for introspection and to draw a line between reporting and editorial policy. Unfortunately, the representative from *Indian Express,* the most culpable of all, decided that discretion was the better part of valour and kept his silence. Some people's thirst for criticism is endless. Now this very daily has a grudge that none of the six letter words so much bandied about earlier were not mentioned even once on the opening day of Gujarat assembly. No condolence motion was passed. Apparently, nine long months of constant media hype on 'genocide' and 'pogrom' was not enough. The dead have been mourned enough and provided for and shall never be forgotten. But Gujarat needs to start on a new path of reconstruction. After all this is said and taken as read shall the media change? Not by the farthest chance. One should not be surprised if some pseudo-secularist leading lights and messiahs of minorityism decide to celebrate another day as an annual day of mourning in line with the 6 December. Unfortunately, the 'pogrom' of Gujarat riots has no fixed date, Godhra has.

The English media in India is being used by the chatterati and our secular mafia. A recent phenomenon much in evidence is the behaviour of the anchor-persons of Star TV news channel towards the leaders or spokespersons of parties whom they consider as sympathetic to Hindu concerns or India's national interest. In *The Big Fight* programme telecast on October 19, 2002, at 8.00 PM during a discussion on India's future options after completing the free and fair elections in J&K, itself a Herculean task achieved by our government and the Central Election Commissioner, the response of a Muslim panelist from Karachi was not only offensive and in bad taste but as was evident was being looked upon approvingly by the anchor person Rajdeep Sardesai. Mr G. Parthasarthi was the only one who was talking in a responsible and mature manner with full knowledge of the ground realities and the desirability of keeping atleast a thought on military option open. The third panelist was talking of a highly utopian scenario of opening a dialogue without the cessation of cross-border terrorism. The panelist from Karachi ended up by declaring that the record of democracy both in POK and J&K has been disgusting, thus equating the colonial status of POK with the near autonomous status of Indian Kashmir. In another 9.00 PM NDTV news bulletin interview on Sunday, Sonia Verma could be seen talking to Mr. Prafull Goradia, not as one asking for views or comments but cross-examining a poor victim accused of heresy and about to deliver judgement for an ordeal by fire at the stakes. The Papal inquisitors could learn a lesson or two from this performance. The other invitee from Congress, Mrs. Margaret Alva was wearing a smile from ear to ear at this inquisitorial attitude of the anchor and her body language. The empathy between Star TV and our secularists was there for everyone to see. In just one week a usurper dictator and destroyer of democracy became a respectable politician. The same story is true about China. Despite nuclear proliferation and suppression of human rights its ruler became a world leader. Mao Tse-tung, a senile aging leader can control the nuclear button, but an active Vajpayee of 76 years could not. That is the bias against India in foreign media. Wherever there is a question of national interest our very own 'impartial', 'secular media' is driven by radical idealism. While foreign correspondents condescend to look down on us, our own media consider deriding their own country as a sign of intellectual freedom and thereby not only harm our national interests but also insult the vast multitudes that constitute Bharat. Immediately after the Gujarat riots the political chorus to remove Modi rose to a crescendo and in parliament unprecedented and unruly scenes of rush to the well were witnessed courtesy Indian TV. A situation came when even the then PM was forced to explain that the fuel to the fire of prolonged riots after Godhra was added by the media coverage and its relentless campaign. Repeated visuals of burning victims, dismembered bodies, charred remains of houses and shops provoked public sentiments in and outside Gujarat. Even the owner of Zee TV Mr. Chandra conceded these facts. He went even further to state that in view of the reporting of Gujarat riots a code of conduct must be drawn and enforced rigorously. Everyday from the beginning of the riots, eyebrows were raised on the role of media and Gujarat Government imposed a ban on Star TV. The questionable role of the media could no longer be dismissed. The political editor of Star TV Rajdeep Sardesai had the temerity to snap that the duty of the media is to present facts, good or bad, regardless of the consequences, suppressing the fact that he had been showing the same visuals again and again on successive dates as new incidents. All this was bound to inflame and lacerate public feelings. It is no coincidence that this TV marathon acted in perfect sync with the more strident demand of the opposition. One feels a sense of dejavu in all this, when one recalls that after Indira Gandhi's assassination her dead body was shown continuously for days together, allegedly for allowing the people to have a last glimpse of their departed leader, but also to extract political mileage out of sympathy generated for the slain leader. Coming to Sardesai, many media magazines have agreed with this proposition, but it is certainly open to scrutiny why overemphasizing gore are the only visual means to convey the news of the riot. Is there no need for restraint on TV or print media?

The famous TV telecaster Nalini Singh in a newspaper Guest Column *TV, Two riots and a lesson*, brings forth with vividity and candour the problem facing a TV reporter and suggested a very reasoned approach. In 1989, she visited Bhagalpur to cover the riots and was told about the massacre of Muslims. She was shown half buried bodies of some thirty victims, putrefying after 45 days of killings. She came back to Delhi to give the coverage to the Director General of Doordarshan, who politely requested her to show the other side of the picture where Hindus were killed, before a complete tragedy could be telecast. While at Bhagalpur she had read the local press clippings screaming, "Muslim students hacked to death by Hindu murderers", and "Hindu sons roasted in their sleep by Muslim murderers", embellished by rumours of more gory details. Rumours, she said, had travelled 'at the speed of thought, plunging the rural hinterland into a communal conflagration'. The silk city lay in ruins. Nalini thought again and visited Meerut to get some inside into Malliana killings of Muslims. She was given the Muslim side of the picture. Deeply moved she visited one Professor Harpal Singh in Meerut. His son, 32 years old Dr. Prabhat, an anaesthetist, while on his way rushing for an emergency to help a Muslim doctor at Hapur to treat a patient was waved to stop by four Muslims who had blocked the road. As the car slowed down, a mob emerged from the bylanes, tied him to the seat and set fire to his Fiat car carrying oxygen cylinders. At 9.00 P.M. the police handed over to Harpal Singh the charred body of Doctor Prabhat tied to the seat in the shell that was left of the car. As the body was being handed over some Muslims neighbours barged into his house seeking protection against some Hindus. Harpal Singh pacified the crowd and saved the Muslims. With tears welling in his eyes the old man mourned for the future of his son's young widow and two children below six years. "From 1989 to 2002, a long wait and the killers of Doctor Prabhat have yet to be punished", cries his wife. The mob frenzy has killed three generations! Should the Prabhat killing also have been shown on the TV to restore balance in reportage? Nalini sums up, "Here is my answer, and this is the invaluable lesson I learnt; in a communal riot there is another side of the picture, always. Viewers need to be shown both simultaneously, however non-seductive the format might be. And we need to expose relentlessly the ugly compulsions at the core-appropriation, dogma, vote-banks, terrorism, and power. To my colleagues and readers who will surely oppose this suggestion, let me stress that reportage and perspective have to be blended seamlessly, or else we, the media, will be stamped by the one label we hate most: biased. Biased and manipulated prophets. And we'll deserve it."

Some time ago our media prophets rose to a man to defend Alex Perry, a *Time* correspondent, who lampooned Mr. Vajpayee, duly endorsed by some members of the Central Press Accreditation Committee. *Times of India* carried an article supporting Perry's case as a fight for the freedom of the press. There are any number of offensive references to India in foreign newspapers and magazines. The *Time* even showed J and K as an independent territory. It is anyone's guess, how long an Indian reporter whose magazine depicts one of the states of US in Mexico can last in the US. Besides the La-affaire Perry, our English media have not literally covered itself with glory in objective and balanced reporting. But they seem to be the one fighting tooth and nail the entry of foreign direct investment (FDI) in print media. What is it that they fear? Competition or better reporting, a thorough job against their slipshod reporting and half-truths? While foreign media is no more obscene and explicit than our own Desi, at least the reader shall have a wider choice to pick from. The *Indian Express, Hindustan Times, Times of India, Hindu,* and *Statesman* have had their day and pontificated for too long. Let other professionals now move in for better or worse. The concern of the local print media that owners of the foreign print will compromise national sovereignty and security does not wash. That they shall coerce local editors to do their bidding need only to look at their own visceral disdain towards the majority community of India and their legitimate concerns. The entire metro cocktail paparazzi, cocooned in their own shell of western culture need not cry fowl if the readers are exposed to the original rather than its badly duplicated copy.

Arundhati Roy, of the Booker prize, the Narmada Bachao Andolan and Delhi High Court contempt case fame, put her acerbic pen on the Gujarat riots on May 6, 2002, issue of *Outlook,* a magazine morbidly anti-Hindu and Sangh Parivar. "Gujarat, the only major state in India to have a BJP government has, for some years, been the petri dish in which Hindu fascism has been fomenting an elaborate political experiment. Last month, the initial results were put on public display. Within hours of Godhra outage, the Vishwa Hindu Parishad (VHP) and the Bajrang Dal put into motion a meticulously planned pogrom, against the Muslim community. Officially, the number of dead is 800. Independent reports put the figure at well over 2000. More than a hundred and fifty thousand people, driven from their homes, now live in refugee camps. Women were stripped, gang-raped, parents were bludgeoned to death in front of their children. Two hundred and forty dargahs and 180 masjids were destroyed – in Ahmedabad the tomb of Wali Gujarati, the founder of the modern Urdu poem, was demolished and paved over in the course of a night. The tomb of the musician Ustad Faiyaz Ali Khan was desecrated and wreathed in burning tyres. Arsonists burned and looted shops, homes, hotels, textiles mills, buses and private cars. Hundreds of thousand have lost their jobs."

"A mob surrounded the house of ex-Congress MP Iqbal Ehsan Jaffri. His phone calls to the Director General of Police, the Police Commissioner, the Chief Secretary, the Additional Chief Secretary (Home) were ignored. The mob broke into the house. They stripped his daughters and burnt them alive. Then they beheaded Jaffri and dismembred him." "The mob broke into the house...... stripping" and bringing almost the description of an eyewitness.

One wonders whether Miss Roy was actually present on the scene, her figure counts are amazing, " two thousand dead as independent sources say." On closer look much of the hot air escapes as the balloon of the lies and half-truths was punctured in a close scrutiny of facts. Jaffri's case has been debunked earlier. She quoted Laloo the eternal "Court Jester" now turned serious, "*Kaun Mai Ka Lal Kahata Hain ke Yeh Hindu Rashtra Hai? Usko Yahan Bhej Do, Chhati Phad Doonga.*" (Which son of his mother says this is a Hindu nation? Send him here and I will tear his chest apart). In her denunciation of Sangh Parivar, Ms. Roy has recklessly used words such as *fascism, pogrom, gang rape, and genocide.* We shall place before the reader the real face of genocide in chapter 10 on Gujarat. She described 1998 Pokhran Test, "Blood thirsty patriotism became openly acceptable political currency", much as Musharraf would like to put it. The *Hindustan Times* describing the Godhra carnage under the title *Gujarat hit by Ayodhya backlash* instead of decrying the horrible burning, combined Godhra with the Ayodhya movement. He almost implied that Godhra was an inevitable nemesis of Ayodhya. Words such as "PM faces trial by Ayodhya heat, Gujarat fire." In another editorial of 6 May 2002 another title appeared "Advani flaunts Hindutva card as the airport at Port Blair was being named after Savarkar."

Despite the verdict of the people of Gujarat against Hindu-bashing, our media's stalwarts refused to reconcile themselves to the Gujarat election results. In an attempt to castigate Hindus in the government once again Stavan Desai, an *Indian Express* correspondent, filed a report in its 22, February 2003 issue with a headline *Same Terror, Different Laws in Gujarat.* He means that POTA which had been applied to all accused in the Godhra case should also be applied to the culprits of Gujarat riots, who mercilessly killed Muslims. Forgetting the reaction factors and mob fury that followed Godhra he seemed to equate an internal law and order problem with PAK inspired conspiracy, which had enlisted local support from willing Muslims. Can there be another example of such skewed perception and irrational advocacy of a minority. Gujarat polls once and for all laid the myth of media objectivity to rest. The English media, print and visual, went ballistic crying for the scalp of one man, Narendra Modi. Far from articulating the concerns of the common man in Gujarat, the media had its own agenda—'Pseudo-secularism' against 'Hindutva'. Long on opinion and short on facts it is they who so surcharged the atmosphere with their rhetoric that the common man was bewildered and confused. Was Gujarat really burning? Was this the only riot in the post-independence or pre-independence India? It was Modi v/s media and democracy. Modi became an industry and the English media and our Marxists and Western clones pulled all stops. They conveniently suppressed the Hindu side of the picture. Alongwith one lakh Muslims there were 40,000 Hindus also in refugee camps. The numbers of Hindus killed and arrested, the recovery of illegal arms and ammunitions from Muslim localities during and after the riots and later the Jagannath Yatra were conveniently ignored. This Janus face of the media was also evident in newspaper articles, periodicals, TV seminars and chat shows. It is unfortunate that a fundamentalist and committed Marxism driven Congress is inexorably moving away from true secularism to minority appeasement. Make no mistakes, India's secularism is in safe hands with the country's Hindu ethos and not because of any constitutional provisions. Hinduism is nothing if not tolerant and secular. Those who in their blind hatred of Hindutva indulge in Hindu-baiting and consider Hindu tolerance as a weakness and provoke and challenge Hindus are bound to reap a bitter harvest.

The negative and inflammatory reporting of the media motivated by commercial needs and increase in circulation does immense harm to the true picture of the nation. Instead of being objective, the newspapers only picked out the failings of the BJP government, unless otherwise influenced through favour or patronage. Every government seems to be a non-performer and riddled with corruption. This inevitably leads to an anti-incumbency factor with a demand for change not knowing that the new dispensation may be even worse. Those who pilloried the BJP government on corruption should realize that beginning from Nehru to Indira Gandhi and her dynasty corruption has been a universal phenomenon. The only exception was the short stint of Lal Bahadur Shastri. It is no secret that the home expenses of Govindballabh Pant, Nehru's home minister, were met by G.D. Birla who also owned the *Hindustan Times,* a paper for whom Congress could do no wrong. If one compares the size of the scams after the Congress governments with those during its long rule the former seem to be peanuts. Even *Tehalka's* much touted revelations on the defence scam have not shown anything more than a few lakh rupees and for all this hype the damage to the defence purchases has been disastrous. For almost three years the Indian armed forces had to do without essential weapons and equipment. There should be some sense of proportion and balance in our perspective towards the misdeeds of the ruling government. The unfortunate part is that the media criticism is selective and governed by the predilection of its management. A political party not in favour with the media is almost invariably wrong. Their achievements go unreported. Some time back on the polio day 20 crore children all over the country were given anti-polio drops. The task was of a magnitude that the numbers immunized cross the population mark of entire Europe. But our newspapers preferred to ignore this. On the other hand, just a few days back an English daily published on the front page some innocuous remarks by Mr. Harikrishan Dalmia, given to the members of Bajrang Dal, that marriage is a wholesome experience and not only sanctified but exhorted by our scriptures. The newspaper flashed in bold print that Mr. Dalmia advocates sex to the Bajrang Dal activists!

This is what Ms. Jaya Jaitley, herself a victim of the tyranny of the media, had to say "A brief look at the manner in which the press dealt with public individuals and whether this adds to the credibility that politics must retain for democracies to survive, or for India to gain respect in various fields, is as important as the issue of increasingly advertisement dominated policies in the media. People in public life, whether in sports, cinema, politics or officialdom have become targets of denigration and negative comment motivated not always by the love of truth but the reasons ranging from promoting rival interests, callous sensationalism, a cynical attitude towards decency and accuracy, personal animosities of some editors and columnists, and the lack of time or interest in verifying or analyzing material."

After this catscan on media activism and their dubious role in the country's polity it would be wise to draw some valid conclusions from the way the English media conducted itself before, during and after Gujarat elections. First the facts Narendra Modi won by a landslide victory in Gujarat. He swam against the tide of media views and crafted a victory that is still being dismissed as a victory of communal poison and divide. For ten months the media pilloried him, as the popular groundswell in his favour and against terrorism kept mounting. Five crore Gujaratis were fed up with the namby-pamby approach of the Congress and the secularist brigade towards terrorism. Media detractors who never tired of squeezing the last drop of nourishment from the post-Godhra violence, were not averse to pointing out that Modi's victory in the Central and West Gujarat lay only in the riot-affected areas. In fact, the Star TV gave a pictorial display of each seat won by the BJP under the category of riot-affected areas and otherwise. If riot-affected areas were so restricted as to deny the credit to Modi for a pan-Gujarat sweep how did it square with their earlier breast-beating that the entire Gujarat was on fire under a state sponsored genocide that was a national shame. The entire media that was cheering for a Congress win did not realize that Gujarat had had enough of the Congress style fissiparous politics, pitting caste against caste and dividing Hindus. L.K. Advani put his finger on the pulse when he said that the results exposed "a disconnect between self-serving prophesies and popular concern." Godhra, Akshardham and terrorism did remain the central issue, despite an eight months delay by an obliging Chief Election Commissioner. The issue of bread and butter are taken as read and are common to all political parties. After all, good governance is an axiomatic responsibility of every government. Did the people have to learn it from the Congress? The media also blundered into towing the secularist line of accusing BJP of pointing a sub-textual association between terrorists and the minority community, thereby harming minority interests, instead of, the so-called virtues of Hindus, whom they excoriate. To the dismay of Congress and its friendly media, terrorism, like all good men, did come to the aid of BJP. Nationalism and security is still a unifying force, much above local concerns, petty interests and even mundane issues of bread and butter. Despite media efforts to belittle Godhra and Akshardham and denounce Hindutva none could be consigned to oblivion or erased from the proverbial short public memory. They remained the central issues. The media politicized the public vilification of state officers and talking in a majority-minority idiom, angered the people of Gujarat. The majority minority conundrum, ear-splitting chant of the Congress and their more than willing cheer leaders, constantly lacerated the feelings of the Hindu community. The media refused to accept Godhra as the ignition switch to Gujarat violence and this denial and rough riding of local popular emotions has permanently put an indelible scar on our English media. The pseudo-secularists were proved wrong, the prophets of doom were proved wrong, the self-styled psephologists, the experts and the analysts on TV channels were proved wrong. Their never ending tirade against Hindutva boomranged; the Ayatollahs' of secularism, who had issued Fatwas were defied. Now the TV bias. The incredible success of the BJP in the tribal belt, some local spokespersons ventured to say, due to the excellent work done by the VHP in opening schools, initiating primary health care and other welfare measures was conveniently switched off from the TV screen. With two or three of their own workers murdered in the run up and soon after the polls, the BJP was accused of violence. The high percentage of polling, above 50%, and the fact that some Muslims also voted for the BJP was dismissed and attributed to a fear psychosis. Vaghela and Congress went to town explaining their rout to the fear generated by the Sangh Parivar and its hard Hindutva agenda. The accepted axiom that a Muslim cannot vote for the BJP implies that those Hindus who do are communal. The TV reporters and even Rajdeep Sardesai after the polls asked Modi a few questions expressing their concern at the demise of secularism. Modi replied that most of the anti-Muslim polarization propaganda was a media construct and asked them to point out one word that he had said against Muslims or about dividing the society. As Modi continued in his scoring spree the media kept hitting self goals. Gujarat should be a lesson for the English media. Report facts, complete facts and do not impose your own opinion and biases, and for God's sake do not think that the public and the voters are fools. They want the truth not your opinions.

Hindustan Times in its editorial on March 14, 2002, warned Indian Government against any pro-active action against Pakistan, now that the American troops were there, "we should not rock the boat." A more disingenuous reason given is that such a move in pursuance of our national security may draw away attention from Gujarat. In other words the focus on Gujarat should persist and the pot should be kept boiling. Put another way, national interests and security should take a second place to the media interest in Gujarat violence. What a perverted view and what an example of unsolicited advice from immature defence analysts. The pros and cons of keeping a large part of Indian army in a state of full alert all along the international border for about 10 months had its own perils and adverse effect on the morale of the army. Our defence analyists agreed that a limited punitive action was called for, but the newspaper experts seemed to know better. Those who have never left their air-conditioned offices on Kasturba Gandhi Road do not know the first thing about the ground realities. Resurrecting the nuclear threat has become a fashion with our so-called intelligentsia. The balance of terror is with us. A Pak nuclear attack can only bruise but Indian retaliation will wipe out Pakistan from the map of the world. Musharraf is no fool to commit hara-kiri. In another TV Chat show *Hot Talk* on Star TV an interview of Shahnawaz Khan, the then Minister of Civil Aviation, was telecast. Star News anchor kept on heckling the minister on Gujarat, a subject for which he was not invited for the interview. He was constantly questioned as to why he did not raise his voice for sacking Modi. The question was inquisitorial; not asking facts but cross-examining the minister in a trial court like a criminal. The anchor was acting as a prosecution counsel. Is the role of journalism and the media confined to pilloring a man not remotely concerned with the incident? He was persistently provoked to react like a Muslim but sadly the minister did not oblige.

The leading English Press has, unfortunately excelled in competitive negative and misleading reporting during the Gujarat riots. Can this government even by mistake do anything correct? Are we a doomed nation? India has endured and prevailed and has shown its military might on 12 March, 1998, and its diplomatic savvy. It has recorded phenomenal growth in the fields of science and technology. One such editor who, letting out his stream, spewing venom on almost everything, and completely exhausted, noted in frustration that his free thought and objective reporting and analysis of national issues has gone unrewarded. There were no kudos for his untiring criticism. Sample this gem. "This government has done more for friendly journalists than all others. Largesse has been showered in terms of Rajya Sabha seats, ambassadorships—spouses, mothers, parents-in-law have been rewarded. A problem with such generosity: its recipients lose credibility, government is back to where it began". A case of sour grapes, Another gem. "If you believe that a fair journalist is a friendly journalist who must also be a darbari, who accepts your gifts, hangs around your living room carrying tales, you will find it difficult to relate to those who would not do such things but may not have sold out to the other side as well." He did not get his lolly, not because of prejudice against him but due to the fact that even the biggest misanthrope in the world can stomach this much negativism and not more. His desperation is born out of a low self-esteem which led to self-inflicted arrogance and disregard for dissenting views. He mentioned that the opposition does not have any newspaper of its own. He does not have far to seek. There are many of his ilk cluttering the print space. Before we close this chapter it would be worthwhile to know how the educated Hindus holding eminent positions in the US perceived our local English media.

"It appears that as in the days of the British, the English media are completely out of sync with the pulse of India. Their shrill response to the BJP victory in Gujarat only ends up alienating the moderate Hindus from the English press. What the Hindus could not achieve in a hundred years the English media has accomplished in just few—Hindu unity. Politics defined by caste lines was never new. The Congress along with the Leftist parties played the caste politics with great success. The division of the Hindu vote was almost complete. As long as the lower caste Hindus perceived the fear of the higher caste, the Congress and the Leftist parties were unstoppable. The erudite English media has to realize that this division was as unacceptable as the division along religious lines. Secularism can survive only if all Hindus and Muslims, Christians, Sikhs etc., are treated equally. Indians and Hindus are secular, otherwise the popular vote share of the BJP in Gujarat would have been higher than the 50% it garnered."

"English media's bias of reading between the lines, adding innuendoes, twisting public speeches, making the word Hindu synonymous with extremism is the catalyst that has made most middle class Hindus turn away from the press. As long as the English media keeps spewing vitriol, the moderate Hindu will keep moving away from moderation. The graceful thing for the press is to acknowledge its biased role and live up to the standards that respectable journals would like to be known by – fair play. Stop berating Hinduism, stop equating Hinduism with ignorance and please stop assuming that intellect is the sole prerogative of the English-speaking people. By demonizing Mr. Modi you are also insulting the intelligence and the good sense of the vast Gujarati electorate. There are lessons for all to be learnt from the voice of the Gujarati people. Mr. Modi has the responsibility of rising above religious lines to try to govern as the leader of the entire state. This is the time for him to reach out to the minorities and start a healing process. This is also the time for introspection by the English press. They were wrong in predicting the results, they were wrong in judging the mood of the people of Gujarat and they are wrong in assuming that it was just the riots that brought the Hindu votes together. Many moderate and educated Hindus are completely fed up with the diatribe against Hindu identity, Hindu causes and Hindu feelings. Failing to understand the Hindu perspective will slowly but surely end up marginalizing the English press the same way the toadies were during and after the British rule."

9

Godhra

Never before in the history of India after the end of the Mughal Rule in 1707AD has a crime of such magnitude been perpetuated by man against man. More people have died in a few minutes due to natural calamities, disasters, manmade or otherwise, and accidents or even by man alone. But there is not a single example where, in a meticulously planned operation without any provocation or affront with a chilling surgical precision a crowd of about 2000 pounced upon 58 innocent men, women and children and roasted them alive in a train. The target was carefully selected, the place and time preplanned and the tools of destruction well chosen. The roots of Godhra lay at Ayodhya. Ever since the destruction of Babri Masjid, a non-mosque structure, on 6 December, 1992, our secularist choristers have never failed to observe 6 December of each successive year as an anniversary of the demolition, a day of mourning for the faithful and by implication a day of national shame for Hindus in general and BJP and Sangh Parivar in particular. Over the years it has acquired the halo of Karbala, the place of martyrdom of Hussein, the son of Ali, the cousin and son-in-law of Prophet Mohammed. The formation of the Babri Masjid Action Committee soon followed and the case went to the court with several senior BJP and Sangh Parivar leaders named as accused. In a yearly ritual the secular brigade went breast-beating and routinely obstructed the proceedings of the Parliament. If they have their way the neo-secularists would have declared 6 December as a national holiday and the day of "mourning and atonement" of an unpardonable sin. With so much sympathy from the secularists and the *'fatwas'* and exhortations of their own mullas and community leaders the psyche of Indian Muslims went into a state of terminally cancerous ulcer. From now on each single stone put near the temple premises, every inch of ground moved or altered, each brick consecrated and offered, each shilanyas performed and sanctified by the *'Dharmacharyas'* and saints, each assembly of Hindus, each move of Sangh Parivar at or around the temple site has not only raised the hackles of our neo-secularists but delivered a bodyblow to lacerate the bruised psyche of some Indian Muslims. In such an ambience a spark can trigger a blazing inferno. Then there is no dearth of agent provocateurs and mischief-mongers within, and an eager and hostile neighbour without, always on the prowl to exacerbate communal passions. Our English print media never lagged far behind and spewed venom on what they called Hindu fascists and fundamentalists.

As the Sabarmati Express left Godhra and chugged along towards its destination hell broke loose. The immediate reaction of many Muslim leaders, English media and secularist loud mouths was to excoriate the innocent kar-sevaks returning from Ayodhya, who according to them had it coming. To these wiseheads it was only retributive justice. First let us see what happened. Around 8.00 AM the Sabarmati Express left Godhra, a station 100 kms distant from Vadodara, on its onwards journey to Ahmedabad. As the train reached the outer signal at Falia, the train screeched to a halt due to a vacuum drop as someone pulled the chain. The driver Rajinder Singh saw a crowd of about 500-2000 people approach the train from the left side as 200 more people closed in from the right side. The coach S-6 carrying kar-sevaks, their wives and children returning from Ayodhya caught fire. As smoke billowed and flames leapt across the length of the compartment, there was hell let loose with the cries of people been roasted inside. Somehow, the doors of the coach were bolted from outside and there was no way to escape. In the blazing inferno 59 people lost their lives. All that remained was a skeleton of burnt beams and every thing inside that could burn was turned into a cinder. Two FIRs were lodged, one FIR by the driver for forcible stopping of the train near signal Falia and the torching of S-6 coach, recording the statement of 400 persons alleged by the media to be VHP activists. The second FIR pertains to another attack on Railway Police Force (RPF) personnel, a couple of hours later, lodged by the complainants, being RPF victims, naming 32 accused. In consequence police arrested Mohd. Hussain Kolota, President of Godhra Municipality and Congress backed independent councillor, Abdul Rahim Danta, Zahur Kala, Abdul Rauf, Siraz Abdul

Jamasa and placed Haji Bilal, another independent councillor into police custody. Another notorious member of this gang Razzak Kurkur who owns a guest house nearby was accused of supplying and carrying petrol. Before the investigation could take even the first steps, our secular media supported by Congress and the Left swung into action and pontificated that there was an altercation earlier between the kar-sevaks and some Muslim vendor at Godhra platform. Some even hinted that the kar-sevaks indulged in eve-teasing, some of them being Muslim ladies! Some even suggested that more than sixty litres of petrol used for burning could not have been thrown from outside and that it was already stored inside. In other words, the kar-sevaks had themselves collected the material for their ordeal and set it afire.

The special investigation team (SIT) rightly pursued the theory of a core group of 200 supported by others, as testified by two Muslim vendors Anwar and Baria at Godhra station. One of them, Baria, deposed that one of the core group members Razzak Kurkur forced him to board an autorickshaw along with 9 others and reach 'A' Cabin near Kurkur's guesthouse called *Amaan Guest House* near Godhra station, load the petrol and carry it to the coach. One miscreant entered S-6 through the connecting gallery. He and the other tea vendor Anwar were the initial prime witnesses. SIT had applied for the attachment of the property of 33 absconders, all Muslims. Poonam Tiwari, a resident of Ahmedabad, is on record having said that she saw a bearded youth with a Muslim cap throw a burning rag into the carriage. That as her father-in-law was stamping on the burning rag with his shoes to put out the fire the rear of the carriage started burning; she ran with her one year old son Ashish to the front door and amidst the stampede and jostling, someone pulled her out of the carriage. As she was about to come out another woman held out her child to be taken out. Her mother-in-law was not so lucky. Her anklets later identified her charred body and Poonam's father-in-law who was burnt to cinders was identified by his dentures. As the train pulled out of the station and came to a halt about half a kilometer later, a volley of stones rained on the helpless victims.

Some crystal gazers went to the extent of saying that it was not only an inside job but was a deliberate attempt by the VHP to extract sympathy and prepare the ground for the revenge killings of Gujarat. The Police were still investigating. While *The Outlook, The Indian*

Express and some columnists shook their doubtful heads, the nation was stunned; nothing like this had happened before. Whom had the innocent children and women hurt? Could the kar-sevaks set fire to their own wives and children? The secular media was skeptical about the cause—that plain and simple, it was the case of minority community hoodlums perpetrating the worst carnage of its kind. The nation knew better. The whole Congress and Left leadership, and our English media maintained a deafening silence. Some even gloated on what had happened. Serves them right; they had it coming; why grieve for the sinners? There was any amount of whitewashing of the crime but the silence of the secularists and their refusal to speak out to condemn the heinous crime was to prove fatal. This was the last straw. Instead of offering sympathy and damnning the perpetrators, the secularists scoffed at the Hindu kar-sevaks and trivialized the hurt to Gujarati pride. Reaction was soon to follow. The wind had been sown and the whirlwind was now ready to be reaped. The Gujarat flames burst out on the Indian scene. Godhra, a Muslim predominant locality and being a stronghold of Muslim League, was known for frequent Hindu-Muslim riots dating back even to 1981. Gandhiji had written an article *To the Hindus and Muslims* in *Young India* of 1928 pleading for Hindu-Muslim unity. He was forced to write again in *Navjeevan* on 11 October, 1928: "Two weeks ago I wrote in *Navjeevan* a note on the tragedy in Godhra, where Sri Purshottam Shah bravely met his death at the hands of assailants. The heading of my write up was Hindu-Muslim fight in Godhra. Several Hindus did not like the heading and addressed angry letters asking me to correct it, for it was a one-sided fight. I found it impossible to accede to their demand. Whether there is one victim or more, whether there is a free fight between the two communities, or whether one assumes the offensive and the other simply suffers, I should describe the event as a fight if the whole series of happenings were the result of a state of war between the two communities. Whether in Godhra or in other places there is today a state of war between the two communities. Fortunately, the countryside is still free from the war fever, which is mainly confined to towns and cities where, in some form or other, fighting is continually going on. Even the correspondents who have written to me about Godhra do not seem to deny the fact that the happenings arose out of the communal antagonisms that existed there. If the correspondents had simply addressed themselves to the heading, I should have satisfied myself with writing to them privately and written nothing in *Navjeevan* about it. But there are other letters in which the correspondents have vented their ire on different counts. A volunteer from Ahmedabad who had been to Godhra writes: "You say that you must be silent over these quarrels. Why were you not silent over the Khilafat, and why did you exhort us to join the Muslims? Why are you not silent about your principles of Ahimsa? How can you justify your silence when the two communities are running at each other's throat and the Hindus are being crushed to atoms? How does ahimsa come there?"

Godhra had always been a tinderbox of communal violence. However much the English media tried to send the investigating team on a fishing expedition by throwing red herrings now and then, the facts were incontrovertible. About 2000 people just cannot materialize from nowhere, all prepared with incendiary material to stop the train and set it on fire. They did not come from long distances, the crowd that assembled in a short time at a pre-determined location at a preplanned time had not come from outside. Indeed there would have been Pak agent provocateurs and ISI men assisted by local organizations such as Student Islamic Movement of India (SIMI), which had lately been very active in Godahra. It was pure and simple a Muslim plot possibly aided and abetted by Pakistan. SIMI is known to have links with international Islamic fundamentalist organizations and was duly banned on May 9, 2002. The Solicitor General S.K. Aggarwal arguing on behalf of the Union Government had admitted before the Tribunal that SIMI aims to utilize students and youths to support and propagate Islamic *Jehad*.

With the Parliament in session and the media going to town with half-truths and innuendos and crying for Modi's scalp for the subsequent Gujarat riots, the opposition stalled the proceedings day after day till their motion was defeated by 94 votes, inspite of Telugu Desam Party (TDP) and National Conference (NC) of the NDA allies abstaining. No one spoke a word about Pakistan's infamous and invisible hand behind Godhra and Gujarat. They kept paying glowing tributes to the secularist English media. If our English media needed a pat instead of a rap on the knuckles, it came from Pakistan, the instigator of violence itself. Who says Pakistan does not have friends in India? In Godhra as has been happening in India all these years even before partition the first spark was lit by the minority and the majority retaliated. The script is not new, the sequence is old; and the story repeats itself over and over again. Minority provocation leading to majority backlash. Hindus left to themselves are and shall remain peaceful as long as the minorities and their secularists godfathers do not provoke.

Peeved by the compulsive venting out of spleen against the Sangh Parivar by some Islamic fundamentalists, particularly Jamal Ansari, Syed Shahabuddin, Hashim Kidwai, and others of this ilk masquerading as liberals many perceptive readers from the land of Mr. Mani Shankar Aiyer felt constrained to rebut some of their rantings. Fortunate, they say, are those who are born in India, a country that has enough space to accommodate different faiths, religions and philosophies. How true! It is only in India that a minority enjoys more privileges than even the majority and accepted as a "state within a state". Can one imagine a large number of members of a majority community being roasted alive in the barbarous manner by some minority hoodlums as has happened in India? Hindus living in our neighbouring countries, professing Wahabi Sunni Islam, Pakistan and Bangladesh, cannot imagine carrying out such a massacre. And would there have been a demonstration in support of the perpetration of such a crime as has been orchestrated in India by our very own elite preaching sermons on secularism. These Muslims are lucky to be born in India where the original inhabitants are treated with disdain, while those of foreign religion preaching hatred between "believers and non-believers" are given prime space in our English dailies. If they had been born in a Muslim country could they have been allowed to write against *Jehadi* terrorists? Could they have perfected the art of running with the hare, read 'secular Hindu' and hunting with the hounds read 'Muslim fundamentalists'. They call themselves 'Muslim Indians' something, which Hindus living in our neighbouring Islamic countries cannot dare.

10

Gujarat

To a proud people, heir to the richest heritage of the greatest civilization known to mankind, that endured an astronomical time span of ten millennia of human existence, humiliated for one thousand years by rapacious invaders crossing the Hindukush to kill Hindus, defile their land, vandalize their temples and shrines, burn and pillage their homesteads, slaughter their men in scores of thousands a day, deprive them of their land and possessions, heap indignities, insults and injuries beyond description, there was no reprieve. To a people trampled upon by merciless foot soldiers of militant Islam for centuries, inveighed, reviled, ridiculed, excoriated by their own 'secular' co-religionists there was no light at the end of the tunnel. Hindu rage had been simmering for five centuries till it boiled over on 6 December, 1992. The demolition of Babri Masjid, raised on the ruins of a temple at the birthplace of Lord Ram, our most revered god, was the rectification of a thousand years of historical wrong and shame. The task carried out by frenzied kar-sevaks long harried, fired at and spat upon by successive anti-Hindu state governments, in their efforts to appease minority Muslim electorate was to become a national disgrace in the lexicon of our Leftist litterati and neo-secularist column writers. 6 December, 1992, far from being celebrated as a day of retributive justice and redemption of national honour, is being remembered as a day of national shame. Can a nation stoop any further? Sure enough, there was a trial by our elite English media, the ubiquitous arm of inquisition and a cacophony of protest by our secularist opinion makers. The punishment was not long in coming. Four state governments including three who had no part in this historical act were dismissed. Taking their cue, Islamic fundamentalists wreaked a heavy vengeance with bomb blasts and indiscriminate murder of innocent Hindus in Bombay, guided by the

Muslim underworld dons, acting on the dictates of ISI and sheltered in the sanctuaries of Pakistan and some Gulf States. This was the cause of simmering rage and discontent among the silent Hindu majority, which lay dormant for a long time. The barometer kept falling till 27 February, 2002, arrived. What our neo-secularist opinion makers and self-styled umpires who lay down the paradigms of political discourse had refused to see was soon to be splashed on the national horizon. The critical mass, so to say, of Hindu discontent had reached and what was required was just a spark. This was provided by a Muslim mob on 27 February, 2002, at 8.00 A.M. As soon as the Sabarmati Express carrying kar-sevaks returning from Ayodhya, left Godhra station for Ahmedabad, it was halted at the outer signal. Here an armed mob with incendiary materials was waiting. The plan had been carefully hatched and the operation meticulously planned. Soon there were shrieks of men, women and children crying for help as smoke billowed out and a towering inferno, engulfed coach No. S-6 and all within. Fifty-eight innocent men with their wives and children were burnt to a cinder. As soon as the news of this ordeal by fire spread in Gujarat, the Hindu discontent long suppressed, ignored, shelved, quashed, pushed aside and swept under the carpet exploded like a bomb. There were many ground zeroes. The fear, frustration and grievances of the Hindus burst out in the open. This was a brief Intifada in reverse, and Gujarat now struck back on its tormentors in open defiance of entreaties for restraint.

What happened in Gujarat for almost six weeks was a determined effort by India's enemies. *Time*, the proverbial India-baiter reported Gujarat riots as a civil war, serving back the same fare, which our overzealous media had been churning out day in and day out. When Prime Minister AB Vajpayee mentioned at Goa, who the attackers at Godhra were and what were their motivations, he was misquoted by the media. Vajpayee did no more than echo the words of Bill Clinton, who had said, "There are a 100 million kids who never go to school. Part of our problem in Afghanistan and in the Muslim world is all these kids could not go to public school, so they went to madarasa where they were indoctrinated instead of being educated", and further "It is no accident that most of these terrorists came from Muslim countries that were not democracies." Gujarat was the funnel through which ISI poured arms, ammunition, drugs and fake currency into Indian heartland, and had every intention to turn Gujarat into another Kashmir. There have been seizures of sophisticated arms and ammunition in Ahmedabad. Touting the riots as unprecedented in the history of Gujarat, our hysterical English media went bellicose against Chief Minister Narendra Modi, baying for his blood. The *Indian Express* gave out lurid details of individuals being killed and some Muslims rendered jobless because their workplace like garages and workshops in Ahmedabad walled city had been gutted by Hindu hooligans. They forgot what had happened in 1969. The paper bemoaned that these jobless Muslim youths had taken to manufacturing crude bombs, which was a flourishing small scale industry; a dozen crude bombs a day could fetch them Rupees 100 or more. But the hazards were high. Between April 14 and 29, there were 67 people injured during bomb making and many died. So this is what the victims of Gujarat genocide were doing, manufacturing to kill Hindus! To quote Dy. Commissioner Zone III R.D. Malkadia, "During a flare up in Kalupur or nearby areas the police finds itself walking into a battlefield. All kinds of bombs explode around you and you don't know where they are coming from. An innocuous looking pipe half an inch in diameter may explode in your face, causing severe injuries."

Ignoring the Muslim violence, the secularist *Indian Express* in one news item focussed on Hindu reprisal screamed 'now, boulders add to Gujarat arsenal'. Two Muslim daily wagers going to work in Dol Bazar area of Kankaria had their head smashed by stones hurled on them and died on the spot. After the above headlines in bold prints the paper went on to mention that explosions also took place in Mirzapur area near Rani Roop Mati Masjid, engineered by Muslims but kept silent on the identity of the culprits and mentioned in passing that a 12 bore pistol with cartridges was also found. This is impartial reporting, as secularist as can be. To an uninformed reader this is hell let loose. But no newspaper or TV channel even once mentioned that more destructive riots had taken place earlier.

Before we come to 1969 riots let us glance first at a the history of riots in Gujarat. Here is an authoritative factoid given by a Gujarat MLA. "The fact is that Gujarat, especially Ahmedabad, Bharuch, Godhra and Vadodara are communally very sensitive. As many as 443 major and minor communal riots have taken place in the past

30 years, of which Ahmedabad has been the worst affected. Hundreds of Muslims were killed in the 1969 riots. Similarly, several people belonging to the minority community were killed in 1985, 1992 and 1995 riots. This time, the Congress and other parties have made it an issue. If the present riots are state-sponsored then what about the riots in 1969, '85, '92 and '95? Who was in power those days and what was the police doing? In 1969, the riots went on for several months. The Congress was ruling right from the district bodies to the Assembly. Would it be fair to say that those were Congress-sponsored riots. You cannot have double standards?". And then the role of Congress and opposition in fanning the flames of violence. "The Congress is fueling communal tension in Gujarat by launching a political agitation against Chief Minister Narendra Modi. There was no single state in the country without communal riots after independence and no state where an agitation was launched against the Chief Minister. I can understand the opposition's demand for the Chief Minister's resignation. But, nowhere has there been agitation of this kind. The Congress agitation only worsened the situation. It is surprising that far from appealing for peace, the opposition led by the Congress has been inflaming passions. Is it only the duty of the administration and the ruling party to bring the situation under control? Does the opposition not have any responsibility? If past administrations have been successful in controlling communal tensions, then why are they recurring every now and then? The Congress has blundered by launching a political agitation in Gujarat. Will the Congress give the guarantee that there will be peace if Mr. Modi is removed? If yes – it is obvious that they are playing to the gallery of the rioters. It clearly shows that the Congress is directly involved with the rioters. I repeat changing the Chief Minster is not a solution to the problem." Now on the prolonged duration of the riots and blaming of ISI, "Several areas in Ahmedabad city have turned into dens for Islamic fundamentalists and ISI agents. This was evident from the fact that the RDX used in Mumbai blasts in 1993 was transported from Kutch to Ahmedabad and moved to Mumbai. Willingly or unwillingly, some of the Muslim youth fell prey to these forces mainly under the influence of *jehad.* They adopt a different strategy. They do not allow the police to patrol. They put their women folk in the forefront to prevent the police from combing

the areas. Attacks on police are not new in these areas. Even in the 1985 riots, several policemen were attacked with petrol bombs. During the present riots, several foreign rocket launchers were used by the mob. The police has unearthed a crude bomb manufacturing company run by fundamentalists. We strongly believe that the second phase of communal riots are being engineered by the foreign forces and fundamentalists." And in the so-called delay in deploying the army here is the official version. "A baseless allegation was levelled at us that we did not move the Army in time. I condemn this. The Congress-led opposition has conveniently hidden facts and indulged in Goebbelean disinformation. The Gujarat Government requested the Centre to deploy the Army on February 28, the day after the Godhra incident took place. The Gujarat Government's request was presented before the Union Cabinet and the Army was deployed in the communally sensitive areas the next morning. As many as 13 companies were deployed on the early hours of March 1. Eight companies were posted in Ahmedabad, 2 in Vadodara, 2 in Godhra and 1 in Rajkot. Another company was kept in reserve. The situation in Ahmedabad had turned normal but, despite knowing these facts, the Congress and other political parties made a hue and cry over the issue just to malign the Union Government." And on the role of the media. "I do not want to comment on the freedom of the press. But, I do feel the media should have been more restrained and observed some restrictions while covering such sensitive issues. Media reports should not instigate or incite people to violence. I remember media reporting during the communal violence in 1969 and 1985. It was difficult to find out who killed whom. The papers did not publish photographs of those killed. I am unable to understand the TV channels repeating the same footage ad nauseam. Is it fair to show violence more than 15 times a day? It would be good for the country if such reporting is prevented."

A significant dimension of the rather prolonged Gujarat riots that was missed by many political observers, our media and even security analysists was the nature of prolonged violence against civil society. With their proverbial passivity and excessive tolerance, verging on cowardice the Hindus in general have no stomach for a sustained long battle. It should have been evident to even the uninitiated that there is all along a foreign hand in this low intensity conflict that can suit only one country – Pakistan. These were no ordinary riots but another form of a proxy war by ISI sponsored agent provocateurs. That continues till today, as indicated by the continuing string of terrorist strikes in various parts of India, including the latest and most audicious out at Ayodhya. The marking on sophisticated weapons, and rocket launchers et al, the ammunition manufactured locally by Muslim youths and supplied by Pakistan, all had the ISI trademark. These were no home grown ordinary riots. But Congress in their zeal to target Hindu organizations went with hobnails where angels fear to tread. Pakistan skillfully used Muslim anger, their weapons and Muslim localities as the base for guerilla type of war against lone Hindu targets, not sparing even the fire brigade personnel. They screamed about Muslims deaths, fires and carnage but totally ignored the Hindu casualties and losses and played the Pak tune using the same language and metaphor. While they criticized the government for international opprobrium they quietly smiled inside, pilloried the government and demanded the scalpel of Modi thus setting a precedent for future to authorize the Central Government to sack the Chief Minister who under-performed and was not liked by the opposition. To subvert democracy by shouting inside the parliament and taking out rallies, heaping every imaginable abuse on the helpless chief minister fighting against every odd in confronting a community acting as a base for ISI's internal subversion. Godhra was forgotten and Gujarat became the focus to pillory the government. Captain Amrinder Singh, the Chief Minister of Punjab, in a silent understanding with 10 Janpath, even refused to send commandos to Gujarat as requested by KPS Gill and accepted by him earlier. All this smacked of politics at its worst; ignoring national interest for narrow party and political gains. As the march of proceedings of Inquiry Commissions et al bumbles along, the whole holocaust has been reduced to a pawn in the game of political upmanship between the two leading political parties of the country.

Indira Gandhi, the icon of Congress, had become paranoid after her Bangladesh victory, which was won by General Manekshaw inspite of her undue interference. It was also a victory handed over on a silver platter by the Mukti Bahini who gave us the most accurate information about the enemy dispositions. Add to this the fact that East and West Pakistan were too far to be strategically defensible.

Having earned the sobriquet of Durga, she overplayed her hand during the Punjab militancy which was altogether a different ball game. It was an insurgency conducted by Indian Sikhs with Pakistan support. There was no civil government, judiciary or political leadership, till KPS Gill was given a free hand by the Chief Minister Beant Singh. The situation in Gujarat resembled the initial stage of Punjab militancy. Ultimately, she paid the price with her life by hurting the Sikh sentiments as she ordered an assault on the Golden Temple at Amritsar. Even in her death with the dead body being shown for days together on the TV the Congress succeeded in dividing the people on religious lines to harvest Hindu votes. Earlier she had propped up Bhindranwale, calling him a religious leader, to break the Akali Dal. An SSP in Amrisar told me that 'Punjab can burn and go to hell, Indira is least concerned as long as she can break the back of the Akalis'. In her effort to raise a Frankenstein for political gains to garner Hindu votes, her plan succeeded but only after her death, as Giani Zail Singh, the President, crowned her son Rajiv Gandhi the Prime Minister even when the Parliament was in session. In the process while the Congress obtained a massive majority in the Parliament in the succeeding elections, 3000 Sikhs lost their lives in the anti-Sikh riots of 1984. This is the Congress record for their so-called communal harmony slogan.

The total loss of lives in Gujarat was around 900, including both Hindus and Muslims and it did not amount to a genocide. The history of riots in India is fairly old. The first recorded riots took place during Holi in 1714 towards the end of the Mughal period. Ahmedabad itself has been the scene of alteast 10 major recorded riots. There was no Sangh Parivar then. For almost three weeks the violence was led by Muslims against Hindus and the bulk of causalties pertain to this period. While the police arrested 34000 rioters, majority of them Hindus, both communities suffered loss of property and business due to arson and looting. Against one lakh Muslims living in the relief camps there were also 40 thousands Hindus rendered homeless and staying in refugee camps. So how does this amount to Muslim genocide?

Fiction writers have invented stories to settle scores with the Sangh Parivar. A woman named Saida 'whose stomach was ripped open and stuffed with burning rags' were the type of hot news aired by the TV and faithfully ventriloquised by the opposition benches in Parliament. 'Foetuses taken out and paraded on sword or trishuls' these were the slogans hurled by our secularists and media managers day in and day out. After close scrutiny and further investigation all these were found to be the products of some fiction writer's morbid imagination; and leading the pack was Arundhati Roy. *The Hindustan Times* February 28 edition reporting on Godhra set the trend for the 'secularist', 'Gujarat hit by Ayodhya backlash' and 'BJP fiddles while Gujarat reels under killing'. On March 1, 2002, again a further venting out of spleen against BJP and Sangh Parivar. In its report on atrocity on Muslims published just two days after Godhra, the paper mentioned but once and that too only in passing the bestial burning of kar-sevaks in Sabarmati Express. The visual media just went berserk in this sprint race to be one up in this 24 hours news coverage to splash gory scenes time and again. And while this concoction of fiction and half truths was being played out the press guild remained uncritical of the media's hawking of gutter journalism. The prolonged and drawn out Gujarat riots and its fury was as much a direct result of Muslim appeasement as the incendiary role of the English media, print and electronic. An insight into the Muslim mindset can be obtained by a news item appearing in the *Indian Express* dated 14 December, 2002, in the aftermath of the assembly elections. Shahwar, the sister of Congress MP Ahsan Jaffri, who on February 28, was burnt alive inside in his flat in Gulburg Society, said, "He called every Congress leader, even Soniaji but nobody came to his help. Two months later, our house too was attacked. We even spotted Congressmen in the mob that was trying to break in and kill us." Her husband Jalian Matree, a retired government officer and a Gujarati poet, agreed saying 'the BJP does it openly and also takes pride in it. The Congress is a bit different because they don't say it openly. Otherwise it is one and the same." Matree scoffed at Congress fielding Vaghela, "he worked for 27 years to make the BJP what it is in Gujarat today. Now he is being projected as our saviour! I don't think ideologies can change so rapidly". He felt that Congress indifference to post-Godhra violence was due to the fact that Muslims do not have enough numbers. Referring to post-Godhra riots, he said, "this was an extreme case, but it's happened earlier too. Jafri's house was gutted in the 1969 riots as well; he and his family survived only because they were not there. This happened under a Congress government. Even our house, then in Krishannagar Housing Colony in Saijpur Moga, was gutted. For us, there is no choice." And finally talking of Congress he complains that they didn't take on Modi for what had happened to us but for political reasons. Even during the rallies they were careful not to attack those who destroyed our lives. They know Muslims had no choice and didn't want to appear sympathetic to us. This is cynicism at its worst; using Muslims only for their votes and then they can go to blazes. That is the true face of secularism peddled in India; so think the Muslims. There has been a concerted volley of criticism from the western nations against India on Gujarat riots. The pitch of this slander campaign and vilification of Hindu organizations has also been on the rise, prompted by the similar language used by our very own desi English media. Most of the slanderous cacophony is heard in the Islamic and Christian majority countries. There have been many riots in the country before Gujarat 2002, but never has the foreign media been so active in its condemnation of violence on minorities. The 1985 riots in Gujarat lasted for three months and hundreds were killed and wounded but no foreign press or country levelled accusations against the Congress dispensation then. It is ridiculous to project Hindu majority culture as another face of Nazism and ascribe the happenings in Gujarat to 'Hindutva' ideology of the state government, allegedly antagonistic to the Islamic minority. The Gujarat violence is being used by the Western media as a means not only to insult Hinduism but to tarnish the image of the country, equating Modi with Millosovich and the VHP with the storm troopers of Nazi Germany. This is the pernicious conspiracy against the honour and sovereignty of India. Working in tandem with foreign media our own media managers, the Congress ideologues and their Leftists pace-setters are not only encouraging but providing nourishment to this assault and interference in the internal matters of a sovereign country. As part of this treasonous campaign, the riot-affected victims were being encouraged to retaliate and instead of dousing the fire an attempt was being made to fuel further violence. Many Muslim organizations were in the forefront of this sustained counter-offensive. When our own politicians welcome foreign criticism, it appears that we have lost all sense of national pride. And how motivated and selective is the foreign criticism is evident from their total silence on atrocities against Hindu minorities in Pakistan and Bangladesh, and the forcible religious conversion of the Hindus and Sikhs in these countries. There were lakhs of Hindus and Sikhs in these countries after the partition. Why is their number not increasing? Where have they all disappeared? More than sixty thousand innocent lives have been lost in the Kashmir valley. Has any foreign country ever severely reprimanded Pakistan? When a country like Britain makes a demand that to solve the Gujarat problem Modi should be removed, is it not a serious trespass into the internal matters of a sovereign nation? Is the European community going to decide who should be the Chief Minister and take away the right of franchise from the people of Gujarat. Colonial arrogance has its limits. Not to be outdone the International Human Rights Commission was also making necessary noises and crying foul. Why did these worthies not visit Gujarat and do a little bit of truth finding? Merely signing the UN resolution on Human Rights gives no one the authority to interfere in the internal matters of a sovereign state. India does not need sermons on religious harmony, secularism and human rights. India did not suffer a 30 years war of religious inquisitions, crusades, Jewish holocaust or Bolshevik purges of millions. Those who live in glass houses should not throw stones on others. In a recent session of the Confederation of Indian Industries (CII) the busy bodies who occasionally get together over sumptuous meals at five star hotels to chalk out the industrial roadmap of India, turned over a new leaf by discussing the Gujarat riots. The concern of the CII, which has had thus far been somnolent on social issues, least of all natural disasters was certainly touching. It woke up to its social responsibilities to discuss Gujarat. But this was an exercise in tokenism. The gesture was indeed touching. Of all the misfortunes plaguing our social fabric they found that Gujarat riots gave them enough food for thought if not follow up action. The concern expressed during the deliberations was confined to violence against Muslim minority. Incidentally not a single member of this august body had visited the riot-effected areas. While the concern expressed for the Muslim refugees was laudable, there was no mention of 40 thousand Hindus living in refugee camps. There was no expression of solidarity with their own business community in Gujarat who had suffered a terrible trauma and closure of most of their industrial units, not to speak of hundreds of crores of rupees in business losses. The other distinguishing feature of this session was that instead of first inviting the prime minister as protocol demands, they asked Sonia Gandhi, the leader of opposition, to address the meeting and make a political statement. They should have known that this was as good as allowing her to use this platform to demand a change of government, which she did. Since when has the CII become a political platform or the Hyde park of India? Vajpayee, who was invited later in full breach of protocol, did not mind and was magnanimous enough to confine himself to offering corrections to Sonia Gandhi's earlier diatribe and thereafter returned to the business agenda. One thought that Hindu-baiting was confined only to political circles. The malaise seems to have infected even the very insides of our industrial fraternity.

For our neo-secularists behind the fig leaf of secular rhetoric everything is fair. It would be futile to look for ideological underpinnings behind their populist polemics and substantive issues in their election campaigns. Congress, the self-styled leader of the secularist pack, during the Gujarat elections of December 2002 did not exactly cover itself with glory. Routed at the hustings, the Congress had only itself to blame. It tried to ride two horses, soft Hindutva with a divisive agenda and putting Kshatriyas, Harijans, Adivasis and Muslims (KHAM) against caste Hindus. And secondly good governance. Thus it fell between two stools. The Hindus did not bite the first one and the second issue was not an issue at all, not being party specific. All parties talk of good governance which after all is axiomatic and mandatory for any party aspiring to govern. To peddle its soft Hindutva, it chose SS Vaghela, an RSS renegade, who did not sound convincing. Incidentally it was the same Vaghela whose government was first propped up by the Congress and subsequently pulled down in October 1997 for bad governance, their present election plank. Their charge sheet read, "the state government has neither provided clean and efficient administration nor has it provided democratic secular government in the state. Unfortunately, the present government has acquired notorious reputation as a corrupt, inefficient, weak, autocratic and whimsical government." An observer who returned back from Gujarat related an off-quoted joke of Laloo Prasad Yadav, the Sancho Panza of Congress who in one of his rallies thundered, "if you vote Congress to power I promise you that I will make another Bihar out of Gujarat". This was the last straw and Gujaratis had made up their mind. But the most vital issue of national security against Pak-sponsored terrorism in a border state, which had suffered the trauma of Akshardham was not only trivialized but mocked at, to spite the BJP and Sangh Parivar. The electorate could not be fooled and they gave their verdict. National security can no longer be ignored. Just as the adjoining state of Maharashtra had produced two national leaders, the moderate Gokhle and Tilak the radical and a true Hindu, so also Gujarat had produced Gandhi and Patel. Hindus knew whom to choose. Cutting across caste lines including even the tribals, it was an unprecedented consolidation of Hindu votes.

We have discussed how the then Opposition stalled the proceedings of the Parliament on the Gujarat riots day after day. It was only after the censure motion against the Government was defeated, 267 against 181 that the debate finally died. The flag-bearers of secularism trying to peddle half-truths as facts, exaggerating Muslim hurts against Hindu losses tried to line themselves up in the ranks of the righteous against the demons of Hindutva and the BJP. No one dared to present the complete picture for fear of losing minority votes. Dissent in a democracy is welcome and a necessary part of the democratic process. John Stuart Mill is reported to have said that even if the complete humanity is on one side and a lone individual thinks differently, it is possible that the single individual may be right. Prophets and leaders of substance have always swum against the tide. The self-styled secularists have done the greatest damage to the cause of secularism and all this for political gain. It is time we define secularism in the Indian context. Gujarat has lent urgency to such efforts. Hindus and Muslims may not intermarry and sup together but they are intimately concerned with the pain and happiness of each other. Being a Muslim should not be a certificate for secularism, just as Hindu identity does not mean Hindu extremism. Have our secularists ever pointed out to the Muslims their mistakes or shortcomings? Have they, along with Hindu violence, seen the brutalities by Muslims in Gujarat? Have they visited the mourners in Hindu homes? Has it ever been recorded by the press or the visual media? The Minority Commission, Human Rights Commission and social services organizations have served only one fare, 'Muslim genocide'. No one cared to understand the agony of Hindu victims.

Which form of justice demands that while ridiculing and calumnising Hindus their religious tolerance is also mocked at.

The Congress sponsored massacre of Sikhs in 1984 is an embarrassment that our secularist friends will prefer not to be mentioned. Peace in Gujarat could not have been possible without a spirit of accommodation between Hindus and Muslims, the very point that RSS stressed in Bangalore, which upset many of our Muslim well-wishers. Was it wrong to state that it is only an accommodative spirit and goodwill of the majority community that can ensure and guarantee the safety and security of the minority community? But there are forces outside, who do not wish this to happen. Their interest lies in keeping the pot of communal violence boiling and our minorities instigated by these vested interests and championed by our secularists, bite the bait and initiate violence. Let us not forget the way Deendaar Anjuman was working at the behest of the ISI to disturb communal amity and demonize the RSS, till an investigation by the Karnataka Police under the Congress rule exposed the plot. Similarly there were any number of secular big mouths protesting against the ban on SIMI for its subversive activities. More on this in a later chapter. Not once did our secularists shed a tear on four lakh displaced Kashmiri Pandits living as refugees in their own country, thanks to the depredation of Pak-sponsored terrorists.

Before we close the survey on, before, during and after Gujarat 2002, it would be worthwhile to see the ground picture and the gut feeling of Gujarati Hindus in general and the much maligned Secretary of the VHP Dr. Praveen Togadia, a practising surgeon in particular. Before Tavleen Singh, an *Indian Express* interviewer, could interrogate Togadia, the latter gave her two books *The Meaning of Glorious Quran* by Mohamed Marmodeup Puckhali and the *Quranic Concept of War* by Brigadier S.K. Malik of Pak Army to read before she could grasp what VHP was up against, warning that if the secularists continue to support *Jehadis*, a civil war in India was a certainty. Now the factoid. He reasserted that Gujarat happened because the secularists camp was silent on Godhra. He even quoted the *Indian Express* newsline that the kar-sevaks were killed since they were coming from Ayodhya.

A brief paraphrase:

- Tavleen shows ignorance of such a news item. Togadia retorts by saying that he has this piece in his laptop. Another newspaper said that not only were they coming from Ayodhya but also shouting slogans. Was that the reason why they were killed? Togadia asked.
- One newspaper mentioned an altercation with a Muslim vendor as a provocation for torching the carriage. If so, why was the train not burnt at the Railway Station, but only after one kilometer where a crowd of 2000 was waiting with kerosene and petrol.
- Many secular newspapers carried false stories that one lady was pulled in the train. That was wrong. Being a medical student of forensic science he could confirm that the coach was not ignited from inside as reported in our secular newspapers; some even suggested an inside job implying that the victims immolated themselves! With this criminal news reporting the newspapers defended the perpetrators of the crime just as they had said Akshardham was a necessary nemesis to Gujarat riots.
- Secularists were defending *Jehadis* after Godhra blaming victims for the violence. After Akshardham all the secularists – probably having learnt a leson from violence – condemned it, they have not established victims of the crimes as the perpetrators.
- Underplaying Singhal's statement that Godhra caused Gujarat, he said "What's wrong in that?"
- Denied its support of violence. Quoted Noakhali and the consequent mission of massacre of Hindus in 1946. This caused reprisals against Muslims in Bihar. Gandhiji visited both places; 750 villages affected by riots, 5300 killed both Hindus and Muslims, three lakh rendered homeless. According to one Muslim it was Congressmen who were burning Muslim homes. There was no RSS or VHP there. On being questioned by Gandhiji the Congressmen sheepishly lowered their eyes in shame. Can the massacre of Muslims in Bihar be blamed on Nehru, the Prime Minister of the interim government? Congressites explained Bihar killings of Muslims as a reaction to the Noakhali Hindu massacre, so what's new? In 1969 Gujarat riots when Hitendra Desai was the Congress Chief Minister and Indira Gandhi the Prime Minister 700 Muslims

got killed. Did anyone blame them? But you have decided to blame Modi because BJP has no right to rule in Bharat since your mindset is absolutely anti-BJP and anti-Hindu.

- To the charge of state-sponsored violence after Godhra, but none after Akshardham. "Two women were ..." Tavleen was cut short by Togadia, "One by one. You have asked why there was no violence after Akshardham. Do you know the difference in the attitude of the secularists after Akshardham and after Godhra? After Godhra they were defending *Jehadis*, blaming the victims for the violence. After Akshardham, all the secularists– probably having learnt a lesson from the violence, condemned it, they have not established victims of the crime as the perpetrators. Not a single Muslim of public standing condemned the violence immediately after Godhra but after Akshardham, all of them condemned it." Tavleen's question and Togadia's answer in original "Any violence should be condemned, it should have no place in civilized society but if violence continues against Hindutva in the name of *jehadi* terrorism, there will be anger. Regarding this incident, I refuse to believe there was any such incident. It is also a tactic of the secularists to defame. And further, first secularists should correct their mindset regarding the Hindu-Muslim problem because secularists have inherited that mindset from Europe, from the German-Jew paradigm. Both were ethnically and culturally separate. Secularists consider the Hindu-Muslim problem within the same paradigm, so they are giving out the wrong perception to both Hindus and Muslims. I hold secularists partially responsible for the divide. Partially I will blame the *jehadis* and partially the politicians. These three are responsible. Hindus and Muslims are not like Jews and Germans because we are ethnically and culturally the same. I recently made a statement that Muslims should have genetic tests conducted – because I am a doctor – and they will find that their ancestors were Hindus. When I say this I am accepting that they are our brothers. Second, secularists should accept that culturally too, we are the same. Islam is not a culture, it's a religion in which so many cultures are there. The culture of an Arabian Muslim, Afghan Muslim, Indonesian Muslim and Indian Muslim is not the same though they may have the same religion. The culture of Hindus and Muslims of Bharat is the same, if we are socially and.... let me complete madam. You are extending your thesis that it will lead to Partition – again this is your thesis I have been reading for the last month. On the contrary in Bharat, Hindus are terrified due to Jehadis and the criticism of the secularists. Tell me a single corner of Bharat in which Muslims are not moving freely with their caps, that they are not practising namaz. And what happened in Kashmir with the Hindus, what happened in Akshardham, what happened in Godhra? But you want to defend Jehadi terrorists, you are trying to establish that the Muslims are terrified. You people are giving Muslims separatist feeling like leftists did in pre-independence India." When she asked regarding VHP, Togadia replied, "because we are a Hindu organisation, we don't need any liking from the Muslims. It is the history of Islam in the last 14 centuries that they have never preferred any Hindu organization. Regarding VHP spreading hatred. Not at all, it is the handiwork of the secularists. Muslims should not feel that we are against Islam". Again, I am telling you we are not against Islam, we are against *jehad*. *Jehad* and India cannot coexist, they have to forget *jehad* and they will get the love of Hindus. We are not against mosques but we are against madarsas which are teaching *jehad* and hatred against Hindus. We believe that there should be legislation in Bharat that anybody practising or professing *jehad* should be sentenced to death because you create a violent atmosphere in Bharat in which Hindus will be killed and in retaliation Muslims will be killed." Regarding the burgeoning base of VHP, Togadia said that "Gujarati Hindus abroad see what's happening in the world. A Gujarati is a middle class Hindu with a lot of exposure to what is going on abroad. As you know the majority of Indians outside India are Gujaratis, so they see what is happening in Saudi Arabia, Algeria, Nigeria, Chad, Chechnya, Holland, France. So Hindus of Gujarat are more aware. Secondly, you know ISI and fundamentalists activities have grown very fast in Gujarat in the past decade. So many AK47s seized, so much RDX, so many people from madrassas arrested, so this has resulted in people joining the VHP to protect themselves."

- To Tavleen's question that VHP is spreading its influence by spreading hatred in Gujarat, Togadia shot back, "I think this is also a secularist thesis that when there is growth of a Hindu organization, you don't see it as a positive thing because you cannot believe that it can be positive. It is not a simple question of a Hindu-Muslim marriage, it is a cultural clash of more than a thousand years."
- And lastly, the final two questions and answers. "For your information, my room partner in medical school was a Muslim and yet he is my friend. It is not a simple question of Hindu-Muslim marriage. Each and every Hindu girl married to a Muslim accepts Islam. Give me ten incidents in which a Muslim has accepted Hinduism. A Muslim boy marrying a Hindu girl insists, she accepts – (and some time kills if she does not)– Islam. It is a conspiracy to Islamize Bharat and for that one lakh Hindu girls are abducted. It is the biggest problem and the process of Talibanisation of the Indian Muslims is going on very fast. What you are seeing is that despite all the efforts of secularists, we Hindu organisations are getting support because of this process of Islamisation of Bharat. We see what is going on in Kashmir, what is going on also in North Bihar, Assam, Bengal, and the western parts of UP."

We have gone into some details regarding this interview to illustrate what the average Gujarati felt about the partisan role played by the English press and how the drum beaters of secularist brigade and Hindu-baiters completely misread the mood of an average Gujarati. With the change of Government at the Centre in 2004, the self-styled consicous keepers have interpreted this routine democratic event as a vindication of their skewed projections of things.

During Gujarat riots in 1969, the media was thoroughly exposed when one of its reporters was rebuffed by a Muslim octogenarian, who replied that if the Hindus had indulged in the slightest violence against Muslims in East Bengal or Pakistan they would have found themselves in jail. The government sponsored media hack did not know which way to look. Incidentally, it was this riot when the much maligned George Fernandes repeatedly visited Ahmedabad to give a healing touch to the suffering Muslims, bringing medicines, milk products and baby food packets for distribution among the riot-affected victims. He even forced the Collector, Ahmedabad, to allow him to visit Behrampura, a Muslim locality deserted by the fleeing Muslims. None of the Congress MPs or MLAs from Gujarat or the big mouths from other parties ever visited the riot-torn areas. All they did then, as they did this time, was to make noises on the security of the Parliament building. One cannot miss the irony when Sonia Gandhi spoke on Gujarat in a debate in the Parliament on April 14, "the NDA has been a passive spectator to the actions of a blatantly partisan Chief Minister who has besmirched the fair name of Gujarat". In 1969, she should have known, her mother-in-law, the Iron Lady, did the same. If anything Mrs Gandhi was more culpable.

Returning to Gujarat 2002, let us see what words the media used for the killing of Muslims in Gujarat: "Genocide of Muslims, Pogrom, Massacre". To set the record straight let our secularist media read the following extracts from the record of genocide perpetrated against the Jews as observed by a real life character in the book *Exodus* by Leon Uris, a compulsory reading for those who use these words loosely. Here it is: "Four centuries of Jew-baiting came to a climax in 1648. During a Cossack uprising half a million Jews were slaughtered;, the frenzy of the slaughtered was such that Jewish infants were often thrown into open pits and buried alive." "The Warsaw ghetto, the largest human stockyard in man's history, one held nearly six hundred thousand people. That number was decimated by starvation, disease, executions, deportation to save labour and finally, assembly line murder in Treblinka. When the Big Action ended, less than fifty thousand remained."

And then the real face of genocide and the Poland holocaust. "Genocide – carried out with the precision and finality of a machine. At first the efforts of the Germans had been clumsy. They killed by rifle. It was too slow. They organized their transport and their scientists for the greater effort. Steel covered trucks were designed to lock in and gas to death prisoners en route to burial grounds. But even the gas vans proved slow. Next came the crematoriums and the gas chambers capable of killing two thousand people in a half hour – ten thousand on a good day in a major camp. The organization and planning proved itself, the genocide proceeded on an assembly line basis. Thousands of prisoners threw themselves on the quick mercy of electrified barbed wire to cheat the gas chambers. Hundreds of thousands who fell to disease and hunger, stacked up emaciated corpses thrown into unmarked ditches, with logs placed between them and gasoline poured over them. And the game of deception that was played to tear children away from their mothers under the guise of resettlement, and of trains packed with the old and feeble. One heard of the lousing chambers where prisoners were given bars of soap. The chambers were gassed and the soap was made of stone. Mothers, who hid children in their clothing, which was hung up on pegs before going into the chambers. But the Germans knew the ruse and always found the little ones. Then there were thousands who knelt naked beside graves they had dug. Fathers holding their heads over the eyes of their sons as German pistols went off in the backs of their heads. *Haupsturmfuehrer* Fritz Gebauer, who specialized in strangling women and children barehanded and who liked watching infants die in barrels of freezing water. Heinen, who perfected a method of killing several people in a row with one bullet, always trying to beat his previous record. Frank Warzok, who liked to bet on how long a human could live hanging by the feet. Was it at Gross Rosen or did they hear Wilhaus' "Death Tango" at Janowska? There were bodies which were melted to fat in the manufacture of soap at Danzig? Death lingered on and on at the displaced person's camp at La Ciotat near Marseillies, France. ... and one heard more names of the land. Danagien, Eivari, Goldpilz, Vievara, Portkunde, Relzee, Chelmno, Majdanik, Treblinka and Sobibor. Kivioli, Varva, Magdeburg, Plaszow, Szebnie, Mauthausen, Sachsenhausen, Oranienburg, Landsberg, Bergen-Belsen, Reinsdorf, Bliziny, Genocide! Fossenberg ! Ravensbrück! Natzweiler! But all these names were small beside the greatest of them all –*Auschwitz* ! Auschwitz with its three million dead! Auschwitz with its warehouse crammed with eyeglasses. Auschwitz with its warehouses crammed with boots and clothing and pitiful rag dolls. Auschwitz with its warehouses of human hair for the manufacture of mattresses! Auschwitz, where the gold teeth of the dead were methodically pulled and melted down for shipment to Himmler's Science Institute. Auschwitz, where an especially finely shaped skull would be preserved as a paperweight! Austchwitz, where the bones of the cremated were broken up with sledge hammers and pulverized so that there would never be a trace of death. Auschwitz, which had the sign over the main entrance: LABOR LIBERATES. Obesturmbannfuehrer Rokita, who ripped bodies apart...

Steiner, who bored holes into prisoners head and stomachs and pulled fingernails and rouged eyes and liked to swing naked women from poles by their hair.

General Franz Jaeckeln, who conducted the massacre of Babi Yar. Babi Yar was a suburb of Kiev and in two days thirtythree thousand Jews were rounded up and shot, to the approval of many cheering Ukrainians. Professor Hirts' Anatomical Institute at Strausburg and of his scientists, and one saw evidence of the deformed women who had been subjects of their experiments. Dachau was the biggest of the "scientific" centres. Dr. Heisskeyer injected children with T.B. germs and observed their death. Dr. Schutz was interested in blood poisoning. Dr. Rascher wanted to save the lives of German air crews and in his experiments on high altitude conditions human guinea pigs were frozen to death while they were carefully observed through special windows. There were other experiments in what the Germans referred to as "truth in science" which reached a peak, perhaps, in the attempted implantation of animal sperm in human females.... Wilhaus, the Commander of the camp at Janowska, who commissioned the composer Mund to write the "Death Tango." The notes of this song were the last sounds heard by two hundred thousand Jews who were liquidated at Janowska. One of them whose hobby was throwing infants into the air and seeing how many bullets he could fire into the body before it reached the ground. His wife was also an excellent shot.... The Lithuanian guards of the Germans who merely clubbed and kicked people to death and the Croatian Ustashis and their violent killings of hundreds of thousands of prisoners too. The lash ! The ice bath! The electric shock ! The soldering iron! Genocide!. The German extermination facilities capable of murdering a minimum of a hundred thousand persons a day in Poland. We do not have the additional numbers who were killed inside Germany. The Polish camps worked at full capacity. New gas chambers and crematoriums were being constructed to increase the rate. That is genocide. Do you want to hear more?

It would be interesting to note what even the erstwhile secularist and liberal and real secular Hindus think of the media upstarts who just pick up a pen and start spewing out hatred of Hindus and even the partners of the BJP- led coalition government. Jaya Jaitley responding to the *Indian Express* of May 16, 2002, in an article published on the editorial page of the same paper of May 18 titled *"We fight your battle—an open letter to General Pervez Musharraf* written by Madhu Kishwar. Strongly objecting to the letter as an insult to those who love India, Jaya Jaitley retorted, "It is doubtful that General Musharraf – the person who, according to a recent report put Pakistan's nuclear programme into action behind his Prime Minister Nawaz Sharif's back, is going to put pen to paper and thank Kishwar for her helpful advice. The assertion and conclusions that Kishwar puts forward must evoke a response from Indians. Unfortunately, her intended audience is the foreign community which loves to take note of the India bashing that Indians do so adeptly." Kishwar's use of the English language deprives 98% of the country's population of sharing her wisdom. According to Jaya, " Kishwar is indulging in hysterics and hyperbole, so is her view that all Hindus are turning into such murderous fanatics that Musharraf's plan to destroy India will be realized by Indians i.e. Hindus. Let us have the honesty to admit the sad truth that Hindus and Muslims attacked each other violently through a series of events that fuelled each group. It is no use ascertaining who used knives and who used acid bombs and AK-47s. To decide who started it all now also depends not on the truth, but on whether you are 'secular' or 'communal', and could take us back to colonial times. Their idea of secularism is certainly not what ordinary Indians know it to be, whether they are from the majority or any minority groups. Let it be absolutely clear to Musharraf and Kishwar that the VHP and Bajrang Dal by no means represent the views of the majority of Hindus, just as SIMI and various maulvis do not represent the inclinations of most Muslims. Did the Khalistanis ever represent the entire Sikh population?"

"It is not so easy for anybody to inject criminality into the bloodstream of the majority or minority community unless there already lie seething imbalances, injustices, perceived or otherwise, economical problems and joblessness which create the climate for violent reactions in any situation. For Kishwar to blame everything on Hindu criminality alone while forgetting to call Godhra any kind of crime and to refer to it merely in passing as something that did not dent the economy of Gujarat must be music to the General's ears. There is so much poison already in the air that even if those inquiring into Godhra genuinely report that it was pre-planned and supported by people inimical to India, it will be attacked as a Hindutva plot to cover up the truth that it was a Hindu plot."

And further the role of the media. "This group which has been peddling the line that everyone in the NDA government is to be hated because they are fundamentalists include the feminist Kishwar, writer Arundhati Roy, media peacock Tarun Tejpal and a handful of journalists and lawyers. They have been screaming ever since this Government came to power and declared its aim of building a strong, resurgent and confident India. This is not an "India is Indira' argument where a person has to love this Government, or any Government for that matter, in order to love this country, but an analysis of how blind hatred of a Government translates into a diatribe that goes far beyond and harms us as a nation. The NDA carried out the Pokharan tests because of the ominous and precarious security environment in the neighbourhood. It has since then effectively overcome all the sanctions and hostility that came in its wake. One would have thought they would be happy that the 'communalists' were finally behaving and doing well. But no! We have Roy suddenly waking up from deep slumber, having missed all the nuclear tests conducted all over the world including Pakistan and China, and declaring herself so alienated from her country of birth that she converted herself into "an independent mobile republic." And finally "Enter Tejpal, who produces a sham expose of defence procurement. He declares with intense pride on his *Tehalka* website that they had destroyed the last sacred cow of the Indian establishment and that his *Operation Westend* was enough for anyone to lose hope in the idea of India. Now we have Kishwar advising Mushrraf not to waste his time destroying India because Indians had all become murderous and would do the work for him. The dastardly attack and killing of over 30 innocent people and Army personnel in Jammu a few days after her open letter was published indicated that the General either doesn't care for her advice or does not read *The Indian Express*. It is indeed sad that Kishwar and her friends have lost faith in this country and its people in their bid to play petulant politics or perhaps for a slice of momentary fame."

In August 2002, two editors of prominent English dailies and Arundhati Roy visited Pakistan on the invitation of a local newspaper there. The statements they made during interviews at Lahore, Karachi and Islamabad, are to say the least, stunning and smacked of unbridled arrogance and treason. Some extracts:

- In India BJP is holding our nuclear policy hostage thus far. Pak should follow suit.
- All of you need not worry about BJP, we the media will sort them out.
- If Muslims are happy in India that is the best certificate for secularism that we have.......
- After Kargil BJP leaders were looking foolish and clueless. It is Sonia Gandhi who bailed them out....
- Every single Muslim of India is a patriot and so we strongly opposed what happened in Gujarat...
- BJP's anti-Pak rhetoric did not bring any electoral gain to them.
- As long as BJP stays in power riots will continue to happen.
- The sole plank of Indian Government in India and the basis of their survival is hatred against Congress.
- The Indian Government is blindly national and poses a danger to its neighbouring countries.
- India should not have taken advantage of the situation prevailing in 1971 and help the creation of Bangladesh.
- Government of India should not have held out a threat of war against Pakistan after the terrorist attack on its Parliament on 13 December, 2001.
- Defence Minister George Fernandes is a suspicious character and a man lying on his nationalistic views.
- We appreciate the Pak position on Kashmir. Conditions can improve but the biggest block to improving the situation is the party in power in India. India should offer complete freedom to Kashmir.
- Just like India-China border dispute there is really no need for a final settlement or solution.
- BJP and RSS have not only demolished Babri Masjid but have raised questions on its very existence as a mosque.
- The Hindu Right is a new form of Rightists who aim to target 14 crore Muslims, and 2 percent Christians. Unlike other Rightists they are dangerous Caesars, because they subscribe to a fascist ideology.

- The ISI was blamed for the Bombay blasts while all this was the work of the Hindu Right.
- Indian leaders missed the historic opportunity at Agra to improve Indo-Pak relations.

The lady writer was in complete agreement with these gentlemen. According to her she was not only an Indian but a world citizen. In her words, " the national flag is just a peace of cloth, which narrows down the mind and it is used to wrap up the dead bodies".

Foreign funds and money does speak. All these three treasonous and wise persons from the East who visited Pakistan are on record in the premier Pak newspaper– *Daily Times* 16 August, 2002, *Dawn* 16 and 19 August, 2002, *The News* on Sunday 25 August and 1 September. In all the statements made by these wiseheads there is not a single mention anywhere of any Pak culpability. In spite of all that is happening in Pakistan, the terrorists playing havoc, massacre of Christians, America baiting, cross-border terrorism, Al-Qaida hideouts receiving support from Islamic extremists and the ISI. Not one word of mention leave alone condemnation. The very fact that vital issues and international concerns like terrorism of which Pakistan is the epicentre were not even touched. The whole exercise clearly planned by Pakistan had only one aim: to make the scribes spit on their own country and tell the International community how right Pakistan and how wrong India is on all issues of national concern. Whatever internal dissensions or differences within religious groups in Pakistan may be, there is one common meeting ground—hatred of India. This trait is singularly missing in India. When Indian journalists travel in India they criticize India, when Pak journalists come to India the theme remains the same, anti-India tirade. Subjects are selectively chosen so that India can be pilloried: Kargil, military coup against Nawaz Sharif, the betrayal at Agra, calling *Jehad* necessary concomitant of Pak foreign policy, active cooperation with Al-Qaida, support to Taliban, and sponsorship of cross-border terrorism are all known issues to this class of visiting professors of political science. There is a grand design behind this, which is financed by foreign vested interests inimical to India. The mindset that feeds on removing all distinctions between BJP-bashing, Hindu-baiting and anti-Indian polemics is a typical secularist facade. Our media plays the tune that it is paid for. Sometimes it is for free, a hobby most attractive to these know alls. Mistaken under the impression that there are a few madcaps 'there, as they are here, who rally against India' they live in their own world of make-believe. The good folks of Pakistan indeed? Did these folks ever criticize their government on Kargil mis-adventure, cross-border terrorism, Bombay serial blasts, IC814 hijacking and for sheltering hundreds of criminals who have caused mayhem in India. No one in Pakistan criticizes their government on any action taken against India. This privilege belongs only to these esteemed intellectuals at large scattering their pearls of wisdom at the drop of a hat.

Details of the performance of this scandal mongering group visiting Pakistan make any self-respecting Indian, who has even an iota of pride in this nation, bow his head in shame. These worthies have not only shamed the nation they have degraded themselves to the lowest level of disgraceful conduct. India could well do without them. All this much hyped and well reported visit brought out only one thing; the unpardonable arrogance and a blind treasonous denigration of one's own country by some of our self-styled media progressives.

The stereotyping of political parties and pinning of labels 'secular' or 'communal' is not based on a reality check but the electoral calculation of those who wish to monoplise Muslim vote-bank. For instance when Congress and Left feel that they stand to gain by a section of Hindu votes and Muslim votes alone do not add up to the magic number, they have no hesitation to use 'soft' Hindutva as they did in the last Assembly elections held in Gujarat. The Congress projected Shankar Singh Vaghela, an old RSS Pracharak and an apostate, as their leader and Sonia Gandhi visited Ambaji temple before starting her election campaign. Some educated and discerning Muslims saw through this duplicity but seemed to be helpless. Why should 'Hindutva' be a dirty word in the first instance? Is it merely a ploy by our neo-secularists to have the best of both worlds; Hindu votes by excoriating what they call the 'lunatic fringe' of the Hindus and dividing Hindus on caste lines to collect whatever votes they can; taking Muslim votes for granted and leaving the sinning 'communal' party, read BJP, to make do with only a fraction of Hindu votes. To quote Francois Gautier, "After Gujarat people could read the sign that good, peaceful non-violent middle class and even lower class Hindus have had it and that they are tired of being made fun of, attacked, bombed, burnt, killed, their women raped, their temples destroyed! What if, rightly or wrongly, it is the portent of things to come, that the next time innocent Hindu women and children are targeted? Hindus might be tempted to take an eye for an eye, a tooth for tooth, the way Israel does at the official level. You may argue that it is a hateful, mad and blind violence, but it is also true that Hindus have been at the receiving end of Christian and Muslim attacks for centuries, that even today 400,000 of them have been made to flee from their ancestral homes in the valley of Kashmir".

The parliamentary debates on Gujarat riots once again exposed the shallowness of the concerns so vociferously articulated in the House. Instead of finding remedial measures to prevent recurrence of such communal violence, the then Opposition party's sole aim was to extract political mileage by putting the ruling party in the dock and trading on human misery. Communal riots were a serious matter and not confined to the BJP ruled states and the cure should be found by going deeper into their root causes. The encouragement to minority separatism must stop and the guilty must be brought to justice. To attribute Gujarat riots to a Hindutva mindset and comparing the latter with Nazism could not only be a fanciful futility but an exercise in self-deception. Hindutva is not only tolerant but enjoins respect for each religion unlike the militant Islam and its Jehadi face. The debate both in the Rajya Sabha and the Lok Sabha completely side-stepped the constructive approach towards prevention and ultimately eradicating the root causes of riots. The politics of calumny is not the answer to the problem. Within 72 hours of the outbreak of violence the army was pulled out from difficult far-off battle positions and deployed in sensitive areas of Gujarat. This is no mean achievement. Mr. KPS Gill, the sole architect of anti-terrorist operational infrastructure and the organizer of a successful effort to eliminate Sikh militancy in Punjab, was dispatched to Gujarat as an adviser to the Chief Minister. Even this did not satisfy the opposition who demanded President's rule despite the fact that there was no breakdown of constitutional provisions. The stone-walling tactics, the repeated adjournments of the Parliament till 7 May, 2002, cost the exchequer Rs. 18 crore. The flag-bearers of secularism and Muslim appeasement had crossed all limits of civilized political discourse. In concert with the media these crusaders of minority rights, far from dousing the fire and applying the healing touch, were busy inflaming communal passions and adding fuel to the fire.

As the storm broke out in Parliament and the political barometer kept falling, a Congress sympathizer and media activist, Praful Bidwai, pathologically allergic to the Sangh Parivar in general and BJP in particular, came out with an article in the May 17 issue of the *Hindustan Times,* titled *From Pokharan to Gujarat.* Pontificating on Gujarat he found a link between 1948 Gandhi's assassination and 1998 Pokharan nuclear blast. Instead of putting the article through the shredder machine before consigning it to the dustbin, some points need to be clarified even to the purblind. Fortyfour years ago, he says, Godse and RSS activists assassinated Gandhi and now Narendra Modi, an RSS Pracharak, a Hindu fundamentalist, and BJP Chief Minister, finds the Muslims a fifth column and deserving of a guilt. First the facts. This gentleman has not read the Home Ministry report which after full investigation under Sardar Patel, the then Home Minister, found the RSS innocent of Gandhiji's murder. It was a canard deliberately spread by another secularist Nehru to score points against Patel and was found entirely unfounded. Godse was not an RSS man. Bidwai castigates VHP for taking pride in Pokharan II, the Hindu awakening to Shakti, the power of missiles and demand for naming India a 'Hindu state'. One doubts the authenticity of the last mentioned demand. India is and shall remain a Hindu majority state, though not a Hindu religious state. Now what is wrong in celebrating the achievements of our industrious scientists, who have placed us in the front rank of nuclear powers. In today's world a nation's worth is measured by its military and economic might. Is Bidwai ashamed of this achievement? He decries the VHP leader Singhal's idea of carrying the hallowed soil of Pokharan to all corners of the country. We should have seen the wave of enthusiasm sweeping the Hindu Non-Resident Indians in the US, who felt one inch taller at the achievement of their motherland. His glee at Godhra, mark these words "today, it is reaping the harvest of the seeds sown by its campaign to build another illegitimate temple, at Ayodhya, fertilized by kar-sevaks who went there from Gujarat in their thousands." So the Kar-sevaks deserved what happened in Godhra. Then he oversteps the limits of his military knowledge by insinuating not only the utter futility of nuclear testing and improving our military arsenal, but criticizing the secrecy behind the explosion. Only those who needed to know, were informed. So much so that even the US was chagrined at the ineptitude of its intelligence not to have known and being taken by surprise. The less the number of our political loud mouths who were informed about these strategic issues in advance, the better. Mr. Bidwai's resentment notwithstanding, RSS was not privy to the secret testing. But Bidwai carries on his tirade, "The decision to conduct the blasts was not taken in the cabinet, following a 'strategic review' or consultations with the defence services. As RSS chief K.S. Sudarshan boasted, it was taken by the Sangh. Only a handful of RSS loyal ministers were privy to it. Indeed, most of our hawkish 'strategic experts' did not advocate actual testing. Never known for much independence they however duly fell in line on May 11 and spun out fanciful *ex-post* rationalizations. Four years on, these appear hollow and fraudulent." Bidwai was also the defence counsel for the NDA partner who too felt that the common agenda did not include nuclear testing. But the NDA members rejoiced wholeheartedly at this national achievement! Then he goes with hobnails on grounds of higher military strategy where angels fear to tread, declaring the utter futility of nuclear deterrence, which to him is against the ethics of war and a barbarous way of meting out indiscriminate punishment on innocent civilians. Why doesn't he preach his sermons to the US, Russia, China and our close neighbour Pakistan? Does he expect us to face two nuclear-armed hostile neighbours, unarmed, with not even a deterrence in place? Squeezing out the last possible drop of the macabre and inhuman from the tragedy of Gujarat carnage for exhibition, he compares it with the barbarity of Chenghis Khan! Those who have read the history of Chenghis Khan's conquest and the massacre of lakhs of civilians in the Muslim kingdoms of Middle East around Bulkh, Bukhara, and Khorasan and Baghdad of the fugitive king Mohmmad Shah of Khorasan will laugh at this comparison. Pyramids of human sculls were raised everywhere celebrating his victory. Did such a thing happen in Gujarat? Those who do not know the first thing about military history should not fool others who do. Half truths are dangerous enough but blatant lies are disastrous. Another profound statement equating Gujarat with a nuclear disaster: "Common to both is the legitimation of genocidal destruction, of a break in the chain of being, of unlimited punishment disproportionate to the threat or crime. Rationalizing a pogrom or worshipping nuclear weapons means banalising evil. Both celebrate revenge and savagery bordering on genocide." There is no sense of proportion. Gujarat 2002 was no different from many other riots before under Congress dispensation; 1985 riots lasted 6 months, 1969 the highest in casualties and many more. Appellations such as masculinity, machocism, virility ascribed to Hindutva are as ill-conceived as the rest of his diatribe. We have discussed Hindutva at some length and need not waste more space here. His swan song, however, needs to be looked into not for its worth but as an illustration of how low our self-styled liberals and humanists can stoop. "Central to this muscular, male supremacist, virulent nationalism is the idea of 'sacrifice' and martyrdom – in the cause of mass destruction. The first South Asian leader who said, "We'll eat grass. But we'll have the bomb", was not Bhutto. It was Atal Bihari Vajpayee, way back in the sixites – with a variation; eating one chapati in place of two, rather than grass. Needless to say, the leaders who pledge such sacrifices on behalf of the people never end up eating grass themselves. They merely prepare the ground for profoundly irrational, hysterical ways of conceptualizing security – by severing the people from the nation. The causal chain that links Pokhran to Gujarat is unmistakable. The first mindset evolves seamlessly into the second. If Gujarat has inflicted unconscionable damage upon India's constitutional order and its claim to pluralism, nuclear weapons have grotesquely perverted our social and economic priorities, promoted crude Social-Darwinist ideas of "survival of the fittest", legitimized unbounded cruelty and degraded India's security." The barb at Vajpayee was a bundle of lies. Vajpayee did advocate production of nuclear bomb even if that meant sacrificing other comforts. One chapatti less perhaps, but the grass sobriquet only applies to Bhutto. Again he strays into politico-military domain, which is not his familiar ground. Does national security sever people from the nation? If there is no security can the nation survive? Can one live with his home destroyed? Then again the illogical linking of Pokharan to Gujarat; one a permanent national security concern and the other a matter of transient communal discord, which can and has happened in many states of the country. Whether one likes it or not, at least in the international arena, the fit happen to not only survive but endure and overcome; the weak only know how to cry on someone else's shoulders and beg for mercy. Incidentally the community Bidwai is pleading for is no sissy, they are known not only for aggression and self-assertion, but also for open hostility and thirst for blood. Cowardice is the virtue of Hindus only, and liberal Hindus at that. And finally with luminaries who speak the language of our hostile western neighbours does India need enemies? When one says that Hinduism is under siege, one does not have to look around for the foreign forces of circumvallation. They are here for everyone to see and there are no countervailing forces around. Hinduism is well and truly under siege.

The outcome of Gujarat elections, while being a rebuff for our neo-secularist thought, also revealed many stark realities that had long been kept under wraps. The first of these was the grand affirmation of Hindu identity and self-respect giving a lie to the media imposed colonial stereotype about the Hindu community being a fractious combine of caste groups; an aggregate so to say of brittle and tissuey elements. The second, that the cost of trifling with Hindu sentiments for garnering votes on the basis of caste division and minority appeasement is going to be electorally unremunerative. Mayawati, the former U.P. Chief Minister, seemed to have noticed the straws in the wind and is already making an effort to broadbase her Bahujan Samaj Party beyond her dalit rhetoric, just as Ms. J.Jayalalitha showed an empathy with Hindu sentiments by enacting a law against forcible conversions. Thus, henceforth, Hindu-baiting is going to be counterproductive. Thirdly, the media heavily biased against Mr. Modi completely failed to read the writing on the wall. Its managers sitting in plush offices in Delhi did not really cover themselves with glory. In fact, everything went wrong with their predictions as the people of Gujarat gave a sharp snub to the Fourth Estate. Fourthly, the complete approach of the English print media that the Godhra tragedy was a richly deserved nemesis for the kar-sevaks because they carried the banners of Ram Janambhoomi and Ayodhya was negated. Even more culpable was the manner in which the Gujarat riots were sought to be delinked from the Godhra carnage and treated as a suo moto orgy of violence by the Hindu community. The electronic media was not far behind, and they tried to whip up minority fears in a manner totally dishonest and provocative. The minorities are under no danger from the majority Hindu community whose tolerance is limitless. The intransigence and intolerance of the minority community towards the native faith of India and the traditions of its past and their insistence on religious conversion will in future impose a heavy cost. The justification of Hindu temples and shrines being attacked by the terrorists will in future be treated as a counterfeit currency. Persistent destruction of Hindu temples for almost a millennia by the Muslim rulers and the latest attack by the Pak terrorists has removed the last fig-leaf of an economic motive that the Marxists ascribed to Muslim iconoclasm. And lastly, Muslims have come to believe that while the 'secular' parties take the Muslim bloc vote for granted, they do not transfer their own Hindu votes to deserving Muslim candidates. This may partially be true but the reality check is that Muslims have very few candidates to offer who can hold out an appeal to the other social groups because of their self-imposed myopia. All in all the inelegant ditching of the Muslims by the Congress, who stood for it, was bound to send tremors in the community.

The people of Gujarat by their verdict gave a snub to the English media, their western clones and the neo-secularists, who had even requisitioned the services of the Chief Election Commissioner (CEC) in the cause of secularism. But what did the people of Gujarat see? Double standards. They saw CEC holding elections in Kashmir under the terrorists' gun and postponing Gujarat elections on flimsy grounds. While three lakh Kashmiri Pandits were denied the right to vote, the Gujarat election was deferred because a few new addresses of Muslims were not available. The CEC banned the VHP yatra, prohibited reference to Godhra and virtually censured Modi's speeches. They saw the media support every word and action of the CEC. While the BJP even once did not utter the word 'Hindutva' during the entire campaign, they saw Congress use 'soft' Hindutva and the media carried their message. They saw the Congress telling the Muslims not to campaign, enter the party office or even wear their Muslims caps. They saw Congress use the sadhus to abuse BJP as an anti-Hindu party. They read the media prophesying relentlessly that Muslims did not vote for the BJP. They saw the Congress widening the caste divide among Hindus to garner votes. They heard the strange secularist logic of the media and the Congress that the Muslims as a strong vote-bank are not only desirable but essential. But different castes being encouraged to vote on caste lines was necessary. They saw the secularists say that denouncing Islamic terrorism was anti-secular. For the Hindus to unite against terrorism is communal, but exhortations to Muslims to defeat a party was secular. Observing the yearly mourning over Babri demolition was secular, but to recall the roasting alive of 58 kar-sevaks was not only anti-secular but illegal. They saw the secularists propaganda premised on the theory that being insensitive to the bruised feelings of the majority is secular, but mere empathizing with the minority feelings is not being adequately secular. They saw these double standards and a single point agenda to defeat the BJP. Consolidation of Muslim votes was secular but dividing Hindu votes was not anti-secular. They have done what Gandhi, the greatest ever Gujarati fought all his life to prevent, division of Hindu society on caste lines and casting away the Harijans from the Hindu fold. The moot question was: Did Modi harvest the hate the secularists created or did the secularists reap the harvest of hate they had sown?

The run up to the outcome of, and the aftermath of Gujarat elections held out many lessons, both short term and long term. The seismic tremors it generated will travel far and wide in the Indian subcontinent, leading to a readjustment of political paradigm and democratic discourse. After a long time, the English media realized that there was no point in demonizing the Hindu community as a whole, and using Narendra Modi as a dartboard for their slings and arrows. Powerful polemics against him were serialized in the media and the column, '*Modimeter*' was just one example. All the media hype against one man who topped their hate list failed to take into account that Modi was only a symptom, and a symbol rolled into one, of a deep churning going on in the majority community. He was no loud mouth upstart but a product of a process that will in future set the ground rules for the exercise of electoral choices. Hindu nationalism will no more be a dirty word. The people of Gujarat and other parts of India will hence forth not accept the thesis that Hindus are restrained by faith to act as bovine onlookers in the face of unwarranted provocation. It was not Modi, who was setting the course but the Hindu upsurge that was driving Modi inexorably to reaffirm Hindu pride. After Godhra, the Hindu groundswell was so powerful that the Hindu-baiting Congress and the secularist brigade had to change gears in an effort to adopt Hindu activism against cow slaughter. Their pointsman, Shankar Singh Vaghela, openly donned a Hindu mantle and used the plank of *soft* Hindutva in full knowledge of the fact that Hindu bashing in Gujarat will not be politically remunerative. This will also upset the electoral arithmetic of those who treated Hindus as an aggregate of various castes to be sliced out for vote convenience. Hindu consolidation, cementing out caste-based faultlines on the one hand and the refusal of Muslims to be treated as permanent clients of the secularist parties on the other spoiled the 'divide and rule' game of the Congress and its fellow travellers. Gujarat has irrevocably demolished the Nehruvian civilizational construct after independence and one leg of his triad of non-alignment, socialism and secularism. The first two have been discredited earlier. The sight of two million people, post-Godhra, comprising urban, educated, middle class and even adivasis and dalits coming on the streets left no doubt in the minds of even the Cassandras that this was a mass movement. It was indeed difficult for the media to grasp the fact that a rich industrial and commercial community seeking material prosperity could jettison the artificial 'secularist' veneer by pursuing a strong Hindu agenda. To the Communists and secularists, the message is loud and clear. There are issues more important than just bread and butter–Hindu pride and cultural self-assertion.

The validity of the Nehruvian consensus on secularism is under challenge. The Gujarat phenomenon was unique on another account. That the Hindu community, which unlike other communities that are at odds with the modern world, has rapidly moved with time in the field of education, trade, industry, information technology, monopolizing the complete motel industry in the US, nicknamed Patel Incorporated, without any assistance from banks, financed by family savings, having established the base camp in material prosperity are not satisfied to stay there. They have achieved much. Now they are readying themselves for the final assault at the summit, to reach 'dharma', the quintessence of the Hindu way of life and the soul of Hindutva. While the geriatric cabal in BJP national leadership was shaking their doubtful grey heads over Modi's derring do's, taking as it were the partisan media frontally, Modi went ahead with his *Gaurav Yatra* calling a spade a spade. His one-liners against the puissant liberalists afraid of even condemning Muslim terrorists at the cost of national security, struck instant rapport with the milling crowds which had come to listen to the *Chotte Sardar.* The *Indian Express* did a caricature of Sardar Patel showing a crow sitting on his head and giving his quotes on Gujarat and communal harmony. The Hindi speaking crowd saw this and their anger registered a new high. While the seniors in Delhi were pussyfooting on the issue of Hindutva and Gujarat's pride, Modi's *Gaurav Yatra* rolled like a juggernaut sweeping away everything in front. Hindu nationalism, national security and the fight against terrorism were not bread and butter issues, but man does not live by bread alone. Modi's candour, sincerity and enthusiasm cast a spell on the milling crowds that came steeped in saffron, welcoming and cheering him. If ever there was a mass Hindu upsurge, this was it. Elections come and go, governments change but the Gujarat elections and the Hindu phenomenon in Gujarat will forever remain etched in public memory.

One would have thought that after the curtains down and the last bit of postmortem completed on the Gujarat elections there would be no fresh outpouring of phlegm or vitriol against Hindutva nor a fresh volley of neo-secularists' verbal pyrotechnics against Hinduism. However this got mired into the labyrinthine quagmire of petty political calculation and callousness that have been for long the dark and pestering hallmarks, of our politico-social life. What is required, honestly, is to redefine Hindutva, by all nationalistic Indians who love their country and understand what Hindutva may mean to its unity and integrity. Hindutva is nothing if not a cementing force binding the plurality of India. Now on what India stands to lose. International relations are built on permanent interests, based among other things on geopolitical considerations. These will remain a constant factor, regardless of the outcome of *any* elections. Second, our moral right on Kashmir valley, 99% Muslim. Is Hindutva anti-Muslim? No it is not. The pro- Pakistan stance of some 12 percent Muslims from the valley will be swamped by the other ayes from India and by the people from the north and south of the valley i.e. Ladakh and Jammu. Have we ever tried to analyze the cause of the almost complete demographic swing in favour of Muslims as the ethnic cleansing of Kashmiri Pandits was going on under the benevolent gaze of the previous secular governments at Delhi, so aptly described by a Kashmiri Muslim Khursheed Wani, "When bullets, blood and fundamentalism made their first inroad into the valley, 1.5 lakh Kashmiri Pandits left their paradise in fear, but 3,000 families stayed back – to fight, to survive and to live or die in their homes. Sadly, more than a decade and a half later, the staying power of these gritty Pandits stands diluted by joblessness, anxiety and loneliness, not to talk of nagging fear. There are no grooms for daughters, no relatives to share family with, no hope of return of the exiled and, of course, distress sale of ancestral properties. And the plight of those who stayed back against all adversity". Hindutva will not generate any new centrifugal forces and in any case even now inspite of the healing touch policy of the Congress and the PDP combine, Pak is calling the shots as far as peace in the valley is concerned. Hindutva will not catalyze Islamic fundamentalism.

The logic that VHP's rath yatra will arouse anti-Muslim and divisive sentiments giving legitimacy to Islamic fundamentalism is again based on premises that only the pseudo-secularists who believe in pampering minorities can conjure up. We should read an article by M. Yusuf Khan, a retired Wing Commander of the Indian Air Force. To him Modi's victory in Gujarat should not be a cause for worry to Muslims in Gujarat or elsewhere. A Muslim feels that Indian Muslims have nothing to fear even in Gujarat where Modi outlines his philosophy of governance— justice for all, appeasement of none. "Muslims want to be a part of all." In his address to the US Committee of Foreign Relations, Mr. Richard Hass stated inter alia that the danger to minorities in democratic countries is much less than those under royal rule or military dictatorships. Referring to India he said, "The role of democracy in providing domestic stability was vividly illustrated by a conversation I had with a Muslim group while visiting India. They explained to me what lies behind the lack of terrorism emanating from India's large Muslim community. Their explanation was that India is a democratic country and Muslims participate fully. And on those occasions when they do not, they have full recourse to the judicial system." The fear of northeast Christian majority faiths severing their ties from India for fear of minority-baiting have been set to rest by the Naga talks of peace and their express desire to abjure violence, not to disturb the electoral process and stay within the Indian Union -- a landmark achievement of the Indian government. The second assumption of their kinship with China, a re-inforcing strength from outside causing minority separatism, is again misplaced. First, there is no such thing as minority- bashing unless one invents a new currency of his own to replace the old one of Hindu-bashing, which was a favourite sport. Nagas are as different, ethnically from Chinese as Tibetans are and even more so from Bangladeshis from where ISI launches its subversive activities against India.

After its debacle in Gujarat elections the Congress in its effort to re-chart its election strategy in the 2004 elections realized that frontal attack on Hinduism or Hinduttva was not going to be electorally remunerative. They came out with a novel premise that "The resolution states, the Hindu *dharma* has nothing to do with the narrow bigoted Hindutva propounded and propagated by the RSS, the BJP and the VHP that distorts the very legacy...". The Congress Working Committee (CWC) resolution reinvented secularism and emphasized that secularism is a battle for rescuing India's religious traditions, teachings and practices from the forces of "bigotries and hate." Brave words for theory but their practice belies this concept. That Hindu bigotry is condemnable, cannot be controverted, but what about their support and often silence on Muslim fanaticism, terrorism and *Jehad*? In this game of semantics they have tried to accept Hinduism but decided against Hindutva, which according to their thinktanks is unacceptable Hindu bigotism or extremism. Even the Supreme Court has given a civilisational content to Hindu, Hinduism and Hindutva and in at least six separate judgments admires the usage of these words, saying that "Hindutva symbolizes tolerance of all other religions". Sanatan Dharma, the foundation of India centric civilisationsal continuum has the inherent capacity to smoothen the angularities of pluralism and remove the possibilities of conflict. It is this Hindutva which inter alia is going to be the USP of the BJP and its saffron allies in the forthcoming assembly elections. When asked by persistent secularist media as to whether he conceded that the Muslims too have contributed a lot to the nation in all walks of life, Dr. Praveen Togadia replied: "Yes, Muslims have contributed to the civilization as well as the culture, but have also contributed Somnath, Pakistan attacks on Indian Parliament and Akshardham. Muslims have also contributed to the youth who are willing to be cannon fodder in the name of *jehad*." Togadia need not have generalized but the gravamen of his charge sheet is not too far off the mark.

In their well-publicized statement Shekhar Gupta and Saeed Naqvi implied, almost in a morphic resonance to Pervez Musharraf, that the massacre of innocent Hindus at Akshardham would not have taken place if there had been no state sponsored pogrom against Muslims in Gujarat. Thus, Akshardham was rationalized as the necessary and inevitable outcome of the Gujarat riots and Hindu "atrocities" against Muslims. These media luminaries suffer from a selective amnesia about the chain of unrelieved massacres and genocides against innocent Hindus by their Muslim conquerors. There is nothing noble or original about the massacre of Hindus at Akhshardham. In the same Gujarat lakhs of Hindus were massacred in the attack on Somnath temple by the great iconoclast Mahmood Ghaznavi and a seven centuries long uninterrupted orgy of violence accounting for eight crores Hindu lives.

Smarting under its disastrous showing in Gujarat election Congress true to form in its effort to seek alibis blamed the NDA for attacks at Kaluchak, Akshardham, Parliament and Raghunath temple holding them responsible for these crimes. In other words hitting a self-goal, just because these events took place while the NDA was in power. Arun Jaitly of BJP duly snubbed them by pointing out that if this premise is carried to its logical conclusion then Congress should be blamed for the assassination of Indira Gandhi and Rajiv Gandhi. In another outburst of frustration Mr. Salman Khursheed declared, "To have equated a possible Congress triumph with Pakistan's aspirations is nothing short of a national betrayal. It denigrates the history of our country since 1885. It insults the people of 15 states who have again put their trust in the Congress. It publicly undermines our confidence and self-esteem as a nation. And most of all, it pretends to give Pakistan a signal that we are a divided country on the issue of terrorism. That is no way to counter terrorism."

The Gujarat verdict was a resounding repudiation of the indifference of our secularist brigade to the twin issue of "Hindutva" or national identity and national security. Both are non-negotiable. To the popular mind, Hindutva and secularism are not exclusive. By giving Hindutva a divisive and discursive currency, the 'liberals' are playing with fire. The Congress in particular had a difficult task, reconciling its minorityism-based electoral calculus with a silence on the terrorist infrastructure provided by the very same constituency threatening the security and sovereignty of our country. In a disclosure of the government it has been mentioned that over 9,000 Pakistani visitors to India have overstayed their visa period and around 3000 are untraceable; 90% of them have given false local addresses. What it means is that thousands of Pak-infiltrators in India are at large and indulging in subversive activities. Earlier, Mr. Mulayam Singh Yadav, the then defence minister, had advocated an open door policy to Pakistani nationals to enter India and treat it as their home. Are the Hindus then not justified in being wary of such wellwishers of the Muslims who can put to stake national security for the sake of minority votes? Time and again, our secularists have fooled Hindus. Double speak, half truths, innuendos, concocting facts. "*suppresio veri suggestio falsi*" 'Oh what a web of lies we weave when first we learn to deceive', said Shakespeare. That should show the mirror to those to whom national security is an unnecessary embarrassment whether it is Godhra, Akshardham, or the Raghunath temple; the targets are Hindu, kar-sevaks or temple pilgrims. All Hindu shrines are potential targets to the militant Islamic fundamentalism whose fingerprints are stained in blood. Hindus do not have to tell the secularists that they are being unduly turned upon. They are under siege, as the nation is under attack from all sides from Pak-sponsored cross-border terrorism. Are the Hindus expected to sit silently and watch their death toll mounting by the day? Are they expected to be mute witnesses to an assault on their pride and national sovereignty?

Our media shows only Hindu rioters attacking Muslims. Did it ever show hundreds of Hindus being gunned down in police firing when they tried to prevent violence? The secularist English media is at it again. Having only partially recovered from the shock of being proved wrong in Gujarat, while some indulged in breast-beating and cursing Hindu extremism, the ostrich species among them are dismissing the Gujarat verdict as a "choice exercised by one electorate in one state, presented with a particular set of alternatives or rather lack of them". One reporter using epithets as "Master divider Modi", "The Badshah of Hate", "Organizer of a massive mandate", chides her comrades for harbouring any doubts on their chosen stand on secularism. In rationalizing the discomfiture of her fraternity, she quoted an example from the US where one Republican senator, Trent Loft, had to resign for making a racial statement, thereby implying that what had happened in Gujarat was a battle of races and the BJP capitalized on the majority race vote-bank. This is the first time in the history of independent India that one is hearing about the Hindu race vote-bank. She bemoans that while, in the US even racial reference is frowned upon, in India political leaders had no compunctions in Muslim-bashing, thereby alienating the whole race.

Such secular, liberal columnists forget that the issue in Gujarat was not Hindu vs Muslim but the choice between minority appeasement and national security. So there were alternatives. A minority, especially in a border state open to depredations from Pak-sponsored terrorism that find support and shelter in many homes, does not have to be appeased. If the coloured people in the US were harbourers of Al Qaida, surely the US response would have been different. In the aftermath of 9/11, even respectable Indians, Sikhs and other Asians came under the scrutiny of US intelligence. This cancerous antipathy to internal security that is eating away at the vitals of our national sovereignty is a chronic ailment of our secularist media. Thus far one only heard of Hindu-bashing, now this columnist has invented another term, Muslim-bashing, another weapon in the armoury of our secularists to fire at Hindus and those who are concerned with national security. Modi had rightly announced a roadmap for governance. "Justice to all, appeasement of none." Gujarat happened because of Godhra, Godhra happened because of intransigence of a section of minority aided and abetted by Pakistan, and this unpardonable intransigence happened because of a refusal to accommodate Hindu aspirations on the Rama temple. A matter of faith and religious pride pitted against the stubbornness and false hurt on the destruction of a non-mosque that stood as a reminder of Hindu humiliation by their Muslim rulers.

We would have dismissed this tirade for what it is worth but some important issues are involved here as also those which show the mindset of the Congress that refuses to learn. First, the history of India. The history of Congress does not start in 1885 though it happens to be its date of birth. The Congress of 1885 was not an organization for the freedom movement but a British creation to confine India's urge for freedom within the four walls of the drawing room. A forum for academic debate to let the Indian elite take off their steam. Those who have studied history know better. Again this period is not the monopoly of Congress struggle as brought out in the chapter 7. There were other great sons of India outside the Congress pale who sacrificed much more than the Congress armchair strategists. Out of the states that elected Congress atleast half had no worthwhile opposition party to challenge them and in the remaining except Madhya Pradesh, Congress rose to power on the anti-incumbency wave, like the high prices of onions in Delhi. The issue in Gujarat was of course the fight against terror. The Congress by stating that Akshardham was the necessary nemesis of Gujarat riots did convey to the electorate the message that far from being fought head on, terrorism was the justified retribution for Muslim lives lost. In other words, every time a riot takes place and some Muslim lives are lost, Congress would smile in approval on Pakistan who would send terrorists inside India to even out the score by taking Hindu lives. Who is dividing the country? The Congress in its selective approval of terrorism or the people of Gujarat ? How would the Congress defend itself when one of its foot soldiers, Prem Shankar Jha made an unconscionable statement that "Akshardham was the first fruit of the poison tree that was sown in the last March." And pray, who lit the detonator for the Gujarat blast, if not the Muslims at Godhra on 27 February? Only the naïve will close their eyes to the real culprits of Akshardham; militant Islam. The terrorists did not wait for Gujarat when they attacked the J&K Assembly and later the Indian Parliament on December 13. Akshardham was a much underplayed version of the serial Bombay blasts. Even during the Gujarat riots there was no dearth of ISI instigated Muslim violence. Crude rocket launchers were used by Muslim mobs in Juhapura, Ahmedabad. Later during the Jagannath *Rath Yatra* a cache of illegal arms was recovered from Muslim localities, where their unemployed youths were manufacturing lethal weapons for revenge attacks like the Palestinian Fedayeens. Akshardham was another explosion of terrorists' violence. This time, against a Hindu shrine like the earlier one at Raghunath temple. It was a sequential terrorists' trail whose starting point was 1997. First came the bomb explosion at the RSS office in Chennai, then the IC 814 hijacking during the Christmas festival and the Holy Ramzan, a *jehad* on the eve of the millennia. Then followed the February 1998 Coimbatore bomb blast targeting L.K. Advani, the killings at Kalucheck, the murder of innocent pilgrims to Amarnath, were all part of the same series of terror. Assault on and destruction of Hindu temples and shrines is nothing new. We had discussed these at great length in chapter 3. This was a never-ending ritual during the Muslim rule. So what's new? But coming back to Gujarat, the violence was the outcome of Godhra. But Godhra is not the only Muslim atrocity against *Kafirs* in Gujarat.

Millennia ago, long before RSS, blamed by some secularists for doing Godhra on itself was even born, the very same Gujarat saw the worst form of vandalism. During the destruction of Somnath temple, Mahmood of Ghazni slaughtered 15 thousand Hindus in a single day. Can Gujarat 2002 match Gujarat 1026? Do Hindus need to be reminded of scores of thousands of the their temples destroyed during the whole millennia from Mohammed Bin Kasim's invasion in 712 till 1707 AD. There was no Gujarat 2002 then. Hindu hurts unredeemed over millennia may have been trivialized by the likes of Satish Chandra and Romila Thapar. But the silent Hindu majority, even the unlettered man of Indo-Gangetic Vedic heartland of yore remembers. He may forgive but he shall not forget. Hindus have a long memory, they never forget. An eminent and true secular thinker like Rafiq Zakaria has not remained untouched by the seismic shock waves of Gujarat aftermath. He seems unduly concerned about the fate of the minorities. According to him, "the secular Hindus are quiet but the communal ones are euphoric. They are happy that they will be able to get rid of the Muslims. If not physically at least paralyze them economically and ostracize them socially. That has been the crux of Guru Golwalkar's teachings. And his followers have faithfully worked to achieve it. They now feel confident they will at last succeed in what they had devotedly wished for. Environment against Muslims seems to be right". But he need not have any misgivings, reassured as he was by his own friends R.V. Pandit and Nanaji Deshmukh. Pandit assured him that, "One of the reasons I support the BJP is because only they can ensure that the minorities have a future. One has to accept that India is a Hindu country. Those who declared it a secular State in 1947 did not understand the obvious fact". The very reason that India has remained secular even after partition is because of its Hindu majority. Look at what happened to Pakistan and Bangladesh. Both theocratic states and not forgetting every Muslim country from Algeria to Malaysia and Indonesia, Middle East not excluded. Let us face the facts. Barring a few honourable exceptions, Muslims in India have neither the capacity nor desire nor the numbers required to make India great. The burden of nation building has to be borne by the majority Hindu community. To do that and face the challenges of the world, the Hindus instead of being a house divided against itself have to unite. Consolidation of Hindus across caste divides is a pre-requisite for any effort at India's resurgence. So Golwalkar was not wrong Mr. Zakaria. Hindu consolidation is a *sine qua non* for the greatness that was once India. Hindutva, the essence of Hinduism, cannot ever be communal. Muslims need have no fears. They are an integral part of this land. They too are a part of the Hindutva whole, the spirit and essence of Indian-ness. The transient stridency of Hindus is not directed against Muslims per se, but against their co-religionists who wish to ghettoise the Muslims in their encysted localities for their votes. Muslims are safe and shall remain so. Let Hindu consolidation not be misunderstood as anti-Muslim. Mr. Zakaria should read the booklet *Sangh Darshan* by Mr. Golwalkar and he will not find a single word against Muslims or any other minority. The boot is on the other foot Mr. Zakaria. It is not Muslims who are under attack. It is Hinduism that is under siege. Hinduism is under siege from its own co-religionists masquerading as secularists. Hinduism is under siege from our English media and western clones. Hinduism is under siege from the Congress and the Left too, arch appeasers of minority and specialists in Hindu bashing. Hinduism is under siege from terrorists from without and saboteurs and subversives from within. Hinduism is under siege from hostile neighbours outside. Hinduism is under siege from caste divides. Hinduism is under siege from evangelizing missionaries and Masjid-Madarsa moles inside. Hinduism is under siege from the messiahs of social justice like Laloo and Mulayam. Hinduism is under siege from traitors among Hindus who weep on foreign shoulders in America complaining against their own people. Hinduism is under siege from foreign borns masquerading as secularists, who scoff at Hindutva, from self-seeking politicians, who ventriloquise the pronouncements from Mian Musharraf. Hinduism is under siege from the merchants of death and destruction who target women and children, cause rail accidents, snuffing out hundreds of innocent lives, attack Hindu shrines and cause explosions in busy city centres. Where do these fanatics or jihadis find shelters? Mosques- cum-Madarsas and Muslim homes. Is it any wonder that the Hindus feel suspicious of some sections of the minority community? After 9/11 George Bush announced that he will flush out the Al Qaida and their terrorist supporters from their holes, smoke them out from their hiding places and ferret them out from their cavernous mountain shelters. In India we have thousands of such hiding places all over the country. What do the champions of Human Rights expect the state to do? Twiddle their thumbs? In a presidential decree Bush authorized the CIA to kill or assassinate the terrorists without recourse to long legal trials. The CIA is also now free to modify and enlarge its list of wanted terrorists. What happens in India? Whose rights are these worthies fighting for - the killers or the victims? Enough is enough said the Hindus of Gujarat. Akshardham where 40 innocent pilgrims were killed alongwith NSC commandos was the last straw.

You cannot push Hindus too far for too long. Nemesis will catch up. It did on 12 December, 2002, people voted not against Muslims but for national security and Hindu pride. Let us remind ourselves that Hindutva was not born out of the womb of electoral politics. It was born ten millennia ago when the first Vedic seers chanted the verses from Rigveda, when in pre-historic India, the first words of the Upanishads were recited and later when Gita summed up the essence of the Vedas and Upanishads at the battlefield of Kurukshetra. Hindutva is the lifeblood of Indian Vedic culture and it does not look for approval from present day politicians, intellectuals, or media managers. Hindu society has been born in this land, lives in this land and shall die here. It has no other place to go, nor a safe retreat or an adopted home in a co-religionists country or society. It has no escape routes. Its past, present and future are dedicated to this sacred motherland and its Karmabhoomi is Bharat. It cannot be equated with any other religion or society. It can co-exist but it cannot be wished or washed away. Hindus have an unalienable claim on Bharat; others are welcome to make it their home, but should not look across the national boundaries for support or sustenance.

In the aftermath of Gujarat a fierce debate has been raging whether India can claim to be a nation and if so can it be called a Hindu nation or a Hindu Rashtra? The debate is futile since etymologically India and Hindu are synonymous and the Indian nation can only be called a Hindu nation. At another level with the weight of our common historical ten millennia old heritage, traditions, culture, value systems the underlying unity that prevails despite local diversities, which are inevitable in a large landmass, can only result in an emotional unity that transcends geographical barriers to make the people of this continent an Indian and Hindu nation. Just sample a few pearls of wisdom thrown by our neo-secularists, ridiculing the concept of a *Hindu Rashtra.* I.K. Gujral, the loud throated chorister of secularist refrain, can see only our diversity and ethnic dissimilarities, different languages and dialects, differing local interests and perceptions to make up a case that far from being a nation, India is an aggregate of conflicting local interests and its pluralistic culture can never allow a synthesis into a national unity. He calls Indian constitution, a human and legal construct, the soul of India, thereby, implying that India had no soul before its enactment in 1950. To have unity in diversity is not a concession. That "Hindutva and Hinduism are both mythical terms, targeted to divide the people, and finally Hindutva as I understand it is an attempt to copy Islamic fundamentalism." How uninformed and misguided can one be even after he has been a prime minister? Enough has already been written earlier about the proverbial Hindu tolerance, the universalism of Hindutva to waste any more space in rebutting these observations. The man, who cannot rise above the parochial Punjabiat, to the spirit of Bhartiyata is not worth wasting time on.

A Hindu nation cannot be a theocracy, but the strongest critics of a Hindu Rashtra are the Communists who unabashedly worked for the creation of Pakistan, a theocratic state, pandered to the worst fundamentalist and obscurantist elements of Muslims in India for their vote-banks. To those who think that democracy is a British gift and 'Hindu Rashtra' would sound the death knell of democracy and dissent, need to realize that long before the British nation was born, and as early as 600 BC ancient India had 60 republics. Democracy is the lifeblood of Hindu ethos. Cassandras need not conjure up spectres of a totalitarian and tyrannical Hindu Rashtra. Jaipal Reddy, the loudest throated advocate of the Congress brand of secularism, misread Golwalkar and accuse the protagonists of Hinduism as obscurantists; and to quote his own words: "the liberal Constitution is the only stumbling block to the 'humongous' effort of the BJP and Sangh Parivar to foist a Hindu Rashtra on our secular polity", little realizing that Hindu Rashtra itself is a secular construct. Make no mistake, India is a secular democracy because its majority consists of Hindus. And finally Javed Naqvi, the prophet of doom, warns, "that Hindu Rashtra will spell trouble for the Indian polity," and for good reason quotes Pakistani papers to buttress his views. A case of pot calling the kettle black.

Now some home truths and facts. While a country is a geographical concept, a state is a political construct, with legal underpinning of laws and constitution, but a nation is a cultural construct based on three pillars. These pillars are, a feeling of reverence for the country, a common sharing of history and ancestors and third, and the most important, a shared value system or culture. Switzerland has three languages, French, German and Swiss and is still a nation, probably the longest living nation in Europe. Philippines has three hundred dialects and not a single national language and still is a nation. Nearer home Pakistan has four distinct languages, Pushto, Sindhi, Punjabi and Baluch. Out of about 180 countries of the world not more than a dozen can claim linguistic or ethnic homogeneity. The integration of 300 separate feuding states in 1870 under Bismarck made a German nation. Nor does race alone form a nation. The British are a mixture of so many races: Saxons, Vikings, Romans, and their kings were imported from Germany, their arch enemy for many years. Prince Albert, an ethnic German and consort to Queen Victoria, was born of a Teutonic stock. Queen Victoria wrote to the King of Prussia a fellow German that it was only the anti-German sentiment which swept England during war which forced the British Royal family to change the venerable dynastic name of GUELPH for the less German sounding Windsor. Commonality of religion and race also do not a nation make nor common economic interests. Look at European Economic Community. Earnest Renan, a French thinker, in his work *What is the Nation* puts it so well, "the soil provides the substratum, the field for struggle and labour, man provides the soul. Man is everything in the formation of this sacred thing that we call a people. Nothing that is material suffices here. A nation is a spiritual principle, the result of the intricate working of history, a spiritual family and not a group determined by the configuration of the earth." He then goes on to say "a nation is a soul, a spiritual principle. Two things, which are really only one, go to make up this soul or spiritual principle. One of these things lies in the past, the other in the present. One is the common possession of a rich heritage of memories; and the other is actual agreement, the desire to live together, and the will to continue to make the most of the joint inheritance. Man cannot be improvised. The nation, like the individual, is the fruit of a long past spent in toil, sacrifice and devotion".

Thus, whether our secularists like it or not there is a Hindu nation that has existed long before secular semantics came to question whether a nation can be a *Rashtra.* It may not have been named Hindu but its underpinnings of a Sanatan Dharma and a precious Vedic heritage is ten millennia old. It is not a term that needs justification for its existence. It is there and has been there. The Hindu nation has a mission for the world also, a value system and a holistic integrated view of the world. The vision and the task is there. Our mission is to complete it.

11

The Threat from without and within

The External Factor

India has a long history of foreign invasions. Small forces of adventurers and soldiers of fortune defeated numerically superior armies due to inadequate response, arising out of internal dissensions, poor battle tactics and strategies, proverbial Hindu fatalism and an enfeebled sense of nationalism. This should not happen again. We shall first briefly deal with the external threats to the Indian state and by implication to Hindu and Hinduism. Instead of getting involved in a discursive discourse on the strategic and military dimensions, which can best be left to specialists, we shall confine ourselves mainly to the politico-military profile of the threat and the counter measures required. Before we proceed, let us state the obvious military wisdom: that a neighbour country should never be taken for granted. Strategic analysis has to take into account the military capability of a neighbour when planning for defence, regardless of its present state of relations with us. What is important is the military potential and capability, not intentions. Intentions can change fast but military potential cannot be created overnight. Therefore, as Kautilya said: "Be wary of your neighbours – they are close to you and can inflict heavy damage". The case of China in 1962 is an example. Repeatedly General Thimmaya, the then Chief of Army Staff, kept warning Nehru of Chinese military build up and road construction in Tibet, only to be snubbed back with the curt reply that 'China is our friend and shall not attack'. History unfolded something entirely different. Even the first world war was thrust upon Germany not because of German hostility against England but because Germany had suddenly emerged as the greatest economic, industrial and military power in Europe. England had no immediate *cassus belli* to fight Germany. But intentions changed and Germany was forced into a war in 1914.

Now a brief defence survey. India is hedged on three sides—by an expansionist China with tremendous nuclear and conventional military might on the north; Pakistan a surrogate of China with enough nuclear arsenal, and almost parity in delivery systems but short on nuclear war-heads, a smaller conventional armed manpower and arsenal in the northwest. And finally Pak-friendly Bangladesh in the east that provides safe operating bases to Pak-sponsored Islamic terrorists. Even on the seaside there are hostile bases south of Myanmar.

Taking China first. Let us face some home truths. China is far superior to India in its conventional and nuclear military capability besides having a much stronger economy. Its $ 40 billion FDI is much higher than our measly $ 2 billion; it exported $ 322 billion worth during the same year when Indian exports stood at only $ 40 billion. It occupies 30,000 sq. kilometers of Indian territory in Aksai Chin (Ladakh), another 5180 sq. kms. ceded to it by Pakistan in Shuksom Valley, 90,000 sq. kms in Arunanchal Pradesh and has no plans to withdraw its claims on this huge chunk of borderland in the foreseeable future. On the remaining 4056 kms. long border as the Line of Actual Control (LAC) under the Border Peace and Tranquility Agreement of 1993, China has kept its options open for further encroachment on Indian territory, under the pretext of its own perception of the delineation of the LAC. This leaves India vulnerable. China till very recently did not recognize Sikkim as an integral part of India and kept the Sikkim issue outside the purview of the LAC resolution, thus, tying up a sizeable part of Indian ground forces in that region and making them unavailable for operations against Pakistan. Thus, while China keeps assisting Pakistan in its nuclear capability it continues to tie up almost half of the quantum of our forces that could be shifted Pak-wards.

The best defence in such an unequal military face-off will be to neutralize Chinese hostility in the north through diplomatic means and maintaining a status quo on the border disputes, abstaining from aggravating postures to enable us to use the troops from north and north-east for counter-insurgency against Pakistan.

Coming to Bangladesh. Dhaka has long been a centre of ISI activities in our north-east. A highly overstaffed Pak mission at Dhaka is in cahoots with their Bangladesh counterparts deriving their strength from the Muslim fundamentalist organizations such as Jamat-e-Islami and other Islamic organizations under the present day Begum Khalida Zia's government of Bangladesh Nationalist Party (BNP). According to a *Time* magazine report, Bangladesh military intelligence maintains contacts with their counterparts in Pakistan ISI and has a long history of supporting rebels across the border. And further over 150 heavily armed Taliban and Al Qaida activists from Afghanistan are said to have entered Bangladesh by boat in December 2001 alone. The Bangladesh terrorist group Harkat-Ul-Jihad-Ul-Islami had long time contacts with the Taliban, ISI and Al-Qaida operating in J & K and has a huge support base in Bangladesh. So also the excessive Pak embassy staff in Nepal is upto no good for India's security interests. India is rightly concerned. Diplomacy with the display of force, strict border surveillance, prevention of ingress through the long and porous border, (more on which later), economic pressure, through a threat of control of its river waters, the lifeline of Bangladesh and display of naval strength in the Bay of Bengal will keep Bangladesh out of harms away.

Next we come to Pakistan. With an adequate number of strike corps including those diverted from North and Northeast facing China to the Western Sector, India will have a superiority in conventional military strength against Pakistan. Though at the army formation levels and above and in air power India has a clear superiority over Pakistan on the Western front from the LOC southwards along the International border upto Kutch, there are weaknesses at the level of fighting units from battalion downwards. The Pak battalions and companies are better equipped and organized than our own units and sub-units. And the war in the hilly terrain of Ladakh, Jammu and Kashmir will be a series of small battles at unit and sub-unit levels. We have to make up for the deficiencies in manpower of both Jawans and young officers at battalion and the company level. It is these officers who lead and suffer the highest casualties. Having said that it should be re-affirmed that in the history of India's battles not one has been lost because of cowardice and ineptitude of our young officers. They have been lost due to other causes; poor high command, bad planning, poor equipment, bad generalship and above all, poor political leadership. In the euphoria of the successful completion of Operation Vijay at Kargil 1999, many embarrassing facts have been kept away from public gaze—the single most important one being the total inadequacy and ineptitude of some of our officers in higher command. While we have taken the media to task in chapter 8 on the issue of Godhra and Gujarat, this is one time that the media did not play foul and for this they deserve due credit. The Kargil intrusion so deep and on such a large scale went undetected for almost one month. Not that the army top brass was not informed. An enquiry was held on this unforgivable intelligence failure but only perfunctorily, and the real culprits were neither named nor brought to justice. Let us face the facts. The first information on Pak troops occupying heights inside LOC, with a view to interdict the lifeline to Ladakh and Siachin, was obtained through shepherds and local Shia population, not well disposed towards the Sunni Pak government. This was confirmed by our patrols and the complete information was passed from the brigade headquarters upwards to the divisional and corps headquarters. But the higher command took no immediate counter-action to eject the intruders. Had a timely action been taken, this task could have been achieved with a smaller force and fewer casualties. But the generals slept. Later, when an inquiry was held, like the maharajas of old, the Army High Command shot the messenger. The very Commander who was crying for early action and despaired of getting the senior formation commanders to get into their act was sacked and the real culprits were allowed to go scot free. This is what we mean when we talk of leading from the front. None of our senior commanders dared to go out of their cushy command headquarters to initiate prompt action and encourage the troops.

Napoleon at the famous battle of Arcola during his Italian campaign, when the advance was halted on the bridge, took the flag from the forward column and was the first to cross the bridge. The rest of his army cheered and followed. The opposing Austrian forces were routed. The same thing happened again at Marengo and Lodi as also the strategic defence of Mantua. It was said that the presence of the emperor at the crucial point in the battlefield was equal to 40,000 troops. So also the typically British, methodical and slow, but the worthy opponent of Napoleon, Arthur Wellesely, later the Duke of Wellington's presence inspired the troops and it was rumoured that the sight of his long nose was equivalent to ten thousand British soldiers. The intrepid cavalry General Sheridon of the Federal Army of the North during the American

Civil War (1861-1865) used to wave his sword and shout at his troops to follow him. Is there any wonder that his cavalry charges were unstoppable like a hurricane? Again our young soldiers did not fail. They fought and died and snatched victory from the jaws of defeat. Our political leadership did even worse. In no textbook of war is it written that the enemy who intrudes and inflicts heavy casualties on our troops almost three times to what he himself suffers, when defeated and forced out of its position is allowed to walk back free into his own territory. There is something called pursuit; these merchants of death pushed by Pakistan had inflicted enormous casualties on our troops. I visited the Army Base Hospital and the Army Hospital Research and Referral Centre. One visit was enough to show how much our troops had suffered. The political leadership in its wisdom allowed the killers from Pak Northern Scouts and Light Infantry to walk back to safety. Our soldiers and young officers felt cheated. The senior Commanders could have wisely told the political leadership that the retreating Pak troops should not be allowed to go without heavy collateral damage. Not one man should have been allowed to go back alive on his two feet. Was it a replay of Gandhiji's non-violence, even during war? Even if the US held our hand we would have been perfectly justified to allow our troops to complete the unfinished task and explain later that the forward momentum of our troops could not have been halted in time. Now we crow about Kargil victory. The truth is that the first part was a disaster; intelligence failure and the inertia of the higher command. The middle part was a glorious vindication of India's pride, thanks to our gallant brave soldiers and the last part was a national shame of our supine political leadership. It is this repeated display of political pusillanimity that encourages Pakistan time and again to cross over to our land and wreak havoc. How long will this one-sided assault on the security of our nation be allowed to continue? One final word before an impression is created that all echelons in our political leadership are effete and suffering from terminal arthritis. The one honourable exception was George (General) Fernandes, the ablest defence Minister that India has had since independence. His visits to forward troops had become legend. The soldiers loved him. Rarely has any of our Defence ministers visited such inhospitable terrain as Siachin so many times. The number of times Fernandes visited forward troops in northwest and northeast can earn him a place in the *Guinness Book of Records*.

Even our much-acclaimed 1971 victory over Pakistan in the East was not much of an achievement when critically analysed. First, Indira Gandhi almost bought defeat by forcing General Sam Manekshaw to attack in April 1971, when the Army was ill-prepared, northern passes providing easy access to China were still not frozen, the monsoon were to play havoc in the marshy, riverine areas of East Pakistan, and the Muktivahini had not collected enough information on dispositions of Pak troops to help Indian troops in their advance. Indira insisted on an immediate attack. Manekshaw advised restraint. When the 'Durga' was burning with impatience in her imperious regal rage, Sam Manekshaw kept his cool and retorted: "Madam if you force me to attack now, the outcome cannot be predicted and a stalemate may result; but if you allow me to attack when I am ready I guarantee complete success." This worked. Though Indira chafed at the delay, Sam stood his ground. The attack started on 3rd December, 1971, at time of our own choosing when the ground was dry for armour manoeuvre, northern passes closed, and the Muktivahini scouts literally led our forward troops to individual bunkers occupied by Pak troops. Success was inevitable. Pincered from three sides, West Bengal, Meghalaya and Tripura on land and assaulted by our Navy from the south, Pak surrender was a foregone conclusion. Some times generals have to discipline political leaders. Political leaders should announce the war aims when diplomacy fails, but the timing and manner must be left entirely to the higher military leadership.

A few words on the proverbial Hindu tolerance, before we turn to Pakistan. If there is one thing the repeated terrorist attacks in India have shown it is the small value we attach to human lives. Indian and Hindu lives are not dirt. How far can our patience be tried? Pak knows the answer; there are no limits. The more India is terrorised the greater becomes its capacity to absorb more. Its self-restraint is limitless. This passivity, a negative legacy of Gandhiji's non-violence and endemic to Hindu society has been internalised due to a mounting toll of human lives in riots, accidents, natural calamities, street brawls and deliberate violence. Some 43 pilgrims killed at Akshardham, 16 rallyists dying in a stampede at Lucknow Railway Station, Kaluchek, Raghunath temple and several other disasters have numbed our senses even as they receive frontline coverage in newspapers. A drunk Salman Khan driving recklessly and killing sleeping people on the footpath of Mumbai or a scion of Nanda family wading through a crowd of innocent bystanders is passe. Bhopal Gas Tragedy is forgotten. Terrorist attacks are treated like a daily normal occurrence. Five Jawans killed today, 10 tomorrow and we go to sleep. The statistics of death through terrorism keep mounting. The then Prime Minister was patience personified and believed in the Biblical adage "that every man be swift to hear, slow to speak, slow to wrath." After declaring zero tolerance against terrorism in 1998, as the graph of terrorist killings rises he silently moved up his threshold of patience and reverted to "Maximum tolerance". The then leader of the Opposition, despite losing her husband to a terrorist's killing wallowed in the same naiveté. Having waited for too long for the US to do our job we have now woken up to the need to bestir ourselves. For long we have lacked a coherent strategy, tactics, and the tools to fight the sophisticated state-sponsored terrorism unleashed by our neighbour and there is no let up. The foreign media view Pak terrorists' attacks on India not within the paradigm of International terrorism, that the world has now vowed to exterminate, but against a India-Pakistan and Hindu-Muslim conflict. While the US has arrogated to itself the right of retaliation even if it means coming all the way across half the world to Afghanistan and Iraq, it has preached a different sermon to India. 'Start talking to Pak'. Hindus and India should have known, that there is no alternative to pre-emption and strong retributive response.

Reverting back to the Pak front; our troops are fine, the higher commanders will pass muster, but the politico-military conundrum at the South Block would be a tangled web, more so with the nuclear option thrown in. We think we have won diplomatic credit from foreign countries by announcing "a no first use policy" on nuclear weapons. Nothing could be more harmful for military success. International laws and UN resolution are those that are meant to be observed by the weak and bent to convenience by the strong. Look at the US war against Iraq and what they have already done in Afghanistan. India still waits for a nod from the west. Every fresh act of terrorism makes our effete leadership wake up and repeat its recorded message stuck in a groove, 'that our patience is not unlimited'. After every assault on our sovereignty a fresh statement raising the threshold of our forbearance is made and a line drawn on the sand. The enemy knows what it means and carries on regardless. The Pak ruling class, civil or military, is deeply infested by fundamentalists, perked in positions of power and influence and dictate state policy. Trapped between a vision and belief and impelled by an atavistic urge they fall back to the certainties of the past and tend to follow the tenets of militant Islam. The military consequences to India can be frightful indeed. It would be interesting to note what Khalid Ahmad, a Pak journalist, has to say "the culture of jehad has been seeping into the Pakistani mind for the past two decades, helped by state propaganda, the rise of the charismatic warrior priest, and the empowerment of those involved in it. In the minds of most people, it began to represent Pakistan in the world outside, not the government or the armed forces of Pakistan. Will it be possible to live without the daily headlines planted in the press about the spiritual superiority of the Islamic warrior in contrast to the evil Hindu empire next door and the global threat of the assumed Western "crusade" against Islam? Columnist Irshad Haqqaqi reproduced in *Jang* (June 1,2002) three letters objecting to his earlier view that Pakistan should listen to the view of world powers. Anwaruz Badr from Karachi said, any stoppage of *jehadi* would be a "betrayal of the thousands of Kashmiris killed by the Indian troops and thousands of women raped by them". The second letter was from Ahmed Hussain from Muzaffarabad, complaining that Haqqaqi had washed his hands off Kashmir, and that America would make Pakistan abandon first Kashmir, then Karachi, Baluchistan and NWFP. The third letter was from lawyer Abdul Hakim Awan from Gujranwala who thought terrorism should be stopped in Pakistan but *jehadi* headquarters in POK should be allowed to continue. The Urdu press has carried such a one-sided opinion over the time that it is difficult to even suggest some flexibility in Pakistan's stance while it responds to India's Kashmir policy". Had there been an effort on the part of newspapers to present a varied picture, Haqqaqi's rational advice would not have aroused the kind of anger one sees in the above letters. The belief that a jehadi or Islamic force is invincible against the 'Kafirs', lends credibility to a certitude of mujahid victory inspite of temporary setbacks. The Jehadi's fervour and mindset is the principal driving force behind Pak adventurism against India, fired by the belief that Allah's wars have only one outcome, victory. But India's announcement of its second strike nuclear capabilities has sown the seeds of doubt in the minds of the soldiers of Islam. Musharraf's prevarications, frequent bluffs, the dichotomy of Taliban and the appeal to some radical groups including parts of his own Sarkari MMA outfits have knocked the bottom out of that overweening bellicosity.

In full knowledge that we shall not be the first to press the nuclear button, Pakistan keeps on raising the ante in the conventional war. Kaluchak, J & K Assembly, Raghunath Mandir, Indian Parliament, Godhra, Gujarat, Akshardham and the religious killings in the Kashmir valley happen with regular periodicity and our top leadership comes with another retaliatory verbal cannonade. And Pakistan keeps bleeding India to death through a thousands cuts. The madarsas in Pak, the factories that produce killer Jehadis are in full operation, as has been comfirmed even by foreign observers. The cannon fodder is limitless; for every jehadi killed in India there are two more to pick up the Kalashnikov or AK 57, cheaply available through narco dollars and Saudi money. A perceptive strategic study will reveal that there is an uncanny similarity of the ideologies of Al-Qaida's Osama bin Laden with those of the ISI sponsored Maulana Masood Azhar. The Jehadi factories in Pak operating in 40,000 to 50,000 madarsas churn out an estimated two million students of which two lakh were fully armed with a backup of another one million waiting to be armed and assigned a mission to kill. Their morale is high and why not. After all Pak got away unscathed from its 13 December 2001 attack on Indian Parliament and defeated the enemy without fighting a war. Indian army stood eye-ball to eye-ball against the enemy on the international border for ten months costing the exchequer Rs 8,000 crore and achieving nothing. In consequence we lost any possibility of surprise in exercising any future military option to deal with Pak provocation. Our strategy planners and our political leadership both failed us, but we should learn from our mistakes. No battle is the last battle, and these are won in the minds of military leaders and their troops.

Pakistan should be told enough is enough. It would still bear reitration to say that cross-border terrorism should cease or else we shall do what the Israelis have been doing. Assassinate the assassins. We need to raise voluntary suicide squads not only from the armed forces but from the vast Hindu youth reservoir that Bal Thackeray talked about; mass participation by the country's youth volunteers. A Hindu call to serve the nation. "Anyone who is prepared to shed blood and make sacrifices for his sacred motherland is a Hindu, regardless of his religion and faith," said Savarkar a long time ago. How much can the army control? How far can it be stretched? Terrorists can attack anywhere at the time and place of their choosing, as their attacks have shown. Thus, we need early intelligence and prompt response, which can only come through a mass awakening and the participation of every able bodied Indian. The safety and the honour of the country comes first. Good governance, development and bread and butter issues are important and necessary but cannot supersede national security. If India as a nation does not exist, what remains? Who shall eat the bread and who will survive to govern or be governed. National security is not an issue that needs debate or mention in party manifestos.

Coming back to regaining initiative, which is vital to military success; the proactive deep penetration to destroy terrorists' camps and support systems must be undertaken early enough, using surprise and secrecy, the strongest weapons of offensive combat. There need be no fear of either a retaliatory conventional or nuclear war from Pakistan even if it comes to that. Conventional war we cannot lose. Nuclear war boils down to a simple outcome provided we forego our fetish of a 'no first use'. If we strike first Pakistan will be wiped out along with its second strike capability. If Pakistan strikes first, encouraged by our 'no first use' self-infliction, even then our anti-missile defence system should neutralise its warheads. There will be some collateral damage if the missile survives and India will suffer some affordable hurts. But once India retaliates with its improved delivery systems and long range missiles and a large stockpile of nuclear warheads Pakistan will just cease to exist. The choice will be with Pakistan, to use or not to use nuclear weapons. We need not, least of all our leadership, develop cold feet from the nuclear possibility. Let us go ahead with our plans and once and for all destroy the terrorists' network in Pakistan even if it means hurting the US feelings and earning their ire, because of the presence of their troops in parts of Pakistan territory to the northwest. The successful strike speedily accomplished will leave the US no option but to reconcile. They may even silently approve, since terrorists are common enemies to both and with the gradual disenchantment of US with Pak double speak and secret support to Al-Qaida and other terrorist organizations, which inspite of being banned are alive and kicking under different names. India will be doing part of the job US wishes to accomplish by eliminating the eastern part of the terrorist empire in POK. The remains of Islamic Jehad have to be buried not in the Indian soil but Pak and POK, its place of origin.

Another factor that gives India an advantage is the full dress rehearsal for a limited or an all out war during 'Operation Parakaram' to achieve surprise, speedy mobilization and occupation of forward battle positions. These would be the operational imperatives. The recently achieved co-ordination with the railways, forward movement of troops, vehicles, missile launchers from railways carriages and firing platforms, tanks and artillery and munitions of war to pre-rehearsed positions, from concentration areas to assembly areas and forming up places, assault through cleared mine lanes, identified and marked on battle maps, movement of bridging material and mine laying devices to breach enemy defences would result in a rapid armoured breakthrough in the plains of Punjab and Rajasthan desert to capture pre-marked tactical objectives deep inside; severing Pakistan from Sindh. The steady push by our mountain formations in the J&K to pre-selected targets and terrorist bases would place the entire western front from LOC to international border in the south right up to the seashore in a state of armed conflict forcing Pakistan to withdraw its low intensity war machine from India back home.

Rising above the limited overview of this war from Siachin to Kutch in the west, one should not ignore what Professor Samuel Huntington called the 'clash of civilizations and making of a new world order'. The America centric Judeo-Christian civilization has its beachhead across the Mediterranean in Israel, the arrowhead of a grand pincer to contain militant Islam as Hindu India provides the other southeastern arm of that pincer. The long-term strategic interest of America centric Judeo-Christian civilization will have a stake in the Middle East, the tinderbox of future conflict between militant Islam and the surrounding civilizations. The only other civilization that can contain this breeding ground of international terrorism and the epicentre of militant Islam would be a Hindu India, placed by a quirk of destiny and geographical accident on its southeastern rim. Thus, in simple terms, Israel led and America centric Judeo-Christian west needs a strong and resurgent Hindu India that could contain this cauldron of Islamic fervour. Other local considerations apart, this is the real scenario that the future is going to unfold. Thus, India and Israel must not only endure but also prevail. After 9/11 the civilizational faultlines are even clearer. Thus, on a long term basis India can only be of help to the US, Europe and Russia, and Indian democracy, a lone flicker of light in the all-pervading darkness of authoritarian dictatorships and monarchies of Islamic middle east, has to be kept burning. On its part India need not be afraid of a confrontation with Pakistan. Rather than allow a cancerous low intensity conflict with cross-border terrorism to drain national strength and enfeeble our country, India should decide to call the shots.

Since the threat of terror is mainly directed against Hindus, the security of India becomes synonymous with that of the Hindus, a point also discussed at some length in the previous pages. In the emerging political scenario after the Cold War and a natural outcome of the clash along civilizational faultlines the Islamic totalitarian regimes are ranged against three circumvallating democracies: the United States, India and Israel. The threat to these from Islamic fundamentalism is real and imminent. Osama bin Laden and his Al-Qaida cohorts as also many other terrorist groups in the Middle East have handed out a '*fatwa*' to wage *Jehad* against these nations. I have dealt with this subject in some details in my earlier book *India and Israel Against Islamic Terror*. Nevertheless, some points need re-emphasis in view of the emerging power equations and realignment of forces. A US-India-Isreal entente against Islamic terror is not only a strategic and civilizational imperative, but also the only way to contain and finally extirpate Islamic militancy from the Middle East and its epicentre in the Pakistan-Afghanistan fertile crecsent. India and Israel have always had a civilizational synergy and convergence of strategic interests, but the US forced by the threat of its own Frankenstein, Al-Qaida, realised only on 9/11 the real dimensions of the worldwide web of terror threatening American interests. Even today the US policy of propping up Pakistan against India on the specious plea of being a frontline ally in its war on terrorism may eventually be found misplaced.

India-Israel relations came out of a deep freeze in 1977 when Moshe Dayan secretly visited India at the invitation of Morarji Desai. Over the years the security concerns shared by the two countries led to discussions under a new paradigm of a nuclear peril, the Islamic bomb, and siege from Islamic terror. This led to a new bipartite unwritten treaty. With the US threatened similarly after 9/11 a trilateral convergence of strategic concerns took a concrete form. During the cold war and under Nehru's policy of non-alignment, which with its Communist leaning and Soviet tilt was not so non-aligned after all, the ideological fixation of the Congress and the Left resulted in a very hypothetical and unrealistic policy prescription. The Jehad emanating from autocratic, radical and dictatorial regimes threatened the interests of all the three democracies even though these may not be totally congruent. A significant factor in cementing the US-India-Israeli ties is the key role played by the Indian and Israeli diaspora in the US under the benevolent gazes of the Capitol Hill, with active support from the US-India Political Action Committee, the American Jewish Committee and the American-Israeli Public Affairs Committee. This effort, incidentally, has a synergy with the Sharon doctrine of India and Israel developing a unique partnership in high technology production. To buttress this effort there is enough diplomatic clout the two countries possess, to resist pressure from those who advocate appeasement and defeatist pacifism, instead of a determined opposition to tyrannical, regressive, oppressive and terrorist forces. The intellectual underpinnings to this political and strategic effort lies in the urge for a joint front against Islamic obscurantism. A reinforcing foundation of the alliance lies in another facet of Sharon's doctrine, that there should be an inherence of civilisational resources and public diplomacy in achieving military victory to more distant horizons like the Torah Talmud and Mishna in the twentyfirst century. The entire corpus of the Jewish scriptures and systems of thought like those of Spinoza, Heine and Maimonides has a morphic resonance with those of Swami Vivekanand, Sri Aurobindo and Tagore. This leaves us with a rich heritage and gives us the ability to focus on the core moral issues arising out of rapid technological changes.

It is most unfortunate that Sharon's official visit during the second week of September 2003, had raised the hackles of the Communist and Muslim groups. These slogan shouters were not concerned with national interest but impelled by religious and partisan politics. In a world of growing pragmatism where empty ideological shibboleths have been consigned to the dustbin of history and nation states aggressively pursue their national interests, in India our national interests have become hostage to an ideological, moral and religious time warp. The Palestinian problem overshadowed our hard security conrcerns as the Shahi Imam of Jama Masjid and Communist red caps ranted and poured venom on Sharon's visit. All this, notwithstanding the fact that our friends in Middle-East oil-rich countries never cared for our energy concerns and the Organization of Islamic Countries (OIC) had never supported our stand on Kashmir in response to our one-sided espousal of the Arab cause. On the other hand Israel had never acted against India.

The red brigade that cannot stand the sight of Sharon for his alleged atrocities against the Palestinians had no moral compunction in rolling out the red carpet in 2001 for the Chinese dictator Le Peng, notorious for his human rights violations. Tienanaman Square is not the only stain on his escutcheon "glorified by genocide". In Tibet alone 6259 monasteries were destroyed causing 1.3 million deaths including 173240 in prisons and 7.5 million Han Chinese planted around 6 million Tibetans to completely change the demographic structure of the state. Then the warmth with which these votaries of Muslim rights in India welcomed Pakistan's President Musharraf at Agra in 2001 cannot be forgotton. Fortunately, this breed of Muslim clerics and Red anachronisms, a stranger to Indian culture and idiom, exists only on the margins of Indian polity. During the 1962 Chinese invasion, Israel stood solidly behind India. In 1965, it secretly sold us mortar bombs after erasing their markings, and laser guided bombs and munitions of war. During the 1999 Kargil conflict also it provided substantial help. After the discard of Nehruvian Left-tilting foreign policy a bilateral relationship has blossomed between the two oldest civilizations of the world that have so much in common and even much more to give and take. The expanding bilateral trade had already touched $1.27 billion mark, almost sixfold during just one decade. This together with defence sales to India amounted to almost $ 5.29 billion in 2003. A nation with the population of six million, less than half of Delhi, is our most reliable defence supplier selling hardware worth $ 1.5 billion a year.

A prima facie matrix of Indo-Israeli defence cooperation is based on enhancing India's power projection in terms of air and naval forces, ballistics missile defence systems (BMD) including Boost Phase Interruption (BPI) technologies as also cooperation in countering nuclear, chemical and biological (NCB) threat from Pak-based terrorist organizations. We must also focus on sea and air-borne effective second strike capabilities to offset the disadvantage of our avowed 'no first strike' policy, all this dovetailing into the US naval interests in the sealanes across South Asia. These trilateral enterprises can be catalysed by the existing successful bilateral US-Israel Funds for agricultural research and developmental infrastructure. Israel's long term strategic naval projection and access to Indian Ocean is in perfect synergy with

India's stress on sea-borne power with a view to guard its 8000 kms long coast line, as also to provide mobile submarine and aircraft carrier sites for launching nuclear weapons in case of a Pak confrontation. Israeli expertise in deterrent radar surveillance and sea to sea missiles can help India develop a credible sea-based nuclear deterrent to have a stabilising effect in the region. With existing bilateral contacts, installation of Israeli equipment in Indian ships and patrolling vessels leading to joint ventures in defence technologies, is the call of the times.

India's support to Israel, a state under siege by a highly articulate international community with a pronounced pro-Muslim and anti-Jewish bias, will help it to break out of the cycle of censure, everytime it attempts to defend its vital national interests assertively. The international approval comes only when it accedes to demands for ever more concessions at the cost of its territorial security. An Israeli leader once exclaimed that international laws are bent to convenience by nations with might and apply only to the weak. Indo-Israeli collaboration should augment and complement and not supplant or replace its reliance on the US and this could follow the pattern of Turkish-Israeli cooperation to dispel any idea of anti-Muslim bias.

If we apply a close scrutiny on our weaponry and its source of supply we shall find that 70% of our defence supplies are Russia based. With our resource crunch India ought to look for a reliable partner who can be trusted not to supply the same weapons to China or Pakistan. The Russian origin of Chinese defence equipment is well known and China in turn meets most of Pakistan's defence needs. Thus Israel fills the bill for a reliable partner for defence supplies, who can be trusted not to sell weapons to Pakistan unlike many other European countries doing business with them. Further, the Israeli package is cost-effective and suits Indian requirements. There is a formidable array of defence equipment that Israel supplies to India. With the induction of Phalcon radar system, Israel would enter into a joint venture to produce unmanned aerial vehicles. It shall meet our demand for sophisticated avionics and electronic warfare systems for our frontline ships and aircrafts. Procurement of laser guided ammunition, specialized infantry weapons including rifles, sophisticated communication systems and weapons for special forces, night vision devices for soldiers and tanks is in the pipeline. Technology transfer to factor indigenisation of India's defence industries will form an important part of this package. Israel is one of the world's best manufacturers of electronic warfare and surveillance systems and will supply these to frontline warships at a cost of about $ 105 million. Its expertise in upgrading will come handy in converting the existing 135mm artillery guns to 155mm caliber as also upgradation of MIG 23, 27 and 29 fleet of fighter jets. This huge defence benefit is not unaccompanied with a rich haul of auxiliary benefits. Improvement of our desert agriculture, plantation of suitable trees for arid areas, drip and other irrigation technology, anchoring of sand dunes, desalination of desert water and harnessing solar energy would be the net gains of India-Israel mutual cooperation.

As we rise above the minutae of weaponry needed to enhance our land, sea and air capability, a clear macro picture emerges positing this natural triple entente of India, the US and Israel subserving their vital national interests against the threat by a resurgent militant Islam. While the US terror concerns cause it to chase Al-Qaida and other world stations of Islamic terror, Israel is under constant attack from Syrian Hamas, Iranian Hizbollahs and Palestinian Fedayeen. These two may not be congruent with India's Kashmir centric concerns. There is no doubt whatsoever that the breeding ground of terror is the Middle East cauldron and its reigning epicentre, the Pak-Afghan belt. Further, there are invisible labyrinthine connections and a process of cross-pollination at work that unites them all, despite a vast geographical spread. The US had battled its own creation of Jihadi Taliban in Afghanistan and now Iraq threatens to be a new base of global Jehad. Thus Indo-Israeli cooperation alone cannot be effective without a winnable US strategy based on a realistic long term vision, rather than expediency and short term gains. The US, India and Israel need to weave this strategy of fighting terror not around ideology but hanging it on the hard pegs of national interest. There are no good or bad terrorists. The only good terrorist is a dead one. The Kashmiri Jehadis are no different from those in Afghanistan, Iraq, Syria or Saudi Arabia. The US as a member of this triple entente should realize that terrorist breeding grounds cannot be fully cleared unless the societies that rear them are deradicalised and democratised. Washington's molly-coddling of Pakistan will not do. Elections in Aghanistan and perpetuating Musharraf's dictatorship in Pakistan will be counter-productive. Despite formidable challenges the US, India and Isreal cannot afford to lose their war against terror. Having earlier routed the Soviet Union in Afghanistan, the growing ranks of Islamic terrorists can now get the only super power bogged down in Iraq and pose a bigger threat to India.

For a few operational bases in northwest and a doubtful support in its fight against Taliban, the US has released their friend Musharraf from Indian pressure during *Operation Parakram* and allowed him to continue his good work of exporting cross-border terrorism into Kashmir. While the US forces were hunting Saddam in Iraq, Powell was busy raising another Saddam in Pakistan armed with weapons of mass destruction (WMD). While India does not have anything to do with the US problems in Iraq, the US shored up Pakistan's military regime and kept its economy afloat by huge tranches of loans, and quietly ignored its export of terror to India. Thus, regardless of whether the Indo-US-Israeli axis comes into shape, India has to fight against terror entirely on its own. Any indirect support from the US must be treated as purely incidental.

The defence collaboration with Israel and the strategic and civilisational imperatives of a triple entente are inescapable. To put it more appropriately in civilisational-politico-strategic terms, Israel is the beachhead of the US centric Judeo-Christianity across the Mediterranean Sea into the Middle East, the heartland of militant Islam. India on the other hand is the great impregnable wall stanching the overflow of this scourge to the Southeast. Thus while Israel, the arrowhead of the gaint pincer of US-centric Judeo-Christianity, can act as the hammer head, India provides the anvil to contain and extirpate the militant Islam extending from Syria to Pakistan.

All this has been mentioned only to highlight that there are great possibilities in the area of diplomacy. Nevertheless, India should prepare to fight its own battle against terror from its own human resources. There is thus an urgent need to raise a young disciplined and voluntary civil defence force, unlike the Home Guards and the Territorial Army units, thoroughly motivated like the revolutionary freedom fighters of yore. Trained in the use of automatic light hand held weapons, they should be our sentries and guards to shed their blood when the need arises for the defence of Mother India. The jehadi can attack any crowded place, railway stations, trains, buses, shopping complexes, temples, religious congregations and pilgrim camps. The targets are unlimited and with local support from a section of minority community providing shelter and intelligence the possibilities are endless. Let us enter again into a new struggle for freedom to rid our land of the jehadi marauders and give a fitting reply not by pleading for help but by using force or *Shakti* as ordained in Gita and be true Hindus, the inheritors of a very cherished legacy of our forefathers. The renaissance of Hinduism in our sacred motherland has not only to sustain itself but overcome all forces against it. That is what Hindutva is all about.

In a recent survey and in a TV seminar most defence analysts agreed that India should exercise its military option of a suitable kind against Pakistan at a time of its own choosing, and in a manner of own choice. The so-called alienation of Kashmiri people already being attended under a new dispensation will look after itself, once the shadow of Pak terror is removed. Let the US sensitivity be a matter of their own concern. India has to address its own security concerns before indulging into the luxury of a public relations exercise and international please-all efforts. In any war, conventional or nuclear, Pakistan has more to lose, notwithstanding the bluff and bluster of Pervez Musharraf. In short, the besieging forces of militant Islam in the northwest, an expansionist nuclear China on the north and a hostile Bangladesh host to Pak terrorists in the east are a challenge that can only be matched by an India united by a strong Hindutva and a patriotic minority support. We shall not discuss any further this aspect on which enough literature already exists, and now turn the focus on the threat from within.

There are many countervailing forces within our home territory that threaten the forces of Hindutva deployed at the barricades of "Fortress Indiana". These have been mentioned separately at length in the previous chapters but a brief review and the compounding effect of these on the health and vitality of Hinduism will be in order. Hindutva is the essence of Hinduism and the foundation of cultural nationalism. All those who live in India regardless of their faith share a cultural affinity, a geographical positioning, caste affiliation within the Hindu fold, commonality of linguistic base, regional affinity and most important of all, a heritage of ten millennia, pre-dating the advent of Islam or Christianity. Change of faith does not alter the DNA code, nor lead to a denial of ancestry or a long attachment to the soil of India. Cultural nationalism is not a negation of other religious identities but an assimilation of all under an overarching national community.

Starting from this premise the position becomes clear and the forces threatening Hinduism can be identified more clearly. Hinduism has not only been under threat but subjected to untold humiliations, massacres, slavery and above all a direct assault on its faith through destruction of their shrines, evangelization and forcible religious conversions. The first Muslim attack on India came in 712 AD, when Mohammed bin Qasim, an Arab invader, carried out a seaborne attack on Sindh along the Baluchistan coast and defeated King Dahir, a local chieftain, on the northwest fringe of the Hindu India. He started a campaign to compulsorily circumscribe Hindu women. When this forcible religious conversion was resisted he got all the population above 17 years massacred. The surviving children and women were enslaved and many sold in the slave markets. Temples were looted; a part of the booty was distributed among the soldiers and a large part set aside as a gift for the Caliph of Baghdad.

After the golden age of Kannauj when the reign of the last great Hindu king Harshavardhana came to an end, for the next four centuries with a regular frequency armed expeditions from Hindukush through Khybar Pass continued under the impulse of Islamic iconoclasm, driven further by the desire to loot the precious Hindu temples and enrichment through sale of prisoners of war, including even innocent non-combatants. During this period there was no evidence of capturing and occupying the sacred Hindu land. It was only from early 14th century when the Delhi Sultanate was established that the process of defiling Hindu lands by conquest and despoilation, killings and conversions gained a momentum all its own till the Mughal rule came to an end in early eighteenth century. The next century belongs to the Marathas and from 1808 AD onwards India came under Pax Britannica. Both Islam and Christianity played havoc with the ethnic faith. It was entirely due to the inherent strength, vitality, resilience and deep roots of Hinduism in its Vedic past that Hinduism survived and refused to die. But the besieging forces instead of weakening, after the collapse of the Muslim and British rule, have raised their ugly head and shall pose a direct threat to Hinduism. Hinduism today faces a threat both from external forces and the enemy within.

Though not yet adopted officially there is a strong case being made by people who matter in the United States that a clear signal be sent to countries that harbour terrorists that they can do so only at a heavy risk to their sovereignty. Saudi Arabia the epicentre of export of Wahabi Islam is under close scrutiny. Also under the scanner should be its worldwide charities amounting to about $ 20 billion that support organizations promoting fundamentalism and religious extremism. Rabita and Matamer, to name just two such charities, are the biggest exporters of Wahabi fundamentalism and are closely watched for imposition of a ban. A Bangladeshi writer Jamal Hassan based in Washington observed that Saudi Arabia has laid out an extensive network of charities and madrasas all over the world heavily funded by their oil money. He went into great details giving the number and locations of such institutions. Seen against this background and the fact that other Islamic fundamentalist and terrorist organizations from Harkat-ul-Mujahideen in Pakistan to Jamat-e-Islam in Bangladesh receive funds and support from Saudi Arabia is bound to cause concern. Lashkar-e-Toiba under a new alias in Pakistan collected funds for Jehadis in Afghanistan, Chechnya, Bosnia and Kashmir.

ISI operatives in Bangladesh are involved in hiring local criminals for smuggling arms, ammunition and narcotics in India as also to provide bases for anti-India activities. While Bangladeshi journalists are hired and recruited by Bangladesh Nationalist Party (BNP) to generate strong anti-India feelings, Pak nationals are being trained to serve as maulavis for indoctrination at mosques and madarsas located along the India-Bangladesh border. The Muslim Tigers in Assam, the Muslim United Liberation Front of Assam, the United People Liberation Front, North Eastern Minority Front and Islamic Front in Manipur have been active for some time. The ISI dispatched two hundred Taliban guerrillas and six Al-Qaida terrorists in Bangladesh where local terrorist group, Tabaliq-e-Jamat, looked after them. Twenty Al-Qaida terrorists were arrested from a mosque in Khulna in January 2002. And above all, insurgent groups operating in North East have found safe havens in Bangladesh, while some of them have even contacts with Al-Qaida and pledge support to them. India should take tough measures against this continuing threat from the east and make it clear to Bangladesh as also to Pakistan that India means business, and that we will ensure that there is a high price tag on supporting terrorism.

In the unrestricted warfare that we are facing from Pakistan by its unabated terrorist Jehad in Kashmir, we may have to resort to a judicious mix of three options open to us: military, quasi-military and non-military. The first two have a greater relevance in the situation of a nuclear standoff, which Pakistan is exploiting to the full. The water weapon is the most effective option available to India as a non-military response. We have all the logic of need and circumstance in our favour. The current Indus Water Treaty (IWT) does not provide an equitable share of waters of the west flowing rivers to J&K, and this is one of the underlying causes for the lack of development in the region. With threefold population increase and repeated droughts, there is a crying need to re-draw the treaty. India is already on record in its request to the United Nations General Assembly in the case of Farakka dispute regarding equitable distribution of waters, that "when a river crossed more than one country each riparian state was entitled to a reasonable and equitable share of an international river." Article XII (4) of Indus Water Treaty stipulates that the treaty can be terminated only by another treaty. We thus have an unfettered sovereign right to renegotiate a fresh treaty in view of the increased water demands since the signing of the earlier treaty in September 1960. There are many hydroelectric projects that have been adversely affected due to prolongation of the treaty, leading to power shortages in J&K. We have two recent precedents to go by. Hungary and Czechoslovakia went to the International Court of Justice (ICJ) due to Hungary reneging on the 1977 treaty of river Danube, in view of her needs of construction of a project on the river. The ICJ ruled on the basis of 1977 treaty, and on the principle of 'equitable utilization of waters'. Thus, Article XII (4) of the IWT permits re-negotiation. The USA and Mexico involved in a dispute over the waters of Rio-Grande referred the case to U.S. Attorney General Harmon, who gave his famous ruling called "The Harmon Doctrine". "The fundamental principle of international law is the absolute sovereignty of every nation against all others within its own territory". Thus India has a sovereign right to the use of the three western rivers—Indus, Jhelum and Chenab flowing into Pakistan, as it deems to be its equitable share. India can hold this jugular to make Pakistan see reason and refrain from its export of terrorism. We shall be doing no more than exercising our sovereign right to use the river waters for the legitimate needs of the people of J&K. If the growth of Pakistan's agro-based economy is stymied it is their problem. They have to choose between parched cornfields and continued unprovoked aggression against India. Rogue nations like

Pakistan understand only the language of force that Gita preaches to all Hindus.

If our leadership is less inhibited by a negative impulse against national self-interest, we can use this water weapon against our hostile neighbour on the east as well. We are gifted with a geographical advantage where a major part of the rivers that sustain the lives and properties of these two countries flow within our own country. What is true of Indus Water Treaty also holds good for the discharge of water from Farakka Dam to Bangladesh where the waters of the Padma sustain the lives in four districts of Kushipur, Faridpur, Jessore and Khulna. At present Padma gets 30,000 cusecs a day regardless of Indian sharing. Any recalcitrance and hostile act against us should bear a heavy cost to the aggressor. Even the threat of withholding extra water that we can ill-afford can bring these countries to their knees.

Mr. K.P. Fabian, a former Ambassador to Italy, once remarked "Water from India terrorism from Pakistan: India cannot accept a state of affairs where life-supporting water flows from India to Pakistan for Pakistan's use under the IWT of 1960, uninterrupted even by the wars of 1965, 1971 and the Kargil war, whereas life destroying terrorism flows in the reverse direction". Another former diplomat Mr. Satish C Sharma has expressed almost identical views: "India cannot supply water to the Pakistani masses so long as Pakistani terrorists continue killing innocent Indians". Let us now look at the enemy within. Despite declaring Pakistan a stalwart ally and a frontline state in their 'War against Terrorism', the US has been careful not to lower its guard against illegal Pak immigrants in their country. Pak nationals in the US have now been brought under the purview of the National Security Entry Registration System (NSEERS), which requires them to register with the local offices of the US Immigration and Naturalization Services (INSO), and have their photographs and fingerprints taken. This move to ferret out illegal immigrants will affect 70-80% of illegal Pak nationals, one thousand of whom have already been deported back home.

A new development in the operations of the international terrorist groups is cross-fertilization among its country's specific centres, devoted to a common cause. Akshardham, Bali and the Moscow hostage crises are but the different heads on a common hydra monster, Lashkar-e-Toiba, which has close links with the Al-Qaida. The Bali bloodbath by Jammati-Islamia, a pan-regional outfit, was first traced at Singapore towards the end of 2001. The Moscow theatre hostage crisis bore clear signs of international transfer of materials, methods and ideology. There were Fedayeens of the Al-Qaida, who masterminded 9/11, present among the 50 Chechen terrorists, who threatened to kill 700 hostage in a Moscow theatre, if the Russian forces were not withdrawn from Chechenya. A terrorist attack is now no more an isolated event but has deep labyrinthine and complex connections of support, structure and functions far away from the splash spot of blood, indistinguishable from the normal social elements.

In a series of articles under the heading *'Cry, O Beloved India'*, a French journalist Francois Gautier has been highlighting many colours of India from its past glory to the present degeneration. It is indeed heartening to see a foreigner residing in India write with such candour and devotion to our motherland. Earlier, Gandhiji too used to write for the paper '*Mother India*'. Above all, it was Bal Gangadhar Tilak and Veer Savarkar, who gave currency to the idea of a sacred motherland India in patriotic tones. Having got our freedom without much human sacrifice, a spirit of complacency has overtaken the post-independence generations. One seldom hears the words *'Beloved India'* these days. But during the emergency of 1975-76, one was forced to mention the words '*Our Beloved Prime Minister*' while referring to the then Prime Minister, Indira Gandhi. The opposition leaders, including RSS, were all in jail. Our secularist press crawled when asked to bend. No function began or ended without the words '*Our Beloved Prime Minister*'. Such were the depths to which the nation had sunk when an individual had become synonymous with the motherland. Some Congressmen still crow Dev Kanth Barua's insult to the nation, by uttering his famous words, articulating the feelings of most Congressmen at that time that *Indira is India, India is Indira.* The sycophants in the Congress even today indulge in the apotheosis of the same icon and its dynasty down to the third generation. It is about time that sons of Mother India instead of worshipping false gods pay their obeisance and debt to the sacred soil of Mother India.

A balanced view of the Muslim mindset was given by Hussein Haqqaqi, a Pak journalist, in the following candid terms. "Decades of repression and authoritarian rule, coupled with the arrogance of elite decision makers, have eroded the spirit of peaceful dissent in almost all of the 57 countries with a Muslim majority population". He goes on to say, "In Pakistan and other authoritarian Muslim countries, the state apparatus wants to control and calibrate peoples, opinions. Political parties capable of mobilizing public opinion have been sidelined through a barrage of propaganda and manipulation of the political system". This is the country India is up against.

In these difficult days, when India is the preferred target of terrorist violence, we need a Vladimir Putin. The Russian President had the courage to take a hard decision and accept the consequences, where Indian leaders would have winced. Despite western pressure to go slow in order to ensure the safety of their nationals caught inside a Moscow theatre, Putin acted with firmness and resolve. With Chechen rebel women strapped with bombs, the lives of people inside were surely at risk. But Putin rightly believed that if he did not surrender to the demands of the Chechen guerrillas, some people may suffer but Russia would emerge stronger. In the process, Russian commandos killed 50 terrorists and took the rest as prisoners with a collateral loss of a few hostages in the theatre. Despite western criticism, Putin brought off his coup with a minimum loss of lives and enhanced the prestige of his nation. Today he is a hero in the eyes of the Russian people. While many in the west and even our so-called 'secularist brigade' in India would wish that he had dealt with them differently, fortunately Putin treated them as they were, just terrorists. Can we expect such a response from our national leadership that is long on rhetoric and short on action? They virtually surrendered Kashmir to terrorists while chanting, "Democracy has won in Kashmir". A state where Sufi Islam prevailed and Hindus and Muslims have lived in harmony for centuries has now become a cauldron of violence, intolerance, bullets and butchery. Is that democracy? They glory in the elections held inside a military fortress where people risked their lives to cast their votes and threw up an unstable and weak coalition government without giving a thought to the four lakh Kashmiri pundits who had to flee their homes under the terrorists' guns to live as refugees in their own country. Democracy has won. Ironically, Mr. Vajpayee known to the press world over and to the opposition in India as a Hindu, buckled to Pakistan without a serious fight. It is disheartening to see a white Christian woman along with a Muslim Ghulam Nabi Azad handing over the reigns of power to Mufti

Mohammed Sayeed, the very man who had got released a number of dreaded terrorists to obtain the release of his daughter Rubaiyya Sayeed. This man is now running a state that was of Shaivism. How does all this contrast with Mr. Putin's brave action at Moscow?

The litany of surrenders to terrorists is endless. The December 1999, IC 814 hijack, made possible due to our negligence, and lack of timely action, where our own External Affairs Minister flew in royal court to deliver the three most dreaded assassins at Kandhar in return for 160 passengers, contrasts sharply with the Russian action at Moscow. IC 814 hijackers had but one pistol and a few knives and there were 160 passengers to overwhelm them. They did nothing but cry for mercy and the government buckled. On the other hand, the Russian hostages bore their ordeal with courage, never cried for help and came out cool and composed on release. The question arises over and over again. Are Hindus cowards? The intelligentsia mocks at Bal Thakeray when he states that Hindus must form suicide squads. Even the Chechen women moving with explosives strapped around their waists ready to die for the cause, however, misguided it might be, were at least brave and not cowards. The point about Hindu cowardice has been made repeatedly and need not be stressed anymore. For centuries, Hindus have suffered massacres, humiliations and indignities but still lack the courage to fight for a just cause. Mr. Vajpayee could only threaten. He did it a number of times when he was Prime Minister. He kept our armed forces on the border for ten long months, costing us Rupees 8000 crores but could not dare take any offensive action.

Pervez Musharraf seems to have had the last laugh. Where Putin acted, our leaders merely squirmed. Look at any place of conflict all over the world. It is Muslims versus the rest. Samuel Huntington's prophecy is coming true. Korea, Chechenya, Israel, Saudi Arabia, a sniper in Washington, Russian hostages, the Bali bombing or the Phillippines, Islamic jihadis are on the move. They are inspired by the Quran – Quran is written in Arabic. Arabic is the language of Saudis through which the Muezzin used to call the faithful to prayers across long distance of desert wilderness. The Arabs are drunk upon their own rhetoric and language. Arab, Arabic and Islam are inseparable, each recreating the other in an undefined process of cross-pollination, till the words are exalted to the level of reality. Islam is a religion devoid of theology. It means submission to the will of God and a total surrender to what He wills or ordains. Though it is difficult to interpret the will of God, Muslim leaders down the ages have conferred legitimacy to their cause from worship to slaughter, all in the name of God's will. The Suras of Quran have a rhythm and a nuance all their own. They proclaim, implore, chant, croon, weep and laugh and the torrential flow of Arabic creates an image that charms. This repetitiveness in Islam overwhelms imagination and calcifies reason. The holy language intoxicates and sanitises the brain in a manner that only the language counts and not its substance. In such an atmosphere, it is easy to understand that the Arab, who for fourteen hundred years had turned inwards upon the spoken words, and numbed his senses to the heat and poverty of the desert, lapped every word of the Mullah. As India faces two Islamic countries on the west and the east, apocalypse is not too far.

Hindus have to shoulder the burden of this *dharmayudh.* While the Cassandras come out with their platitudes to rationalize Islamic violence and the cynics argue till the cows come home, India has only one choice and destiny, a strong resurgent Hindu nation capable of fighting Islamic jehadis head on. All great men with a mission have made history. India has a mission. But is still searching for a leader. Let her not be disappointed. Instead of adopting a tough proactive stand every time a terrorist act is perpetuated in India by Pakistan, there is a tendency to run to Uncle Sam and cry on his shoulders. The time has come for taking some hard hitting measures. Our pleadings to the US to declare Pakistan a rogue state have come to naught. A lot of water has flown over the Yamuna since our New Year gift of handing over three dreaded terrorists, the hijackers of IC-814. Those who took the government to task for releasing Masood Azhar were equally cynical about the shooting of two terrorists at Ansal Plaza to avoid a blood bath. The police was accused of staging an 'encounter' shooting of two prisoners already in custody. Either way the government was damned. Masood Azhar's release should have taught India that rather than whining before the International community, the time has come for unilateral action against terror. The then Deputy Prime Minister, L.K. Advani, said as much though belatedly in Thailand. While we were fiddling, President Bush has given the CIA a *carte blanche* to kill terrorists figuring on their list, with permission to add new names as deemed fit. This order authorizes the CIA to eliminate terrorists without seeking prior presidential approval. This is the type of hard line we have to follow.

An unnoticed but slow and steady growth of the Muslim population in India is one of the potential sources of communal strife, internal subversion and threat to India's internal security. The Hindu feeling of insecurity on this count alone is not entirely unfounded. Here are the facts. Even during the British rule from 1881-1941, the increase in Muslim population was much higher than that of the Hindus. From a figure of 75% Hindu population against 20% of Muslims, the balance changed to 69% for the Hindus and 24% for the Muslims. An increase of 4% for the Muslims against a decrease of 6% for the Hindus leading to a 10% difference in growth rate. In the Census of 1961 after independence, when Hindus registered an increase of 2.5%, for the Muslims the increase was 8.5% leading to a disparity of 6% in their growth rates. Some experts put the present Muslim population in India at 16% of the national total. At this rate, in another 112 years, Hindus will become a minority in their own homeland. If we add to this the continuous influx of Muslims from Bangladesh and Pakistan, variously estimated at 2-5 crores, the situation causes concern. Along with two fast growing nations on our east and west, even Nepal that had no Muslim population is showing an increase mainly due to the spread of madrasas along the Indo-Nepal border. As opposed to this the Hindu population in Pakistan decreased from 17% in 1948 to just about 1% today. Likewise, in Bangladesh it has come down from 14% in 1971 to 10% in 1991. During British rule in 1891, the Census Commissioner O'Donnell had forecast that in the coming 620 years, Hindu population would disappear from India. Colonel V. N. Mukherjee put the time span to only 420 years. A forecast in 1998 predicted that at the present rate of demographic change, the Muslims would outnumber the Hindus in 316 years. The latest census figure, once again have under scored the disturbing truth and trends. It is about time that our policy planners take note of this rapidly increasing rate of growth of the Muslim population in India, as also the illegal influx of Muslim migrants from the east and the west. Samuel Huntington had stated that among the world religions, the dubious distinction of the fastest population growth goes to Islam. A militant Islam with its ever-increasing ranks is a threat to the world. Hindu concern on this phenomenon cannot be ignored and our neo-secularist minority appeasers will learn it the bitter if they refused to see the inevitable consequence of this multiple Muslim growth. If unchecked, after another 316 years if not earlier, our neo-secularists will themselves become a threatened species, with no Hindu majority to castigate or crucify.

The signs of Islamabad's plan to widen the cleavage between the two main communities can be read clearly in the hidden links between Godhra, Gujarat and Akshardham. The temple attack was an outcome of terrorism feeding on communal hatred and divide. This is just the beginning, there is much more in store. A prominent indigenous terrorist cum religious organization to give shape to this design is Ahle Hadis, based in western Uttar Pradesh. It was a madrasa set up in 1990 by Maulana Afiq, with branches all over the country. Flush with funds from Saudi Arabia, the institute can afford to keep one-third of its students on scholarships, while poor students are offered a yearly stipend worth Rs. 13,500. It promotes Wahabi Islam, born out of Saudi Arabia, rigidly adhering to the orthodox interpretation of the Prophet's teachings. It is also affiliated to Markaz Dawana 1-Irshad, a Lahore based extremist religious group and a wing of Lashkar-e-Toiba. The ugly face of Ahle Hadis first came to view after investigations in the great serial train blasts following the demolition of Babri Masjid in December 1992. Intensive raids were carried out and Dr. Ansari, a qualified doctor and an active member of Ahle Hadis, was found to be the mastermind behind the serial explosions in five trains in just one night, 5/6 December, 1993. Tunda, a resident of Pilkhuwa, Uttar Pradesh, who escaped the CBI dragnet was involved in the Bombay serial blasts in March and December 1993 and was also a suspect in the plot to blow up the dais of West Bengal Chief Minister, Buddhadeb Bhattacharya during his public speech at Dumkal, in Murshidabad district, West Bengal, on 22 December, 1994. He was later also involved in the explosion in the Jhelum Express on 3 December 1996, and serial blasts at Rohtak and Panipat in January 1997. Tunda's operations in Haryana and West Bengal could not have been possible without local bases. These were provided by Ahle Hadis of which Tunda was an active member. Tunda then did a disappearing trick and floated a rumour that he had died, his dead body being found near a railway track a few years later, The points-man of Lashkar–e–Toiba's operations, he was reporting directly to the Lashkar's chief of India's operations Azhar Cheema who worked directly under the Commander of Military Operations, Zaqu-ur-Rahman Lakhvi. Tunda came on the police radar screen when one of his new recruits from Bangladesh, Syed Abu Nasir, was found working from the network that mostly served Ahle Hadis. It was Tunda's associate Aftab Ansari, arrested in Dubai and extradited to India in May 2002, who exposed Tunda's Ahle Hadis, ISI, LeT and Al-Qaida link. The prime accused in the kidnapping of a Kolkata businessman Partha Roy Burman and the attack on the US consulate in Kolkata, he was also later dispatched to Mohammad Atta, the suicide pilot bomber of the 9/11 attacks. The money trail passed through the ISI chief, Lieutenant General Mohammad Ahmad, later sacked, and Omar Shiekh who was a close aide to Abu Zubaidah, the Al-Qaida Chief of Operations who escaped the US bombings in Kandhar to Peshawar to be arrested by the FBI in early 2002.

Aftab Ansari and Omar Sheikh had been friends during their incarceration in Tihar jail. The arrest in Delhi of LeT operatives Ahmed Bakshi and Farhan Ahmed Ali from West Asia on their mission to India to recruit young Muslims from Gujarat to launch revenge attacks, laid bare the last link between Tunda and Ahle Hadis. Indoctrinated by LeT by showing photographs of the Gujarat riots, these two came prepared for instigating revenge killings of Hindus. While Bakshi was trying to set up a tanker business as a front for transporting arms and explosives, Ali contacted Hafiz Mohammad Tahir, Ahle Hadis Secretary in Moradabad, for recruiting young Muslims from the Gujarat riot-affected areas. In the last four years, the network of Ahle Hadis has reached Kutch. It is the organizations like Ahle Hadis and SIMI who on ISI command are keeping the communal cauldron boiling and the terrorism alive in India. The Indian state will do well to keep these subversive organizations under closer scrutiny and defang them.

One of the major internal threats to the social fabric of India where two communities have to live in harmony is the series of pontifications and divisive statements made by the articulate club of the silent Muslim minority. The wise words of Mr. N. Jammal Ansari have been discussed earlier. In a godly revelation that seems to have prompted him to offer some pearls of wisdom through a letter to the editor in *The Pioneer,* dated 6 February, 2003, he holds forth that Muslims taught Hindus to 'cook food, eat spices and wear stitched clothes and gave them a 'concept of architecture, city planning and accounting.' The statement is a blatant travesty of truth but shows the typical Muslim mindset whose historical memory does not go beyond the birth of the Prophet and Islam. Belonging to a community whose 95% members are Hindu converts to Islam, his statement reflects the representative voice of the opinion makers of his community. We will trash the first part of his statement by referring to Indian history down the millennia discussed in chapter 2. As early as the time of Harsh Vardhana, Indian cooking, weaving of stitched clothes and use of spices was quite common. In fact the spices were not only used in India but also exported ever since Vedic times. There are innumerable references to cinnamons, pepper, cardamom and cloves in Vedic texts. Each king had a *bhojshala* where the best spiced food was cooked for the king and his guests and even the ordinary householders. Regarding architecture, he should refer to the Harappan township's elaborate roads, aqueducts, baths, storehouses, amphitheatres and other artefacts in the newly discovered township off the Gulf of Cambay, dating back to 7500 BC. He should also remember that it was his own co-religionists who destroyed the finest temples and shrines of his Hindu ancestors from 700 AD onwards. Regarding knowledge, it is futile to repeat our repertoire of the Vedic ages. With self-appointed spokesmen of the Muslim community intent upon perverting Indian history and denying their pre-Islamic past, is there any surprise that the assimilation of Muslims in India seems to be a daunting task.

The biggest threat to Hinduism and India is the presence of a large number of illegal immigrants or foreign bodies within the body system of India and its solution brooks no delay. A country already victim to a savage cross-border terrorism sponsored by Pakistan, needs not only physical internal secularity but a psychological reassurance that the transfusion of illegal immigrants that provide life support to subversive elements within and without is completely flushed out. Firm measures are called for not only to restore the confidence of the besieged citizenry but to eliminate the adverse fall out on the national demographic structure, as also to cleanse the national system of the cancerous moles having extranational loyalty. As of now, according to government statistics, there are in India around 20 million illegal Bangladeshi immigrants and 13,500 Pak nationals who have overstayed their visas and are not traceable. They are, obviously, not here for the development of the country. The Ministry of Home Affairs would have been right in restricting the entry of Pak nationals to only three cities as mandated by the Simla agreement by overturning the anti-national decision of the earlier Gujral government, to ensure that no further illegal immigrations take place. The issuance of national identity cards (NIC) cannot be delayed any further. The MHA had then made a statement that 285 lakh such cards will be issued to immigrants in 13 sensitive states from 1 April 2003 onwards. This will require a close centre-state intelligence tie-up, establishment of multi-agency centres in states and formation of state task forces with adequate power to detect and deport the illegal foreigners. The need for a more vigilant and corruption-free patrolling on land borders and coastal waters cannot be overemphasized. The past weakness, a result of vote-bank politics has to be ruthlessly overcome. There is an unending stream of Bangladeshi migrants entering Assam, north eastern states, West Bengal and Bihar, thanks to the apathy of the state administrations, politically motivated inertia, due to the use of migrants as an electoral constituency as happened in Assam and West Bengal. Unfortunately, considerable damage has already been done by local state governments through the issuance of ration cards to these extra hungry mouths, thus adding to food shortage and poverty that the nation can ill afford. As has been pointed out earlier, due to this perpetual influx, the demography of the whole of Assam and border districts of West Bengal and Bihar has completely changed in favour of a Muslim majority with disastrous consequences. With the effete Congress Government in Assam and an anti-Hindu government in West Bengal, it is difficult to see how this inflow can be checked. With such unwilling state governments a deportation drive will remain a pipedream. With Assam having a 158 kms border and West Bengal and Bihar about the same length, the deportation drive and issuance of NIC can be delayed only at a grave peril to national security.

These infiltration attempts from our eastern neighbour Bangladesh into Indian territory raise certain serious questions about the security of our country. In the first week of February 2003, an attempt was made to push through 213 Bangladeshi nationals in the guise of snake charmers into Indian territory with the active connivance of Bangladesh Rifles (BDR). The attempt was forestalled by the timely action of the Border Security Force and Bangladesh Rifles had to send the infiltrators back into their country. However, Mr. Shamsher Mohin Chaudhuri, their Foreign Secretary, instead of being sorry about the affair blamed India for pushing Bengali speaking Indian Muslims into his country. Later, Bangladesh's Foreign Minister, Maitztir Morshed Khan, after receiving a rebuff in Washington regarding strict restrictions imposed by their Naturalization and Immigration Services (NIS) upon foreign Muslims including recording of finger prints, had to vent out his spleen through a visit to Calcutta on January 24. There he wished to seek audience with Chief Minister Buddhadeb Bhattacharya to sort out the infiltration problem on the Indo-Bangladesh border. This dubious approach to talk to a State Chief Minister instead of the Central Government on a national issue was aimed to drive a wedge between the Centre and West Bengal Government, in full knowledge that the Left Front Government in West Bengal was not in tune with the Centre. Undoubtedly, there has been rapid increase in the infiltration from Bangladesh into India and West Bengal during the last few years. Bangladesh also acts as a safe haven for the insurgents from North-East whom Bangladesh calls freedom fighters just as their co-religionists give the same appellation to the Kashmiri militants. During the last meeting of Indo-Bangladesh Joint Working Group, New Delhi had handed over to Dhaka a list of 88 insurgents including Sanjit Dev Burman of the All Tripura Tiger Force and Anup Chetia and Paresh Barua of the United Liberation Front of Assam, who are being accorded hospitality in Bangladesh. The fundamentalist Islamic mindset of elements of Bangladesh Nationalist Party (BNP) openly encouraged by Begam Khaleda Zia are known to have an antipathy towards India and have given shelter to Al-Qaida members fleeing Afghanistan. Heavily armed fundamentalist Islamic Militia like Harkat-ul-Jehadi-Islam has a strength of about 1500, flourishing and in good health in Bangladesh. The significance of the timing of the sudden rise in infiltration from Bangladesh into India cannot be missed. It ties down a large part of our BSF forces making them non-available for contingencies of internal security in Jammu & Kashmir, where with the melting of snows, the level of militant activities is bound to increase. Thus, Bangladesh in full knowledge of Pakistani designs and in full co-operation with them will attempt to push in more illegal immigrants into India, banking on the less than serious concern over this from the Left controlled West Bengal Government.

In an attempt to encircle India, Pakistan and Bangladesh have entered into a clandestine agreement for 'Joint Security Co-operation' to funnel more terrorists into our troubled North Eastern states, where there are already 16 insurgent groups fighting guerrilla war for almost two decades against the Indian state. They aim to fuel the ethnic and cultural turmoil through financial help, supply of arms and training their cadres. As per intelligence reports till some time back, Bangladesh was secretly increasing contacts with Pakistan and China, by giving bases for operations to the Pakistan ISI. As a result of increasing ISI assistance, there were a total of 139 camps functioning there, 99 belonging to North Eastern ultras and the rest to ISI and Bangladesh Directorate General Frontier Intelligence (DGFI). Some captured North Eastern ultras admitted to the existence of the training camps in Sylhet, Kishanganj, Bogra, Ranipur and Mymensingh districts manned by ISI instructors. Let us now look at the minutae of this insidious attack of Bangladesh. The 4000 kms. long porous border has a number of entry points into India, one of these being at the zero line at Satgachi, where the incursions took place. At a rough estimate, given by the then Deputy Prime Minister, L.K. Advani, the number of illegal immigrants into India will be about 15 million. This is a fact which was accepted even by the former Home Minister of India, Mr. Indrajeet Gupta, in whose time the figures stood at over 10 million. The problem of infiltration would not only cause economic disaster to Indian economy by having extra mouths to feed and employ, but will also help boost the Dhaka economy. The remittances from illegal Bangladeshi immigrants back home amounts to a whopping Rs. 15,000 crores per year. Working on the basis of Rs. 30/ a day saved by a Bangladeshi per day in India, we can add to this thousands of crores in cash and kind involved in smuggling, which accounts for a regular traffic of five lakh cattle heads per month from districts bordering Bangladesh. Some districts of West Bengal are less affected by immigration due to local Indian tribals' appearance being different from the infiltraltors but south Bengal districts more than make up for these deficiencies. Murshidabad is the biggest district accounting for Satgachi type incidents. There is a need to complete the border fencing, installation of neon lights and reduction of distance between watchtowers. Lohapur village in Birbhum and Chuapur Haat in Murshidabad district are the major transit points including night shelters for cows and camels in transit located there, all at a nominal charge of Rs. 15/- per animal per night. As per the latest estimates, upto 7th February, 2003, over 10,000 cows from North Bihar and Bengal were waiting at Chuapur

Haat in Murshidabad district for transportation to Bangladesh. During one fortnight alone, BSF seized four trucks of medicines, mobile phones, etc., worth Rs. 5,01,39,428 and 1032 cattle heads, and ten camels worth Rs. 67,00,000. As a result, BSF arrested 771 Bangladeshis and 36 smugglers in Murshidabad, Nadia, 24 Parganas and Malda districts alone in addition to shooting 39 smugglers in transit. The actual figure of smuggled goods probably is 10 times the figures mentioned above. The smugglers have an elaborate network with informers and moles within Indian territory, who alert them in time against BSF action. Any BSF personnel who perform their duty strictly are targeted by lodging false cases against them as the police is pressurized by politicians to file these FIRs.

The direct consequence of this cattle trade is a thriving leather and processed meat industry in Bangladesh for export to Middle East. Politicians are not above encouraging this illegal trade into Bangladesh and reverse infiltration both damaging the economy of our country and improving that of Bangladesh. Thus the fencing of the open border brooks no further delay; but that itself is a problem. The local vested interests are dead opposed to it since this will dig a hole into their pockets. District Magistrate of Malda speaking on the issue of the border fencing said that "such was the agitation that we could not even put a shovel to dirt." The problem does not stop here. Every third or fourth sex worker in Kolkata and Mumbai comes from Bangladesh and Nepal through touts stationed across the border, often under political patronage. In addition, there are a large number of Bangladeshi women serving as maid-servants in India at one-third the rate of local domestic help. This has resulted in 25% increase in crime and burglary in Kolkata and its suburbs during the last few years. Most of the crimes in 24 Parganas are committed by suspected Bangladeshi immigrants. Due to this never-ending stream of illegal immigrants from Bangladesh, the Hindu Bangladeshis who came during the partition and formed the Left Front Government vote-banks have suddenly changed sides and are lining up with the Hindutva forces. Though the Muslim infiltrators have remained faithful to the Left forces, the backlash against them is bound to play a decisive role in future elections.

Now the minority angle: The Baptist Minister Jerry Falwell declared Prophet Mohammed a terrorist and riots flared up in Sholapur in the state of Maharasthra. He did not consult the local people of Sholapur before handing out a judgment. *Sahmat*, a Communist front organization, called Rama and Sita, brother and sister, but there was no squeak or protest in support of the hurt caused to Hindu sentiments. The editor of *Hans,* a Hindi literary monthly, Rajendra Yadav tried to prove that Sri Hanuman was a terrorist, but no action by the government or a reaction by the Hindu community followed. The process of suppressing the truth on the sacrifice of the great Hindu heroes has continued with a view to appease minority sentiments. Hindu patriots have been regularly derided and declared enemies of the nation. The demand for ban on cow slaughter was dubbed as communal; 58 kar sewaks were burnt alive at Godhra and our secularists kept silent. It is this silence that has encouraged the tendency to reap political profit from an anti-national platform. If this was not so the riots would not have flared up in Sholapur. The President of Muslim Personal Law Board (MPLB) takes exceptions to the Bombay High Court judgement ordering population control. They do not accept the permissible marriageable age decided by the government. Why? Because they can get the famous Supreme Court judgement on Shahbano case overturned through an obliging secularist Congress government by bringing an amendment to the Constitution in a quiescent parliament. If they could defy even the Supreme Court, why would the President of MPLB care about defying the Bombay High Court in order to increase Muslim population manifold through government offered facilities? That is one form of internal threat.

Today, many who think alike with the MPLB are worried; they are also worried over the strident anti-Hindu rhetoric of the Communists camp, which they feel is striking at the foundation of Hindutva. In other words Hindu-baiting may not be a useful exercise after all and may prove counter-productive, since the Hindu backlash may consolidate the Hindu ranks creasing out even the caste distinctions. The realization seems to have dawned on them that if the protagonists of Hindutva are to be kept weak, Hindu sentiments need not be hurt beyond a point. A Muslim lady belonging to *Sahmat*, lately in the US, made all out efforts to prove that the culprits of the Godhra massacre were totally innocent. Communist character has been traditionally anti-national right from the days of partitions, to Pak position on Indian nuclear testing, India-China border disputes to Kargil and Pakistan sponsored terrorism. They went ballistic against J. Jayalalithaa for her ordinance banning religious conversions by fraud, force or allurement in spite of the fact that similar laws have been in existence in many Congress ruled states. According to a survey carried out during the British rule in Tamil Nadu (earlier Madras Presidency) each district used to have thousands of local language schools. They were all destroyed since the education there with a strong national content was the chief roadblock to the enslavement of the country. Anti-Indian sentiments even today flourish on the premise that the Hindus have no organizational abilities, their religious beliefs and thoughts are so disparate as to be almost irreconcilable in the absence of a unifying force, a popularly acceptable leadership and political awakening. And to crown it all, anti-Hindu forces are getting a tacit support from their foreign godfathers.

Even the big churning process initiated after 9/11 WTC bombing has not solicited an unqualified condemnatory response from the Islamic world. The reasons are many. The moderates in Islamic countries have not been able to mount the necessary offensive against the obscurantist militant Islam. The perception of being exploited by a covetous West is all-pervasive and the feeling of oppression and exploitation is complete. Osama bin Laden still remains the hero, voicing the concerns of the under-dog, and America is perceived as an exploiter of Muslim oil resources, an enemy of Islam and a world gendarme. Al-Qaida has succeeded in its propaganda war against the US. There is an unprecedented level of hatred against the US policies and values it stands for. Confronted with a formidable foe, Muslims have sunk their differences and decided to remain united against the common enemy. During the last half century, the moderate Muslims have been pushed to the fringe by the new breed of political activists of the *Salafi* or *Wahabi* creed, that challenge the western values and promote a simplistic utopian Islam. The rise to prominence of *Salafis* after 1970s owes much, firstly to the loss of credibility of the moderates in Muslim lands and secondly to the political and economic failure of secular national polemics of most Arab states, along with the rise of brutal authoritarian regimes and the brainwashing of the younger generation at the mosques as centres of opposition. Thirdly, the accumulation of petro dollars by Saudi Arabia and Gulf Sheikhdoms, who spend billions of dollars to promote Salafi Islam to the neglect of traditional centres of Islamic education. In India during August

2000-2001, Saudi Arabia spent huge sums of money on the creation of madrasas and schools that propagate their brand of Islam, study of religious sciences and offer scholarships for study in Saudi universities. According to their own statement the Saudi monarchy has spent billions of dollars on financing 210 Islamic centres, more than 1500 mosques, 200 colleges, 2000 schools for "educating Muslim children in non-Islamic countries across the world". The influence of Saudi Arabia during the last three decades in re-shaping the landscape of the Muslim world cannot be ignored anymore. While in Pakistan Sufism is under attack from Salafism, in India too the Hanafi scholars of Deoband and Nadwa, frown upon the traditional Indian Islamic beliefs and practices under inspiration from the Saudi Islamic view. The Saudi monopoly over Arabic media and censorship of religious views criticizing Salafism is highly visible. As the moderates are squeezed out to find shelter in the west after a process of marginalisation, the Salafi resonance with current Muslim concerns and perceived injustice of it all, creates a disenchantment with western value systems and the so-called modernity. The Salafism has clear cut thoughts and very ingenious answers to most Muslim problems and its muscular Islam having a contemporary macho appeal is going to define the contours of modern Islamic identity.

The silent majority of Muslims is not so silent after all. Some of their more vocal leaders even now forcibly assert that Islam does not approve killing and that Quran forbids the murder of innocents, amounting to the murder of mankind, and that forced conversions are against the tenets of Quran. Many verses in Quran itself contradict these two statements, not to speak of 14 centuries of *jihad*. M.J. Akbar in his book, *The Shades of Swords* avers that the *Jihad* is the signature tune of Islam, without which Islam would have been different. The famous Islamic scholar, Alfred Guillaune in his book *Islam* mentions that Prophet Mohammed declared that war is a sacred duty in Islam as he led his followers to attack the Meccans and adds that "this fight figures largely in Muslim tradition and in the Quran and must be regarded as the foundation of all subsequent success of Muslim army." Regarding conversions, Thomas W. Arnold in his book *The Preaching of Islam* says: "It is established without doubt that forced conversions have been made by Mohammedan rulers and it seems probable that Aurangzeb's well known zeal of his faith had caused many families of northern India to attribute their change of faith to this. In the Deccan .....that Tipu Sultan forcibly converted sundry families and sections of the population."

All this is enough evidence to prove that Islam is an intolerant religion, particularly when seen against what Sir William Muir has to say in his book *The Life of Mohammed:* "the sword of Mohammed is the most stubborn and implacable enemy of civilization. Liberty and truth that the conversion has crushed, have lost their meaning". Fifty-seven years after the 16th August, 1946, Suhrawardi's call of Direct Action, meaning action against Hindus, the same is being carried out clandestinely in the bylanes of Kolkata, through networking and the use of pamphlets. The area of operations of the notorious triple – Topala, Tiljala and Tangia—is a haven for the deadliest criminal elements. Thanks to police indifference the shady junk hovels and begrimed student lodges in Tapsia and Raja Bazar bylanes have turned into SIMI strongholds and Bangladeshi hideouts for their subversive activities. The Bangladeshi illegal immigrants from Narainganj, near Dhaka, are all huddled up here, having escaped detection by the BSF. They sympathise with SIMI, which according to them is a progressive student movement in India, a secular country. Near Gobindo Khatik Road, near Tangra, famous for its Chinese delicacies, is another cluster of madrasas, whose teachers keep in daily contact with shady characters who cross the border under the protection of SIMI activists, whose tentacles have by now extended to north and south 24 Parganas. Most madrasas are unregistered and inspite of being denied affiliation are still functioning, most of these at Saptagram in south 24 Parganas have been receiving huge financial aid from Middle East countries for years. As per MHA sources, the Islamic development fund in Middle East countries has sent one lakh dollars to the madrasas between 1998 and 2001 of which 80 percent has been utilized for humanitarian causes such as the rehabilitation of anti-social elements. The SIMI activists here keep regular contact with their counterparts in North Bengal, forcing the Chief Minister to state that ISI has been inducting and training Indian moles in North Bengal, planning subversion and are facilitated by a porous border.

According to a report at least 100 SIMI activists have fled to South Bengal hiding around Kolkata after being forced to flee North Bengal under police pressure. Most of the SIMI moles had even recruited agents to the Bangladesh based militant groups HUJI, while some had sought shelter at Ithar, Islampur and Malda madrasas as large numbers have moved to Bashirhat in Golgunj, and Hassanabad in North 24 Parganas. Some escapees from North 24 Parganas and their prime movers in Bangladesh frequently cross the border over to Bangladesh leaving no room for doubt that the hardcore notorious elements are not likely to give up their Kolkata habitat. A small vessel carrying arms from Malaysia entered Indian waters via the port city of Chittagong in Bangladesh, some time ago. It unloaded its cargo inside the Sunderbans causing serious concern to our intelligence agencies regarding unchecked subversive activities of SIMI.

The Iraq war also holds many lessons for India. Carefully watch your national interest before you go to the market with your unsolicited views. It is very easy to win a war but difficult to win the peace. Our leaders in all the Indo-Pak wars have proved this truism by squandering away the gains of war on the negotiating table. A change of regime in Iraq is not necessarily to India's disadvantage. One less among the Muslim states, the possible harbourers of Islamic terrorists that threaten Judeo-Christian Hindu civilizational configuration and less Islamic control on the world oil resources. The ineptitude and obsolescence of our Ministry of External Affairs (MEA) mandarins is matched only by the naiveté and old hang-up of our so-called military strategists and experts so often seen on the TV chat shows or expressing their profound thoughts in newsprints. According to this class who derive their strategic foresight from the golf fields of Delhi, Iraq war should have lasted six months. What with the invincible Republican Guards, the Fedayeens, suicide bombers and close combat amongst falling debris in the streets of Baghdad, the US troops would be fighting hell. All these predictions were made on April 5, 2003. As it was, the fighting came to an end just within four days i.e. on 9 April, 2003. They were proved wrong earlier too in the first Iraq war of 1991. Does the nation have sound military advice available to its defence planners? Our legislators fare no better. They took two precious days' time quibbling about the words to condemn or deplore the US action in Iraq and finally came up with a magic change of word in Hindi "Ninda". All this when the war was over. Could there be a better example of a futile exercise in semantics and diplomatic vacuity. How does a change of guard in Iraq adversely affect Indian interests? Why can't our big mouths learn the virtues of silence on issues that do not directly affect us. Nehru's legacy of being the custodian of world morality refuses to die. What has our non-alignment, read pro-Russian and anti-Americanism, and espousal of Arab cause given us? For sixty years we have been trying to please Muslim countries starting from the Khilafat movement, the sequel to which was the massacre of Hindus by Mopla Muslims in Kerala, supporting Palestine and condemning Israel. And the result, more madarsas and Jehadis raised through Saudi Arabian money. And how are we treated in these Muslim countries? Just like second-rate citizens. The incident in Malaysia of the torturing of our IT professionals and the expulsion orders of three million Indians from Saudi Arabia was the harvest. If only we could have been more friendly with America, post-World War II the US instead of befriending Pakistan would have been more favourably disposed to us, as was evident as an exception, during the 1962 war with China. Has any group of Indian Muslims ever openly declared that they are Indians first and Muslims later? That Kashmir is an integral part of India and finally have they ever expressed their gratitude for being treated as a highly pampered minority, by willingly withdrawing their claim on Ayodhya?

India's policy towards its neighbours has been suffering from a self-accusatory syndrome amongst the media and our elite, amounting almost to a neighbourhood complex. A nation that does not care for its interests and self-respect not only loses the respect from others but opens itself to their depredations and ridicule. Improvement of relations with our neighbours, a favourite refrain of our myopic liberals, is not a one way street. Except for a short duration of Rajiv Gandhi and Narasimha Rao's government that has been the story of India. Vajpayee lost his diplomatic innocence after Lahore and Agra and had to change course. The nadir of our diplomacy was reached during the short terms of V.P. Singh, Deve Gowda and Gujral. Pak proxy war, Nepal's extortion of concessions in trade and transit, and Bangladeshi demands for excessive Ganga waters were the harvest of this "give and not take policy". Bangladesh reciprocated our friendly gesture by pushing in illegal immigrants, while Gujral's request for the use of transit facility through Bangladesh to access our north-eastern states was summarily rejected. All the hugging and smiles at SAARC meeting at Male ended only in an intangible vacuity, the so-called goodwill. Pakistan upped the ante on Kashmir. Gujral left a diplomatic legacy, which, shorn of its Panchsheel rhetoric, meant that India being big must give its small neighbours whatever they ask. We have forgotten what

Kautilya had said on treatment of neighbours. 'The "soulless enemy" intent on harming us must be destroyed at all costs. The friendly neighbour or well wisher must be helped, but the one whose intentions are not clear must be placed on the watch list.' Caution and circumspection, not sentimental moonshine must be the watchwords and the state must be strong, with its national interests superseding notional popularity gains. There should never be a grovelling supplication. The illegal migrants issue with Bangladesh must be met head on. In fact India went to war with Pakistan in 1971 for pushing back just one million refugees back to the erstwhile East Pakistan, while today we have more than 20 million Bangladeshis with us. While strengthening our border vigil, and reining in corruption in the border control agencies, we must stop handing out political patronage to illegal immigrants for vote-bank politics. To the bleeding hearts at home and the authorities in Bangladesh a clear signal must go that poverty and unemployment at home will no more be accepted as an alibi for accepting surplus hungry mouths. India's territory and resources are a sacred trust for our coming generations and not a free lunch for outsiders.

A confirmation of the secular character of our nation and a correct assessment of the Muslim invaders, Mahmood Ghaznavi in particular, came from some plain talk of Mohammad Khatami, President of Iran, during his visit to India as the chief guest at the Republic Day Parade in 2002 when he said that " Ghaznavi, who during his military expeditions looted and plundered a number of places in India including Somnath temple, had expansionist designs." And that he was "the raider and military adventurer who did not represent Islamic ethos and ideology". And finally on India's secular credentials despite the bogey of 'Hindu Rashtra' raised by our secularist big mouths, "Iran pays great tribute to India for maintaining a secular and democratic character. India is a great family where people of all religions have complete freedom."

The biggest scourge of Hindu society as has been mentioned earlier is the caste system. Though evolved around the noble ideas of distribution of work it need not have ossified into a hierarchy based on birth. There are encouraging signs that Hindus have realized the evils born out of the perpetuation of this disgraceful cancerous sore that has eaten into the very vitals of our society. The cure lies not only in its immediate abolition but also empowering those who have suffered the tyranny for ages. There is only one caste for Hindus and that is

Hinduism, one culture, Hindutva and only one civilizational ethos born out of the Vedas. The earlier attempts at permitting the caste divide to continue and giving the lowest caste a grand name of Harijan was an exercise in escapism. It is no wonder that many dalits take offence to the use of this distinctive appellation. Mahatma Gandhi who gave currency to this word did not fully grasp the fact that instead of assimilating the dalit into a Hindu monolith it would perpetuate this scourge and in time prove counter-productive. Gandhiji's idea was indeed noble. But in glorifying them as a man of God, he did not remove scavenging, by no means a desirable activity.

The broadside fired by the secularist brigade against *Manuvadis* after the lynching of five dalits in Haryana wrongly accused for skinning a dead cow some time ago assumed serious dimensions. No sane Hindu can ever justify this act. Not confirmed but reported on the TV and the press, the families of these five miserable victims had decided to convert to Buddhism. No Hindu can object to this act of desperation. But the moot question is, can their lot improve by a change of religion and will they receive their due respect in the society where they live? Unfortunately the lot of a dalit Hindu converted to Christianity and Islam remains the same, so much so that the segregation virus has contaminated these two so-called egalitarian faiths too. The new dalit Muslims and dalit Christians are demanding reservations. Somehow change to Buddhism was a smoother process since a dalit Hindu does not have to disown his past and change his God and his Sanatan values. Buddhism was born out of Hinduism and has the same corpus of divine knowledge and religious teachings except for a change in rituals. If the Hindus shun their divisive prejudices against all sections of their faith, there is no reason why most of these converts cannot come back to their old fold. Quantum decrease in the Hindu fold and a corresponding increase in Buddhism will not change the civilizational contours of India. Even so it is the duty of all right thinking Hindus not to alienate their disadvantaged lot and drive the weak and the helpless to conversion by apathy, humiliation and condemnable violence.

Having said that we should realize that such heinous acts have been committed in our society under many other pretexts. Whether it is Maoist communists against Ranbeer Sena and vice versa or Peoples War Group (PWG) against innocents in Andhra Pradesh, Naxalites elsewhere, Bodo and ULFA militants in Assam against helpless migrants from other parts of the country, all these are intra-Hindu conflicts and must be condemned with the same severity. It is a wake up call for the Hindus that atrocities against the weaker sections is a crime and unless put to an end immediately may lead to serious consequences. The very survival of Hinduism is at stake. Those who rail at *Manuvadis* do not know the first thing about *Manu Samhita* and the man. Manu, the first man, gave us the moral code like the one Moses gave to Israelis. It clearly stipulates that caste is not by birth but by action. With time and human aberration the system has been badly distorted. It is not Manu who has failed Hindu society but the misguided practitioners of Hinduism who have failed Manu. Hinduism has to reform itself and follow what Vivekanand had said on untouchablity. "Therefore our solution of the caste question is not degrading those who are already high up, is not running amock through food and drink, is not jumping out of our own limits in order to have more enjoyment, but it comes by everyone of us, fulfilling the dictates of our Vedantic religion, by our attaining spirituality, and by our becoming the ideal Brahmins. There is a law laid on each one of you in this land by your ancestors, whether you are Aryans or non-Aryans, Rishis or Brahmins, or the very lowest outcasts. The command is the same to you all, that you must make progress without stopping, and that from the highest man to the lowest pariah everyone in this country has to try and become the ideal Brahmin. This Vedantic idea is applicable not only here but all over the world. Such is our ideal of caste as meant for raising all humanity slowly and gently towards the realisation of that great ideal of the spiritual man who is non-resisting, calm, steady, full of worship, pure, and meditative. In that idea there is God".

No society is altogether free from religious imperfections, divisive practices and human frailties. Hindus owe it to themselves, their proud culture and priceless heritage to periodically cleanse themselves of evils that creep up under alien influence.

It is no secret that it was a secularist messiah and self-proclaimed champion of probity in public life, who Mandalised Hindu society and exacerbated caste conflicts. His mantra of social justice and empowerment of the lower orders has produced just the reverse effect—social unrest, exacerbation of caste conflicts and agitational politics, all with the sole aim of achieving a favourable electoral calculus. The other issue of personal probity in public life lies in tatters as this gentleman flies ever so frequently on public expense to London hospitals for his treatment, which was easily available in India. There are many others who have followed his example wasting enormous amount of public money. Beside living in a spacious and expensive bungalow in New Delhi's prime metro land even while out of office and retaining houses all over the country, V.P. Singh is alleged to have deprived even an Army officer's widow of her own property by retaining it as a residence at Lucknow. Call yourself a secularist and loot the country. Another such secularist ex-PM made a killing of hundreds of crores of rupees during the last few days of his brief tenure by getting a number of contracts signed post haste. Still another secularist PM during his short stint of six months amassed huge wealth and had no compunctions in occupying a trust property near Delhi till he was evicted under the orders of the Supreme Court. Still another farmer's son became PM and made similar gains by bribing. Can one find a blemish on the escutcheon of the great secular dynasty, one of whose stock became PM and was equated by one of her adoring psychophants with India. She declared that corruption was a worldwide phenomenon, while her younger son plundered the taxpayer's money. Another secularist PM whose son was involved in the Urea scam had the dubious distinction of presiding over the largest number of financial scams in independent India. His obliging finance minister had the gall to describe the one thousand crore rupees security scam as a systemic failure. All these worthy secularists used Indian Air Force planes for private purposes and never paid till the outstanding dues amounted to Rs. 70 to 80 crores. They were all let off the hook by an ever obliging bureaucracy, which wrote off this amount as incidental expenses thus defrauding the taxpayer. These are the illustrious secularist breed that strut about as paragons of probity in public life. As with our leaders so with the foot soldiers of this secularist brigade. This is another threat from within to the country and its majority Hindu community.

Before the ink could dry on the Ansal Plaza incident where our human right activists, were baying for the blood of Delhi Police for their preemptive shooting of two terrorists. Unfortunately, an impression has gained ground that the area of concern for the NHRC is confined only to the human rights of the terrorists and the lives of innocent people is just so much collateral damage. Kashmir provides ample evidence of this sad prejudice. Sad but true. While the killings of the terrorists should be a cause celebre our breast beating human rights activists level accusations and the security forces are singled out for condemnation and insult. Engaged in a thankless job under severe restrictions to protect those who throw mud at them, they have no rewards, only opprobrium. Soldiers killed in ambush or killed through remote controlled explosive devices is not news anymore. The Delhi paperazzi is not concerned. There are no mournings or rallies by our charmed circles in Delhi when innocent women and children, sometimes sleeping villagers are mercilessly beheaded or brutally killed. Not a squeak from our chatterati. The hypocrisy of it all is not only maddening but disgraceful. Those who pillory VHP keep quiet when temples are attacked. Did anyone ever try to understand, why only temples are the targets and never any mosque? When our soldiers try to kill terrorists holed up in the sanctum sanctorum of a Raghunath temple by storming the temple no one takes notice, but when they attack a mosque to rid the holy place of terrorists protests are raised at the India International Centre. It is about time we call an end to this charade, which has put the government on the defensive and tarnished the image of our soldiery, the best in the world. It is a signal to the terrorists and subversives that they can have a free run, and take shelter in a mosque; they have enough friends inside India. That is not the way to fight terrorism. Have we lost our virility or resolve? Before we can take the enemy without we have to defang this anti-Hindu and anti-national element. The *Indian Express* in one of its issues came out with headline "*Mole on the blast sends village reeling into a nightmare*" and followed this up by the subtitle column *Probe turns into police witchhunt, taking heavy toll on normal life*. The mole of the Mumbai blast that the police was investigating was the handiman of ISI-assisted local terrorists. On receiving intelligence Police went to Borivilli village in Patgaon and arrested one Adilkot, a former activist of SIMI, and ten others. While Investigation was still in progress, our loud mouths prejudged the issue and held a media trial of the police not bothering about the culprits. With media managers acting as paid referees is there any hope of bringing about internal secularity?

Another threat from within is the white man's complex, a legacy of the colonial rule and love of the white skin (*gaur varna*) a tribute to the mythical Aryan invaders. Even after 56 years of independence this reverence for white skin refuses to die. Bill Gates comes up to the help of AIDS victims and the world press discloses that India has the largest reservoir of HIV Positives accounting for 25 million cases! Most of it is fancy. None of the three primary causes of AIDS, i.e. homosexuality, hypodermic syringe used by drug addicts, and prostitution is so abundant in the vast Indian heartland. NGOs and western interests thrive on magnifying the problem to obtain aid from abroad and line their pockets. The Indian fascination for white skin cuts across different age groups and party lines.The seeds of the white man's superiority, sown by Macaulay, have borne fruit and the myth of the Aryan invasion has much to do with it. The lesser mortals, the so-called dark skinned Dravidians, were driven south and the aliens lorded it over and all this led to an imaginary Aryan-Dravidian divide. This in turn led to the complete alienation of the south from north. We have discussed all this in some details in chapter 2 and need not dwell on this further. Besides a glorious past, even today half the people in the Silicon Valley belong to Indian origin and thirty percent of all doctors in the UK are Indian. Add to this the fact that we are the world leaders in information technology (IT). Let India throw out the complex of white skin, remember that while white is wishy washy, brown is beautiful. Centuries of self-abnegation and excessive tolerance have led the Hindus and Indians to develop a low self-esteem and image deficit syndrome, what the Americans would strategically call *armed suasion.* No wonder foreigners treat us in a shabby manner. The (low paid) Indian staff in Delhi embassies is commonly addressed as bloody Indians. The recent death of a driver employed by the Embassy of Senegal, a tiny African country, by the son of the Ambassador was a case in point. The Ambassador was not even apologetic. The treatment of our IT professionals in Malaysia and subsequently in Belgium and the deprivation of the majority Indian community in Fiji show us how the world looks at us. We have enormous resources and one of the best skilled manpower in the world and yet our image is smaller than reality. This low self-esteem is imposed on us not only by the world outside but our own English educated elite and the media. Can one ever imagine an Indian painting of the Prophet even in his full robes and his daughter Fatima or the Virgin Mary in the nude? This is what precisely is happening in India. Our gods are a sport for everyone to mock at and kick around. An M.F. Hussein, a commercial artist turned intellectual painter, the toast of the metro rich, who is commissioned to paint murals on the grand interiors of their palatial homes, can take liberties with Indian goddesses. He has painted Goddess

Saraswati and many others in the nude and even Sita has been shown in the nude in an obscene posture, sitting on the tail of Hanuman. Can national degeneration go further? In an Islamic or Christian country he would have been guillotined long ago and yet Hasnaim Kaif and his ilk are allowed to freely vilify Hindus and ridicule their culture in our very secular India.

Besides the open Pak hostility which is the biggest threat to Hinduism and India from outside, the internal threat posed by cross-border terrorism sponsored in the state of J & K, is the biggest security concern of India. The policy to bleed India to death by a thousand cuts, most of which are confined to the state of J&K, is the cancerous sore that has persisted over three decades. During this period India has fought three wars with Pakistan—in 1947, 1965 and 1971—but the root cause of the problem remains. Pakistan intransigence has spawned a highly effective low intensity conflict during the last two decades coinciding with an increase in cross-border violence with the support of internal anti-India elements in the valley itself. After the rigged elections of 1987 the frustration of the Kashmiri youth, abetted by Pak supply of arms and training, created the Kalashnikov culture, blurring the distinction between the foreign mercenaries and the local insurgents. Kashmir cauldron has been on the boil, resulting in the loss of over 40,000 lives. It took the centre more than a decade to take action against the separatist elements in J&K whose complicity in fostering terrorism was never in doubt. At last just before the All Party Hurriyat Conference (APHC) was about to strike out, the central government suspended the passport of Hurriyat Chairman Mirwaiz Omar Farooq and Yasin Malik, among others. The Mirwaiz had asked the Organization of Islamic Countries (OIC) Conference to impose economic sanctions against India's "illegal occupation of Kashmir" and was due to leave for Dubai en route to the US. All this was a part of APHC denigrating India at every possible international forum, including an anti-India tirade on BBC's *Hard Talk* Programme. The hardcore APHC members are openly subverting India's security, pose a big security risk and, being in ISI's permanent payrol, receive huge funds for anti-India activities, their so-called indigenous struggle for freedom. This secessionist group is the chief promoter of anti-India publicity in the international fora. It is never too late. This Pak mouthpiece which whips up anti-India sentiments from mosques and other platforms was the main hand behind the expulsion of Kashmiri Pandits. Nemesis has at last caught up with them. Any party which stands in the way of tackling terrorism and betrays the trust of the people can be branded as condoning anti-national activities. Terrorism is the burning issue today, whether Congress likes it or not. The attack on institutions of the civil society, parliament, temples, educational institutions, public transport systems, homes, market places, are planned by saboteurs and subversive elements, aided by Pak ISI. They find shelters in minority ghettos, biding their time to strike out and deliver their death cargo. The nation should stand up and crush these jehadis. National security is not a part time job. The earlier our political parties realize this truth the better. The main culprit here is the soft approach to terrorism advocated by the Congress whose coalition in J&K under Chief Minister Mufti Mohammed Sayeed released 26 hardcore militants as part of his policy of "the healing touch". Osama bin Laden has many admirers not only in Islamic countries but in many parts of India as well, all Muslims. This is proved by the number of flags, banners, pictures and photographs prominently displayed in many parts of the country. Even in the Jamia Millia Islamia campus a number of Osama bin Laden admirers were arrested while holding a meeting to glorify the achievements of the world's most wanted terrorist.

Inspite of brave words and calling Pakistan a terrorist and rogue state, there is little evidence of any tough and concrete diplomatic, military, quasi-military and non-military response from India. We whine and implore the international community in general and the US in particular to redress our grievances and come to our help. Even after years of being in power, the new dispensation i e NDA was not without its shrill and strident rhetoric. It seemed to be bogged down under the weight of the old Congress foreign policy of the Nehru-Gandhi dynasty. Our bureaucracy that still carries this baggage seems to be out of sync with the popular mood. Thanks to our Nehru-Gandhi fostered External Affairs mandarins, our policy towards Pakistan still lacks clarity and direction. Military and strategic experts having overruled deep air strikes inside POK on terrorist infrastructure as being unproductive and impractical, there is no evidence of any other strong option being adopted. Our MEA bureaucracy seemed tentative and circumspect whenever it comes to dealing with Pakistan. This pussyfooted approach is in consonance with the views of the 'Lahore Club' in Delhi, an ante-diluvian species that is still breathing. This august body, though a hopeless minority, is exceedingly sentimental and nostalgic about Pakistan, seems to have considerable clout with our MEA mandarins. The leading lights of this exclusive club are Mr. Kuldeep Nayyar and I.K. Gujral, both hailing from the land of the five rivers. It is time our political leaders and diplomatic community speak in one voice and expose Pakistan for what it is, a rogue state, and deal with it accordingly with the kidgloves off.

It would be platitudinous to repeat the need for an intense nationalistic fervour and patriotism at a time when India is facing challenges both from the outside and inside. With the exception of the Sangh Parivar and the Right, this spirit seems to have been an embarrassment to the Congress, the secularists, the liberals and the Leftists. What degeneration! The Indian Diaspora can serve as an example to our home-grown choristers of trans-national loyalties and blind votaries of globalization. Only Hinduism with strong underpinnings of Hindutva, like Judaism and Zionism can unleash forces to sustain a vigorous patriotism and nationalistic fervour. Our Sanskrit speaking forebears had exalted the land of their birth to the pedestal of their mother that even excelled the heavens – "*Janani Janamabhomisch Swargadapee Gareeasi.*"

12

Breaking Free

In the earlier chapters we have discussed the essence of Hinduism, our precious Vedic heritage, the chronic malaise of historical negationism that has plagued the Hindu society, neo-secularism, that is cancerously eating away Hindu vitality, and minorityism that has spelt disaster to Hinduism in India before, during and after Independence. We have also seen the slow and steady depletion of Hindu strength due to mass religious conversions. We also held up the mirror to the people and the organizations, which claimed exclusive rights on patriotism, and struggle for freedom completely ignoring those great sons of India, whose only fault was that they were Hindus and did not subscribe to the Congress ideology of non-violence. The suffering and ultimate sacrifice along which they went in their revolutionary fervour and patriotism is a heritage lost to the present generation. We have seen the traitorous role played by a large part of our English media culpa, the tragedy of Godhra and the explosion of Hindu anger in Gujarat. We have taken note of the existing forces that threaten India from outside and the enemy within. All these forces stacked together mount a formidable challenge to Mother India and its life breath, Hinduism. And Hinduism is under siege. If Hinduism is to die what is left of India? But it shall never happen. A civilization that has withstood adverse weather for almost a millennium cannot be easily wished away. But there is no room for complacency.

Let us first eliminate the threats looming against Hinduism and purge the system clean to nourish it back to health. In the following pages we shall re-emphasize some issues that have to be attended to without further prevarication. Firstly, before Hindus embark on any effort at self-improvement and nation-building, they should ask themselves the question, who are they? There is a Jewish saying, "know from where you come before you know who you are and where you are going, you must know from where you come". The answer is given in chapter 1. Recently, a Muslim lady after the conclusion of Iraq war wrote an article on what Baghdad means to her. The word conjures to her the vision of the great Babylonian empire, the golden era of Nebuchedrazzar, Hammurabi, Harun Ul Rashid, the Sumerian empire and the glory of the Caliphate that was the birthplace of all human knowledge. Readers may refer to Chapter 2 and note that Vedic India had a far richer and more ancient heritage. In fact, it was the fountainhead of all that flowed east and westwards. One cannot escape the past. Perpetual striving for better present and building for a bright future does not necessarily mean living in the past. History inflicts a cruel nemesis on those who refuse to learn from it. Hindus must learn from history. They should not forget the series of defeats they suffered in the troubled history of its last millennia. They should not forget the slaughter and the catastrophes inflicted on the nation. To those Hindus who tend to forget their historical shame and wait for the world to take note and help them must read these lines from Menachim Begin, once Prime Minister of Israel, "Indifference – that is the danger. Humanity might claim that it was at least progressive when it could be aroused on account of injustice to a single Dreyfus in Paris to a Sacco and Vanzetti in America; to a Dimitrov in Berlin. Humanity will retrogress into the darkness of savagery if it remains unconcerned about the fate of millions of 'Dreyfuses' or if it fails to produce as it has failed during these terrible years—a single Emile Zola. And if humanity at large is threatened by the enemy called indifference, how much greater is this threat to the Jewish people? That is why the most solemn warning for Jews as for Gentiles speaks to us in Kipling's immortal words, 'Lest we forget!'

They should not forget the days of Islamic rule of Delhi Sultanate when torture and bestiality were as common as Friday prayers. They should not forget the hissing sound of the swift arcing Saracen blades that slit across hundreds of thousands of Hindu throats spurting blood on the streets of Delhi. They should not forget the rape of Hindu princesses inveigled into the harems of the Turko-Mughal rulers. The Jews remember their holocaust in Europe and also the indifference of the world community to their sufferings. To quote Begin again: "Dark night, the darkest of all nights, descended on the Jewish people in

Europe. One million five hundred thousand Jewish children were transported in the death trains to the gas chambers. Millions of men and women were shot, or drowned, or burned, or gassed or buried alive. When man becomes a beast, the Jew ceases to be regarded as a human being". How many Hindus have to be slaughtered by the Islamic militants before they say enough is enough? Again to quote Begin, when Descartes said; "I think, therefore I am, he uttered a very profound thought. But there are times in the history of peoples when thoughts alone do not prove their existence. A people may 'think' and yet its sons, with their thoughts and inspite of them, may be turned into a herd of slaves or into soap. There are times when everything in you cries out: your very self-respect as a human being lies in your resistance to evil."

When will the Hindu soul cry out for action against the assault on their national honour and pride. How long will they act as bovine witnesses to the despoliation and desecration of their holy shrines, the assault on their religion and the trampling down of their culture, beliefs and values? Centuries of oppression have weakened the spirit of our people. There are two types of people; there are those who are acted upon by history. They, unlike what Christ had said, 'do not inherit the kingdom of heaven', but there are others who refuse to submit and decide to act upon history. They are the ones who rule the kingdoms of this world. Countless brave hearts, the noble sons of Mother India have sacrificed their blood and lives so that this land becomes free. Let their lives and blood not go waste. There are enough footprints on the sands of time, left by our forebears, which show us where to go. Let us not repudiate their priceless legacy. Cherish it, preserve it, and let it inspire us to greater deeds to make India great. The spiritualism of our sages that still runs in our blood should not make us atavistic and effete. We should also listen to the call of the times and the world around us, to become Karmayogis and make this nation great. A great pedigree should propel us ever forward to make us the masters in the arts and sciences of the world. Hindus bear an enormous responsibility on their shoulders.

Undoubtedly, today Hinduism is under siege both from forces without and within. We have dealt with these in the previous chapter and know how to deal with them. There can be no true friends without true enemies. Unless we hate what we are not, we cannot love what we are. These are the old truths we are painfully rediscovering after a century and more of sentimental cant. Those who deny them deny their family, their heritage, their culture, their birthright, and their selves! They will not lightly be forgiven. We will have to prove our enemy wrong, especially those outside that think that one Muslim or a jihadi is equal to ten Hindus. Hindus will have to show by action, not by rhetoric that they have no equals. How can ten millennia of its glorious existence as the leader of the world, the oldest and the most advanced civilization known to mankind and the dispenser of all knowledge spiritual and secular to mankind be wiped out in just one-tenth of its life-term? India is still alive and shall endure as along as Hinduism lives. Hinduism being Sanatan has no beginning nor end. The recent signs of self-assertion by a section of the Hindus is a mere ripple, a transient reflex action, and a warning, so to say, to the forces intent upon destroying its culture. Their protest is merely to remind. The misguided secularists, English media and the elites should take note that in a Hindu majority country nurtured by the blood of Hindus, Hindus shall be trampled upon no more. To fire that spirit of Hinduism there needs to be a frenzy of patriotism and a devotion to its values and national symbols. Ram cannot be just wished away. It is our most precious heritage and national possession.

The Babri structure was a standing challenge to Hindu pride. The Hindu rage that kept simmering for five centuries at last boiled over on 6 December 1992 and demolished the symbol of its shame. The shrine belongs to Hindus and cannot be bargained away. Dr. Chaim Weizmann, one of the founding fathers of Israel and Zionism, when he saw the miracle in the desert that the Zionists had worked said, "to be a Zionist it is not necessary to be mad, but it helps". To those decrying Hindu fervor and patriotism and an abiding attachment to their faith let this be a warning.

In the troubled past millennia of Hindu history excessive tolerance has fostered a kind of cowardice and timorousness that has been internalized as a virtue. In a more dispassionate analysis a question may be asked, tolerance against what? Admittedly tolerance is an effort to put up with something that is unpalatable or offensive. In other words, the object that is to be tolerated has a negative connotation. But why tolerate something that is offensive and not try to overcome or remove it? That would be a more logical approach. When Hindus are constantly harangued to exercise tolerance they are being indirectly told to accept unpleasant facts, opinions or even assault on their dignity. Hinduism has never disallowed dissent. But the gospel of tolerance thrown at Hindus pre-supposes that the other party is the aggressor to whom Hindus have to acquiesce. Unfortunately, that has been the history of Hinduism in the last ten millennia of its existence. And this tolerance must be shown by choice not by compulsion against a faith that had no regard for this religion and considered it not only inferior but an abomination. If that is the type of tolerance now expected of Hinduism, it is too late in history. Tolerance is the virtue of the weak. And its excessive dose has already made India a soft state. Even Swami Vivekanand railed at Hindus against this softness. "This softness has been with us till we have become like masses of cotton and are dead. What our country now wants are muscles of iron and nerves of steel, gigantic wills which nothing can resist, which can penetrate into the mysteries and the secrets of the universe, and will accomplish their purpose in any fashion even if it meant going down to the bottom of the ocean and meeting death face to face."

Enough water has flown in the Ganga since the era of mute submission to tyranny was forced on them. Reliance or undue reliance on the moral restraint of the enemy is no part of strategy. Hindus need not depend on the goodwill of the forces inimical to the nation. The time has now come to reassert the Hindu pride and dignity without any further compromise or humiliation. In the rapidly changing kaleidoscope of Indian polity from one election to another, political formations trim their ideological sails to the prevailing winds of public opinion. Except for those who swear by Hinduism the other parties have no permanent ideology, only permanent interests; to stay in power. The secularist brigade switches positions across the spectrum from Muslim appeasement and Hindu-baiting to soft Hindutva and religious tokenism. But the abiding commitment of the Left as also the English-speaking elite and media is and shall always remain antagonistic to Hinduism for reasons we have discussed in the earlier chapters.

The Indian Communists have always tended to look for identity beyond the national borders. The ceremonial burial of the International Communism and its socialist ideology has shocked them into an identity crisis and withdrawal symptoms. Trapped between grand delusions of the past and their present irrelevance they have in the true Quixotian manner taken to attacking windmills. Since they cannot attack another monotheistic, totalitarian and monolithic system like Islam, their alter ego, Hindus and Hinduism come to them as easy targets.

The Jews who constitute a tiny two percent of the US population have, by sheer hard work and loyalty to their adopted land, pulled America by its shoulders and made it the greatest military and economic power, ranked as the one and only superpower. Their contribution in almost all fields of human endeavour is unmatched. They have produced the largest number of Nobel laureates in the world. But here in India with the exception of Parsees and Bohras the share of the largest minority is minimal. What has the Muslim population forming 15 percent of our total population contributed to the building of our nation? If all the efforts at nation-building have to come from the Hindus and rightly so, is there any justification to revile, vilify and slander that community? Even the so-called Hindu extremists have one abiding faith; patriotism and glory to the nation. Call it *Gaurav* or the faith to make India great. Today, many educated Muslims are questioning the motivation behind the ghettoisation of their community by the so-called secularists in keeping them backward and uneducated. Hindus have no grudge against their Muslim brothers and wish them well and invite them to join the national mainstream to better their own lives and cooperate in the effort of nation-building. Who stops them? The accusing finger shall point to our self-styled secularists. Our secularists behind their mask can stoop to any depths to grab power and enrich themselves. A Laloo Yadav can plunder his state exchequer and even stoop to misappropriate funds for the purchase of fodder. The Left government in Bengal can liquidate countless people to stay in power. The unscrupulous secularist changes his ideals and loyalties to suit electoral requirements; whether it is minorityism or soft Hindutva or Garibi Hatao, everything goes. He has a wide ideological space to manoeuvre, but the so-called saffron brigade is bound to its agenda of patriotism and cultural nationalism. The bread and butter issues, of course, have to be addressed and should form the common denominator of the programmes of all political formations. Being a Hindu does not mean neglect of economic development, territorial security and the other national issues. It is the despised and vilified staunch Hindu Diaspora in the west and Middle East that is doing India proud and not any of our secularist windbags. So let us not denigrate Hindus and Hinduism.

With 85 percent share in the population of the country, the Hindus have a legitimate and unquestionable concern with India's present and future. What happens to India affects the Hindus most. Should they continue to crawl as insects and worms in their country or should they live with dignity and pride? Their concern with the country is not only legitimate but an inalienable right and duty, rolled into one, and their strong patriotism is but natural. Any person or group that dallies with India's destiny cannot be a friend to the Hindus. Hindus have a lineage ten millennia old. Is it fair to ask them to denounce or forget their ancestors? The past shapes the present and builds the future. The Hindus with the world's richest heritage behind them can and should shape a great present and build a glorious future. Our forefathers have given Hindus an idea, a dream to be fulfilled, a land to be consecrated and consummated in its highest glory. Let us not fail.

It is a common saying that the Jews believe that they have priority rights over sufferings. Three thousand years of a homeless existence, genocide, pogroms, and every kind of indignity heaped on them has failed to snuff out the Jewish faith in their religion and destiny. They thought, "evil will destroy itself" but the evil continued destroying the Jews, and still they clung to their faith. Their tormentors have been consigned to the dustbin of history, but Jews and Judaism endure. Hinduism too suffered countless massacres, pogroms, genocides and humiliations for over one thousand years from Islam and Christianity. But the Hindu faith outlived its oppressors. Today we need that intense faith and devotion to the Motherland if we wish to earn the respect of the world. Our present generation, totally rudderless and adrift, feeding on consumerism, lives from day to day without a vision of what India could and should be. Our TV serials dole out vulgar exposures, lewd gestures, obscene tunes and a soulless spectacle titillating the basest of human impulses. Why don't they soar high as an astronaut, climb the Everest, win a gold medal for India in world Olympics, earn a Nobel prize, make contributions to sciences and arts and achieve excellence in human endeavour? Is hip swinging the ultimate in human achievement? We have to move fast and forward to reach and excel, to level up with the other world leaders and the superpower. India is one of the lowest rated countries in any index of human development. Should we waste time in trivialities or get down to the serious task of nation-building? There is no other choice in the world of today. Achieve or perish. Hindus have to develop that fiery zeal to defend their motherland at all costs. It is not merely the job of the armed forces. Every single man who hears the call of the land and reveres the sanctity of its soil is a fighter. People who are afraid to die are of no use, living or dead. The tiny North Korea can challenge the Western world, if they tamper with its nuclear programme. Their stand may not be wise but it is brave. Small Iraq defied the US might for the last one decade and has gone down fighting again in the last war. No tears need be shed for Saddam's decline but every Iraqi will still strive for his land. Can we say the same about our luxury seeking drawing room paper tigers, who can roar but cannot bite? Just read these lines; how tiny Israel, a nation state yet to be born, prepared itself against seven Arab armies waiting around to pounce on a minuscule population of the Jews to destroy them. Against all military wisdom the Jews decided not to wait for the inevitable attack but strike out. Here is the opinion of a military expert on the relative strength of the Jews and the Arabs: "The Jews have four or five thousand Palmach troops and a paper army of fifty thousand in the Haganah, but they only have ten thousand rifles. The Maccabees can put a thousand men out, no more, with light arms. They have no artillery, their air force is three Piper Cubs, and their navy is those illegal immigrant runners tied up at Haifa. The Jews are outnumbered in soldiers forty to one, and in area five thousand to one. The Haganah has turned down my advice and advice of every military man who has told them to pull in to a tight defence line. They are going to fight it out at every moshav, every kibbutz, and every village. That means Gan Dafna, too. Do you want to hear any more?"

It would be one man in millions in any age, any culture or country who through some mysterious working of forces within his soul would stand unafraid against any odd. It is that one man in millions whose indomitable spirit cannot bow. It is that one man in millions who will not submit to tyranny and inspire the millions in his country to follow him. Mother India needs men of raw courage to turn into heroes. It needs the birth of new leaders and the force of ideas. This sacred soil will give birth to leaders of will, who do not wait for history to create events but those who are prepared to make history. The world cannot foresee those hidden forces which propel men of destiny to achieve the seemingly impossible. The process of cross-pollination of cause and effect, down the lane of history, has an alchemy that throws up a cause, a leader and a vision at critical moments. For India that moment has arrived.

In the field of education the grandees of the former New Delhi intelligentsia patronized by the earlier Congress Governments rise as choristers to chant anti-Hindutva carols and perform rituals to exorcise away the imagined ghost of saffronization, Hindu chauvinism, bigotry and superstition from the national educational scene. The secularist parivar, a legatee of Macaulay to whom Hindu India was a pagan wasteland, consider Hinduism as an occult cult redeemed somewhat by Raja Rammohun Roy. To them Hinduism is the dangerous product of crypto zoology, which unless reined in will swallow all minorities, dalits and these progressive themselves.

The Hindu Diaspora in Britain and the US is acutely conscious of its ethnic identity and cultural roots. They do not blindly ape the ethnic inhabitants of their adopted land and keep intact their umbilical cord to Hindu Dharma in India and are touchy about being called Asians, a wider generic term that includes both Pakistan and Bangladesh. They even took the BBC to task on this issue. With an inward awareness of their cultural and spiritual tradition and value systems they wish to retain their Indian roots. They castigate the new commercial breed of swamis and godmen of different *sampradayas*, who in a bid to protect their turf promote sectarianism. They celebrate their festivals with great religious fervour and Hindu solidarity. Indian history, commentary on Gita and Upanishads and books on the lives of our national heroes are in great demand. They crave for authentic history untainted by the brush of our very own respectable "Marxist historians of JNU faculty". The young among them are so upbeat and possessed with a clarity of vision that they are converting white youth to Hindu Dharma to share its essence. Though the earlier gurus did not insist on formal conversions, they did permit the British youth to share the treasures of Sanatan Dharma, such as Yoga, meditation techniques and Hindu philosophy.

A large number of countries in the world are struggling to define themselves in terms of ethnicity, culture, religion, geography and history. Europe is Christian, though parcelled out into Roman Catholicism and Protestantism; in addition the countries have different ethnicity, history, language and economic concerns which they are now trying to synthesize. The North and South Americas are a melting pot of civilizations. Islamic countries of the Middle East are trying to erase political boundaries imposed by colonial powers, and draw new lines. Trapped between the forces of Shia and Sunni Islam on the one hand and Arab nationalism on the other, they are a conglomeration of various ethnic ancient civilizations. In the process they are torn between the forces that pull them towards their pre-Islamic past. Sumer of Akkad in the Tigris valley of Mesopotamia, the old kingdom of Egypt in the Nile valley and Zoroastrianism of Persia challenge the logic of Pan-Arabic Islam. India, however, is twice blessed in its history and geography. Its mountain sheltered north and a sea girded south allowed its pristine Vedic culture to flower and send deep roots into the soil of Bharat, uninterrupted by foreign invasions for almost eight and a half millennia leading to the longest civilizational continuum on this planet. Regional dialects, diversities and divides notwithstanding, our souls still vibrate to the signature tune of a ten millennia old existence unparalleled in the world. Let Hindus drink deep of this elixir and fortify themselves for the task of nation-building.

Hindutva just cannot be wished away. The refulgent mass of knowledge, wisdom and truth and its Weltanschauung of syncretic ecumenism bequeathed by our Vedic sages have lighted mankind in its way through long periods of darkness in human history. To quote Mark Twain, "India is the cradle of human race, the birthplace of human speech, the mother of history, the grandmother of legend and the greatgrandmother of tradition. Our most valuable and most instructive materials in the history of man are treasured up in India." The 'Fortress Hinduana' has repelled assaults of many a battering ram and slings and arrows of hostile religions hovering around. It will do so again, it will also withstand the treacherous darts and daggers of Lilliputean forces of neo-secularism, Marxism, minorityism and historical negationism within. Hinduism cannot remain under siege for long. It has to break free and break free it will.

A Select Bibliogaphy

1.	A. Murray and T. Titus	-	*Indian Islam*
2.	Arun Shourie	-	*Eminent Historians*
3.	Arun Shourie	-	*Missionaries in India*
4.	Arun Shourie	-	*Harvesting Our Souls*
5.	Alfred Guillaume	-	*Islam in History*
6.	Alain Danielou	-	*Histoire de l' Inde*
7.	Sri Aurobindo	-	*Foundations of Indian Culture*
8.	Sri Aurobindo	-	*India's Rebirth*
9.	Balbir Punj	-	Articles
10.	B. R. Ambedkar	-	*Thoughts on Pakistan*
11.	Durga Das	-	*Correspondence of Sardar Patel*
12.	Prof Daniel Pipe	-	*In the Path of God*
13.	David Frawley	-	*Arise Arjuna*
14.	David Frawley	-	*Path of Divinity*
15.	David Frawley & N. Rajaram	-	*Vedic Aryans & Origins of Civilization*
16.	Eliot and Dawson	-	*Muntakahabu–L–Lubab*
17.	National Centre of Social Research (7 French authors)	-	*Histoire de l' Ind moderne* 1994/ *Paris*
18.	Menachim Begin	-	*The Revolt*
19.	Francois Gautier	-	*Arise O India*
20.	F. K. Durrani	-	*Meaning of Pakistan*
21.	Feuerstein, Kak & Sidenberg	-	*In Search of the Cradle of Civilization*
22.	Giri Lal Jain	-	*The Hindu Phenomenon*

23. Harold Lamb - *Babur The Tiger*
24. H. G. Wells - *The Outline of History*
25. H. M. Eliot - *History of India as told by its own Historians*
26. Jawaharlal Nehru - *Discovery of India*
27. Kautilya - *Arthashastra*
28. Koenraad Elst - *Negationism in India, Concealing the Record of Islam*
29. Prof. K. M. Lal - *Growth of Muslim Population in India*
30. Ludlow - *History of British India*
31. M. R. A. Baig - *Preaching of Islam*
32. N. Raja Ram - *Ancient India and Vedic Aryans*
33. Romilla Thapar & Perceival Spear - *Penguin History of India*
34. Mahatma Gandhi - *Young India*
35. Roger Pol Droit - *Le Oubli de l' Inde (The Forgetting of India)*
36. Sir William Muir - *The Life of Mahomet*
37. Syed Qutub - *Voices of Resurgent Islam*
38. Sitaram Goel - *Hindu Temples: What happened to them* (Vol. I & II)
39. Subhas Majumdar - *The Islamic doctrine of Permanent War*-1994
40. S. K. Malik (Brig.) (Pakistan) - *The Koranic Concept of War*
41. Selections from the Works of Swami Vivekanand - *Swami Vivekanand*
42. Thomas W. Arnold - *The Preachings*
43. T. P. Hugee - *The Dictionary of Islam*
44. V. Shankar - *My Reminiscences of Sardar Patel*
45. Praful Goradia - *The Saffron Book*
46. Praful Goradia - *Muslim League's Unfinished Agenda.*
47. Ram Swarup - *Understanding Islam through Hadis*

48. Will Durrant - *The Story of Civilization* – Part I- Our Oriental Heritage

49. James Todd (Col.) - *Annals & Antiquities of Rajputana.*

50. Prof. Harin Srivastava - *Sawarkar – Five Stormy Years*

51. Kanhaya Lal Talreja - *An Appeal to Hindu Law Makers*

52. Vincent Smith - *The Oxford History of India*

53. Pandit Sunder Lal - *Bharat Mein Angrezi Raj*

54. Ved Vyas - *Bhagwad Gita*

55. Oxford World Classics - *Holy Koran*

56. Oxford University Press - *The Holy Bible*

57. Hussein Sayyed Nasr - *The Heart of Islam*

58. Mustaq Naqvi - *Partition – The Real Story*

59. K. S. Lal - *The Legacy of Muslim Rule in India*

60. Bruce B. Lawrence - *Sheltering The Myth*

Index